OBJECT-ORIENTED SYSTEMS ANALYSIS AND DESIGN WITH UML

ROBERT V. STUMPF
California State Polytechnic University, Pomona

LAVETTE C. TEAGUE
California State Polytechnic University, Pomona

PEARSON

Prentice Hall

Upper Saddle River, New Jersey 07458

Library of Congress Cataloging-in-Publication Data

Stumpf, Robert.
    Object-oriented systems analysis and design with UML/Robert Stumpf,
Lavette Teague.
      p. cm.
    Includes bibliographical references and index.
    ISBN 0-13-143406-3
    1. Object-oriented programming (Computer science) 2. Sysem analysis.
3. System design. 4. UML (Computer science) I. Teague, Lavette C.,
1934- II. Title.

QA76.64.S78 2004
005.1'17—dc22

2004011907

Executive Editor, MIS: Bob Horan
Publisher: Natalie E. Anderson
Project Manager: Kyle Hannon
Editorial Assistant: Robyn Goldenberg
Senior Media Project Manager: Joan Waxman
Managing Editor: John Roberts
Production Editor: Renata Butera
Permissions Supervisor: Charles Morris
Manufacturing Buyer: Michelle Klein
Design Director: Maria Lange
Design Manager: Patricia Smythe
Interior Design: Dorothy Bungert
Cover Design: Kiwi Design
Illustrator (Interior): Matrix Publishing Services
Director, Image Resource Center: Melinda Reo
Manager, Rights and Permissions: Zina Arabia
Manager: Visual Research: Beth Brenzel
Manager, Cover Visual Research & Permissions: Karen Sanatar
Manager, Print Production: Christy Mahon
Full-Service Project Management: Carlisle Communications
Printer/Binder: Courier–Westford
Typeface: 10.5/12 Janson Text

Credits and acknowledgments borrowed from other sources and reproduced, with permission, in this
textbook appear on appropriate page within the text.

Microsoft® and Windows® are registered trademarks of the Microsoft Corporation in the U.S.A. and other
countries. Screen shots and icons reprinted with permission from the Microsoft Corporation. This book is
not sponsored or endorsed by or affiliated with the Microsoft Corporation.

Pearson Education LTD.
Pearson Education Singapore, Pte. Ltd
Pearson Education, Canada, Ltd
Pearson Education–Japan

Pearson Education Australia PTY, Limited
Pearson Education North Asia Ltd
Pearson Educación de Mexico, S.A. de C.V.
Pearson Education Malaysia, Pte. Ltd

10 9 8 7 6 5 4 3 2 1
ISBN: 0-13-143406-3

CONTENTS

PART TWO   OBJECT-ORIENTED SYSTEMS ANALYSIS   69

CHAPTER 3: SYSTEMS ANALYSIS — BUSINESS EVENT ANALYSIS   70

CHAPTER 4: ESSENTIAL USE CASES AND SYSTEM SEQUENCE DIAGRAMS 96

CHAPTER 7: ## INFORMATION SYSTEM DESIGN 181

Chapter 8: PROGRAM DESIGN — INTERACTION DIAGRAMS 218

Chapter 9: PROGRAM DESIGN — DESIGN CLASS DIAGRAMS 258

Object-oriented software is here to stay. Object-oriented methods are the preferred way of developing new information systems. In industry the Unified Modeling Language (UML) has become the standard notation for modeling object-oriented systems during analysis and design.

College and university curricula are currently making the transition from structured tools and techniques for information systems analysis and design to those based on the object paradigm. This paradigm will soon be the norm for instruction in information system development.

This book is an introductory text which presents the concepts and methods of object-oriented systems analysis and design. It is intended for a one-quarter or one-semester object-oriented analysis and design course at the undergraduate level, ideally preceded by an introductory course in object-oriented programming. In addition, it might also be suitable at the graduate level in an MBA or Information Systems Management program. It should be especially useful in Computer Information Systems programs which provide considerable depth of experience in systems analysis and design at the undergraduate level and which may even teach the first programming and systems courses at the sophomore level.

This book is a rigorous yet readable analysis and design text. It is addressed to an information systems major who knows relatively little about computers and the business environment. The book provides an introduction to the process of information system development along with a thorough grounding in object-oriented tools and techniques. It stresses principles that will outlast the anticipated rapid changes in specific tools and techniques. It also emphasizes non-technical dimensions of business decision-making that affect information systems and the crucial role of communication skills.

We link information systems analysis and design issues to general systems theory and a domain-independent view of design. We provide a description of the system development process which is the context for the activities of analysis and design. We offer detailed discussion and extensive examples of how to use the UML models in system development. We do not assume that the student has any background in object-oriented programming, as desirable as that may be.

Important features of the contents include:

▌ basic concepts of general systems theory.
▌ the context for systems analysis and design — both the system development process and the organizational context.
▌ a description of the system development process which includes the Rational Unified Process.
▌ an explicit step-by-step procedure for both object-oriented analysis and object-oriented design.
▌ event analysis as the principal technique for generating a system-level model.
▌ UML as the modeling standard for object-oriented analysis and design.
▌ a layered model of at least three tiers as the best practice for system architecture.
▌ a clear pedagogical separation between analysis and design.
▌ an explicit discussion of the nature of design and the design process and their relation to software development.

- a comprehensive overview of system design which includes database design and user interface design as well as program design.
- an emphasis on design practices which facilitate re-use of models and objects.
- design by contract using patterns as the approach to program design.
- two chapters on user interface design — one on design principles with a section on the use of color and one on detailed modeling of the user interaction, featuring state transition diagrams.
- chapters on information gathering and reporting as well as software project management.
- a case study continuing through the text for presenting explanatory examples.
- two additional case studies as a source for project activity assignments.

In addition to the case presented in the body of the text, each chapter contains learning objectives, a list of key terms, review questions, and exercises. There is also a glossary drawn from the list of key terms. Beginning with Chapter 3, the end-of-chapter material includes project assignments based on two additional continuing cases — a hotel and a car rental company.

The presentation of the material facilitates the use of software tools for UML modeling as well as interactive development environments in connection with the course but will be independent of specific software packages.

In any introductory discussion there is a tension between conceptual clarity and conveying what system developers do in industry. In practice, software development can be a complex and messy process, not nearly so neat and well-ordered as the world of textbooks. Yet, as one of our colleagues said to us recently, "There are two kinds of people who develop object-oriented systems, those who understand objects and those who don't." Our priority in this book is to help students understand objects.

In our presentation we make a sharp distinction between analysis and design. Our analysis models are restricted to concepts in the problem domain. We enter the realm of design when we model software in terms of objects and their behaviors. Even though experienced developers may do analysis and design together or allow analysis models to evolve into design models, especially in an iterative process, at least they are presumably aware that they are doing so.

We also present and discuss examples in some depth so that the reader can learn to apply the models and techniques instead of only knowing about them. Where we make inevitable simplifications in the interest of clarity, we try to make these simplifications accurate even though we may ignore some of their subtleties and complexities.

The organization of the book provides a conceptual overview of system analysis or design followed by a presentation of the necessary tools and techniques. Then the application of the techniques in the analysis or design process is presented, using a continuing case — a university registration system.

Some other analysis texts discuss the technique of event analysis; few make it the driver for the analysis process. We make system-level event analysis the starting point for use cases in the object-oriented environment.

Ideally, a comprehensive treatment of system design should include all three principal subsystems of a computer information system — the application programs, the data base, and the user interface. Practically, database design is usually covered in a separate course. Thus we focus on system-level design, program design, and user interface design. However, for the sake of conceptual completeness, we summarize the major issues in designing an interface to a data base.

The chapters on user interface design incorporate visual and perceptual design principles as well as precise software engineering models.

Our book consists of four parts. Part I (Chapters 1–2) begins with a broad discussion of information systems for business and the system development process. Chapter 1 introduces some important concepts from general systems theory and applies them to describing business systems and information systems. Chapter 2 presents the Unified Process for information system development, identifies the major deliverables produced by the process, and describes the roles of the participants.

Part II (Chapters 3–5) covers object-oriented systems analysis. Chapter 3 provides an overview of systems analysis and presents system-level event analysis as the primary technique for initiating the analysis process. Chapters 4 and 5 describe the UML object-oriented analysis models — use cases and use case diagrams, system sequence diagrams, system contracts, and models of the problem domain. These chapters show how object-oriented analysis methods are applied in the process of stating users' requirements for a computer information system, using a university registration system as a running example.

Part III (Chapters 6–12) covers object-oriented system design. First, it provides an overview of system design and the information system design process. Chapter 6 discusses fundamental concepts and principles common to all design disciplines. Chapter 7 states the goals of information system design and surveys the components used to implement an information processing system. It relates the activities of system design to the information system development process and examines the roles and skills of a system designer. It presents system design as comprising three sub-problems — program design, user interface design, and database design.

Chapters 8–10 address object-oriented program design. Chapter 8 discusses critical characteristics of the object software paradigm and introduces basic design patterns used to appropriately assign responsibilities to objects. It then presents interaction diagrams — collaboration diagrams and sequence diagrams — introducing the essentials of the UML conventions required to read, understand, and develop them. Chapter 9 discusses UML design class diagrams and criteria for design quality as well as techniques for specifying methods.

Chapter 10 deals with issues regarding the interface between object-oriented software and object-oriented or relational data bases. Design of the data base itself is outside the scope of this book.

Chapters 11 and 12 are concerned with designing the user interface — the detailed form and structure of the messages crossing the automation boundary. We stress a basic approach and fundamental principles which can be expected to endure when devices and details change. We encourage the designer to take a broad perspective rather than being immediately constrained by what is familiar. Chapter 11 provides the context for user interface design, summarizes important design principles and guidelines, and applies these principles to the design of reports and displays. Chapter 12 presents state transition diagrams for modeling the interaction between user and computer. It also addresses the connection between the user interface and the application layer.

Part IV discusses other activities which support the products and processes of systems analysis and design. Chapter 13 discusses methods of information gathering and reporting. Chapter 14 deals with the management of object-oriented software development projects.

There is also an appendix which summarizes for reference the most important UML conventions.

THE SUPPLEMENT RESOURCE PACKAGE: WWW.PRENHALL.COM/STUMPF

A comprehensive and flexible technology support package is available to enhance the teaching and learning experience. All instructor and student supplements are available on the text's Web site: www.prenhall.com/stumpf.

▌ *Instructor's Manual.* The Instructor's Manual includes teaching objectives, answers to questions and exercises at the end of the chapters, and teaching suggestions. It is available on the secure faculty section of the Stumpf Web site.

▪ *Test Item File and TestGen Software.* The Test Item File is a comprehensive collection of true–false, multiple-choice, and short answer questions. The questions are rated by difficulty level and the answers are referenced by page number. The Test Item File is available in Microsoft Word and as the computerized Prentice Hall TestGen. TestGen is a comprehensive suite of tools for testing and assessment. It allows instructors to easily create and distribute tests for their courses, either by printing and distributing through traditional methods or by on-line delivery via a Local Area Network (LAN) server. TestGen features Screen Wizards to assist instructors as they move through the program, and the software is backed with full technical support. Both the Test Item File and TestGen software are available on the secure faculty section of the Stumpf Web site.

▪ *Power Point Slides.* PowerPoint slides are available to or which illuminate and build on key concepts in the text. Both student and faculty can download the PowerPoint slides from the Stumpf Web site.

▪ *Materials for Your Online Course.* Prentice Hall supports our adopters using on-line courses by providing files ready for upload into both WebCT and Blackboard course management systems for our testing, quizzing, and other supplements. Please contact your local PH representative or mis_service@prenhall.com for further information on your particular course.

ACKNOWLEDGMENTS

We appreciate the comments of our colleagues and students, whose suggestions over the past two years have made this a better book. We also acknowledge the thoughtful and valuable insight of those who reviewed the manuscript:

Rob Anson, Boise State University
Bettina Bair, Ohio State University
Dirk Baldwin, University of Wisconsin–Parkside
Martin Dion Benes, DeVry University
Qing Cao, University of Missouri–Kansas City
Gail Corbitt, California State University, Chico
Terry L. Fox, Baylor University
Robert Grenier, Augustana College
Marilyn Griffin, Virginia Tech University
Wayne Huang, Ohio University
Lakshmi Iyer, University of North Carolina–Greensboro
Fred Neiderman, Saint Louis University
Bonn Oh-Kim, Seattle University
Alex Ramirez, Carleton University
Anthony Scime, SUNY–Brockport
Nedal Seyam, DeVry University
Ed Sullivan, Indiana University–Purdue University Indianapolis
Craig VanLengen, Northern Arizona University
Te-Wei Wang, Florida International University
Connie Wells, Roosevelt University
David Woodruff, University of California–Davis

In particular, we are grateful for the involvement of Bob Horan from the time the project began. His encouragement and support have been critical to its completion as well as to whatever success it may have.

Robert V. Stumpf
Lavette C. Teague
Pomona, California
March 23, 2004

INTRODUCTION TO INFORMATION SYSTEM DEVELOPMENT

The digital computer has transformed our society since the middle of the past century. Computers and information technology have changed the way we work and learn and play.

This book explains how to analyze users' requirements for information systems and how to design software. It is oriented toward information systems for businesses, and for their counterparts in government and not-for-profit organizations, and it takes its examples from applications which support such organizations. Nevertheless, the principles and techniques of systems analysis and design presented here are applicable to all kinds of computer information systems. In particular, these techniques include the use of the Unified Modeling Language (UML), which is a widely accepted standard notation for describing object-oriented software.

In general, systems analysis is a process of learning about and describing users' requirements for an improved system. System design is a process of describing a solution to those requirements. Both analysis and design, which are common activities in many disciplines, work to satisfy people's needs for useful systems.

For example, the architects and engineers who design a building must determine the types and sizes of the spaces required by the occupants. They must also learn how the spaces need to be related to each other in order to function well for their intended use. Then the designers can organize the spaces in three dimensions and define the structural, mechanical, and electrical systems (and others) which compose the completed building. The architects construct physical models as well as computer simulations of what the building will look like. The engineers construct mathematical models to calculate the expected performance of the systems which they are designing. The possible solutions are limited not only by the laws of physics, but also by the size, topography, and geology of the site as well as by building codes and other government regulations.

Similarly, automobile designers will start from the expected use of a new vehicle and the marketing profile of the prospective purchaser to define the required size of the interior and the trunk as well as the desired amenities. They must take into account the ranges of shape, size, and weight of the passengers. Then they can determine the sort of power train needed for this particular model. The designers will make sketches and build physical models to study the vehicle's appearance and styling. They may calculate the aerodynamics of the vehicle with mathematical models and may compare the calculations with wind tunnel tests on a physical model. They may simulate the behavior of the vehicle

INTRODUCTION TO INFORMATION SYSTEM DEVELOPMENT

and its passengers during a crash. The design is constrained by the manufacturing process as well as by safety regulations, fuel economy, and air pollution standards.

So, too, the developers of information systems for business must first understand the business reasons for a new system. They must then learn and record the users' more detailed requirements — what the system must do in order to serve its purpose within the organization. Based on these requirements, they may define the software for the new system. They, too, will use models which help them envision how the software will work and which will guide its construction by the programmers.

The two chapters in Part I establish the context for the analysis and design of object-oriented information systems.

Chapter 1 introduces both the conceptual and the organizational contexts for system development. It defines and illustrates basic terms used in describing and modeling systems. It discusses what all systems have in common, using a variety of examples from many fields of human endeavor. It describes how people solve problems in many domains. It then applies these general system concepts to the description (and development) of computer information systems. Every information processing system contains components which perform three types of functions — they move information, store information, and transform information. The way these components are organized and interact defines the structure of the system.

Chapter 1 also examines the organizational context for business information systems, providing an overview of the information needs of businesses as well as major applications of computers to business information systems. Manufacturing businesses are heavily dependent on information to monitor and manage their performance as well as to support management decisions; service businesses are often even more dependent on information processing systems.

However, systems analysis and design are part of a larger cycle of system development and use. Chapter 2 presents the managerial and developmental contexts for systems analysis and design — the information system development process — as well as the roles and responsibilities of the various participants in this process. A request to change an information processing system and an evaluation of the desirability and feasibility of the proposed change are followed by a requirements analysis. The result of this analysis — a statement of users' requirements — poses a problem to be solved by the system designers. Their solution is then programmed, tested, and delivered to the system's users for integration into the operation of their organization.

INTRODUCTION

We live in a systems age. Many of the most challenging and amazing human achievements since the mid-twentieth century are the result of our ability to apply systems thinking. The landing on the moon, the eradication of polio, and the Internet are only a few examples.

This chapter defines basic systems concepts and applies them to the description of information systems. It also presents a systems overview of business organizations and summarizes their need for information as well as the business activities supported by computer information systems. It provides a foundation for the more specialized activities and techniques of object-oriented systems analysis and design explained in detail in Parts II and III.

LEARNING OBJECTIVES

After mastering the material in this chapter, you will be able to

▌ Explain how systems thinking helps address the complexity of developing an information processing system.

▌ Define a system and identify the function, components, and structure of familiar systems.

▌ Understand the relationship between a system and its environment, or context.

▌ Explain the role of an interface.

▌ Give examples of information system components which perform the functions of transformation, transmission, and storage.

▌ Explain the difference between essential and implementation descriptions of a system.

▌ Describe some of the major roles of information in a business organization.

▌ Explain the major steps in a problem-solving or decision-making process and how systems analysis can be understood as problem solving.

COPING SUCCESSFULLY WITH COMPLEXITY

Systems analysis and design are challenging and complex activities. They challenge us intellectually as we attempt to understand a system and describe it conceptually. They require creativity as we solve users' problems. They involve us in changing how people and organizations carry out their work. Analysis and design can also be complex in practice as we coordinate the efforts of the participants in system development. When developing computer information systems, we must cope with the complexity inherent in our world in spite of our human limitations.

Systems analysts are often called on to investigate an unfamiliar situation and recommend what should be done. The problems to be investigated may be poorly understood, and the analysts may have little background in the specific problem areas to be studied. They must learn as their work proceeds. Methods of systems analysis must provide ways to overcome lack of structure and understanding as well as ways to cope with complexity.

To deal with complexity rationally and wisely, we must first discover — or impose — some kind of order. Finding or creating order and structure permits us to understand a situation, communicate that understanding, and then take appropriate action. For centuries, thinkers have debated about the extent to which the world we experience incorporates some inherent structure and the extent to which we impose order on our experience in order to perceive and understand it. Human language, so closely connected to human thought, is one of the great organizers of experience. It is also a principal means of communicating, sharing, and understanding our experience. Precision in thought and language, as well as effectiveness in oral and written communication, is critical for systems analysts and designers.

In creating new computer information systems, we need to make good decisions in spite of change and complexity. We must take into account not only the fluid and disorganized nature of the world around us, but also the limitations of the human mind. Psychologists of perception tell us that we can maintain only a very small number of "chunks" of information (about five to nine) simultaneously in our short-term memory. They also point out that in a fixed period of time we can absorb far more information visually than we can verbally.

Then how do we cope with complexity? We structure and we simplify. We simplify in a variety of ways — we:

▐ Limit the extent of our interest;
▐ Select the important or essential features of a situation and ignore the rest;
▐ Break up what is large until it consists of pieces of a manageable size;
▐ Examine things iteratively, a few at a time, until we have considered everything of interest;
▐ Review and refine our ideas to improve them; and
▐ Use visual modes of thought whenever we can.

Systems analysis requires us to limit the area of study, abstract the essential features of reality, divide a complex whole into parts of intelligible and manageable size, and model a system to show the relationships among its components.

Before further describing and illustrating these means of simplification, it is important to introduce and define some terms which will enable us to think and talk more effectively about systems of all kinds.

WHAT IS A SYSTEM?

One of the most general and powerful notions of order and structure is that of a system. A *system* is an interrelated set of components which are viewed as a whole. The components work together to perform a function or to achieve an objective. The function and objective of the system are usually closely related to the point of view and interests of the person looking at the system.

A system has **components,** the basic parts or elements which make up the system. It also has a **structure,** which defines the way in which the components are organized. There are a variety of useful ways of thinking about the structure of a system. Sometimes it is described as the arrangement of the components, sometimes as the relationships which link the components, and sometimes as the rules which describe the interactions among the components.

The **function** of a system is what the system does — the task, activity, or work which the system performs. The **objective** of a system is the human goal or purpose which the system serves in carrying out its function. Many systems perform multiple functions and serve several objectives. Consider the following examples of systems.

The solar system comprises our sun, nine major planets and their moons, and a belt of minor planets or asteroids between Mars and Jupiter. The behavior of this system follows the physical laws of gravity. The position and motion of each planet relative to the sun are described by Kepler's laws:

1. The orbit of each planet is an ellipse with the sun at one focus.
2. Each planet moves along its elliptical path in such a way that a line joining the center of the planet to the center of the sun sweeps out equal areas in equal times.
3. The square of the time it takes each planet to complete one orbit is proportional to the cube of its mean distance from the sun.

A baseball game has as its major components the two teams; the umpires; the playing field; the ball, gloves, masks, and other equipment; the actions of the players; and the score. The rules of baseball define the valid ways in which these components may be arranged and may interact. Because the rules define the permissible relationships among the components (the system structure), they are an essential part of the system. The function of the game is playing baseball; in this case, what the system does is defined only in terms of the system itself. A baseball game may accomplish many objectives: to provide exercise and camaraderie for amateur players, to provide employment for professional players and managers (as well as hot-dog vendors), to entertain the fans, to provide an occasion for betting, and so on.

A bicycle system consists of a rider, two wheels, a frame with handlebars, a seat, pedals, and a chain to connect the pedals to the wheels. The function of a bicycle is to transform the circular motion of the cyclist's legs into linear motion. The principal objective is to transport the rider from place to place. However, a bicycle may also provide exercise, recreation, sport, or competition.

SYSTEM STRUCTURES

A few familiar structural patterns — hierarchical, matrix, and network — occur frequently in systems. However, as the examples above should make clear, there are a great many systems whose structure cannot be adequately described in terms of these three relatively simple forms of organization.

A **hierarchical system structure** is one in which every system component except one is immediately subordinate to exactly one other component (called its superordinate). A familiar example is the management structure for a corporation, such as that shown by the organizational chart in Figure 1.1. Each person in the company reports directly to only one person, but a supervisor may be responsible for several subordinates. In Chapter 5, we will see that a model of the problem

FIGURE 1.1 Hierarchical structure: Organizational chart

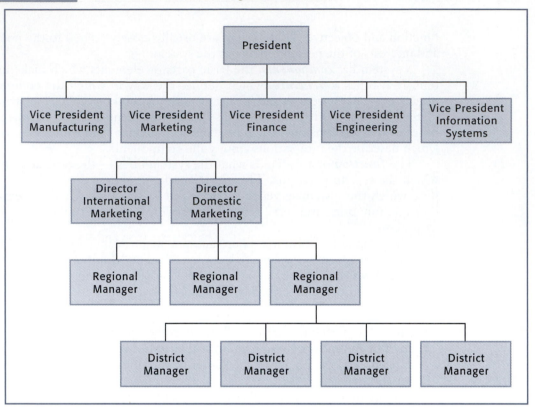

FIGURE 1.2 Nested hierarchy: State map

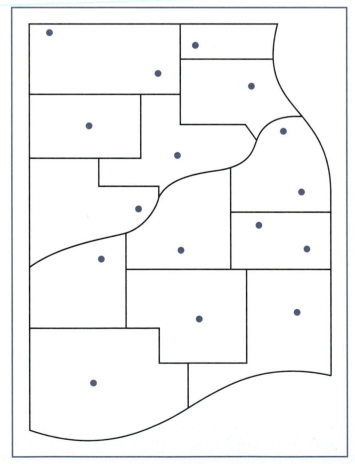

domain may contain a hierarchy of concepts. Figure 1.2 shows a state map. In this state, each city is contained in only one county, and the counties in turn are contained in the state. This figure illustrates why some hierarchical systems are called **nested.**

A hierarchical structure is sometimes called a **tree structure** because it can always be represented in the form of a tree. A hierarchy tree is usually upside-down, as in Figure 1.3, with the **root** at the top and the **branches** extending down; the elements at the ends of the branches are sometimes called **leaves.**

A **matrix structure** is one in which the location of the components is determined by a combination of two or more factors. The matrix form of organization is found in many businesses. In architectural and engineering firms, this structure is based on both project assignment and professional disciplines (see Figure 1.4). Each project has a manager, while each discipline has a department head responsible for allocating personnel and providing them with additional technical expertise and support. In Chapter 2, we will see that the Rational Unified Process for object-oriented software development has a matrix structure.

A network structure consists of a set of **nodes** (or points) connected by **arcs** (or links or lines). The arcs permit **flows** between pairs of nodes in specified directions. An interstate highway map (Figure 1.5) is one example of a network. In Chapter 8, we will see network structures used to model interactions between software objects.

FIGURE 1.3 Tree structure

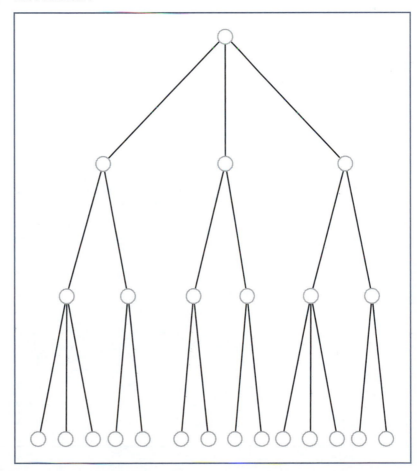

FIGURE 1.4   Matrix structure

		Project 1	Project 2	Project 3	Project 4	Project 5
DISCIPLINE	Architecture					
	Structural					
	Mechanical					
	Electrical					
	Interiors					

HIERARCHIES OF SYSTEMS

When we wish to investigate a system, how do we isolate it from the complexity of the environment in which it is embedded and with which it interacts? One of the difficulties is that many systems come in hierarchies. A system within a hierarchy can be viewed as a *subsystem* — as part of a more inclusive system. There is always a temptation to expand

FIGURE 1.5   Network structure: Interstate highway map

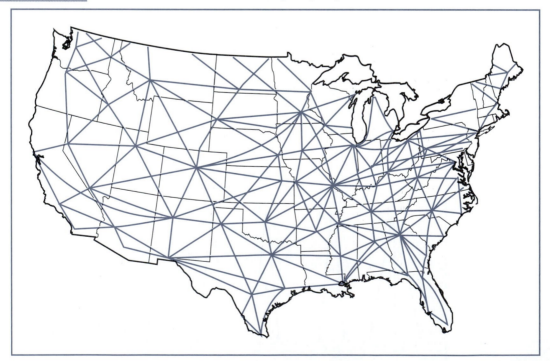

our area of study to obtain a more comprehensive perspective. On the other hand, it is always possible to shrink the focus of our study to look at finer and finer detail. If we continue to expand the area of study, the problem becomes unmanageable, or we fail to solve it because we never finish studying it. These dilemmas, which occur in the design of physical systems as well as information systems, are captured in John Eberhard's story of the doorknob.[1]

> One anxiety inherent in design methods is the hierarchical nature of complexity. This anxiety moves in two directions, escalation and infinite regression. I will use a story, "The Warning of the Doorknob," to illustrate the principles of escalation.
>
> This has been my experience in Washington when I had money to give away. If I gave a contract to a designer and said, "The doorknob to my office doesn't have much imagination, much design content. Will you design me a new doorknob?" He would say "Yes," and after we establish a price he goes away. A week later he comes back and says, "Mr. Eberhard, I've been thinking about that doorknob. First, we ought to ask ourselves whether a doorknob is the best way of opening and closing a door." I say, "Fine, I believe in imagination, go to it." He comes back later and says, "You know, I've been thinking about your problem, and the only reason you want a doorknob is that you presume you want a door to your office. Are you *sure* that a door is the best way of controlling egress, exit, and privacy?" "No, I'm not sure at all." "Well I want to worry about that problem." He comes back a week later and says, "The only reason we have to worry about the aperture problem is that you insist on having four walls around your office. Are you sure that is the best way of organizing this space for the kind of work you do as a bureaucrat." I say, "No, I'm not sure at all." Well, this escalates until (and this has literally happened in two contracts, although not through this exact process) our physical designer comes back and he says with a very serious face, "Mr. Eberhard, we have to decide whether capitalistic democracy is the best way to organize our country before I can possibly attack your problem."
>
> On the other hand is the problem of infinite regression: If this man faced with the design of the doorknob had said, "Wait. Before I worry about the doorknob, I want to study the shape of man's hand and what man is capable of doing with it," I would say, "Fine." He would come back and would say, "The more I thought about it, there's a *fit* problem. What I want to study first is how metal is formed, what the technologies are for making things with metal in order that I can know what the real parameters are for fitting the hand." "Fine." But then he says, "You know I've been looking at metal-forming and it all depends on metallurgical properties. I really want to spend three or four months looking at metallurgy so that I can understand the problem better." "Fine." After three months he'll come back and say, "Mr. Eberhard, the more I look at metallurgy, the more I realize that it is atomic structure that's really at the heart of this problem." And so, our physical designer is in atomic physics from the doorknob. That is one of our anxieties, the hierarchical nature of complexity.[2]

---

[1] Mr. Eberhard was working at the time for the National Bureau of Standards.
[2] John P. Eberhard, "We Ought to Know the Difference," in Gary T. Moore, ed., *Emerging Methods in Environmental Design and Planning* (Cambridge: MIT Press, 1970), 364–65.

FIGURE 1.6   System context diagram

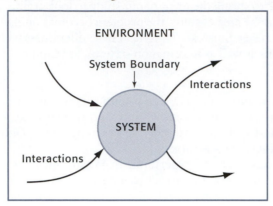

SYSTEM BOUNDARIES

You have to draw the line somewhere. It is undesirable, if not impossible, to be concerned with the entire world and to try to solve all its problems at once. In any specific situation, the scope of our system should be sufficiently inclusive and our system description should be sufficiently detailed to serve our purpose. But the more we extend the scope, and the more detail we include, the more complex the system becomes. Yet there is always the temptation to enlarge the scope and increase the amount of detail, as Eberhard's story has illustrated.

In practice, where to locate the system boundary is often one of the most difficult decisions an analyst has to make. The *system boundary* (Figure 1.6) defines the limits of the system. Inside the boundary is the system, the part of the world to be studied, described, structured, and, usually, changed. Outside the boundary is the *environment,* or *context,* the part of the world to be ignored except for a few important interactions at the boundary between the system and the environment. A diagram such as Figure 1.6, which shows the system, its environment, and perhaps selected interactions between them, is called a *system context diagram* or *context diagram.*

The term *interface* is often used to describe an interaction — between system and environment, between two systems, or between two components of a system, as shown in Figures 1.7 and 1.8. The basic geometric analogy for an interface is that of Figure 1.7, where the area of interaction appears as a zone of contact. In Figure 1.8, however, the interfaces or connections between components are shown as lines or arcs; in this case, the representation has lost the underlying image of touching.

MODELING AND REPRESENTATION

Once we have identified a system as being of interest to us, limited the area of interest by defining the system boundary, and established which interactions between the system and its environment are important, we must decide how to describe the system. We must reduce the complexity of the system description by further simplification.

Producing a simple system description involves **abstraction** and **selectivity.** The two major approaches to constructing or presenting system descriptions are *aggregation* and *decomposition.* The resulting description is usually a *system model,* communicated and manipulated through one or more *representations.*

FIGURE 1.7   System and subsystem interfaces

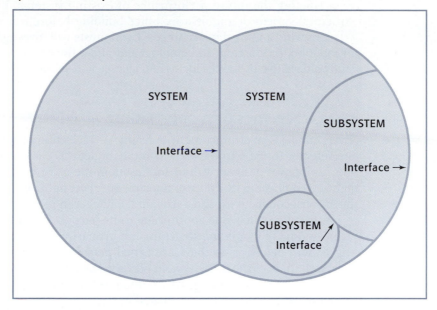

THE NEED FOR SYSTEM MODELS

System descriptions, or models, serve several purposes in system studies. At the most basic level, a model is used to understand the system — to grasp conceptually what the components are and how they interact to carry out the system functions and objectives. Closely related is the use of a model to communicate this understanding of a system to others. The more clearly we understand, the better we can communicate; and clearer communication can result in improved understanding. We use models to study the behavior of a system because it is usually impossible or impractical to deal with the

FIGURE 1.8   Interfaces as connections

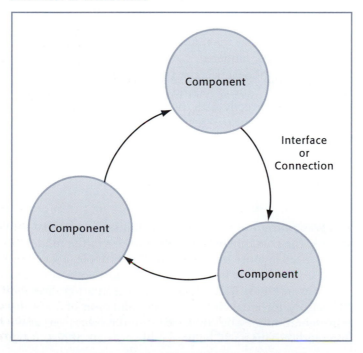

system directly. This is especially useful in understanding the behavior of new systems or predicting the future performance of existing systems. Engineers will model the structural system of a multistory office building before it is constructed to study the effect of wind and earthquake forces. Economists will investigate how changes in levels of inflation, production, and employment affect the economy. Models may be used to study alternative proposals for system change and select the best.

CHARACTERISTICS OF A GOOD MODEL

Every model is an abstraction from reality — a selection of system characteristics which are relevant to the purpose for which the model was constructed. In modeling a building, an interior designer will be interested in the color and surface texture of a wall, a lighting engineer in its ability to transmit or reflect light, an air conditioning engineer in its thermal conductivity, and a structural engineer in its weight and the load it can carry.

A good model is one appropriate to its purpose. Some models, such as the engineer's model of a building structure, are primarily oriented to simulating or predicting system behavior — these are called *performance models.* They are judged by how well they approximate system performance. Other models, such as the plans and specifications for a building, are oriented to constructing the system. These are often called *specifications* and are evaluated in terms of their adequacy for constructing the system, and primarily in terms of completeness and consistency. For example, construction documents for a building are complete if all the components of the building are described and are consistent (they are consistent, for example, if beams, ducts, and lights are not shown occupying the same space).

Good models also support the process of systems analysis and design. This is usually a highly interactive process, so the models must be easy to manipulate, change, and throw away. In this respect, a mathematical model of a building structure, such as a set of simultaneous equations, may be preferable to a graphical model. A quick sketch of the exterior of a building may be better for an architect than a three-dimensional scale model, and a diagram of the locations of emergency exits may be preferable to a photograph of the interior of an airplane. Graphic models greatly aid us in imaging or visualizing a system. They take advantage of the higher rate of information transfer through the eye. They permit a simultaneous perception of the system in contrast to verbal models or descriptions, which must be perceived sequentially in time.

Good models are also felt to be **natural.** They incorporate properties in such a way as to emphasize the inherent similarities between the model and the essentials of the system being modeled.

The best models become **transparent** to their users. That is, the users are able to "see through" the model, so that when they manipulate the model, they appear to be interacting directly with the system. In short, the model does not get in their way. To be sure, this transparency is partly the result of skill and much practice on the part of the user, but a natural system description which supports the visual imagination greatly facilitates the achievement of transparency.

REPRESENTATION

A *representation* of a model is a graphical or physical way of displaying or demonstrating the components and relationships in the model. Sometimes a model may be represented in more than one way. For example, a set of rules for making decisions in given situations may be depicted in the form of a table, as in Figure 1.9, or in that of a tree, as in Figure 1.10. The two representations are equivalent, in that both show the actions to be taken for each combination of conditions. Because of this, either representation may be converted into the other; yet, as we might expect, sometimes one representation will be preferable because of how we intend to use it.

FIGURE 1.9 Structure of a decision table

	1	2	3	4	5	6	7	8	9	10	11	12	13	14	15	16	17	18
Recent Sales Activity	F	N	S	F	N	S	F	N	S	F	N	S	F	N	S	F	N	S
Inventory Level	H	H	H	O	O	O	L	L	L	H	H	H	O	O	O	L	L	L
Perishable	Y	Y	Y	Y	Y	Y	Y	Y	Y	N	N	N	N	N	N	N	N	N
% Change	0	–10	–15	0	0	–5	+5	+5	0	+5	–5	–10	+10	0	–10	+15	+5	0

NOTATION

Sometimes there are also alternative notations. A **notation** is a symbolic way of describing a system. For example, in describing the moves in a chess game, different sets of symbols may be used to denote the pieces and the squares of the chessboard. The international algebraic notation has replaced the more traditional English notation. (See Exercise 1–5 for details.)

GENERATING A SYSTEM MODEL

There are two principal approaches to generating a system model—*aggregation* and *decomposition*.

Aggregation and Synthesis

Aggregation is a process of assembling a system using a set of elementary components, often called **primitives**. This "kit-of-parts" approach is like fabricating a building out of bricks, mortar, lumber, and nails, or stringing a necklace of beads, or organizing complex patterns of information out of 0s and 1s. It proceeds from the parts to the whole and is thus frequently characterized as a **bottom-up approach**. (Think of constructing the foundation of a building first or looking at an organizational chart from the most detailed, or bottom, level.) This process is known as **synthesis**, a word whose Greek roots mean "put together" and whose Latin equivalent is **composition**. Thus, synthesizing a chemical compound and

FIGURE 1.10 Structure of a decision tree

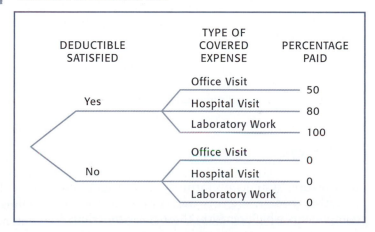

composing a symphony are both referred to as bottom-up activities in which something new is created.

Decomposition and Analysis

Decomposition, on the other hand, proceeds from the whole to the parts. This approach **partitions** a system into its constituent elements, much as an artist rents an empty loft and organizes the space into distinct areas for painting, exhibiting paintings, cooking, eating, sleeping, and bathing. A developer takes a tract of land and **subdivides** it into lots. Decomposition is characterized as a *top-down* approach, as when an organizational chart is read from the top down, beginning with the chairman of the board. The classical term for decomposition is *analysis,* meaning to "break up." Analysis is most often conceptual rather than physical. We describe system structure by distinguishing, isolating, or identifying the components.

ANALYSIS AND SYNTHESIS—COMPLEMENTARY APPROACHES

Clearly, analysis and synthesis proceed in opposite directions and take opposite points of view, yet in practice they are complementary. In many situations, system models are generated through a combination of analysis and synthesis. In this sense, what is frequently called **systems analysis** requires synthesis, and **system design,** often considered a synthetic activity, requires analysis. When we have a job to do, we work from the bottom up, from the top down, and from the middle in both directions. The result is what matters. If we master both analytic and synthetic techniques, we can selectively apply each of them in generating system models.

Aggregation and decomposition have been discussed in relation to generation of models. These same approaches are useful in presenting a system model. However, the model, once developed, exists independently of the developer. When the model has been completed, it may be impossible to tell which approach was used to generate it. Moreover, the most effective way to present a system description does not necessarily match the approach used in its generation.

LIMITATIONS OF SYSTEM MODELS

Because every model is an abstraction, a description of reality selected to carry out an objective, it is limited. It is limited by the aspects of reality omitted from the model, the relationships among system components ignored by the model, and the degree to which the model approximates reality. The systems expert is aware of these limitations. It can be just as important to know what a model does *not* show as what it does show. It is important not to apply a model outside its intended domain without being aware of the situation. Thus, throughout this book, we will emphasize the limitations of the system models presented.

Expertise in the systems field is built on a broad knowledge of system models as well as facility in applying them to specific situations. Expertise is also based on the ability to see a system from multiple perspectives, to see the whole as well as the parts, and to exercise sound judgment.

FUNCTIONS OF AN INFORMATION SYSTEM

Information systems perform three principal functions — they transmit information, they store it, and they transform it. A model of an information system contains components which perform these three functions.

COMMUNICATION

Systems whose chief function is to transmit information are usually called communication systems. Communication systems move information from person to person or from place to place. Speech is the oldest and most fundamental form of human communication. Like all communication systems, it involves three types of components. A transmitter (the vocal apparatus) encodes information into elementary units (the sounds or phonemes). Then a signal or sequence of these encoded units (sound waves) is sent via some information-carrying medium (the air). A receiver (the ear) decodes the signal (the sounds) and reconstructs the meaning of the message based on a set of rules (the syntax and semantics of the language).

Communication problems arise through a faulty transmitter (a speech impediment), faulty transmission (perhaps due to noise or interference), a faulty receiver (lack of attention or partial deafness), or problems in encoding or decoding (neurological or linguistic disabilities).

Other familiar communication systems are the telephone, the radio, and television. The telephone encodes sounds (primarily speech) into electromagnetic signals, which are transmitted through wires, through the air in the form of microwaves, and now through glass filaments in the form of light. The radio transmits music as well as speech by means of airborne signals. The television, whose signals are also transmitted by air or cable, adds pictures to music and speech.

STORAGE

Messages in a communication system are inherently transient; without a means of storage, there is no enduring record of the information. Carvings in stone, impressions in soft clay, ink on parchment, pencil on paper, phonograph records, photographic film, and sound and video recordings on magnetic tape — all these are different ways of capturing information in a relatively permanent way.

In English and other Western languages, for example, the spoken language is recorded using an alphabet — a set of written symbols. A letter or combination of letters from the alphabet represents each sound of the language. The symbols can be recorded with pencil, pen, or some other marking device on paper or some other surface. When this is done, a transient sequence of sounds has been converted into a permanent sequence of graphic symbols. The symbols are decoded visually into the sentences of the original utterance. But, surprisingly enough, when reading a book or newspaper, it is not necessary to utter the sounds. Thus (even without speed reading), information retrieval through reading is considerably faster than information transmittal through speech or information recording through typing or writing. Through techniques such as micrographics, using microfilm or microfiche as the storage medium, and electronic storage, using silicon chips or optical discs, information storage today has become not only permanent, but also extremely compact.

TRANSFORMATION

As we have seen, even the transmission and storage of information often require a conversion from one information-carrying medium to another. However, when we speak of transforming information, we are usually referring to a change in the content of the information rather than a change in the form of the information or in the medium which carries it.

From this point of view, we may say informally that a transformation is a computation or calculation. The result of the calculation is derived from known information by following a known procedure or set of rules. For example, given a list of purchases

FIGURE 1.11   Example of a transformation

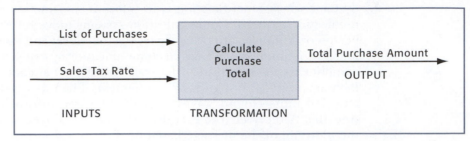

at a grocery store, the sales tax rate, and the rules for addition and multiplication, it is possible to calculate the total amount of the purchase. The price of each item on the list is summed; then the amount of the sales tax is computed by multiplying the tax rate by the sum of the prices of the items purchased; and, finally, the amount of the sales tax is added to the sum of the prices of the items purchased, giving the total amount of the purchase.

The list of purchases and the sales tax rate are called the *inputs* to the transformation. The total amount of the purchase is the *output* of the transformation. We say that the output is **derived** from the inputs. The rules which describe the transformation are known by a variety of names. *Procedure* is probably the most generally useful, although other terms are also used in more specialized contexts. Figure 1.11 is a diagram of a transformation, showing its inputs and its output.

INFORMATION PROCESSING SYSTEMS

An information processing system is an information system which performs transformations. (Indeed, the word *process* is often used as a synonym for transformation.) Most information processing systems also need to store information and transport it from one part of the system to another. Thus, most information processing systems perform all three of the functions discussed above — transmission, storage, and transformation.

However, the essential function of an information processing system is to respond to what happens in the world outside the system. The identification of significant occurrences in the outside world and the desired response of the system constitutes the activity called *event analysis,* discussed in Chapter 3. In general, an information processing system responds to an event by carrying out one or more transformations of information. These transformations derive some desired information (the outputs) from some known information (the inputs). The specific information contained in these inputs and outputs depends, as discussed above, on the specific human objectives to be accomplished by the system and the specific context in which the information processing system occurs. We shall return to this topic later in the chapter.

For example, a simple payroll system will derive employee paychecks from time cards containing the number of hours per week each employee has worked and from the salary or hourly wage of each employee. The payroll system will also need information from which to calculate the amounts to be withheld for federal and state income tax and for contributions to the social security system. Other desired system outputs may include the annual statement of earnings and withholding (Form W–2) for each employee and the summary of withholding for all employees, which the employer sends periodically to the federal and state governments along with the amounts withheld.

DESCRIBING A COMPUTER INFORMATION SYSTEM

When we model an information processing system, we expect to describe it, as we do any other system, in terms of its components, their arrangement or relationships, and their functions. An information processing system consists of components which transport or transmit information, components that store information, and components that transform information. The system boundary separates the system from its environment and identifies the points of contact (the interfaces or connections) between the system and its environment.

MANUAL AND AUTOMATED SYSTEMS

Thus far, everything we have said about information processing systems has been independent of the technology used. We have given examples of manual systems as well as those assisted by sophisticated technology. Strictly speaking, every information processing system is based on a technology. The ancient abacus and the mechanical calculators of the late nineteenth and early twentieth centuries are technological aids which increase the speed and accuracy of computation. But the invention of the electronic computer about 1940 and the subsequent advances in the technology for information transmission, storage, and transformation have indeed revolutionized information processing systems. These advances have made economical a wide variety of applications of electronic computers.

The desire to use computers for a wide range of information processing tasks is what makes the study and understanding of information processing systems of great practical benefit and not merely of theoretical interest (although what is merely of theoretical interest today often turns out to be of great practical benefit tomorrow). To be sure, the same concepts are useful in describing any information processing system, whether manual or automated, and the study of a manual system may lead to improvements in it. Nevertheless, the reason for carefully analyzing a manual information processing system usually turns out to be the hope that replacing it with a computerized system will significantly enhance the system's effectiveness.

Consider, first, a digital computer as an automated information processing system. Within the system boundary, information is transmitted, stored, and transformed in electronic form. At the system boundary are the interfaces between the computer and its environment — the human world, in which information is stored in words, numbers, and pictures, and transmitted orally and visually. These interfaces are devices for capturing data (such as keyboards, microphones, digitizers, touch-sensitive panels, and optical scanners) and devices for displaying data (cathode ray tubes, voice synthesizers, plotters, printers, and the like). Within the system, there are storage devices with a wide range of capacities and a wide range of access times. These may include various levels of memory, magnetic and optical discs, tapes, and so on. And there are various devices for information transformation — logical and arithmetic processors in a variety of possible configurations. Connecting these components are channels, cables, wires, buses, and other paths through which information can flow from one component to another. Finally, there is a way to control and coordinate the various components so that they can work together to perform the information storage and transformation in the desired sequence (or in some cases in parallel).

Thus far, all the computer components named have been part of the hardware. But a computer information processing system also comprises software, the programs which direct the operation of the hardware. Some of these programs manage the hardware resources — naming and cataloging information and allocating it to the storage devices, allocating time and space to various users and jobs in a multiuser or multijob system, and accounting for the usage of the system by the various users and jobs. These programs constitute the **operating system.**

Most computers are general-purpose information processing systems. The hardware provides a limited set of low-level operations for storing and transforming information. These operations must be combined in the proper sequence to perform the specific transformations of interest to a person or organization in the world outside the computer. That is, a general-purpose computer must be converted to a special-purpose computer. The computer software which adapts general-purpose hardware so that it carries out specific transformations or functions required by a user or group of users is called *application software* or *application programs*.

A MATTER OF EMPHASIS

Every description of a system, as we have seen, involves a selection of essential or significant characteristics. In our discussion of computer information systems, we have identified the transfer, storage, and transformation of information, as well as the control of these functions, as the significant features. Each is essential. Which of these is most important?

Currently, there are several points of view, each with a different emphasis. The most traditional view emphasized the sequence or flow of control within a program. More recent approaches to describing computer information systems have either given priority to modeling the requirements for stored data or emphasized the flow and transformation of information. Structured analysis and design emphasize data flow and transformation and are best suited for systems which will be implemented using a procedural programming language such as COBOL. Object-oriented analysis and design address systems which will be implemented using an object-oriented language such as Java or C ++ .

In many respects, the structured and object-oriented approaches to systems analysis and design are complementary. The advanced student will do well to be familiar with them all. However, the first step is to understand one approach well and be able to use it. In this introductory text, we concentrate on object-oriented analysis and design.

ESSENTIAL AND IMPLEMENTATION DESCRIPTIONS OF SYSTEMS

As we have noted, system description involves abstraction. The most concrete description of a computer information system includes the manufacturer, the model and serial numbers of each piece of hardware, its capacity and speed, and perhaps even the color each cabinet is painted. It also includes a facsimile of each document containing input to the system and each report produced by the system. But we can imagine a specific set of application programs, such as the payroll system mentioned above, which produces the same outputs from the same inputs, yet runs on entirely different hardware — different in color, made by a different manufacturer, using different storage devices of different sizes and speeds. We can also redesign the input documents and reformat the output without altering their information content or changing the kinds of transformation required. And yet, in spite of these obvious external differences, we intuitively feel that these are essentially the same system.

That is why we distinguish between *physical* and *logical* system descriptions. In analyzing computer information systems, we need both kinds of system description. The terms **physical** and **logical** have long been widely used in a variety of contexts at a variety of levels of detail. For this reason, when describing information processing systems, many practitioners prefer the terms *essential* and *implementation*. These words state more directly the contrasts discussed below and will be used throughout this book.

FIGURE 1.12   Implementation versus essential system descriptions

Implementation (Physical) Description	Essential (Logical) Description
Non-essential	Essential
Shows form	Shows content
Concrete	Abstract
Implementation-dependent	Implementation-independent
Technology-dependent	Technology-free

The distinction between a description of a system's implementation (physical) and an essential (logical) system description may be explained in terms of five pairs of opposites, as shown in Figure 1.12.

Consider the time cards in a payroll system. The color of the cards is a physical detail. It doesn't matter whether the cards are printed on white or gray or cream stock. But suppose that the cards are color-coded: The hourly employees' cards are white, and the salaried employees' are blue. This may be a great convenience for those involved with the time cards, but the particular colors chosen are not essential. Any two easily distinguishable colors will do. The decision to color-code the time cards is a choice of the form in which the content (the classification of employees as hourly or salaried) will be shown. It is only one of many ways in which the distinction between the two types of employees can be implemented; thus, it is implementation-dependent. Alternatively, the color-coding is one possible concrete realization of the abstract employee classification.

Similarly, the information on the time cards can be rearranged or formatted in a variety of ways without altering its content.

So a description of a system's implementation incorporates physical features; an essential system description is independent of the way in which the system is implemented. An implementation description mentions specific technologies; an essential system description avoids prescribing technologies. An implementation description includes the form in which information is stored or arranged; an essential system description focuses on the information content. An implementation description includes accidental, superficial, and non-essential features, as opposed to what is essential. Thus, an implementation description views the concrete characteristics of a system; an essential description sees it abstractly.

COMPUTER INFORMATION SYSTEMS FOR BUSINESS

Now that we have described the function and structure of computer information systems in general, it is time to look specifically at the use of these systems in business. This section takes a systems view of business organizations. It summarizes their need for the information as well as the support which computer information systems provide to their business activities.

Information systems are frequently classified by the kinds of applications which they support. These broad areas of application include science, research, engineering, design, manufacturing, accounting, and finance. Clearly, any or all of these functional areas can be found in business organizations.

Traditionally, each of these areas has been associated with characteristic data and computations. Scientific, research, and engineering applications were typified by small amounts of data and extensive, complex, floating-point computation. Design applications added the manipulation of complex geometry. Manufacturing applications used computers to guide the paths of cutting tools or to monitor and control production process equipment. Monitoring industrial processes or research experiments required real-time readings from instruments measuring the values of critical variables. Accounting and financial applications, on the other hand, needed only simple calculations, exact to the penny, but with large files of data.

Early hardware and software were intended for either scientific or commercial applications, and the two types of systems were generally incompatible. As computers became more compact, less expensive, and less demanding in their physical environment, leading to their more widespread use, these traditional distinctions have become blurred. Scientific and engineering applications use increasingly large databases. Business applications incorporate extensive statistical analyses and continuous monitoring of inventory levels. Word-processing and document-editing systems, curiosities in the 1960s, now give support to people working throughout an organization. Microcomputers, distributed computing, and color graphics displays provide further capabilities for a variety of computer applications.

A SYSTEMS VIEW OF BUSINESS

A business provides products and services to the public or to other businesses. There are two principal types of businesses — *industrial* or *manufacturing* firms, which manufacture goods, and *service* firms, which sell or distribute products made by others or which provide a variety of other services. Some organizations expect to make a profit; others are non-profit. Government organizations are public rather than private but are similar to business organizations in many respects, especially with regard to their use of information.

Figure 1.13 shows a context diagram for a manufacturing business. Its environment includes the government, which establishes the legal and regulatory framework; other businesses which supply materials, parts, and services; competing businesses; and customers. There are also the stockholders or owners and those who have lent the company money, such as bondholders, banks, and insurance

FIGURE 1.13   Context diagram for a manufacturing business

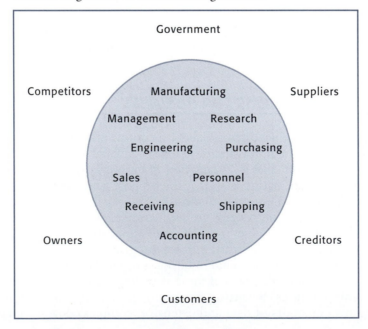

companies. The business itself comprises the management, the manufacturing functions (which are primary), and the supporting functions (which are secondary but necessary), such as research, engineering, purchasing, sales, personnel, receiving, shipping, and accounting.

Figure 1.14 shows the major functional units of a typical manufacturing business as well as the flows of material and information between these units. [3]

The material required in the manufacturing process is purchased from suppliers. Deliveries from the suppliers are received and stored as inventory until used by manufacturing to make finished products. The goods produced are then sold and shipped to customers, perhaps being stored while awaiting sale or while in transit.

The major information flows help coordinate and control the flow of material through the manufacturing process. Marketing receives orders for goods from

---

FIGURE 1.14 Major information and material flows in a manufacturing business

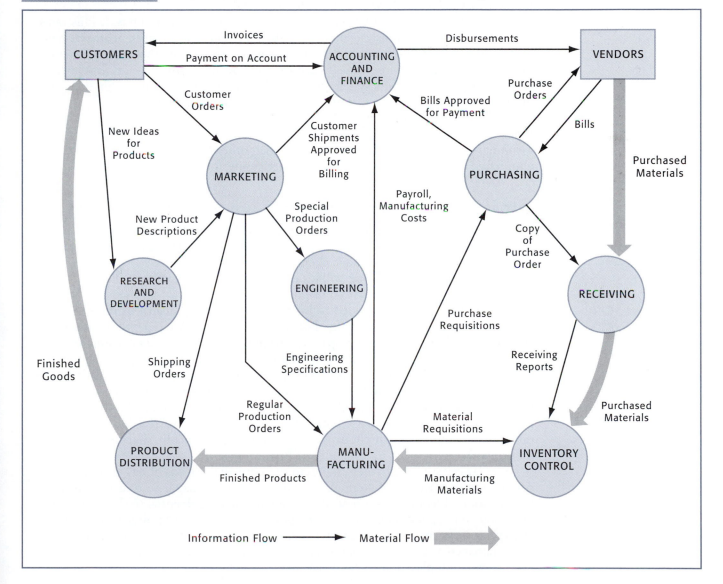

---

[3]Figure 1.14 is based on Figure 2.7 in Robert J. Thierauf, *Systems Analysis and Design: A Case Study Approach, second edition* (Columbus, Ohio: Charles E. Merrill, 1986), 52.

customers. Information about those orders goes to Product Distribution, so that the goods can be shipped, and to Accounting, so that the customers can be billed. Information from Marketing about the level of sales goes to Manufacturing to specify the desired level of production and the product mix. Engineering may be required to prepare specifications to guide the manufacturing process for special orders. As material is needed for the manufacturing process, Manufacturing requisitions it through Inventory Control from the stock on hand or, if it is not available in inventory, asks Purchasing to buy it. Purchasing in turn orders material from suppliers as needed to maintain the desired inventory level or to fill special requests from Manufacturing. Copies of the purchase orders go to Receiving to be compared against deliveries arriving from suppliers. Accounting sends invoices to customers and pays the bills from suppliers after Purchasing has approved them. Accounting also pays taxes, records and monitors the costs of doing business, and provides the company's management with information about its profitability. Research and Development takes ideas for new products and turns them into prototypes for commercially viable products.

Figure 1.14 is deliberately simplified to present an overview. Thus, it illustrates one of the benefits of an abstract model. Deliberately simplified to present an overview, it shows only major flows of material and information supporting the primary function of Manufacturing. A more detailed view would show other information flows which provide feedback within the system. Some of the important functions within the organization, notably Management and Personnel, do not appear at all.

A diagram presenting an overview of a service organization would show fewer functional units than Figure 1.14. There would be no Manufacturing function transforming material into finished products. Which other flows and functions would be eliminated would depend on the types of services performed.

INFORMATION — THE KEY TO OPERATING AND MANAGING A BUSINESS

Operating and managing a business require information. Some information is required to carry out the operations on a continuing basis. What parts are required to make Product Y? Do we have them in stock? Where can we buy them? How much will they cost? How long will it take to get delivery? Is there a discount if we order in quantity? If we pay within five days?

Other information is needed to monitor the financial health of the business. What is our current level of profit? Is our debt too high? Are our production costs competitive? Are our customers paying promptly? Are our assets earning an adequate rate of return? Is our share of the market increasing?

Still other information is used to support long-range planning and decision making. What are the trends in the economy and in our markets? What kinds of capital investments, if any, should we make, and when? What will be the effect of introducing a new product? Of reorganizing our sales territories? Of accelerating our research and development program? Of revising our profit-sharing and retirement plan?

Similar questions, whether related to the immediate needs of day-to-day operation or the perspective of strategic management decisions, arise in every business organization. The information needed to answer them is essential to the production of goods and the provision of services as well as to the continuing vitality of the enterprise. Information is increasingly being regarded as a major corporate resource to be managed as wisely as people, materials, equipment, and money.

Information plays four major roles in a business:

1. It helps carry out the production and service functions of the organization.
2. It measures and monitors the performance of these primary business functions and the other functions which support them.

3. Based on these performance measurements, it helps the organization control its operations in order to meet performance targets.
4. It supports management decisions to improve the business by modifying the organization or changing its objectives.

In any business, these last three tasks — monitoring, control, and decision support — are almost exclusively information processing activities. In many service organizations, such as insurance companies, law firms, advertising agencies, and market research groups, even the primary function of the business is information processing. Only in such areas as manufacturing, distribution, and maintenance are the primary business functions material- and energy-intensive rather than information-intensive.

PROBLEM SOLVING AND DECISION MAKING

Information is used to monitor, control, and support decisions at almost every level in a business organization, from the concerns of daily operation to the long-range strategic decisions of top managers. Information produced by monitoring the activities of the business can be used to identify a discrepancy between what is happening and the expected performance of these activities. Such a discrepancy between actual and planned performance indicates that there is a problem. Indeed, the philosophy of management by exception provides for continuous monitoring but limits the reporting of information to those situations in which performance varies from what is planned or expected.

Correcting a problem is a process which culminates in a decision. The decision specifies what action to take to change the undesirable situation and eliminate the problem. Thus, problem solving and decision making are closely related processes; problem solving leads to decisions, and effective decision making requires consideration of the underlying issues or problems.

For the purposes of presentation, the problem-solving process may be described as a sequence of steps. In reality, however, there is considerable flexibility in the ordering of the steps and in the amount of effort devoted to each step, depending on the situation. These steps are listed in Figure 1.15 and described in greater detail here.

1. *Identify the problem.* This step involves examining the situation in order to be able to state clearly what the problem is. The problem statement implies the conditions which a solution must satisfy. These conditions are known as **constraints**.
2. *Generate possible solutions.* In general, problems may have many solutions. Considering several dissimilar solutions is likely to produce a better result than considering only a single proposal. In this step, several possible solutions are proposed. Each solution is described in sufficient detail to carry out the remaining steps in the problem-solving process.

FIGURE 1.15	Steps in the problem-solving process

1. Identify the problem.
2. Generate possible solutions.
3. Eliminate the proposed solutions which do not solve the problem.
4. Evaluate the expected performance or behavior of each proposed solution.
5. Compare the alternatives to select the best solution.
6. Plan how to implement the solution which was selected.
7. Implement the solution.
8. Evaluate the performance of the solution after its implementation.

3. ***Eliminate the proposed solutions which do not solve the problem.*** Each proposal is checked to see whether it satisfies the constraints of the problem. If not, it is rejected or modified until it becomes acceptable.

4. ***Evaluate the expected performance or behavior of each proposed solution.*** The remaining proposals are evaluated qualitatively and quantitatively with respect to the most important factors affecting the choice of the best proposal. These factors are called evaluation ***criteria.***

5. ***Compare the alternatives to select the best solution.*** As a result of the evaluation, the relative advantages and disadvantages of the proposals can be compared and the best one selected. At the end of this step, the best solution is known; the appropriate decision can be recommended. However, people in business make decisions in order to act — whether the action is immediate or requires considerable planning and preparation. Effecting the solution requires that additional steps be taken.

6. ***Plan how to implement the solution which was selected.*** This step includes everything which must be done to make the proposed solution a reality. If the solution involves extensive or complex changes to the organization, schedules and budgets must be prepared, resources allocated, and responsibilities assigned for implementing the solution.

7. ***Implement the solution.*** In this step, the decisions and plans are effected.

8. ***Evaluate the performance of the solution after its implementation.*** Finally, the situation is monitored to determine whether the actions taken have solved the problem and whether the anticipated improvements have been achieved.

In the broadest sense, systems analysis is a discipline which analyzes problems, estimates the implications or consequences of various courses of action, and recommends what action to take to solve problems. In a business organization, the analysis of information systems is also directed toward improving these systems so that they provide better support for business activities. All aspects of business rely increasingly on computer information systems to assure timely and accurate data displayed in a useful form.

STRATEGIC INFORMATION SYSTEMS

To an increasing extent, information systems, especially those supported by computer technology, are playing a strategic role in many organizations. A strategic information system is one which is essential to the survival of the organization, creates or maintains a significant competitive advantage, provides a major enhancement in the value of a product, or enables the achievement of a high-priority corporate goal. Systems which directly support a company's core products or services may be essential to organizational survival. A network of automated teller machines is essential to the operation of a retail bank today. The classic competitive strategies — providing the highest quality, dominating a market niche, and being the low cost producer in a market — can be effectively supported by information systems. The first automated airline reservations system — SABRE, developed by American Airlines — provided that carrier with a significant advantage over its competitors. Just-in-time delivery of parts to the production line depends on sophisticated computer systems to provide timely information.

SUMMARY

Systems analysts must cope with complexity and lack of structure in the environment in which they work. In order to do this, they simplify and provide structure.

Thinking about the world in terms of systems is one of the most general and powerful ways in which humans provide order and structure. A system is a whole comprising interrelated components organized according to a structure. Most systems perform one or more functions and fulfill human purposes or objectives. Common types of system structures include hierarchies, matrices, and networks.

Our world can be viewed as a hierarchy of nested systems — capable of infinite expansion, on one hand, and divisible into subsystems of smaller and smaller scope, on the other. Establishing system boundaries to limit the area of study is one of the most difficult tasks in systems analysis. The system boundary separates a system from its context, or environment, and locates the interfaces between the system and the environment.

A system model is a selective, abstract description of a system. It is used to understand an existing system, to simulate or predict future system behavior, and to construct a new system. System models are generated through two complementary processes — analysis and synthesis. Analysis works from the top down, decomposing or partitioning the whole into its constituent parts. Synthesis works from the bottom up, constructing the whole by combining or aggregating primitive elements.

The simplifications introduced by system models allow humans to think and act effectively in complex situations in spite of human limitations. Yet models have their own limitations. The wise user respects them when exploiting the conceptual and practical power of systems thinking.

Information systems perform three principal functions — they transmit information, they store it, and they transform it. However, the essential function of an information processing system is to respond to what happens in the world outside the system by carrying out one or more transformations of information — by deriving some desired outputs from known inputs. Every information processing system can be described abstractly in terms of the components which move, store, and transform information.

The description of an information processing system may range from highly implementation-dependent to highly abstract. An essential system description is independent of the technology with which the system is implemented. A description of a system's implementation includes the form in which information is stored or arranged; an essential system description focuses on the information content. An implementation description includes accidental, superficial, and non-essential features rather than what is essential. Thus, an implementation description includes the concrete features of a system; an essential description sees it more abstractly.

Both manufacturing and service businesses make extensive use of information to carry out and support their activities. Information is increasingly being regarded as a major corporate resource to be managed as wisely as people, materials, equipment, and money. Information plays four major roles in a business:

1. It helps carry out the production and service functions of the organization.
2. It measures and monitors the performance of these primary business functions and the other functions which support them.
3. Based on these performance measurements, it helps the organization control its operations in order to meet performance targets.
4. It supports management decisions to improve the business by modifying the organization or changing its objectives.

Monitoring, control, and decision support are almost exclusively information processing activities. Monitoring the operation of a business often leads to the recognition that there are problems to be solved. Problem solving and decision making are closely related activities which lead to improved ways of doing business. Systems analysts can assist businesses in solving problems and making decisions. In particular, their analysis of information systems can provide improved monitoring, control, and decision support.

Information systems can often provide an organization with a strategic, competitive advantage.

KEY TERMS

component *5*

environment of a system *10*

interface *10*

subsystem *6*

system *4*

system boundary *10*

system function *11*

system objective *5*

system structure *5*

REVIEW QUESTIONS

1-1. State some human limitations which make it difficult to deal with poorly structured complexity.

1-2. Name three types of system structures, and give an example of each.

1-3. What is the difference between a system model and its representation?

1-4. What is the difference between a representation and a notation?

1-5. List four characteristics of a good model.

1-6. What is the difference between aggregation and decomposition?

1-7. What type of model is used to
  a. Describe or predict system behavior?
  b. Present a consistent description of a system in sufficient detail for the system to be constructed?

1-8. Define analysis and synthesis. How are these concepts related to aggregation, decomposition, and system modeling?

1-9. Name the two types of outputs of a business.

1-10. Name the functions included in a typical manufacturing business. Which of these are primary and which are secondary?

1-11. List four major roles of information in a business.

1-12. State and explain briefly the steps in the problem-solving process.

1-13. What are the three principal functions performed by information systems?

1-14. How does an information processing system differ from a communication system or a filing (information retrieval) system?

1-15. How is a transformation related to its input and output?

1-16. What are the principal components of a computer information processing system? Name some input and output devices. Which components of a computer information processing system carry out transformations? Name several types of computer software and briefly describe the purpose of each.

1-17. What approach to modeling information processing systems is emphasized in this book?

1-18. Explain the differences between essential and implementation descriptions of an information processing system. Do we ever find information in a purely essential form? Why?

EXERCISES AND DISCUSSION QUESTIONS

1-1. Draw a diagram depicting a system. On it, label the following: system, subsystem, component, system boundary, environment, and interface.

1-2. Based on Figure 1.16, draw a more abstract diagram showing state, county, and city as a nested hierarchy of subsystems.

1-3. In Figure 1.5, which shows a highway network, identify the components of the system. Which are nodes, and which are arcs? What is flowing through the system? How can the flow be measured? What does the length of each arc represent? Can the length of an arc be measured in more than one way?

1-4. Draw a context diagram for a system with which you are familiar, such as the educational system in which you are a student, or the company for which you work, or a piece of equipment, or the solar system. (*Hint:* It will be similar to the diagram you completed for Exercise 1.1 but will show specific features of the system you have selected. Also see Figure 1.6.)

1-5. Describe a series of moves in a chess game in two notations — the traditional English descriptive notation and the international algebraic notation. You may wish to consult a book on chess for an explanation of these notations. What are the advantages and disadvantages of each notation?

1-6. Consider the games of chess and checkers as systems. What components do they share? What components differ? Could the descriptive chess notation be easily used for checkers? Could the algebraic notation? Is a king identical in both games? Why?

1-7. Frequency (pitch) and duration are important aspects of musical sound. Explain the conventional notation used for each in a musical score.

FIGURE 1.16　　State map

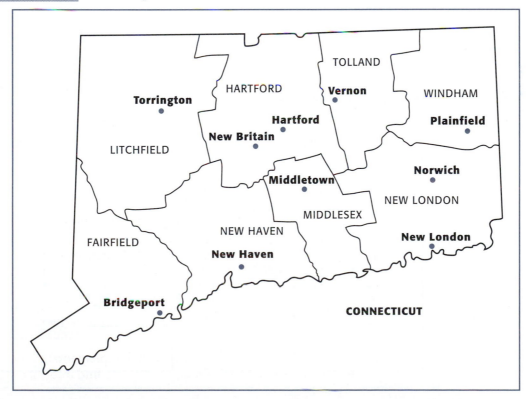

1-8. a. The meter (rhythmic structure) of poetry is described in terms of a primitive called a *foot*. Shakespeare's plays are written in ***iambic pentameter***. Explain what this means and what approach to system description has been taken.

   b. Other poetic forms incorporate both meter and rhyme. Find an example of a ***sonnet*** and explain its structure.

1-9. State some differences in function between a banking business and a manufacturing business. That is, which functions shown in Figure 1.14 are not applicable to a bank, and which functions in a bank are not applicable to a manufacturing business? List some specific products and services of a bank.

1-10. For each of the four major roles played by information in a business:

   a. Select an organization with which you are familiar.
   b. Identify a document or other collection of information used by the organization.
   c. Explain how the document is used by the organization to fulfill its role.

1-11. In the light of businesses' need for information, what does **information resource management** mean, and what purpose does it serve?

1-12. Identify some examples of strategic information systems other than those mentioned in the chapter. Discuss what strategic value they contribute to the organization.

1-13. Figure 1.17 is a schematic diagram of a computer. Explain the purpose of each component shown in terms of information transmission, storage, and transformation.

1-14. Figure 1.18 shows a system controlled by *feedback*. How does feedback affect the relationships among input, output, and transformation? Interpret Figure 1.18 as a diagram for a heating system which includes a thermostat.

1-15. In Figure 1.18, identify some of the points at which feedback could be used to control the system. At each point, state what information could be obtained and how it could be used to control the system.

1-16. On August 14, 2003, the most extensive electrical blackout in North America affected much of the Midwest, New York, and eastern Canada.

FIGURE 1.17   **Schematic diagram of a computer**

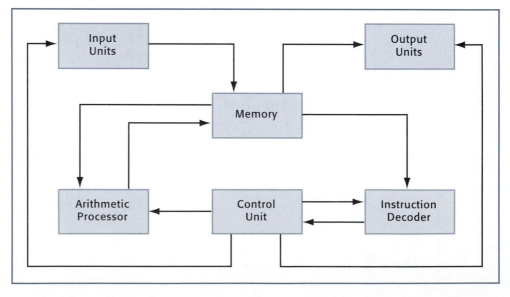

FIGURE 1.18   System controlled by feedback

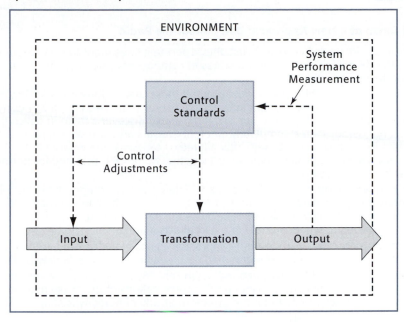

What was supposed to happen if part of the system was overloaded or if nearby portions of the system failed? To what extent was this approach successful, and to what extent was it a failure? What other system became overloaded with demand as a result of the blackout? In order to prevent future blackouts, to what extent does a solution depend on technical improvements to the power distribution grid, and to what extent does it depend on factors in the environment?

1-17. Consider the article in Figure 1.19 about the shift to systems biology:

a. Explain the "shoot-the-radio" approach to understanding a system.
b. Why does the author call this approach reductionist?
c. How does the article support the understanding of systems presented in this chapter?
d. What perspectives have ecologists taken on biological systems?

FIGURE 1.19   Biologists Hail Dawn of a New Approach: Don't Shoot the Radio

Biologists Hail Dawn of a New Approach: Don't Shoot the Radio

How would a team of biologists fix a radio? First, they'd secure a large grant to purchase hundreds of identical working radios. After describing and classifying scores of components (metal squares, shiny circles with three legs, etc.) they'd shoot the radios with .22's.

Examining the corpses, the biologists would pick out those that no longer work. They'd find one radio in which a .22 knocked out a wire and triumphantly declare they had discovered the Key Component (KC) whose presence is required for normal operation. But a rival lab would discover a radio in which the .22 left the Key Component intact but demolished a completely different Crucial Part (CP), silencing the radio. Moreover, the rivals would demonstrate that the KC isn't so "key" after all; radios can work fine without it. Finally, a brilliant post-doc would discover a switch whose position determines whether KC or CP is required for normal operation. But the biologists still can't fix the blasted radios.

For those of you who haven't looked inside a radio lately, the Key Component is the wire connecting the external (FM) antenna to the innards of the radio, the Crucial Part is the internal (AM) antenna and the switch is the AM/FM switch. Biologists can't repair radios because the part-by-part approach fails to describe the radio as a system — what's connected to what and how one part affects another.

Biologists' affinity for the one-part-at-a-time approach, argues biologist Yuri Lazebnik of Cold Spring Harbor Laboratory on New York's Long Island, who dreamed up the radio analogy, is "a flaw of biological research today."

For that, thank the events of 50 years ago today. On Feb. 28, 1953, James Watson spent the morning at his Cambridge, England, lab piecing together cardboard representations of the "base pairs" in the DNA molecule. With that, he and Francis Crick realized that the master molecule of heredity is shaped like a spiral staircase, or double helix.

This discovery ushered in the era of the gene and gave birth to a new field: molecular biology. The study of living things became a science in which progress meant describing the smallest bits possible, usually one at a time — one stretch of DNA, one RNA, one protein. The double helix, Harvard University naturalist E. O. Wilson once said, "injected into all of biology a new faith in reductionism" — a "shoot the radio" approach.

Don't misunderstand. Molecular biology was a rousing success. It reached its pinnacle with the sequencing of the human genome. But all good things must end, and there are signs that biological reductionism is one of them. It's pretty clear that making a parts list for an organism, even if you annotate it with those parts' functions, is no more adequate to understanding the complexity of a living thing than is listing the parts of a Boeing 777. Instead, you have to ask how all the parts fit together and work together.

The new approach is called systems biology, and it represents a huge departure from the reductionist paradigm. "Biology undergoes these revolutionary waves from time to time, after which nothing ever is the same," says biologist Eric Davidson of the California Institute of Technology, Pasadena. "This is one of those times."

Systems biology analyzes a living thing as a whole, not one gene or protein at a time. "You have to look at all the elements in a living system to understand how they function," says biologist Leroy Hood. His seminal work on DNA-sequencing technology fell four-square in the reductionist camp, but in co-founding the Institute for Systems Biology in Seattle in 2000 he became one of the first and most prominent defectors.

Not surprisingly, the system approach represents an unsettling shift that "is not exactly welcomed" by many biologists, says Mr. Lazebnik. Partly, that's because "doing systems biology requires a huge change in the research culture," says Prof. Davidson. "In traditional molecular biology, each scientist works on his own gene, but the systems approach requires determining the effect of every gene on every other. You have to give up this 'my gene, your gene' stuff."

But the payoff could be tremendous. At MIT, quantitative models showing the interconnections among cellular components — much like the wiring diagram for a computer chip — promise to predict unexpected properties of anticancer drugs such as Herceptin, says MIT's Peter Sorger. With any luck the models will predict how to tailor cancer treatment to individual patients.

Adapted from Sharon Begley, "Biologists Hail Dawn of a New Approach: Don't Shoot the Radio," *Wall Street Journal*, 21 February 2003, B1. © 2003 Dow Jones & Company.

LEARNING OBJECTIVES

After mastering the material in this chapter, you will be able to

- Describe the overall structure of the Rational Unified Process for information system development.

- Name and explain briefly the phases of the Rational Unified Process

- Describe how its nine core disciplines contribute to the Rational Unified Process.

- Explain the difference between incremental and iterative system development and discuss why the system development process should be both incremental and iterative.

- Identify the different types of users of information systems.

- Discuss the principal roles and responsibilities of users, analysts, designers, programmers, and quality assurance staff during system development.

- Appreciate the principal skills required of successful systems analysts and designers.

- Explain the important categories of system feasibility.

- Prepare an economic feasibility analysis as part of a business plan.

INTRODUCTION

In the previous chapter, we discussed computer information systems — in general and in relation to the information needs of a business organization. We also enumerated some of the kinds of applications software available for business.

But every system of application programs has to be developed. The development of an information processing system is a process, carried out as a project, which has the system as its product. The process begins with the identification of a need for a computer information system and ends with a system which operates routinely and effectively to support a business organization.

Clearly, each project to develop an information system should occur as a part of a comprehensive information systems plan for the entire organization or enterprise. Such a plan must be driven by and consistent with the strategic goals and business plan of the organization. Information systems planning identifies the information systems and technology required to carry out the business plan, including the necessary data, people, software, and hardware. It also establishes priorities among system development projects as well as allocating the people, money, and equipment required for each project. Careful planning and coordination are necessary if the resources devoted to information systems are to support the organization effectively. This book focuses on individual system development projects, but the importance of enterprisewide planning must always be kept in mind.

The information system development process provides a conceptual framework for presenting and understanding the activities involved throughout a project to develop an information system. This system development process, sometimes known as a system development life cycle, also provides a management framework for scheduling and coordinating a system development project and for monitoring its progress.

Among writers on information system development, there is little uniformity in defining and describing the system development process. There is broad general agreement on the overall process but differences in the terms used to describe it. There is a reasonable consensus about the very detailed tasks, but considerable variation in how these tasks are related within the process. Unlike older fields, such as the sciences and engineering, information systems analysis and design has no universally accepted technical language. Moreover, object-oriented software has spawned its own ways of describing the process.

In this chapter, we present an overview of the Rational Unified Process for information system development, which incorporates current approaches to object-oriented system development. But you are cautioned that others may view or describe the process somewhat differently, and we encourage you to look behind differences in terminology to find the conceptual similarities and differences.

THE RATIONAL UNIFIED PROCESS FOR SOFTWARE DEVELOPMENT — AN OVERVIEW

Figure 2.1 depicts a simplified overview of the information system development process. It assumes the most comprehensive situation — a project to develop custom-made software. It is a simplification of a software development process developed at Rational Software Corporation by Jacobson, Booch, and Rumbaugh.[1] This process is commonly known as the **Rational Unified Process (RUP)**, or merely the **Unified Process**.

According to Jacobson, Booch, and Rumbaugh, the product of system development is a **software system**. It includes all the information necessary to represent it in machine- or human-readable form to the computer, the users of the system, and the participants in the development process.

FIGURE 2.1   **Phases, disciplines, and iterations in the Rational Unified Process**

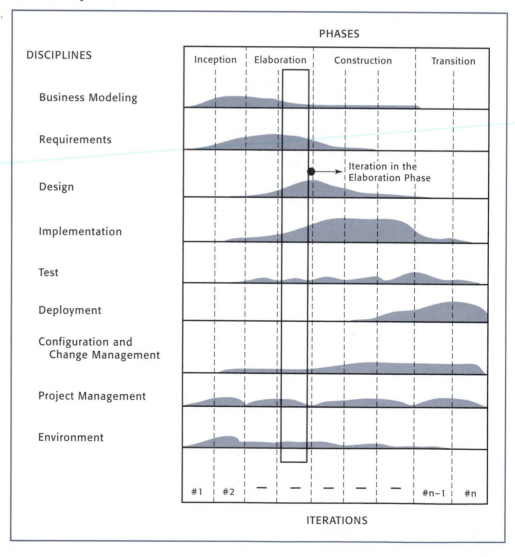

---

[1]Ivar Jacobson, Grady Booch, and James Rumbaugh, *The Unified Software Development Process* (Reading, Mass.: Addison-Wesley, 1999). See also Phillipe Krutchen, *The Rational Unified Process: An Introduction*, 2nd ed. (Boston: Addison-Wesley, 2000).

There are four *phases* in the Unified Process:

1. **Inception** (Make the Business Case)
2. **Elaboration** (Define the System Architecture)
3. **Construction** (Construct the System)
4. **Transition** (Integrate the System with the Using Organization)

Each phase produces a well-defined set of *artifacts*, or work products. These phases are described later in this chapter. Note that we could use a slightly modified version of this development process to describe the process of creating many other new systems, such as a house or an automobile. (See Exercise 2–5.)

Contributing to the work of each phase are nine core **disciplines:**[2] A *discipline* is a sequence of development activities with related artifacts which produce a result of value.

Figure 2.1 shows the phases and the core disciplines in each phase.[3] It does not show the information used to manage the process or any of the more detailed activities within each phase.

The nine core disciplines are:

▌ **Business Modeling** (Re-envision and Re-engineer the Organization)
▌ **Requirements** (Define the User Requirements)
▌ **Design** (Design the System)
▌ **Implementation** (Write the Software)
▌ **Test** (Test the System)
▌ **Deployment** (Integrate the Software into the Using Organization)
▌ **Configuration and Change Management** (Manage the Artifacts of the Evolving System)
▌ **Project Management** (Manage the Development Process)
▌ **Environment** (Support the Development Process with Processes and Tools)

The Unified Process provides a very sophisticated framework for describing system development. Note that Figure 2.1 has a matrix structure. The rows show the disciplines in sequence from top to bottom. The disciplines are people-oriented and refer to the specialized skills and activities of software development professionals. The columns show the phases in time sequence from left to right. They are project-oriented and organize the development process into a plan for completing related activities. The phases may be further subdivided into *iterations*, as shown by the vertical divisions within each phase. This structure of disciplines, phases, and iterations permits considerable flexibility in tailoring the process to a specific project.

The sophistication and flexibility of the Unified Process also introduce considerable complexity, which makes it harder to explain. In order to simplify our presentation, we will first discuss the core disciplines and the phases as independent dimensions of development. We will then describe the importance of iterations in the Unified Process.

In this chapter, we have chosen to explain the names of the disciplines and phases with infinitive phrases, in keeping with the best traditional practices of systems analysis. Although longer, these names are clearer and may avoid some of the confusion caused by the wide variations in naming the phases of a development process.

---

[2]Until 2001, these disciplines were called **workflows.**
[3]Adapted from Kruchten, *The Rational Unified Process*, 23, Figure 2.2

CORE DISCIPLINES OF THE RATIONAL UNIFIED PROCESS

This section discusses the nine core disciplines of the Unified Process. It describes each briefly, including an illustration of typical artifacts from most of these disciplines. These artifacts are explained in detail in Parts II and III. This book is primarily concerned with the Requirements and Design disciplines because they are the disciplines most heavily involved in object-oriented analysis and design.

In the discussion below, an explanatory phrase follows the name of each discipline in order to clarify the work of that discipline.

BUSINESS MODELING (RE-ENVISION AND RE-ENGINEER THE ORGANIZATION)

This discipline addresses an organization's need to improve or re-engineer its business and its business processes.[4] It is concerned with understanding the organization and its current problems. It seeks to identify opportunities for improvement. It helps develop a new vision for the organization as well as a model of the business which will realize that vision.

Merely automating business processes as they are currently done may not be the best way to benefit from information technology. As Hammer has expressed it: "Automating a mess yields an automated mess."[5] Significant improvements are possible if a business modifies its processes before automating them. Business process re-engineering examines business processes in terms of the value they add. Some processes (or steps within a process) add value to the customer; others add no direct value to the customer but add value by helping manage the business. Those processes which add no value to either the business or its customers should be eliminated. Thus, modeling and improving the entire business and its processes may precede the definition of users' requirements for an information system.

Although this book does not deal with business re-engineering, many of the Unified Modeling Language (UML) models and modeling skills presented in it are also applicable to the activities of business modeling. In the case of a single application, the business model focuses on the application domain.

REQUIREMENTS (DEFINE THE USER REQUIREMENTS)

The Requirements discipline focuses on finding out what is to be built for the users of a system. This discipline has traditionally been known as systems analysis. It identifies, refines, and structures the users' requirements for the proposed system. Identifying requirements may involve understanding the system context as well as describing the features needed in the system.

In the Unified Process, the system context may be expressed as a model of the problem domain — the business or application area to be supported by the system. (Domain models are discussed in Chapter 5.) Figure 2.2 is an example of a domain model; it shows important concepts in a university student registration system.

The requirements to be identified are both functional (what the system must do) and nonfunctional (constraints or performance expectations). Requirements are expressed in terms of use cases (see Chapter 4), which describe explicitly what the new system must do. Figure 2.3 is a use case diagram for the Public University Registration System; it depicts the people who interact with the system and the processes they need to use.

---

[4]Michael Hammer and James Champy, *Reengineering the Corporation: A Manifesto for Business Revolution* (New York: Harper Business, 1993).
[5]Michael Hammer, *Making eGovernment Work*, (Hammer and Company, 2001), 11.

FIGURE 2.2   Example of a domain model

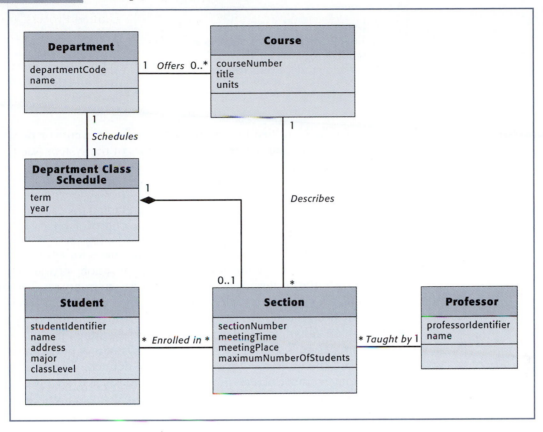

FIGURE 2.3   Example of a use case diagram

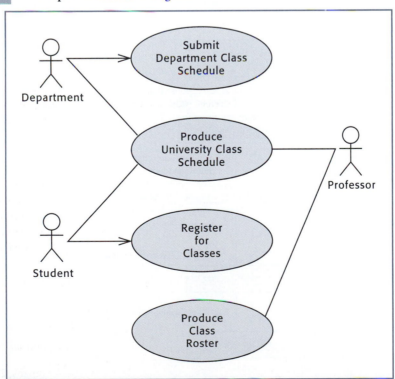

FIGURE 2.4   Example of an event list

> 1. Department submits its class schedule.
> 2. Time to produce university class schedule.
> 3. Student registers for classes.
> 4. Time to produce class roster.

Use cases may be identified by finding the significant events or occurrences in the system's environment and the expected responses of the system (see Chapter 3). Figure 2.4 shows an example of an event list.

Object-oriented systems analysis is described in detail in Part II.

DESIGN (DESIGN THE SYSTEM)

The requirements refined during analysis become the basis for system design. The Design discipline is responsible for designing the application software for a system which will operate in the hardware and system software environment. This discipline must also design the related manual procedures. Once the system-level interfaces have been decided on, the system design can be partitioned into a program design problem, a database design problem, and a user interface design problem.

The program design is specified as one or more systems of program units; all the program units and the interfaces between them are defined. (Figure 2.5 shows the interactions among software objects in response to a message from a student requesting registration in a specific section of a course.) At the detailed level, the logic of the

FIGURE 2.5   Example of a collaboration diagram for the operation requestSection

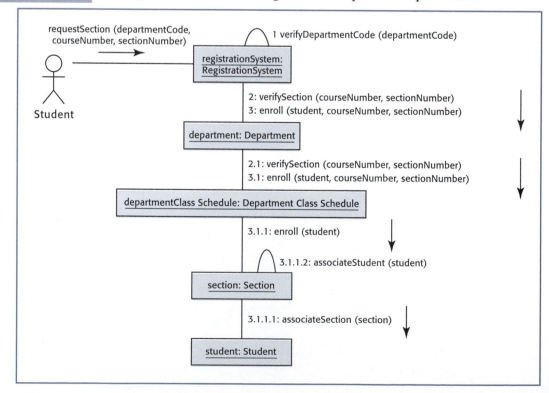

operations performed by each program unit is specified. The design is also adapted to fit the hardware selected for implementing the system.

Also, the structure of the database is defined, and the interface to the database is designed.

In addition, the details of the dialogue or interaction between users and the automated part of the system are defined, and the final form of inputs and outputs is determined. Draft versions of critical user documentation are prepared as part of the system design process.

Object-oriented system design is described in detail in Part III.

IMPLEMENTATION (WRITE THE SOFTWARE)

The Implementation discipline plans the software components to be coded during each iteration. These software units are coded and tested individually. Then they are integrated into an executable system so that they can be tested as a system.

TEST (DEVELOP AND CARRY OUT THE SYSTEM TESTS)

This discipline plans the tests required in each iteration. An *integration test* is conducted for each group of components constructed during an iteration. A *system test* occurs at the end of an iteration and involves the entire system.

The performance targets established in the requirements specification are used to develop detailed and specific tests of acceptable system performance. These tests determine whether the system as constructed by its developers satisfies the users' requirements.

Designing the tests includes creating test cases, which define what to test; describing test procedures, which state how to perform the tests; and writing code to automate as much of the testing as possible.

Finally the tests are carried out; defective builds may require redesign or recoding to correct the defects.

DEPLOYMENT (INTEGRATE THE SOFTWARE INTO THE USING ORGANIZATION)

Deployment is the primary discipline involved in the Installation phase. It conducts the *beta test*. In beta testing, a small number of users try the product and report defects and deficiencies to the developers. The developers correct the defects and may also incorporate some of the suggested improvements in the version of the product for general release. The Deployment discipline also installs the software throughout the organization, trains the users, and converts existing databases as required.

CONFIGURATION AND CHANGE MANAGEMENT (MANAGE THE ARTIFACTS OF THE EVOLVING SYSTEM)

This discipline manages the artifacts produced during system development. It is concerned with the product and the process as well as project management. *Configuration management* deals with the various versions of consistent sets of related artifacts. *Change request management* is responsible for managing requests for change, assessing their impact, and tracking approved changes. Figure 2.6 shows an example of a change request form. *Project status and measurement* extract information about the development process for use in project management.

FIGURE 2.6   Project change request form

Project Change

Number _____

Requested by: _____ Request Date: _____

Reason for change:

Attach affected models, diagrams, and descriptions

Attach cost-benefit analysis

Disposition: Accept

           Defer until _____
                           Date

           Reject for the following reason:

Lavette C. Teague, Jr., and Christopher W. Pidgeon, *Structured Analysis Methods for Computer Information Systems* (Chicago: Science Research Associates, 1985), 318, Fig. 15-4, which has been adapted.

PROJECT MANAGEMENT (MANAGE THE DEVELOPMENT PROCESS)

This discipline plans all the phases of a software development project from inception to transition. It also plans each iteration in detail. It is concerned with identifying and managing the risks associated with development. It tracks and measures the progress of a project in order to detect problems as well as to provide a basis for estimating resource requirements for future projects. Important issues in project management are discussed in Chapter 14.

ENVIRONMENT (SUPPORT THE DEVELOPMENT PROCESS WITH PROCESSES AND TOOLS)

This discipline provides and supports an organization's software development environment. It selects, acquires, installs, and configures software development tools. It provides guidelines for individual projects. It is responsible for improving the organization's development process and supports that process with technical and administrative services.[6]

PHASES OF THE RATIONAL UNIFIED PROCESS

This section describes the four phases of the Unified Process, as shown in Figure 2.1. Each phase organizes the work of the appropriate disciplines to produce the necessary artifacts or deliverables. Associated with each phase are evaluation criteria used to determine whether the project should advance to the next phase. Each phase terminates in a ***milestone*** marked by the delivery of a defined set of artifacts. (Some of these evaluation criteria and artifacts are listed in Figure 2.9.)

Figure 2.7 depicts a timeline for the phases of a project for developing an initial version of a system. It assumes that the project is of moderate size and requires a moderate amount of effort.[7] The horizontal axis shows the approximate percentage of the time spent in each phase; the vertical axis shows the approximate percentage of the resources used in each phase.

In the discussion below, an explanatory phrase follows the name of each phase in order to clarify what happens in that phase. The descriptions summarize the goals or objectives of each phase. We also discuss briefly the principal artifacts of each phase in order to suggest what is done to accomplish these objectives.

| FIGURE 2.7 | Distribution of time and resources to develop the initial version of a system |

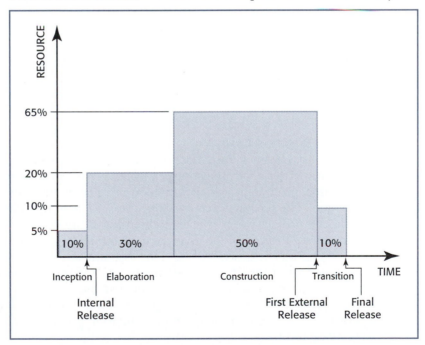

---

[6]Readers who are familiar with the traditional system development life cycle will note that the Requirements, Design, Implementation, Test, and Deployment disciplines correspond closely to the major components of the life cycle. Business Modeling is a preliminary or preparatory discipline, and the remaining disciplines support and manage the development process.
[7]Adapted from Kruchten, *The Rational Unified Process*, 64, Figures 4.5 and 4.6; 128, Figure 7.4; and 129, Table 7.1.

1. INCEPTION (MAKE THE BUSINESS CASE)

The principal goal of the Inception phase is to obtain agreement among the stakeholders about the objectives for the system development project. The principal artifacts produced during Inception are directed toward establishing feasibility. Feasibility addresses, from a variety of points of view, whether the proposed project can be completed to the satisfaction of the stakeholders. We discuss the topic of feasibility in more detail later in this chapter.

At this stage in the development process, the system description is necessarily so general and sketchy that economic evaluation is extremely imprecise. What is really addressed here is whether the proposed system promises sufficient potential benefit to invest the additional resources necessary to complete the Elaboration phase.

The proposed project may also be evaluated to determine its compatibility with the goals of the using organization.

The most important artifacts produced during Inception are a vision document, a use case model (see the example in Figure 2.3 and the explanation in Chapter 4), a description of a structure for the system, an initial business case, a risk assessment, and a project plan. These artifacts are described briefly below.

In addition, the Inception phase may produce a proof-of-concept *prototype* to demonstrate to users or customers that the system will be able to support their business objectives. A prototype is a partial implementation or simulation of what the completed system will be like. In some cases, a prototype may be used to assist in the assessment of risk or feasibility.

Vision Document

The vision document organizes the requests from all the stakeholders in the new system. It summarizes the project's requirements, its key features, and its major constraints.

Critical Use-Case Model

The use case model defines the scope of the system and its functions. It depicts all the people who will interact with the system and the processes in the system which they will need to use. This model emphasizes those processes which are critical to system acceptance and which will drive the major design decisions.

Initial Business Case

The initial business case describes the business context for the project as well as the business criteria for project success. These criteria could include desired increases in revenue, profitability, or market share as well as in product quality or customer satisfaction. The success criteria must be measurable so that they can be used for evaluating the project when it is completed (or along the way). The business case also contains a forecast of the financial implications of the project.

This business case will state the assumptions on which the project is based and the expected return on investment (ROI) if the assumptions prove to be true. These assumptions must be confirmed at the end of the Elaboration phase, when the project scope and cost can be estimated more accurately. The estimates are revised at the end of each iteration and each phase and should become more accurate each time.

Candidate System Architecture

The initial business case requires initial estimates of the expected cost of the proposed system. The cost will depend not only on the scope of the system but also on the structure of the system. This structure is commonly referred to as the system architecture (sometimes as the software architecture). The *system architecture* is the set of significant decisions about what the software components are and how they are to be organized. It specifies the most critical subsystems and defines their relationships with each other.

While the usage of the term continues to be somewhat hazy and inconsistent, Kruchten provides the following summary of the way system architecture is understood in the Unified Process:

Architecture encompasses significant decisions about the following:

■ The organization of a software system.
■ The selection of structural elements and their interfaces by which the system is composed, together with their behavior as specified in the collaboration among these elements.
■ The composition of these elements into progressively larger subsystems.
■ The architectural style that guides this organization, these elements and their interfaces, their collaborations, and their composition.

Software architecture is concerned with not only structure and behavior but also context: usage, functionality, performance, resilience, reuse, comprehensibility, economic and technological constraints and trade-offs, and aesthetics.[8]

The description of the system architecture produced in the Inception phase is called the ***candidate system architecture***. It is only a tentative proposal for the way the system can be organized, describing a structure which appears to be promising and workable. It will be refined further or replaced by a more suitable architecture during Elaboration.

Initial Risk Assessment

Software development is full of risk and uncertainty. The initial risk assessment identifies and prioritizes the most significant obstacles to the successful completion of the project. Eliminating or reducing these risks is a key element in planning the project and is discussed further in Chapter 14.

Initial Project Plan

The project plan describes the sequence in which the system functions will be defined, designed, and constructed as well as the schedule and budget for developing the system. The plan must consider the uncertainties and risks inherent in the project and their impact on the schedule and budget.

The initial project plan shows the number of iterations planned for each phase. It also sets a date for the milestone at the end of each phase.

2. ELABORATION (DEFINE THE SYSTEM ARCHITECTURE)

The goals of this phase are to define a system architecture which can serve as the basis for subsequent system development and to produce a more reliable project plan and cost estimate.

In practice, developing a reliable cost estimate may require assumptions about the details of the system based on experience, or it may involve partial implementation of some of the system. There may be significant risks which could cause the schedule or cost to change. A list of these risks accompanies the estimate so that their impact can be quantified if necessary.

The Elaboration phase includes a substantial amount of analysis — establishing the use cases which describe the users' requirements to be supported by the system

---

[8]Kruchten, *The Rational Unified Process*, 84.

architecture. It also incorporates the design and initial implementation of the most important portions of the system, as shown in Figure 2.1.

The principal artifacts produced during Elaboration are directed toward realizability. The use case model is extended. The proposed system architecture is developed into an executable prototype. The most critical use cases are programmed. The vision document, the business case, the risk assessment, and the project plan are revised based on what has been learned in the Elaboration phase. A detailed plan for the Construction phase is prepared. If desired, a preliminary users' manual may be produced. Some of these artifacts are described briefly below.

The result is an agreed-on scope and basis for completing the development. After this point, changes to the scope of the system require formal approval.

Architectural Baseline

The *architectural baseline* is an internal release of the system. It is an initial implementation of the system architecture — a small, lean, working version which serves as the foundation for continued development.

Use Case Model

The use case model captures the functional requirements for the system. By now, it identifies all the use cases, with descriptions of most of them. **Supplementary requirements** are added to the use case model to capture the nonfunctional requirements and to record any requirements not associated with a specific use case.

Project Plan

The project plan now includes the entire project, with milestones, iterations, and evaluation criteria for each iteration. It also includes a more detailed plan for the Construction phase.

3. CONSTRUCTION (CONSTRUCT THE SYSTEM)

Following the Elaboration phase, the system is constructed.[9] The Construction phase produces an operational system ready for beta testing in a user or customer environment. During construction, the development proceeds iteratively and incrementally, as discussed later in this chapter. This phase is, in effect, a software manufacturing process. All the required features are developed and incorporated in the software product. The emphasis is on managing and controlling the process in order to optimize costs, schedules, and quality.

Constructing a computer information system involves coding, testing, and debugging each of the program units. These program units are coded, tested, and debugged individually. Then they are combined incrementally. That is, only one program unit at a time is added to the previous combination, and its interfaces to the rest of the system are tested. If there is a problem, it is located in the newly added program unit or in the interfaces. This continues until the entire system has been tested.

Final versions of the users' manuals are developed in parallel with the software. Operations manuals and reference manuals are produced for both the manual and the automated portions of the new system.

During system construction, users and analysts observe the system as it evolves. Thus, they have tangible evidence of progress. It is also possible that

---

[9]The phase of the development process in which the system is constructed is widely called "implementation." However, in other contexts, "implementation" refers to integrating the new system into the using organization. In the Unified Process, "implementation" refers to a core discipline which writes the code for the software.

they will catch design and construction errors. Depending on their technical abilities, some of the analysts and users may be invited to participate in development walkthroughs.

4. TRANSITION (INTEGRATE WITH THE USING ORGANIZATION)

The goal of the Transition phase is to place the software in the hands of its users. The product is released for beta testing. After the documented and tested software has been delivered by the developers and accepted by the users, it must be integrated into the using organization. This requires training of the users, delivery and installation of any additional hardware, conversion or creation of the files or data bases for the system, and possibly a period of parallel operation of both the old and the new systems. At the end of the Transition phase is a postimplementation review, which may result in modifications and minor enhancements to the system.

Testing

Testing during the Transition phase includes beta testing, as mentioned above, and acceptance testing. *Acceptance testing* is carried out by users to confirm that the system satisfies their requirements.

The performance targets established in the requirements are used to develop detailed and specific tests of acceptable system performance. The performance requirements are expressed as a specific set of tests which will decide whether the system is acceptable. If the system passes all these tests, it is considered to be acceptable by the users.

The acceptance tests establish measurable standards of system performance. In principle, they are passed or failed as a whole, although in practice some tests may be considered as less important, and therefore the acceptance standards may be relaxed somewhat if the system does not meet them exactly. Review, use, and evaluation of the users' manuals and other system documentation should be part of the acceptance test.

The acceptance tests may be generated before or in parallel with system design. The designers' task is to anticipate and achieve the required system performance. It is important that the designers know what the tests will be because the tests provide the standards for evaluating the system design.

Acceptance tests make an important contribution to quality control in system development. To be effective, quality control must begin in the early stages of system development. Quality control involves continuing evaluation of the system requirements and of what is being produced in response to those requirements.

Ideally, people who have no analysis, design, or construction responsibilities for a system should define these acceptance tests. In this way, there is an independent interpretation of the system requirements as stated by the analysts. In addition, systems designers and constructors are prevented from setting the standards by which their own work will be evaluated. In many situations, however, analysts prepare or help prepare the acceptance tests because they are most familiar with the users' requirements. Users are consulted if necessary to clarify the requirements statements.

Training

The users and their managers need to be trained to operate the system. They need to understand the interface between the manual and automated procedures for the new system. User training aids required at this stage, such as manuals, examples, videotapes, computer-aided instruction, and demonstrations or simulations, will have been prepared in advance.

Conversion

Conversion to the new system also occurs during this phase if there is to be a period of parallel operation of the current and new systems. Database conversion could also occur at this time if acceptance tests do not require building the entire new database.

Certainly there may be appreciable technical problems when moving to a new computer information system. Database conversion alone can be overwhelming when converting from a manual, paper-based system to an online, interactive database management system. If the conversion is spread out over a period of time, users who were promised that the new system would be much more efficient and productive are likely to be dismayed at the extra effort required. What these users fail to realize, whether they were told or not, is that the benefits of efficiency and productivity come after database conversion.

Other Activities

Other activities required for this phase may be dependent on the approach taken to system testing. In some large or geographically dispersed systems, initial system installation and testing may be limited to users in one region or area. In such situations, the installation of the new hardware or software in the other regions may follow the initial tests.

Users should anticipate some difficulties during system start-up as they learn their new tasks and procedures. The more these difficulties are minimized through user involvement in system development, well-designed user interfaces, proper user training, and cooperation among all the participants, the better the transition will be.

Once the system is operational in its intended organizational setting, some refinements to the software and user procedures may be needed in order to correct errors or to clarify misunderstandings. Sometimes the software must be "tuned" to improve its performance. After the period of transition and integration is over, a postimplementation review should be held to evaluate whether the original system objectives as well as the users' requirements and performance targets continue to be met.

Postimplementation Review

After the new system has been integrated into the organization, routine system operation begins. The start-up and learning period is over, and users are familiar with the system. Both manual and automated procedures are working smoothly and normally. The anticipated benefits of the new system are available to the organization on an ongoing basis. It is now time for a postimplementation (or postinstallation) review. This review, which normally occurs three to six months after full operation begins, assesses the successes and shortcomings of the system development. Two specific areas are included in the review — *system performance* and *project performance.*

In evaluating system performance, two questions are addressed:

> **Have the operational expectations for the system been met?**
>
> **Have the predicted benefits been achieved?**

The answers to these questions indicate whether or not the users got what they expected and whether or not the specified system requirements are still being met. This review is especially important if acceptance tests were not made with the system at full load or with the full data base. It helps identify any bottlenecks in the system and determines whether the execution time or response time of the automated system should be reduced. Even if the stated requirements are satisfied, unanticipated requirements or problems may be discovered by the review.

The project review assesses the technical performance of the system developers and builders. It also gathers data that can be used to determine resource requirements for future projects. In judging project performance, the following questions are asked:

> **Were the stated project goals and objectives achieved?**
>
> **What is the relationship between estimated and actual development costs and schedules? What are the explanations for any variances?**

These questions deal with what happened in the project and why it happened.

When the system is constructed and delivered in several versions, there will be a postimplementation review for each version.

Care must be taken to keep the review from turning into a witch hunt. The emphasis should be on giving an honest, accurate, and dispassionate evaluation of successes and failures. Then the documented successes can be repeated and the failures avoided on future projects. This review process provides critical feedback so that both users and analysts can learn from the effort. Otherwise, it will be easy to commit the same errors in the future.

If the postimplementation review finds a discrepancy between the system's performance and the specified system requirements, it will be necessary to correct the deficiencies (or relax the performance requirements). But, in many cases, even though the evaluation is satisfactory and the system is operating effectively, there may be a need for subsequent modifications. Minor changes may become necessary to accommodate changes in hardware or operating systems. Other modifications may be required as a result of changes in the business environment, such as new government regulations, increased customer expectations, or actions of competitors. Users seldom remain content, especially if they are being exposed for the first time to the power of an effective computer information system. Early successes usually create pressure to enhance the usefulness and augment the scope of a system.

Defining Requirements for System Enhancement

A good job of system development often leads to requests for system enhancement. Satisfied users have an increased understanding of the potential of computer information systems. As a result, they may ask to add "just this one more thing." The ad hoc incorporation of many new features can compromise a system design which did not anticipate them. Major system enhancements should be treated as a new system development project.

CONTRIBUTION OF THE DISCIPLINES TO EACH PHASE

In principle, the Unified Process permits all nine disciplines to contribute effort to each phase. In practice, the distribution of effort among the disciplines differs from phase to phase, as shown in Figure 2.1. During the Inception phase, most of the time is spent in the Business Modeling and Requirements disciplines. In the Elaboration phase, most of the time is spent in Requirements and Design. The Design discipline overlaps Elaboration and Construction. Most of the time spent in the Implementation and Test disciplines occurs during the Construction and Test phases.

ITERATIVE AND INCREMENTAL SYSTEM DEVELOPMENT

Traditional approaches to system development often attempted to satisfy all the system requirements with the initial version of the system. In the case of large systems, the development process could take several years. Moreover, these systems often failed to meet users' expectations. A long system development cycle has become increasingly problematic in today's dynamic business environment. Users are unwilling to wait to see tangible results and insist on realizing benefits from their investment in systems in the short run. As a result, large systems are usually constructed, tested, and delivered in versions. The initial version furnishes users with an important subset of the system's ultimate capabilities; each subsequent version adds a group of additional capabilities.

Thus, system development has become increasingly iterative and incremental. Development is *iterative* if it allows for the reworking of a part of the system. Development is *incremental* if it is organized as a series of builds. As Richter expresses it:

> Incremental development improves the process (by dividing it into phased builds), whereas iterative development improves the product (by providing for the reworking of any part of the design or implementation that is flawed).[10]

Figure 2.1 shows that the Unified Process is an incremental and iterative process. Once the business case has been made and the system architecture defined during the Inception and Elaboration phases, the system is constructed in short *iterations* (or *builds*). Only a few new capabilities are added to the system during each iteration. Each iteration results in a working (though initially limited) system. As soon as the new system has a wide enough scope to benefit the users, it is put into production. The technique of event analysis, explained in Chapter 3, divides a system into independent parts and can help identify what should be done in each development iteration.

TIMEBOXING

One specific technique for iterative system development is called *timeboxing*. It fits a development phase or cycle into a limited period of time called a *timebox*. The timebox is usually between two and six weeks.[11]

For example, in a build cycle, the system developers are expected to complete one cycle of analysis, design, construction, and testing. The scope of the work is limited to what can be accomplished in the specified time frame. If the work gets behind schedule, then its scope is reduced so as not to exceed the time limit.

Figure 2.8 illustrates the concept of a timebox.

PARTICIPANTS IN SYSTEMS ANALYSIS AND DESIGN

Figure 2.9 summarizes the previous discussion of the Unified Process. It tabulates the phases in the development process, the participants in each phase, the products resulting from each phase, and the criteria used to evaluate the satisfactory completion of each phase. The participants with the most intensive involvement in each phase are shown in capital letters. The evaluation criteria are presented as questions to be answered affirmatively before proceeding to the next phase. If the answer to any question is "No," then parts of previous phases may have to be done over, or the development or use of the system may have to be discontinued.[12]

---

[10]Charles Richter, *Designing Flexible Object-Oriented Systems with UML* (Indianapolis, Ind.: Macmillan Technical Publishing, 1999), 362.
[11]For very large, complex projects with large teams, a timebox could be as long as three to six months. However, there can be shorter iterations within this period.
[12]For additional details, see Kruchten, *The Rational Unified Process*, as well as Jacobson, Booch, and Rumbaugh, *The Unified Software Development Process*.

FIGURE 2.8   Timebox for a build cycle

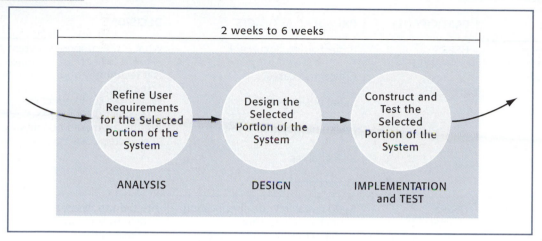

This section discusses the participants in the system development process, emphasizing their roles and responsibilities in systems analysis and design.

We have said that systems analysis is the process of studying a system — separating the system from its environment as an object for study by identifying the system boundary, determining the components which make up the system, and describing the rules which govern the interactions among the components. In a practical situation, analysts study a system to detect and correct deficiencies, to improve system performance, or to forecast the effects of changes to the system or its environment. Thus, the purpose of systems analysis becomes to investigate systems problems, determine explicitly what constitutes a solution, and recommend a course of action which will lead to system change.

In the context of computer information systems for business, this means investigating problems related to an organization's use of information; stating precisely the users' requirements for information processing systems (including what portions should be automated); determining explicitly the system inputs, outputs, and transformations as well as the tests for satisfactory system performance; and recommending to management what action to take to change the system.

Although other system development people are occasionally involved, there are two principal groups of participants in systems analysis — users and analysts. What are the major roles and functions of each group, and how do the members of both groups interact?

TYPES OF USERS

"The user" is a simple, convenient abstraction which often distorts or suppresses important perspectives on system development. It is better to recognize at the outset that there are several groups of users of a computer information system with different needs and concerns. Each group, in its own way, is able to stop, delay, sabotage, or ignore the completed system. Ignoring their differences is a frequent cause of failure.

DeMarco identifies three types of users — the hands-on user, the responsible user, and the system owner[13] — to which we add a fourth — the beneficial user.[14]

---

[13] Tom DeMarco, *Structured Analysis and System Specification* (New York: Yourdon, 1979), 14.
[14] Lavette C. Teague, Jr., and Christopher W. Pidgeon, *Structured Analysis Methods for Computer Information Systems* (Chicago: Science Research Associates, 1985), 50.

FIGURE 2.9

Phases, participants, artifacts, and decisions in the Unified Process

PHASE	PARTICIPANTS	PRINCIPAL ARTIFACTS	DECISIONS
1. Inception (Make the Business Case)	USERS ANALYSTS	Project vision document Critical use cases Initial business case Preliminary system architecture Risk analysis Project plan	What is the proposed system going to do for each of its major users? Is it technically and organizationally feasible? What risks could affect its feasibility? Are the estimated benefits worth the expected costs?
2. Elaboration (Define the System Architecture)	USERS ANALYSTS DESIGNERS programmers	System architecture specification (includes hardware characteristics and system software characteristics) Initial Implementation of critical use cases Reliable project schedule and cost analysis Refined project plan	Are the use cases, system architecture, and project plans stable enough? Are the risks under sufficient control to commit to developing the entire project? Is the construction phase plan adequate? Is the project still economically feasible?
3. Construction (Construct the System)	DESIGNERS PROGRAMMERS QUALITY ASSURANCE analysts users	Intermediate builds of system at each iteration Documented and tested version of the completed system with users' and operations manuals	Do the software units work and meet the specified requirements? Is it still technically, operationally, and economically feasible? Is the documentation for the completed system accurate and adequate? Is the system ready for delivery to the users? Are the stakeholders ready to take delivery of the system?
4. Transition (Integrate the System with the Using Organization)	USERS analysts designers quality assurance	Report of completed acceptance tests Operational system Postimplementation evaluation report	Do the acceptance tests show satisfactory compliance with all the stated performance targets? Has the system passed all the user acceptance tests? Has the accepted system been smoothly integrated with the operations of the organization? Is the system still meeting the specified performance targets?

System Owner

The *system owner* is a high-level manager and decision maker for the business area supported by the system, usually with profit-and-loss responsibility. In some organizations, the cost of information system development is centrally funded. In others, development or operations costs are recovered from those supported by the system. Or the system owner may allocate funds for system development as well as its continuing operation. A system owner for a sales analysis and forecasting system, for example, might be a vice president for marketing.

The system owner's principal concerns are:

1. Wise use of company resources in system development and operation;
2. Top management's understanding of and support for the system;
3. Compatibility of the system's objectives and functions with the goals of the organization as well as with those of the part which the system owner manages;
4. Delivery of a working system on schedule and within the budget;
5. Satisfaction with the system on the part of all the other types of users; and
6. Protection from liability due to use or misuse of the system by incorporating auditability, adequate controls, and appropriate security.

Responsible User

The *responsible user* is a low- to middle-level manager with direct day-to-day operational responsibility for the business functions supported by the system. A responsible user for an accounts receivable system which records customer invoices and payments, produces monthly statements, and identifies overdue accounts would be the manager of the accounts receivable section.

The responsible user's principal concerns are:

1. A system of appropriate scope for correct and detailed support of the operations which he supervises;
2. Smooth integration of manual and automated procedures;
3. Timely and understandable reports and other system output;
4. Adequate training and documentation for hands-on users;
5. A reliable and dependable system;
6. Enhanced productivity at an acceptable cost; and
7. Satisfaction on the part of the hands-on and beneficial users.

Hands-On User

The *hands-on user* is a person who interacts directly with the data capture and data display devices for the system. In a batch system, these users may be part of the data processing or computer operations staff rather than part of a group responsible for the business-related functions supported by the system. In an online or partly online environment, those who enter data and receive output at a terminal are directly supported by the system. An example of a hands-on user at a savings and loan association would be a teller who uses a terminal to enter deposits and withdrawals and to find out customer account balances.

The principal concerns of the hands-on user are:

1. Ease of system use, with procedures which are well documented and easy to follow, and with effective error detection and correction features;
2. A reliable and dependable system;
3. Well-designed equipment and workstations to reduce the level of fatigue and stress; and
4. Increased personal satisfaction with working conditions as a result of the system.

Beneficial User

The *beneficial user* is one who has no direct contact with the automated system but who receives output from the system or provides input to the system.[15]

A beneficial user of a banking system is a depositor who receives monthly statements and cancelled checks. Note that a depositor using an automated teller machine becomes a hands-on user.

---

[15]"Beneficial" is used here in the sense of one who receives the benefits from something, as does the "beneficial owner" of stock, in contrast to the owner of record.

The principal concerns of the beneficial user are:

1. The quality of service provided by the system;
2. Understandable and usable reports and other system output;
3. Security and privacy for confidential personal information; and
4. Appropriate error detection and correction features with effective response to problems by hands-on and responsible users and system owners, who do not blame the computer for system inadequacies.

It is also clear that a single individual may belong to more than one of these four categories, especially in small organizations.

ROLES, FUNCTIONS, AND RESPONSIBILITIES OF USERS

During systems analysis and development, users have — or share — the responsibilities and functions shown in Figure 2.10.

The decision to adopt the new system must eventually be made by all types of users. In many situations, however, as a beneficial user, an employee or a customer may have little leverage beyond going elsewhere. Relating the need for the system to the goals, policies, and objectives of the organization is ultimately the responsibility of the system owner but may also require the participation of the responsible user.

In large organizations, it is rare for a single user or type of user to have a complete understanding of the entire system. Detailed knowledge and understanding must come from the beneficial users within the organization as well as the responsible user. Users have a responsibility to communicate — to give thoughtful, considered, honest responses to the analysts' requests for information. Evasion, concealment, and even well-intentioned erroneous information all work against the overall best interests of the organization.

Corporate goals are not always consistent; the desires or needs of various users may be incompatible. Sometimes it is possible to tailor the data collection or the presentation of information to different groups of users. But the responsible owner must resolve fundamental conflicts if possible. Otherwise, a decision from the system owner is required.

During Inception, users, along with other stakeholders, review the vision document and the business case. During Elaboration, they also review the

---

FIGURE 2.10 Responsibilities of users

1. Deciding to incorporate the automated system into their way of doing business
2. Relating the need for the system and its functions to the goals, policies, and objectives of the organization
3. Knowing and understanding the business functions supported by the information processing system
4. Serving as a reliable information source
5. Establishing priorities and resolving conflicts among system objectives and among users' requirements
6. Reviewing, understanding, and approving the system development documents which define users' objectives and requirements
7. Reviewing the system at milestones and making abort or continue decisions
8. Allocating the necessary resources to the system development process
9. Deciding among alternatives, making trade-offs, and evaluating relative costs and benefits
10. Providing support for desired change and continuing pressure for change

artifacts containing more detailed statements of requirements. In the later phases of system development, users may also review user-oriented manuals and documentation.

The last several user responsibilities shown in Figure 2.10 are in management areas — supporting change, making decisions, and allocating resources. Allocating the necessary resources to the system development process is the responsibility of the system owners or their superiors. This responsibility includes making key people available to the process as well as ensuring their timely interaction with the analysts. It also includes providing adequate funds for system analysis and development. Successful projects have strong, well-communicated psychological commitment on the part of management, especially the system owner. Continuing accessibility of system owners and responsible users to the analysts for purposes of communication, involvement in decision making, and interaction throughout the process are all vitally important.

ROLES, FUNCTIONS, AND RESPONSIBILITIES OF ANALYSTS

Analysts also have many roles and functions in information system development. Many of these are technical — requiring a knowledge of system concepts and expertise in system development techniques. Others are nontechnical — especially involving the business dimensions of the system or the interpersonal and human aspects of the development process. All the tasks of the analysts are directed toward an informed and adequately supported user decision to proceed with system development based on a precise statement of requirements.

Responsibilities of Analysts

Analysts have the principal responsibilities shown in Figure 2.11.

In serving as a conscience for the development effort, the analyst helps other participants recognize negative as well as positive impacts of the information processing system under development, especially as they affect people in the organization. The analyst helps everyone to keep the development effort in perspective — as a part of the business and as the prelude to ongoing system use.

Required Analysis Skills

To carry out these responsibilities, an analyst requires the following skills or attributes:

1. **Facility with the tools and techniques of analysis.** Technical competence is also a major basis of credibility with other participants in the process.

FIGURE 2.11   Responsibilities of analysts

1. Assuring the technical quality of the products and procedures of systems analysis (as described in Part II)
2. Determining (with the aid of other participants in the process) the implications — technical, economic, psychological, and organizational — of decisions about the scope and kind of automation
3. Facilitating communication and understanding among the other participants in the process
4. Providing effectively organized information to support user decisions leading to the development of the best computer information system for the organization
5. Acting as an advocate or ombudsman for the users, especially during design and acceptance testing, to ensure that users' requirements stated in the system specifications are satisfied in the later stages of system development
6. Acting as a conscience for the development effort

2. *The ability to master complexity.* The analyst has to be able to assimilate large amounts of information; to distinguish among fact, opinion, hearsay, and conjecture; and to identify what is relevant.

3. *Facility at abstract thinking.* This includes the ability to generalize from limited and incomplete information without losing precision and concreteness of detail.

4. *Language and communication skills.* Much of the work of analysts is interpreting the significance of information and translating each other's technical jargon for users and system developers. Effective written, oral, and graphic communication is essential.

5. *Information gathering skills.* The analyst must be capable of extracting information from a wide variety of sources, assessing its relevance and reliability, and organizing it in useful structures.

6. *Interpersonal skills.* The analyst needs to inspire confidence and develop effective working relationships among the participants in the system development process.

7. *The ability to function effectively in new situations, to tolerate a high degree of ambiguity and uncertainty, and to function with imperfect information.* The analyst must often work with information which is deficient in quantity and quality, incomplete, imprecise, or redundant.

8. *Sound judgment and common sense.* The analyst must maintain a sense of perspective and make reasonable recommendations and decisions.

Do these requirements seem impossibly demanding? Perhaps so. Few people are equally competent or effective in every skill area. Thus, systems analysis is often a team effort so that the strengths of the team members can complement and support each other. That is why the process of system development must be carefully organized and why peer review of work products is built into effective system development methods.

ROLES OF USERS AND ANALYSTS DURING DESIGN

During design, users and analysts may be called on to help plan the continued system development. They may be asked to set priorities for delivering various portions of the automated system. Analysts and users may also serve as consultants to the development team by interpreting the requirements specification. This role is essential when ambiguities, omissions, or errors remain in the specification despite everyone's best efforts. They must be corrected as they are discovered.

The responsibility for designing the interface between the manual and automated parts of the system is often given to the designers of the manual part of the system. Since this is such a critical interface, all the design groups, the users, and the analysts must agree on its design. Recently, this has become such an important consideration that some analysts include a specification of the style or format of the user-computer interface as part of the requirements specification.

Users and analysts may also both be involved in the development of documentation and training aids.

USERS AND ANALYSTS — A SYNERGY

During analysis, as we have seen, users serve primarily as information sources and decision makers. Analysts serve primarily as decision facilitators by clearly stating system requirements and their implications for the organization. Each group has its own responsibilities in the process, but system development at its best is truly a joint effort. Neither group has a monopoly on imagination, innovation, or

FIGURE 2.12   Responsibilities of designers

1. Reviewing the requirements specification to verify its completeness and consistency
2. Notifying users and analysts of any deficiencies found in the requirements specification
3. Assuring the technical quality of the products and procedures of system design
4. Facilitating communication and understanding among the participants in design
5. Defining design alternatives and selecting the best
6. Assuring that the design can comply with the performance standards of the requirements specification as well as those of the system acceptance tests
7. Coordinating the design with decisions about the hardware and system software environment
8. Determining the implications of their designs for system performance and construction
9. Assuring that the system as designed is still technically, economically, and operationally feasible

wisdom. Experienced analysts often acquire a wealth of business knowledge, and the keenest insights into better systems often come from dedicated and imaginative users. Working together in close interaction with effective communication, users and analysts can achieve superior-quality computer information systems for business.

ROLES, FUNCTIONS, AND RESPONSIBILITIES OF DESIGNERS

Designers are the primary participants in system design, with analysts, users, and programmers playing supporting roles from time to time. Figure 2.12 shows important responsibilities of designers.

In spite of the best efforts of users and analysts, the requirements specification produced during systems analysis may contain errors, omissions, ambiguities, or inconsistencies. The earlier these problems are detected and corrected, the more efficient the design process will be. When design begins, the relevant requirements should be reviewed. Users are the final authority on the system requirements; analysts assist them by stating the requirements in a form usable in design and by explaining the implications of the requirements for the completed system. Deficiencies in the statement of system requirements found during design must be reported immediately to the users and analysts who can correct them.

A design is feasible only if it satisfies the stated requirements, particularly as demonstrated by its passing the acceptance tests. Designers need a repertory of performance models to predict that the completed system will behave acceptably. Designers must be concerned not only with acceptable performance but also with realizability.

System failures often occur at critical interfaces. The interfaces between the application software and its environment can be especially critical, particularly if the application software designers do not make decisions about the hardware/software environment.

Because of system complexity and performance trade-offs, design changes made to satisfy users' requirements and acceptance tests may sometimes make a system too expensive or cause technical or operational problems with the system. Designers must be alert to these possibilities and inform users and managers when such undesirable implications of design decisions occur. Ease of modification is also an important design consideration.

Information system design usually involves a team of designers as well as other participants. A common understanding of the design problem and the evolving solution is essential. Effective communication helps create and maintain this common understanding.

Producing the best system design entails consideration of a variety of alternatives using a systematic means of evaluating and comparing them. Designers are expected to incorporate current professional standards and current methods in their work products.

Required Design Skills

Among the skills most valuable to a system designer are the following:

1. *Facility with the tools and techniques of design.* The designer should be accomplished in creating and using the various models and representations used in system design.
2. *Working knowledge of several design methods with expertise in at least one.* The designer should know how the design models are related to the design process in a systematic way. In addition to mastering the predominant method used by his organization, the designer should know when other methods may be more appropriate and be able to communicate with designers who use other methods.
3. *The ability to master complexity and to sense the key issues in a design problem.* Good designers are able to simplify complexity through appropriate abstraction and structuring. Through a combination of intuition and insight, they can identify the most difficult issues or critical decisions in solving a design problem.
4. *Familiarity with good current design practice.* Good designers stay abreast of the state of the art.
5. *Creative imagination.* Creativity allows designers to propose new design alternatives and to make the best use of new technology as it becomes available.
6. *The ability to defer decisions to an appropriate time in the design process.* Premature commitment to low-level decisions can unduly restrict the variety of alternatives considered and thus reduce the quality of the resulting design.
7. *The ability to reach closure on design decisions.* Designers can be so eager to continue improving a design that they are psychologically unable to commit themselves to design decisions. The result can be ineffective use of design resources and inadequate time to work out the detailed design.

ROLES, FUNCTIONS, AND RESPONSIBILITIES OF PROGRAMMERS

Programmers make their major contribution to system development after systems analysis and design. Their primary responsibility is to construct the system. They write and debug the code for the necessary software. The role of programmers in systems analysis is usually minimal. However, programmers are secondary, yet important, participants in system design. Among the roles they may play are those shown in Figure 2.13.

FIGURE 2.13	Responsibilities of programmers

1. Notifying designers of any deficiencies found in the design
2. Assessing the realizability of a design in differing hardware or software environments
3. Evaluating the flexibility and reusability of the software components
4. Predicting system performance

FIGURE 2.14	**Responsibilities of the quality assurance staff**

1. Establishing standards and policies for quality assurance throughout the system development process
2. Monitoring compliance with software quality standards
3. Obtaining measurements of the quality of the software and of the performance of the development teams
4. Conducting independent tests of the completed software

Programmers may review the design for errors, inconsistencies, and incompleteness. They may help designers determine how easy it will be to program the software and how adaptable the software will be to different operating environments.

One of the goals of design, especially object-oriented design, is to define reusable software components. Programmers can contribute to evaluating the design from this perspective.

Good performance models for software are lacking in many areas. Programmers can contribute their experience to help predict system performance.

ROLES, FUNCTIONS, AND RESPONSIBILITIES OF THE QUALITY ASSURANCE STAFF

Analysts, designers, and programmers all have a responsibility to produce quality systems and software for the users. In addition, quality assurance professionals provide an independent assessment of the system's quality throughout the development process. Responsibilities of the quality assurance staff appear in Figure 2.14.

The achievement of quality software cannot be an afterthought. Practices which lead to quality software must be built into the entire development process. These include periodic reviews of the work produced to identify defects and inconsistencies and to assure that they are corrected. They also include standards and procedures for testing software.

The quality assurance staff provides an external check on the extent to which the organization's standards are incorporated into developers' practices. Unbiased measurements of time, cost, and quality for a project are more likely if outsiders make them instead of the project team. The quality assurance group can perform this role. The quality assurance group can also manage the system acceptance tests, arranging and overseeing the user participation in these tests.

Two important areas of concern in the system development process are related to the necessary introduction of change into an organization and to the investigation of the system's feasibility. These areas are addressed in the remaining portion of the chapter.

INTRODUCTION OF SYSTEM CHANGE

Information system change often introduces significant organizational change. Users and analysts need to work together to formulate a plan which provides incentives for both types of change. In discussing how to plan for organizational change, Athey points out that acceptance of a new system depends on the attitudes of the group of people affected by it. He summarizes the major factors affecting the acceptance of a new system:

The more **pressure** on the acceptance group to make a decision, the more likely the group will be to try something new.

The greater the **relative advantage** the recommended solution has over the present system solution, the more likely it will be accepted.
The greater the **goal congruence** among the acceptance groups, the greater the likelihood of the new system acceptance.
The better the match in the **behavioral change** required to that which is desired, the more likely the new solution will be implemented.[16]

When planning for system conversion and integration, these factors can be used to increase the likelihood of success. The plan for system change can induce pressure to change, demonstrate the relative advantage of the new system, promote common goals among the acceptance groups, and minimize the amount of behavioral change required.

By addressing these organizational behavior issues as well as the technical issues, users and analysts can increase the probability of a smooth transition from the existing system to the new one.

FEASIBILITY

Not every desire for system change is worth pursuing. The effort involved in developing an information processing system is considerable. Before this effort is undertaken, the stakeholders in the project ought to be sure that the venture is worthwhile. The Inception and Elaboration phases, described earlier in this chapter, focus on determining whether a system development project can or should be undertaken and carried to completion.

The activities of these phases address the issue of *feasibility*. They help make explicit the *constraints* on the system and its development — **the conditions which must be satisfied for the system to be acceptable**. A system which satisfies all these constraints is said to be **feasible**. Also made explicit are the *criteria* for evaluation — **the characteristics which are used to compare alternatives for a proposed system**. (Constraints and criteria were discussed in Chapter 1 in the context of problem solving.)

QUESTIONS ADDRESSED

Informally, consideration of feasibility leads to questions such as the following.

> **What benefits is the system expected to provide for its users and major stakeholders?**

A new system should produce additional value for its users and stakeholders — something not adequately provided by the current system. There may be a problem with the system as it is currently operating. On the other hand, the system may be adequate at present but not able to serve the anticipated growth of the business or provide satisfactory service in the future. The organization may recognize an opportunity to service new markets, to add new services, or to enhance its competitive advantage. In other cases, new government regulations or intensified competition may necessitate the system change.

> **What specific objectives is the proposed system to achieve?**

---

[16] Thomas H. Athey, *Systematic Systems Approach* (Englewood Cliffs, N.J.: Prentice-Hall, 1982), 261.

Which costs are to be reduced, and by how much, for the new system to be considered acceptable? What features of the system will be used to evaluate qualitative improvements? How many orders per day is the system expected to process next year? Five years from now? How many years do we expect the new system to operate before making further significant changes or replacing it?

There are three generic objectives for new systems — to reduce cost, to increase revenue, and to improve the quality of products or services. These all may lead to increased profit; how this profit is used varies with the organization. Nonprofit groups may choose to reduce revenues or expand services; a profit-making organization may invest in research or increase its dividend. The three generic objectives must be made as specific as possible for each project in order to establish useful targets for system development.

What are some promising alternatives for an architecture of the new system?

If the desired system cannot be built, trying to develop it is futile. There must be a reasonable probability that a new system can be constructed which will satisfy the stated constraints. If similar systems already exist, the chance of success is high. If the proposed system or significant subsystems are being constructed for the first time, the risk is considerably higher. The initial comparison of alternatives is rapid and highly selective.

What is it likely to cost to develop the new system?

The quality of information available is usually low, and therefore the variability of estimates of costs, benefits, and performance, as well as of system development, is high.

The project plan describes the sequence in which the system functions will be defined, designed, and constructed as well as the schedule and budget for developing the system. The plan must consider the uncertainties and risks inherent in the project and their impact on the schedule and budget.

The selection of a system architecture depends not only on the initial list of feasible alternatives but also on estimates of the resources necessary for system development, especially those resources committed to system architecture definition, before the more detailed cost estimate can be produced.

CATEGORIES OF FEASIBILITY

An analysis of a project's feasibility considers that project from a variety of perspectives. The constraints of a project are commonly grouped into several categories.

1. *Technical feasibility* addresses whether construction of the proposed system is within the state of the art.
2. *Resource feasibility* addresses whether the resources required to construct and deploy the system are available when they are needed.
3. *Organizational feasibility* addresses whether the system can work in the culture and power structure of the organization. The mere fact that the system has been developed does not mean that anyone will use it. (See the article in Figure 2.19 and Exercise 2–15 at the end of the chapter.)
4. *Economic feasibility* addresses whether the investment in the system is a worthwhile use of the organization's resources. Ideally, the benefits of the new system

are greater than the cost of developing and operating it. And from a financial standpoint, the organization's return on its investment in a new information system should exceed the return on other uses of the organization's capital. However, in some situations, the capabilities of the new system are essential if the organization is to continue in business. For example, it is hard to imagine a retail bank which provides its customers with no access to ATMs. In that case, the economic goal may be to minimize the cost of such an essential system.

5. *Schedule* or *temporal feasibility* addresses whether the system can be developed and implemented in time to meet the business needs of the organization.

Resource feasibility, economic feasibility, and schedule feasibility are closely linked. All are dependent on a cost estimate and schedule for the proposed development project. An analysis of economic feasibility is usually the most complex of the three, as it involves considerable calculation. Thus, the next section discusses this analysis in detail.

ECONOMIC FEASIBILITY ANALYSIS

Economic feasibility analysis estimates the value of an investment of any sort using accepted financial measures. The most important of these measures are the net present value (NPV), the break-even point, and the return on investment (ROI). If the results of the analysis are unsatisfactory, the project is said to be economically **infeasible**.

Net present value compares the costs of the new system with the financial benefits it will bring. The costs and benefits of developing and operating the new system are projected over several years. Future costs and benefits are discounted to take into account the time value of money, as discussed below.

Management is interested in how long it will take to recover the costs. This is called the *break-even point*.

The *return on investment* is the ratio of the overall net present value of the project (that is, the net present value of the benefits minus the net present value of the costs) to the net present value of the costs.

CALCULATING ECONOMIC FEASIBILITY

The best way to understand this is with an example. This book contains a continuing case study called the Public University Registration System. We use this system here to provide an example of economic feasibility analysis.

Description of the Current System

For our example, we will assume a paper-based registration system. Each department in the university fills out a paper form listing the classes it will offer the next term. The data from these forms is entered into a computer system. Then the complete schedule of classes offered is printed and mailed to the students. When students register, their request for classes is a paper form. Students bubble in their desired courses and turn in the registration forms for processing by the existing computer system. The computer then processes the requests and prints a student class list for each student. Finally, a class roster for each section is printed for the professors. There is also a process for adding and dropping classes, but it will not be considered in this analysis.

Description of the Proposed System

The proposed new system will be Web-based. The departments will enter their class offerings on line. The schedule of classes will not be printed but will instead be available on line. Students will request their desired courses on line as well. No student class lists or class rosters will be printed by the university. Instead, the students and the professors will print them from the Web.

FIGURE 2.15　Estimated recurring costs of the existing Public University Registration System

Public University Registration System
Recurring Costs of the Existing System

Item	Annual Cost
Hardware maintenance	$ 18,000
Software maintenance	70,000
Paper and supplies	24,000
Postage	8,000
Clerical labor	150,000
Total recurring costs	**$270,000**

Estimates of Costs and Benefits

In order to compare costs, one needs to compute of the cost of running the present system as well as the cost of operating the new system. It costs $270,000 a year to run the existing paper-based registration system. Figure 2.15 itemizes the components of this cost. It is estimated that a new Web-based system will cost $462,000 to build and $132,000 a year to run. (See Figures 2.16 and 2.17.) Figure 2.18 tabulates the costs and benefits over the period of analysis.

Clearly, the new Web-based system will save $138,000 each year, but there is the initial cost of the new system to consider. Dividing the cost to develop the new

FIGURE 2.16　Estimated costs to develop the new Public University Registration System

Public University Registration System
Development Costs for the Proposed System

Item	Cost
Hardware purchase	$ 50,000
Communication upgrade	50,000
Software development	350,000
Internet connection	12,000
Total development costs	**$462,000**

FIGURE 2.17　Estimated recurring costs of the new Public University Registration System

Public University Registration System
Recurring Costs of the Proposed System

Item	Annual Cost
Hardware maintenance	$ 8,000
Software maintenance	70,000
Paper and supplies	5,000
Postage	0
Clerical labor	25,000
Internet connection	24,000
Total recurring costs	**$132,000**

system ($462,000) by the savings incurred each year ($138,000), we obtain 3.35 years (about 3 years and 4 months) to recover the cost — that is, to break even.

Present Value Considerations

There is a big problem with the above calculation! It does not take into account that money saved or spent in the future is not as valuable as money saved or spent today. For example, suppose that you work for a business and the owner agrees to pay you $1,000 for writing a computer program. After the work is completed, the owner says, "Do you mind if we pay you a year from now?" After realizing that a loan at 10 percent will cost you $100 for one year, you would most likely say, "Only if you pay me $1,100 then."

Let us do the arithmetic on this analysis. We will call the *present value* of the payment "PV" and the *future value* of the payment "FV." We will call the 10 percent "i" for *interest rate.* All of these terms are standard usage for financial analysis.

Then we can compute the future value of $1,000 for one year as follows:

$$FV = PV + (PV \times i) = PV \times (1 + i)$$
$$1100. = 1000. + (1 \times 0.10) = 1000. \times 1.1$$

2.1

FIGURE 2.18   Worksheet for economic feasibility analysis

Economic Feasibility Analysis
Public University Registration System

Row		0	1	2	3	4	5
1 **Years**		0	1	2	3	4	5
Benefits							
2 Net Economic Benefit	$ -	$ 270,000	$ 270,000	$ 270,000	$ 270,000	$ 270,000	Totals
3 Discount Factor (at 8%)	1.0000	0.9259	0.8573	0.7938	0.7350	0.6806	
4 PV of Benefits	-	250,000	231,481	214,335	198,458	183,757	
5 NPV of all Benefits	-	250,000	481,481	695,816	894,274	1,078,032	$ 1,078,032
Costs							
6 One Time Costs	(462,000)						
7 Recurring Costs		(132,000)	(132,000)	(132,000)	(132,000)	(132,000)	
8 Discount Factor (at 8%)	1.000	0.9259	0.8573	0.7938	0.7350	0.6806	
9 PV of Costs	(462,000)	(122,222)	(113,169)	(104,786)	(97,024)	(89,837)	
10 NPV of all Costs	(462,000)	(584,222)	(697,391)	(802,177)	(899,201)	(989,038)	$ (989,038)
11 Overall NPV							$ 88,994
Break-Even Analysis							
12 Yearly NPV Cash Flow	(462,000)	127,778	118,313	109,549	101,434	93,920	
13 Overall NPV Cash Flow	$ (462,000)	$ (334,222)	$ (215,909)	$ (106,361)	$ (4,926)	$ 88,994	
14 Interest Rate	0.08						
15 Project breakeven occurs between years 3 and 4							
16 Breakeven ratio = (($93,920-$88,994)/$93,920) =1.049							
17 Breakeven will occur at 4.05 years							
18 Overall ROI = Overall NPV/NPV of all Costs							0.0900

A similar computation can also be done for two years:

$$FV = PV + (PV \times i) + (PV + PV \times i) \times i$$
$$1210. = 1000. + (1000. \times 0.10) + (1000. + 1000. \times 0.10) \times 0.10$$
$$1210. = 1000. + 100.00 + 110. \qquad \qquad 2.2$$

We can then apply some simple algebra and obtain a formula for the future value of a payment for two years:

$$FV = PV + (PV \times i) + (PV \times i) + (PV \times i^2)$$
$$FV = PV + (2 \times PV \times i) + (PV \times i^2)$$
$$FV = PV(1 + 2 \times i \times i^2)$$
$$FV = PV(1 + i)^2$$

This formula can be extended to n years as

$$FV = PV(1 + i)^n \qquad \qquad 2.3$$

Then by dividing to obtain the present value,

$$PV = FV / (1 + i)^n \qquad \qquad 2.4$$

The expression $1 / (1 + i)^n$ in equation (2.4) is called the ***discount factor.*** It depends only on the interest rate and the number of years. When multiplied by any FV, it yields the corresponding PV.

Now we realize that money earned next year is discounted, and each year after that it is discounted even more. Specifically, $1,000.00 is worth only $909.09 now, if it is not received until next year and if it is earning interest at a rate of 10 percent. That is, the present value of $1,000.00 paid next year is $909.09, assuming a 10 percent interest rate.

In order to present the economic feasibility analysis, we commonly develop a worksheet for ROI. (See Figure 2.18.) To understand the table better, note that there are six columns numbered 0 through 5. The column for Year 0 contains the values of benefits and costs which occur before Year 1 begins. The other columns contain these values at the end of Years 1 to 5. The rows are grouped as follows. Rows 2, 4, and 5 show benefits. Row 5 is a cumulative summary of all the benefits. This is an annual savings of $270,000 after use of the old system is discontinued. Note how the present value of the $270,000 goes down each year. In fact, in Year 5, the benefits are worth only $183,757.

Rows 6, 7, 9, and 10 show costs. Row 10 is a cumulative summary of all the costs. The major cost is the $462,000 up-front cost of developing the new system, which occurs in Year 0. The recurring cost of the new system in this example is $132,000. However, in Year 5 this cost is worth only $89,837. Note that all costs are negative, indicated by enclosing them in parentheses.

The discount factors for Years 1 through 5 at an interest rate of 8 percent are shown in Rows 3 and 8.

Now we can recompute the break-even point using benefits and costs discounted for time. This is done in the last rows, Rows 12 and 13. Row 12 is the sum of the benefits and costs. Row 13 is a cumulative summary of Row 12. The break-even point is now shown to be 4.05 years (about 4 years and 1/2 month). Recall that, without considering time, the break-even point was calculated at 3.35 years. The reason that it takes longer to break even is that the benefits in later years are worth less, while the development cost occurs in Year 0, so that its cost is never discounted.

The return on investment (Row 18) is

$$ROI = \$88,924 \,/\, \$989,038 = .0900 = 9\%$$

With this information, we can make an informed decision as to whether the new system is economically feasible or not. A break-even point in just over four years seems attractive enough when other advantages are considered. These advantages are not easily measured. They include a system which is expected to be easier to work with as well as to provide better response times to students and faculty.

ASSUMPTIONS AND SENSITIVITY ANALYSIS

An economic feasibility analysis is fraught with uncertainty. The calculations are based on many assumptions. These assumptions should be stated explicitly. If they prove to be incorrect, the system may become infeasible. One way to deal with some of the uncertainty is to use a spreadsheet for the calculations. Then we can repeat the calculations with different assumed values for costs, benefits, interest rates, or time periods. In this way, we can find out (at least informally) how sensitive the analysis is to changes in the numbers. If conclusions about feasibility do not change much when the inputs change, then it may not matter much how accurate the assumed values are.

EVALUATING THE FEASIBILITY ANALYSIS

By definition, an economic feasibility analysis considers only those benefits which can be quantified in terms of dollars (or another currency). Such benefits are called *tangible benefits.* A system may have other benefits which cannot be quantified, known as *intangible benefits.* Then the evaluation of economic feasibility must consider whether these intangible benefits are worth their cost.

The feasibility analysis is part of the business case, which is developed during Inception and then refined throughout the system development process.

SUMMARY

Information system development is usually organized as a set of specific projects within an enterprisewide information systems plan. This information systems plan is coordinated with and driven by the organization's overall business plan. The information system development process provides a conceptual framework for understanding and managing an information system development project.

The product of system development is a software system. It includes all the information necessary to communicate it to the computer, the users of the system, and the participants in the development process.

The system development process for custom software development presented in this chapter is a simplification of the Rational Unified Software Development Process. The Unified Process consists of four phases:

1. Inception (Make the Business Case). The goals of the Inception phase are to develop a vision of the system, define its scope, and make a business case for it.
2. Elaboration (Define the System Architecture). The goals of this phase are to define a system architecture which can serve as the basis for subsequent system development and to produce a more reliable project plan and cost estimate.
3. Construction (Construct the System). The Construction phase produces an operational system ready for delivery to users. During construction,

the development proceeds in a series of build cycles — each constrained by a timebox.

4. Transition (Integrate with the Using Organization). In the Transition phase, the product is released for beta testing. After the acceptance tests are passed, the system is fully deployed. Any necessary conversion from the old system takes place, user training is completed, and the system is used in its operational setting. A postimplementation review may lead to modifications, and continuing use may identify desirable enhancements.

At the end of each phase, there is a management decision as to whether to proceed to the next phase. Eventually, the system may be superseded by a new one.

The work within each phase is done by nine core disciplines — Business Modeling, Requirements, Design, Implementation, Test, Deployment, Configuration and Change Management, Project Management, and Environment.

- Business Modeling is responsible for identifying opportunities for making fundamental improvements to the organization and its business processes as well as for modeling the application domain.
- Requirements focuses on finding out and structuring what is to be built for the users of a system.
- Design specifies the software units and their structure.
- Implementation codes and debugs the software.
- Test defines the tests and test procedures and carries out the testing of the software.
- Deployment is responsible for delivering the system and integrating it into the using organization.
- Configuration and Change Management manages the artifacts produced during system development. In addition to configuration management and change management, it includes measuring and reporting on the project and its status.
- Project Management is responsible for planning the project, managing risks, and measuring the progress of the project.
- Environment provides and supports an organization's software development environment.

The system development process is iterative and incremental. Each phase is divided into iterations, each of which adds capability or refinement to the system. The system is constructed in builds and delivered in versions. The development process described here is necessarily generic. This process must always be tailored to the specific needs of each system development project.

There are two principal groups of participants in the process of systems analysis — users and analysts.

The group of users includes four types of people — beneficial users, hands-on users, responsible users, and system owners. Each user type has somewhat different interests in a computer information system and a different perspective on the system and its development. Users are responsible for establishing policies for the conduct of their business and for making business decisions about the information processing systems which support their organization. Strong user support and involvement and wise user decisions are essential to successful computer information system development and use.

Systems analysts, often working in teams, carry out both technical and nontechnical roles in system development. They are responsible for a technically competent statement of the users' requirements. They must also understand, interpret, and communicate these requirements to all the other participants in the process. Facility with abstractions, superior communication skills, the ability to act effectively in unstructured situations amid complexity and uncertainty, and sound judgment and common sense are the most important characteristics for systems analysts.

System designers review the requirements and notify users and analysts of any deficiencies. They are responsible for the technical quality of system design and its products. Designers facilitate communication and understanding among the participants in design. They propose new design alternatives and determine the implications of their design decisions for system performance and construction. They must assure that the design is technically, economically, and operationally feasible; that it complies with the requirements; and that it can pass the system acceptance tests. They must also coordinate the design with decisions about the hardware and system software environment.

During design, users and analysts resolve deficiencies in the statement of requirements, set priorities for construction, and may evaluate the user interface. Programmers may consult on questions of system realizability and expected performance. Quality assurance staff monitor the development process throughout and provide measurements and tests which are independent of the development team.

The business case for the proposed project incorporates an analysis of its feasibility. The constraints on a project are commonly grouped into the categories of technical, resource, organizational, economic, and schedule (or temporal) feasibility. An economic feasibility analysis usually calculates the net present value, the break-even point, and the return on investment.

KEY TERMS

acceptance test *43*	milestone *39*
architectural baseline *42*	net present value *57*
artifact *33*	organizational feasibility *57*
beta test *37*	phase in the Unified Process *32*
break-even point *58*	present value *60*
build *46*	resource feasibility *57*
candidate system architecture *41*	return on investment *58*
constraint *56*	schedule feasibility *58*
criterion *56*	system architecture *40*
discipline in the Unified Process *32*	technical feasibility *57*
economic feasibility *57*	timeboxing *46*
feasibility *56*	Unified Process *32*
future value *60*	

REVIEW QUESTIONS

2-1. What is the product of information system development?

2-2. Name the four phases in the Rational Unified Process.

2-3. Who are the major participants during each phase?

2-4. What are some of the major decisions to be made during each phase?

2-5. What are some of the major products of each phase?

2-6. What are the nine core disciplines which may occur during any phase? Is the effort in each of these disciplines distributed evenly in all the phases?

2-7. Explain the difference between incremental development and iterative development.

2-8. What is the purpose of a proof-of-concept prototype?

2-9. What activities occur during a typical build cycle of the Unified Process?

2-10. What is the role of users and analysts during system construction?

2-11. Who has the primary responsibility for integrating the new information system into the using organization? What steps can be taken to encourage a smooth transition to the new system?

2-12. What is the purpose of system acceptance tests?

2-13. What is the purpose of the postimplementation evaluation? What two aspects of system development are assessed?

2-14. What two groups are the principal participants in systems analysis?

2-15. Name the four types of system users. For each of them, list at least four concerns with regard to a computer information system.

2-16. List at least eight responsibilities of users during system development.

2-17. List at least five responsibilities of analysts during system development.

2-18. What skills does a systems analyst require?

2-19. State at least seven responsibilities of system designers during information system design.

2-20. State at least five desirable skills or attributes of system designers.

2-21. Identify some of the responsibilities of users, analysts, and programmers during system design.

2-22. What is the purpose of a feasibility study? What are some of the questions addressed in a feasibility study?

EXERCISES AND DISCUSSION QUESTIONS

2-1. Why are there different major participants in the development process during the different stages?

2-2. Who decides whether the test at the end of each phase has been passed?

2-3. Which of the products of the system development process presented in this chapter are primarily information? Which are not primarily information, and what are they, then?

2-4. The description of the system development process in this chapter is an abstraction of a very complex process. What components of the process have we chosen to abstract? What aspects of the process have been omitted? What features of the process are included in Figure 2.9 but are not shown in Figure 2.1? What features are discussed in the text of the chapter but not shown in Figure 2.1?

2-5. How would you modify the development process shown in Figure 2.1 to make it fit the development and use of a different type of system (such as a house, a dress, or a constitution for a club) instead of an information processing system? How would that development process reflect both the similarities and differences between the two types of systems?

2-6. Why is it important to consider several alternatives for a new system?

2-7. Why is the current system usually desirable as one alternative? Under what circumstances could the current system not be considered?

2-8. Information processing system development is said to be an iterative process. Support this assertion by discussing it in terms of the organization of the phases of the Unified Process as well as in terms of the relationship between the phases and the core disciplines.

2-9. Discuss an academic term (semester or quarter) as an example of a timebox.

2-10. Explain why the users' responsibilities described in this chapter are theirs rather than those of the analysts.

2-11. Explain why the analysts' responsibilities described in this chapter are theirs rather than those of the users.

2-12. Technical competence alone is sufficient for developing a successful computer information system. Do you agree or disagree? Why?

2-13. Discuss why each of the analyst's required skills is needed. How do these skills reinforce each other?

2-14. Discuss why successful system development is usually a team effort involving analysts, designers, programmers, and the various types of users.

2-15. Consider the article on postinvestment auditing of IT projects in Figure 2.19.

  a. What is return on investment (ROI)? Why is it estimated or forecast at the beginning of an information system development?

  b. In what situations might an initial ROI forecast be unnecessary?

  c. Why do many companies avoid a postinvestment audit to determine whether a completed information system project has achieved the expected ROI?

  d. Why did the hospital's IT team decide to conduct an ROI audit while the new system was being deployed rather than waiting until after deployment was complete?

  e. Relate the decision to audit during deployment to the use of iterations in the Unified Process. Does what happened confirm the approach of the Unified Process?

FIGURE 2.19	Assume Nothing: Audit Instead

Assume Nothing: Audit Instead

The IT manager who assumes that a technology investment will meet or exceed an economic or return on investment (ROI) forecast reminds me of the anecdote about the economist trapped in a burning building. "No problem," he says. "I'll assume a fire hose."

One of the most damaging assumptions an IT manager can make is that the cost savings or revenue increases forecast in an ROI exercise will materialize on schedule, or at all. Yet most organizations don't bother to confirm that all the economic returns depicted in a forecast actually materialize. Too often, after the project has gone live, the thinking goes: "The forecast is irrelevant because the project is done — let's move on."

What's likely lurking behind the absence of postinvestment auditing at most companies is fear that the real-world results will fall below forecast.

There are ways to conduct a consistent, repeatable postinvestment audit, and no one need fear being shot at dawn. Audits are an effective component of IT management because they allow developers to learn about the outcome of a project and use this knowledge to make improvements.

The maximum value from an IT investment isn't realized from simply confirming that the returns match the forecast, but rather from improving the technology asset's performance should it turn out that the returns are lower than planned — which is often the case with more strategic kinds of technology requiring process and organizational change.

Consider the example of a hospital that decided to expand its business. Instead of doing the lab work of hospital patients only, it took on referral business from physicians and clinics as a way to increase revenue by leveraging unused lab capacity in the off hours. This was a big-risk, big-payoff project, involving an investment in people, processes, and technology — an ideal candidate for a postinvestment forecast validation.

The hospital correctly anticipated that the specialized lab management software it rolled out to support this venture might introduce some business-process incompatibilities that could drag down forecast ROI. However, it had little understanding of exactly what those incompatibilities would look like and how they would affect returns. The hospital's IT team decided to conduct an audit concurrent with technology deployment. It could have waited to audit the returns until after deployment, but the risks were high enough that it sought to catch any operating dysfunction quickly.

The audit team discovered soon after the platform went live that the software collected far more data than it needed for referral patients. The system required lab workers to capture 20 data elements from each patient with a lab order. This demanding screening was optimized for in-hospital patients, but for referral patients, the lab really needed only a few pieces of information, such as name, age, and insurance carrier.

The dysfunction wasn't catastrophic, but it clearly could have compromised the volume of referral patient traffic the lab was equipped to handle. Having discovered through an audit the operational tension between the needs of the patient referral service and the information acquisition overkill of the software, the IT organization recognized the potential drag on revenue and went to work immediately on a code fix.

Today, this lab is a $7 million profit center for the hospital. In the absence of an audit, it would have been less profitable, because lab personnel would have continued to collect too much information from its patients.

Adapted from John Berry, "Assume Nothing: Audit Instead," *Computerworld*, April 7, 2003, 43.

PART TWO

OBJECT-ORIENTED SYSTEMS ANALYSIS

Part I introduced fundamental systems concepts and provided an overview of the information system development process for object-oriented systems. Part II is devoted to the analysis of information systems. The major task of systems analysis is specifying the users' requirements for an information processing system.

It is common to organize the system requirements as a set of models which describe what the system must do to accomplish the requirements. Chapter 3 presents the process and products of systems analysis. It introduces the technique of system-level event analysis as the starting point for developing overall system models. Chapters 4 and 5 describe object-oriented analysis models — use cases and use case diagrams, system interaction diagrams, models of the concepts in the problem domain, and contracts for the system operations. The Unified Modeling Language (UML) is the modeling standard. These chapters show how object-oriented analysis methods are applied in the process of stating users' requirements for a computer information system, using a university registration system as an example.

SYSTEMS ANALYSIS — BUSINESS EVENT ANALYSIS

3

INTRODUCTION

Specifying the users' requirements is the major task of information systems analysis. In the previous chapter, we identified the roles and responsibilities of the various participants in the process of information system development. In this chapter, we begin with a closer look at what is involved in specifying users' requirements, emphasizing what is common to all methods of systems analysis. We then present an overview of a process for the analysis of object-oriented systems and explain the technique of business event analysis, the first step in this process.

After mastering the material in this chapter, you will be able to

- State and discuss the goals of systems analysis.
- Characterize a statement of system requirements as well as the process of systems analysis.
- Define the term *event* and understand the implications of this definition.
- Explain the difference between a temporal event and an external event.
- Give appropriate names to events and recognize whether or not an event is named appropriately.
- Carry out a business event analysis for a system and present the result in an event table.

SPECIFYING USERS' REQUIREMENTS

Systems analysis may be characterized in terms of its goals, its procedures, its products, and its tools and techniques.

GOALS OF SYSTEMS ANALYSIS

The principal goals of systems analysis are listed in Figure 3.1.

PRIMARY GOAL

The primary and fundamental goal of systems analysis is to state accurately the users' requirements for a new information processing system accurately.

An accurate statement of users' requirements is **explicit**. It is documented and open to all the participants in system development. No one has to read between the lines, and there are no hidden assumptions. It is also **complete** in all the essentials of concern to the user. It covers all the system requirements and the entire scope of the processes to be carried out by the computer. All the information entered, stored, transformed, and output is specified. The requirements statement is **unambiguous**. It leaves nothing vague, fuzzy, or subject to more than one interpretation by the reader. It must be **consistent**. There are no undetected or unresolved conflicts and incompatibilities built into the requirements specification. Requirements are **precise** and **specific** and are presented clearly and definitely. They are sufficiently detailed that nothing crucial has to be filled in later. They are expressed in terms which are tailored to the specific tasks of a specific system for a specific group of users rather than in general terms, which could address a variety of other situations.

SECONDARY GOALS

Growing out of the primary goal of accurately specifying the users' requirements are several related secondary goals, as shown in Figure 3.1.

Understanding the Users' Requirements

Accurate specification is impossible unless requirements have first been understood. Systems analysis is a process by which users and analysts help each other reach an understanding of the system requirements that is sufficient for their accurate specification. This implies an understanding of all those dimensions of the users' business which affect or interact with the information processing system. It may require a knowledge of how things are currently done before deciding how the system should

FIGURE 3.1	Goals of systems analysis

Primary Goal:

To state accurately the users' requirements for a new information processing system.

Supporting Goals:

1. To understand the users' requirements.
2. To communicate the current understanding of the proposed system.
3. To prevent expensive mistakes.
4. To state a design problem.
5. To state the conditions for system acceptance.

be changed. Incremental system development allows analysts to refine their understanding of the users' requirements.

Communicating the Current Understanding of the Proposed System

Successful communication is a prerequisite to successful system development. A mutual understanding of the users' requirements is achieved through interaction and communication among users; among analysts; and among users, analysts, and others involved in developing a system. Communication makes understanding explicit and shared. If I cannot express my requirements so that you can understand them, it usually means one of two things: that I do not really understand them myself (in which case communication may lead us both to my requirements) or that I alone am able to act on my understanding (no one else can help me until we are able to communicate).

Preventing Expensive Mistakes

DeMarco has characterized systems analysis as a defensive activity, offering the following maxim:

> The overriding concern of analysis is not to achieve success, but to avoid failure.[1]

In practice, a perfect statement of users' requirements is unlikely to be fully achieved. Nevertheless, the methods of systems analysis attempt to reduce the number of omissions, inconsistencies, and undetected errors as well as to minimize their impact on information system development. There are no guarantees of success. But the penalties of failure can be minimized by preventing mistakes, detecting errors as soon as possible, and correcting those errors quickly. The later in the information system development process changes are made, the more expensive they become.

Stating a Design Problem

An accurate statement of users' requirements is not an end in itself. It is the basis for designing an information processing system which will satisfy those requirements. Thus, systems analysis must provide system designers all the information they need in order to specify an executable system of computer programs that will correctly carry out the required transformations.

Stating the Conditions for System Acceptance

How can users be assured that the information processing system, as delivered by its developers, will in fact meet the stated system requirements? There must be explicit performance requirements for the new system. These performance requirements will be used to test the completed system — to determine whether or not it is acceptable. They may be quantitative or qualitative, but they must be measurable or observable.

CHARACTERISTICS OF A STATEMENT OF SYSTEM REQUIREMENTS

These characteristics of the requirements statement serve to achieve the goals of the analysis process.

- It is **graphic**, using diagrams to present the system structure — taking advantage of the most effective form of human communication.
- It is **partitioned**. The diagrams organize the system model into comprehensible parts so that its structure can be understood and communicated.

---

[1]Tom DeMarco, *Structured Analysis and System Specification* (New York: Yourdon, 1979), 9.

> ▌ It is **nonredundant**. With "a place for everything and everything in its place," the requirements statement is friendly toward change. Minimum redundancy supports the many revisions necessary during an iterative analysis process, accommodates change during system development, and facilitates modifications after the system is in production.
>
> ▌ It is **accurate**. As discussed above, it is rigorous, precise, clear, consistent, and complete.
>
> ▌ It is **minimal.** It eliminates non-essentials and omits what can be decided later or left to the discretion of the system designers or implementers. However, it must not omit details which will result in rejection of the system by the users.

THE PROCESS OF SYSTEMS ANALYSIS

The major activities within the analysis portion of system development are introduced here and described further in the remainder of Part II. First, we wish to highlight the more important general characteristics of the analysis process.

CHARACTERISTICS OF THE ANALYSIS PROCESS

Systems analysis shares the characteristics of the system development process presented in Chapter 2. Thus, analysis is inherently **iterative**. It is a process of gradual refinement, beginning with a comprehensive, high-level view of the system and continuing until all the necessary details have been filled in. Analysis also focuses on specific parts of the system to limit the amount of complexity from moment to moment. There is a need for correction when errors are detected. There is a need for revision when users' requirements change. Iteration is also necessary because achieving understanding through communication requires considerable interaction.

Effective analysis is **systematic** in order to produce a complete and consistent set of requirements in spite of the complexity of a system. It is based on an organized body of skills and techniques for producing the necessary system models. Analysis must be dynamic so that it can respond to and accommodate change as well as complexity.

The process of analysis is also **inseparable from its tools and techniques**. Conceptually we distinguish between the process and the tools, but in practice, they go together. The tools and techniques are integral to the process. They are the natural by-products of doing analysis. Documentation produced during analysis is not created artificially or after the fact. Rather, it is essential to achieve the goals of stating users' requirements accurately, understanding users' requirements, and communicating during an inherently interactive process.

SYSTEMS ANALYSIS AND THE UNIFIED PROCESS

As discussed in Chapter 2, in the Unified Process, systems analysts participate throughout system development. They have the primary responsibility for the Requirements core discipline, as the Unified Process speaks of requirements rather than analysis. However, their greatest involvement is during the first two phases — Inception and Elaboration. The need to establish a stable system architecture means that most systems analysis is completed by the end of Elaboration. Analysis activities during a build cycle in Construction are primarily intended to refine the system or to correct misunderstandings.

FIGURE 3.2   Procedure for object-oriented systems analysis

> Step 1. Identify the business events and make an event table.
> Step 2. Identify the use cases and produce a use case diagram for the system.
> Step 3. Write a use case narrative describing the system's response to each business event.
> Step 4. Draw a system sequence diagram for each use case scenario.
> Step 5. Produce a domain model showing the concepts, attributes, and associations in the problem domain of the system.
> Step 6. Write a contract for each system operation.

A PROCEDURE FOR OBJECT-ORIENTED SYSTEMS ANALYSIS

This chapter and the two which follow explain a procedure for object-oriented systems analysis. For the purpose of explanation, this procedure is presented as a sequence of six steps, as summarized in Figure 3.2. The first step is described in this chapter. The remaining steps are explained in Chapters 4 and 5.

In practice, experienced analysts often carry out some of the steps simultaneously. As the various steps are carried out, it often becomes obvious that the work accomplished in previous steps must be revised as a result of what is learned in later steps. This is consistent with the iterative nature of the system development process.

OBJECT-ORIENTED ANALYSIS – MODELS IN THE PROCESS

The process of object-oriented analysis is closely tied to the models developed during the process.

- To describe, understand, and communicate the requirements for an information processing system means to identify the events to which the system must respond. This results in an event model, which may be presented as an event table. (See Figure 3.6 for an example.)
- To investigate the required system response involves writing narratives of the use cases associated with each event and revising them until an accurate statement of the users' requirements has been achieved. Use cases and their descriptions form the use case model of the system requirements. System sequence diagrams show the form and content of the system inputs. (See Chapter 4.)
- To understand the application domain and to define the users' requirements for stored data entail preparing a domain model, which shows the relevant concepts, the attributes which describe each of those concepts, and the associations between concepts. (See Chapter 5.)
- To define the outcomes of the procedures for carrying out the system's response requires writing a contract for each message which the system receives from its environment. (See Chapter 5.)

Figure 3.3 is an overview of the models used in object-oriented analysis. It shows the sequence in which the models are produced as well as the relationships among the models. Figure 3.3 assumes that the system is simple enough for a single diagram or table to show the entire system. If it is not, these diagrams may need to be partitioned in order to be legible and communicate effectively to their readers.

FIGURE 3.3	Models used in object-oriented systems analysis

MODEL	IMPORTANT COMPONENTS	RELATIONSHIP TO OTHER MODELS
Event Table (1 for the system)	Event	
Use Case Model Use case diagram (1 for the system)	Use case	At least 1 use case per event
	Actor Association	Actors and associations are shown in the event table
Use case narrative (1 for each use case)		
System Sequence Diagram (At least 1 diagram per use case)	Actor System (black box) Message	Structure and content of messages from an actor are derived from an expanded use case narrative
Domain Model (1 for the system)	Concept Attribute Association	Derived from the set of use case narratives
System Operation Contract (1 per message from actor to system)		Derived from • Expanded use case narrative for the corresponding use case narrative • Domain model

THE UNIFIED MODELING LANGUAGE

Most of the models produced in object-oriented analysis use a notation for models of object-oriented systems known as the Unified Modeling Language (UML). In this book, we introduce the basic elements of the UML as we explain how to carry out object-oriented analysis and design. A brief history of the UML appears at the beginning of Chapter 4.

TECHNIQUES OF OBJECT-ORIENTED ANALYSIS

It is clear that systems analysis must include techniques for modeling and modifying the system requirements. Maintaining an information system model as it evolves through many iterations is a tedious and exacting task, especially when carried out manually. Integrated Development Environments (IDEs) now permit system developers to create, modify, and maintain the system model in a computer, carrying it from analysis through design and construction.

Important techniques used in object-oriented analysis are:

▮ *Information-Gathering Techniques.* The basic techniques of gathering information, such as interviews, observations, and questionnaires, are common to all approaches to systems analysis. These are discussed in Chapter 13.

▮ *Event Analysis.* Event analysis (described in this chapter) is a technique for identifying system-level requirements. It views an information processing system as providing preplanned responses to significant occurrences in the system's environment. It is the starting point for object-oriented analysis.

▮ *Use Case Modeling.* A use case model presents the required interactions between the system and its users. Initially, each use case is the counterpart of one of the events identified previously. A use case model consists of a diagram showing which users participate in which use cases as well as a narrative of the expected response of the system as each use case unfolds. Use case modeling is explained in Chapter 4.

■ *Domain Modeling Techniques.* These techniques are used to obtain a minimal, nonredundant, coherent, comprehensive view of the problem domain, as presented in Chapter 5.

■ *Walkthroughs.* A walkthrough is a technique originally associated with structured analysis methods. It is equally valuable in object-oriented system development. A walkthrough is a bug-identification session for an information processing system description. It is a peer review by systems analysts and users which focuses on finding errors. This serves the goal of detecting mistakes as soon as possible so that they can be eliminated.

EVENT ANALYSIS FOR OBJECT-ORIENTED SYSTEMS

Event analysis is Step 1 of the procedure for object-oriented analysis outlined in Figure 3.2. Event analysis is a powerful technique for identifying what users expect a system to do. In our approach to object-oriented systems analysis, event analysis initiates the analysis process and drives the development of the other models of object-oriented systems analysis. The remainder of this chapter explains event analysis and applies it to a university registration system. The university registration system example continues throughout Parts II and III.

In object-oriented analysis and design, it is important to be sure that the actions carried out by the objects occur in the proper sequence. It is also important to partition the system's behavior into manageable parts by determining which sequences of actions are independent. Viewing a system in terms of events provides a useful perspective. It helps to sequence and coordinate the system's dynamic behavior and to identify system responses which are independent of each other.

For example, consider some of the banking transactions which may occur at an automated teller machine. A customer may deposit funds, withdraw funds, or transfer funds between accounts. Informally, each of these transactions may be regarded as an event. The customer initiates the transactions, provides the system with the necessary data, and expects a predictable response. These transactions can occur independently, in any order.

At the system level, event analysis considers the purpose of an entire information processing system to be responding to a selected set of occurrences in the system's environment. The system is organized to produce preplanned responses to what happens outside it.

Event analysis works by composition, or synthesis, rather than by decomposition. At any one time the analyst and user focus on a small, and thus manageable, portion of the system. Event analysis helps bypass details of the implementing technology, resulting in a closer approximation to an essential system model. This is consistent with the incremental nature of the system development process.

Event analysis[2] is also known as event modeling or event partitioning. Each of these terms emphasizes an important aspect of the process:

■ **Event analysis** stresses the need to identify and understand each of the situations in the environment to which the system must respond.

■ **Event modeling** notes that the completed system model is the aggregation of models of the system's response to individual events.

■ **Event partitioning** recognizes that the basis for the decomposition of the model is the independent nature of the events. The resulting model will thus consist of independent behaviors, connected only if they require shared access to stored data.

---

[2]For a fuller treatment of event analysis, see Paul T. Ward and Stephen J. Mellor, *Structured Development for Real-Time Systems*, 3 vols. (New York: Yourdon, 1985, 1986).

CONCEPTS AND DEFINITIONS FOR EVENT ANALYSIS

Event analysis involves a few basic concepts — events, event flows or control flows, and a means of recognizing events.

EVENTS

An *event* is an occurrence which takes place at a specific time and initiates or triggers a predetermined response from the system.

Events are categorized as **external, internal,** or **temporal,** depending on whether the occurrence takes place outside the system, inside the system, or only at a predetermined time. (The interaction at the user-computer interface may also be represented in terms of events.)

An *external event* is an event which occurs outside the system boundary. Examples of external events are as follows: "Student registers for classes," "Customer buys item," and "Guest registers at a hotel."

An *internal event* is an event which occurs inside the system boundary. For example, an internal event occurs when the quantity of an item of inventory falls below the reorder point. Internal events are important in real-time systems as well as to coordinate the dynamic behavior of objects in a system. However, internal events are not covered in this book.

A *temporal event* is an event which occurs at a prespecified time. The most common examples of temporal events are those which trigger periodic outputs. For example, every Friday afternoon or at the first of every month, it is time to produce employees' paychecks. Or an accounts receivable summary is expected on the manager's desk by 10 A.M. on each Monday morning.

RECOGNIZING EVENTS

Understanding system behavior in terms of events takes a **stimulus-response** perspective. The basic pattern of operation of an event-driven system is as follows:

▌ The system does nothing until triggered by an event; it sits and waits for an event to occur.
▌ When an event occurs, the system responds as completely as possible.
▌ After the response is finished, the system continues to wait until something else happens.

For example, consider a vending machine which dispenses tea, hot chocolate, and a variety of coffees. The machine sits in the hallway until someone drops some money in the coin slot. The purchaser presses a button to select the desired beverage (and perhaps additional buttons for extra sugar or cream). The machine then dispenses the beverage (and may return change).

When the coins are entered, the machine recognizes that an event has occurred — a customer wishes to buy a beverage. The signal from the coin slot to the machine is the event flow. In order to dispense the desired beverage, the machine needs two pieces of data — the specification of the beverage and the amount paid. Pressing the beverage selection button tells which drink is desired; the coin slot senses the amount paid. Given this information, the machine can respond appropriately.

From the perspective of event analysis, the system is like a giant vending machine, waiting for buttons to be pushed or coins to be inserted before it springs into action.

In order to respond to an event, the system or some object within it must be able to recognize that the event has occurred. The occurrence of an event generates an event flow. This *event flow* (sometimes called a *control flow*) is a signal or message which notifies the recipient that a particular event has occurred.

In the case of an external event, the incoming message must also contain specific data about the event in order for the system to respond appropriately.

The system may recognize either directly or indirectly that an event has occurred. **Direct recognition** is possible when the occurrence of an event always sends an information flow to the system. The arrival of a withdrawal request informs the bank transaction processing system that a customer wishes to make a withdrawal. Similarly, a flight request tells the airline reservation system of a desire to book a seat. Temporal events are noticed by looking at the clock and the calendar.

Indirect recognition requires the system to infer the occurrence of an event from the inputs it receives. For example, data from the environment may be compared with internally stored values, or the system may calculate or simulate what is going on outside.

BUSINESS EVENT ANALYSIS

Depending on the analyst's purpose and the stage of the system development process, events may be identified at a variety of scales and levels of detail. For example, "Customer makes a deposit to a bank account" is a very high-level, large-scale event occurring at the system level. On the other hand, "Deposit option selected" (by the customer's pressing an ATM key) is a low-level, small-scale event. It describes one detail of an implementation of a system which responds to the system-level event "Customer makes a deposit to a bank account."

When investigating system requirements, we are primarily interested in events at the level of the system as a whole. For our purposes, we will refer to these system-level events as *business events*.

As noted earlier, event analysis views an information processing system from the perspective of *stimulus* and *response*. The **stimuli** are system inputs — messages or signals which report on occurrences in the environment of the system. Some **responses** are system outputs; each output is a predetermined message or signal produced when a specific input or combination of inputs is received. Other responses store data in the system's internal memory.

For example, a withdrawal from a bank account causes the amount of the withdrawal to be subtracted from the account balance. At the end of the month, this transaction will be itemized as part of the account statement. A request for an airline reservation leads the reservations clerk or travel agent to search for an available flight, quote the applicable fare, record the reservation, and perhaps even issue a ticket and boarding pass. Reading a drop form causes a university registration system to remove a student from a class and generate a request for a refund of fees, if one is due.

Event analysis creates a system description by identifying:

1. The events to which the system is expected to respond,
2. The incoming message (event flow or data flow) associated with each event,
3. The desired response, and
4. The actions or behaviors required to generate the response for each stimulus.

Figure 3.4 shows an external event as a whole as seen from outside the system.

The system inputs and outputs are the **only** means of **communication** between the system and its environment. It is often helpful to think of the system as a *black box*. What happens inside is hidden. The only way the system can learn about what takes place on the outside is by receiving messages which contain the essential information about what has occurred. The only way the outside world can perceive the system's responses is through messages coming from inside the box. Perhaps we should imagine that a telephone and a fax machine are the media for exchange of

FIGURE 3.4   External event and its components

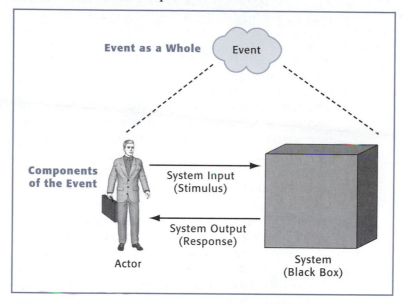

information between the black box and the world outside. Using this analogy, we can understand the role of stimulus and response. The value of the conversation comes from the information transmitted.

These messages, like all information flows, may be classified as either event flows (also known as control flows) or data flows.

EVENT FLOWS

An *event flow* is an information flow which contains no application-specific data. An incoming event flow merely notifies the system that a specific event has occurred and triggers the system to respond. Any data essential to the system's response is already stored inside the system. Temporal events always generate event flows. Examples are Friday-Afternoon, First-of-the-Month, and Time-to-Produce-Account-Statement.

Occasionally, there may be an outgoing event flow to initiate an action in the environment or to report to the environment that the system has completed its response. Examples are messages such as "Successfully Completed" and "Unable to Complete."

DATA FLOWS

A *data flow* contains application-specific data elements with specific values which describe details of the event. In the banking example mentioned above, the Withdrawal Request might consist of:

▌ Account Number,
▌ Withdrawal Date, and
▌ Withdrawal Amount.

The Flight Request for an airline reservation might include:

▌ Passenger Name,
▌ Number in Party,
▌ Date of Flight,

- Preferred Time of Day,
- Class of Service, and perhaps
- Preferred Airline.

An incoming data flow serves two purposes:

1. Its arrival triggers the system to respond.
2. The flow contains the data essential for the system to produce the required response. (Or, if some of the information is already stored in the system, the flow contains the additional essential data.)

In this case, a separate event flow to report the occurrence of the event and initiate the system's response is unnecessary.

An outgoing data flow transmits the system's response to the environment. It may be as simple as one or two data items or as complex as an elaborate report.

DESCRIBING BUSINESS EVENTS

When carrying out event analysis, it is critically important to be extremely precise with the language used to identify and describe business events. Unless the language is clear, the point of view on which event analysis is based can be compromised or lost, and the analyst can become confused. Descriptions must be phrased so as to clearly distinguish events from non-events. It is usually easy to recognize a situation associated with an event; it may take practice to refer to each type of event in appropriate language.

In order to be precise when describing an event, focus on the event as a whole rather than on its parts. Remember that an event is **not** any of the following components:

- A system input. An input is a message that tells the system what it needs to know about an event, a stimulus to which the system must respond, but it is not the event itself.
- An action or response of the system. It is true that the system must carry out an action or behavior to respond to an event, but the event is independent of the response. It occurs whether or not the system responds adequately.
- A system output. An output is a message produced by the system in responding to an event, but it is not the event itself. It is not always necessary for the system to produce an output when it responds to an event.

We are concerned with temporal and external events. Each of these event types has a characteristic style of description.

DESCRIBING A TEMPORAL BUSINESS EVENT

A temporal event description begins with the phrase "Time to . . . " or "It is time to . . . . "

An example of a temporal event description is:

- Time to produce employees' paychecks.

Note that this is not the same as "Produce employees' paychecks," which describes an action of the system — what the system does when the event occurs — rather than the event. This distinction is crucial.

Other examples of temporal business events are:

▌ Time to produce a customer's bank account statement.
▌ Time to cancel a hotel room reservation which was not guaranteed for late arrival.
▌ Time to produce class rosters for instructors.

Note that when a temporal event is named, the predicate of the sentence usually refers to a system output — the message describing the system's response to the event.

DESCRIBING AN EXTERNAL BUSINESS EVENT

An external event description is a complete sentence in the active voice.
Examples of descriptions for external events are:

▌ Customer makes a withdrawal from a bank account.
▌ Passenger requests an airline reservation.
▌ Student drops a class.

Note that when an external event is named, the subject of the sentence will refer to a person, organization, or system in the environment, and the predicate of the sentence often refers to a system input — the message reporting the essential information about the event. Sometimes the predicate may refer instead to the desired system output.

IDENTIFYING ACTORS

An *actor* is a person, organization, or system which interacts with a system. An actor may generate a system input or receive a system output.
To identify an actor means to:

▌ Find out which people, organizations, or systems in the environment provide each system input or receive each output.
▌ Give the actor a name.

The name of an actor is a noun or noun phrase describing the actor. The actor who initiates a Registration Request is a Student.

IDENTIFYING SYSTEM INPUTS AND OUTPUTS

Identifying a system input or output means doing two things:

▌ Finding out what information associated with an event is entering or leaving the system and
▌ Giving the input or output a name.

The name of an input or output should be a noun (or noun phrase) which describes the information contained in the input or output. For example, in a university system, Registration Request is a good name for the input containing a student identifier and the list of desired sections.

At a minimum, all the system outputs, as well as the system inputs, should be identified and named. Sometimes an event will result only in storing data within the system, producing no associated output.

Traditionally, the inputs and outputs are considered as flows of data. Their composition is specified using a notation for data structure.[3] In object-oriented systems, inputs are specified as messages. Outputs may be specified either as messages or as output objects. The specific information content of system inputs and outputs will be defined in Step 4, discussed in Chapter 4.

When identifying the events, the actors, and the system inputs and outputs, it is often useful to tabulate the results in an *event table*. Figure 3.6, in the example which follows, shows an event table in the recommended format.

AN EXAMPLE OF EVENT ANALYSIS

How do we apply the procedure presented above to create an event model? Let us illustrate event analysis with an example based on a student records system for Public University.

BACKGROUND: THE PUBLIC UNIVERSITY REGISTRATION SYSTEM

The schedule of classes for each term is produced in advance of the preregistration date according to a timetable prepared by the Records Office. By a date contained in the timetable, each department in the university must submit a list of classes scheduled for the term in question. These lists are combined to form a printed class schedule. The schedule is distributed free to each department office and to each professor; students must buy theirs at the bookstore.

During the preregistration period, students request the classes they would like to take, using a touch-tone telephone. Each class request contains the student's identifier and the identifier of the class for which the student wishes to register. If that class is not available, the student may try to enroll in a different section of the same course or in another class. After a student has registered for as many classes as possible (up to the maximum number of units permitted), a class list is printed for that student. It shows the classes in which the student has been enrolled.

A class roster, containing a list of the students' names and identifiers, is printed for the professor teaching each class. The list is ordered alphabetically by the students' last names.

EVENT MODEL FOR THE PUBLIC UNIVERSITY REGISTRATION SYSTEM

The event analysis for the Public University registration system and the resulting event table are discussed below.

Identify the Business Events

First, we identify the business events and make a list of them, as shown in Figure 3.5.

There are four events:

1. *Department submits class schedule.* In spite of the fact that the registrar schedules a time for this event, it is still an external event. The system cannot respond until it receives the information contained in the class schedule. The arrival of the scheduled date by itself is not sufficient to permit the system to respond. The Department Class Schedules are submitted individually by each

---

[3]See Lavette C. Teague, Jr., and Christopher W. Pidgeon, *Structured Analysis Methods for Computer Information Systems* (Chicago: Science Research Associates, 1985), ch. 7.

FIGURE 3.5   Event list for the university registration system

> 1. Department submits class schedule.
> 2. Time to produce university class schedule.
> 3. Student registers for classes.
> 4. Time to produce class roster.

department. (That is, the submission of each department schedule is considered to be a separate occurrence of the event "Department submits its class schedule.") The information is stored in the system for future use.

2. *Time to produce university class schedule.* This is a temporal event. The University Class Schedule cannot be produced until the last Department has submitted the required information.

3. *Student registers for classes.* This is an external event. The system registers a single student for as many classes as possible and produces the Student Class List. The enrollments are recorded within the system. Note that the system has enough information to produce a student's class list as soon as that student has registered. There is no need to wait until all students have registered.

4. *Time to produce class roster.* After all students have registered for their classes, the stored data is used to produce the Class Rosters. (Strictly speaking, a Class Roster can be produced as soon as a section has been filled.)

We could easily identify other events for this system, such as "Student drops classes" or "Community college sends transcript." However, we have limited this example to four events which are central to the registration system. In Exercise 3–12, we extend the list of events.

Identify the Actors

In order to identify actors, we need to know who supplies the system with inputs or receives outputs from the system.

In the external event "Department submits class schedule," we realize that a department provides the registration system with information about the schedule of classes which the department plans to offer. This tells us that Department is an actor for the event. We also note that the subject of the sentence describing the event is "Department." If external events are properly described, the subject usually names the actor providing input to the system. Similarly, Student is the actor supplying a list of requested classes in "Student registers for classes."

Who receives system outputs? Event 1 has no output. In Event 2, Departments, Professors, and Students receive the University Class Schedules. In Event 3, the Student receives a Class List. Class Rosters (Event 4) go to the Professor who teaches each class.

Thus, the actors for these four events are Department, Professor, and Student.

Identify the System Inputs and Outputs

For now, we merely identify and name the system inputs and outputs. Their detailed definition is deferred to Step 4 of the object-oriented analysis process.

In the Public University Registration System, there are two inputs — Department Class Schedule (Event 1) and Registration Request (Event 3). We give each a name describing its information content. There are three outputs — University Class Schedule (Event 2), Student Class List (Event 3), and Class Roster (Event 4). Note that a good description for a temporal event includes the name of its output.

Note that we must distinguish between the input Department Class Schedule (Event 1) and the output University Class Schedule (Event 2).

FIGURE 3.6   Event table for the university registration system

EVENT NUMBER	EVENT DESCRIPTION	SYSTEM INPUT	ACTOR PROVIDING INPUT	SYSTEM OUTPUT	ACTOR RECEIVING OUTPUT
1.	Department submits class schedule.	Department Class Schedule	Department		
2.	Time to produce class schedule			University Class Schedule	Student Department Professor
3.	Student registers for classes	Registration Request	Student	Student Class List	Student
4.	Time to produce class roster			Class Roster	Professor

It is convenient to expand the event list into an event table. For each event, the event table includes the associated actors, inputs, and outputs. Note that the event table describes the system response in terms of an output, if there is one. What the system must do to produce the response is described in a use case narrative. Use case narratives are explained in Chapter 4.

Figure 3.6 shows the event table for the registration system.

HINTS ABOUT EVENT ANALYSIS

Effective event analysis requires building an essential event model, modeling the system's complete response, and isolating individual events.

BUILD AN ESSENTIAL EVENT MODEL — IGNORE THE TECHNOLOGY OF IMPLEMENTATION

In Chapter 2, we introduced the distinction between essential and implementation models. Throughout systems analysis, we want to produce essential models which ignore the system's specific technology. In building an essential event model, we ignore how the system is or could be implemented.

For example, one event in a banking system is "Customer makes deposit." The essential system requirement in this situation is that the customer provide funds in some form and of a known amount for deposit to a valid account. In response, the customer ultimately receives a receipt for the transaction.

It does not matter whether the customer hands the deposit to a teller, puts it in a deposit envelope and then in a slot in an ATM, drops it in a box in the bank lobby, mails it, or sends it by carrier pigeon. Similarly, the receipt can be provided by a teller, dispensed by the ATM, or mailed. What the bank is required to do is essentially the same in spite of the superficial differences in the technology for transmitting the deposit to the bank and for returning the receipt to the customer.

Decisions about the implementing technology are design decisions. Analysts should not assume what these decisions will be. They should state the requirements in a way which will allow a variety of implementations.

MODEL THE SYSTEM'S COMPLETE RESPONSE

It is often helpful to assume that the internal technology of the system is perfect. That is, we assume that messages move instantaneously within the system, responses are carried out immediately and without error, and stored data is never lost or unintentionally altered. This helps us model the complete response of the system to each event. It also helps to isolate individual events, rather that lumping them together.

When we fail to model the system's complete response to an event, we are likely to split what is really a single event into two or more fragments. In general, the response should include everything the system is able to do with the information it has at the time.

For example, in the event "Student registers for classes," the response is not complete until the system produces a Student Class List. After a student has enrolled in all the open sections which were requested, the system knows everything necessary to generate the Student Class List. Therefore, producing a Student Class List is not a separate event; it completes the event "Student registers for classes." The fact that the university may currently mail the class list a week after the student registers should not change the essential event model.

An output should not be separated from the event it completes unless the system's environment or a conscious policy decision by the system's users requires a delay.

ISOLATE INDIVIDUAL EVENTS

An opposite problem arises when several separate events are mistakenly combined. Sometimes this is caused by failure to recognize the need for a delay between the events. Sometimes the analyst fails to notice that the system lacks enough information to produce an output, and the output is prematurely incorporated into another event instead of being modeled separately. At other times, the analyst erroneously assumes that two events must occur together when in fact they may occur separately.

For example, "Time to produce university class schedule" must be a separate event. The system does not have enough information to generate the entire university class schedule until all the instances of "Department submits class schedule" have occurred. Only then is all the information in the university class schedule stored in the system.

In a restaurant, "Patron pays bill" is a separate event from "Patron orders food" because the bill is the output which completes "Patron orders food." The amount of the bill is unknown until it is presented to the patron.

SUMMARY

Systems analysis may be characterized in terms of its goals, its procedures, its products, and its tools and techniques.

The principal goal of systems analysis is to state accurately users' requirements for a new information processing system. Systems analysis is an iterative process, which is inseparable from its tools and techniques.

This chapter introduces a six-step process for object-oriented analysis. The first step is event analysis, which produces an event model. The remaining five steps provide a method for producing object-oriented analysis models — a use case model, system sequence diagrams, a model of the problem domain, and system operation contracts. This method starts with the events identified in the first step and uses the graphic symbols of the Unified Modeling Language. The six steps are:

1. Identify the business events and make an event table.
2. Identify the use cases and produce a use case diagram for the system.
3. Write a use case narrative describing the system's response to each business event.
4. Draw a system sequence diagram for each use case scenario.
5. Produce a domain model showing the concepts, attributes, and associations in the problem domain of the system.
6. Write a contract for each system operation.

An event is an occurrence which takes place at a specific time and elicits a predetermined response from the system. An event generates a message which notifies a system that an event has occurred and triggers a predetermined response. There are three types of events: external, internal, and temporal.

Event analysis views an information processing system from the perspective of stimulus and response. The initial goal is to identify the business events to which the information processing system must respond. Then the analyst begins to understand the system's response by identifying the messages which pass between the system and its environment. During this process, the analyst may also define the information content of the system's inputs and outputs.

Event analysis creates a system description by identifying:

1. The events to which the system is expected to respond,
2. The stimuli (inputs) associated with each event,
3. The desired response (outputs or stored data), and
4. The behaviors essential to produce the response for each stimulus.

The results of event analysis are presented in an event table. Viewing a system and the objects which compose it in terms of events provides a useful perspective. It helps both in sequencing and coordinating the system's dynamic behavior and in identifying system responses which are independent of each other.

KEY TERMS

actor *81*

business event *78*

control flow *77*

event *77*

event flow *79*

response *78*

stimulus *78*

REVIEW QUESTIONS

3-1. What are the goals of systems analysis?

3-2. List important characteristics of an accurate statement of users' requirements for an information processing system.

3-3. List three characteristics of the process of systems analysis.

3-4. Name the models produced during object-oriented systems analysis.

3-5. Explain the difference between an event and each of the following:

a. System input
b. System output
c. System response

EXERCISES AND DISCUSSION QUESTIONS

3-1. Explain how each characteristic of a statement of system requirements mentioned in this chapter helps achieve the goals of systems analysis.

3-2. How do information-gathering techniques and walkthroughs further the goals of systems analysis?

3-3. Discuss some of the impacts of lack of clarity, inconsistency, incompleteness, and lack of rigor on a statement of system requirements.

3-4. Explain the difference between temporal events and external events in terms of the type of stimulus for each (data flow or control flow) and possible system responses (output or storage of data).

3-5. Must every temporal event produce a system output? Why?

3-6. Why do we focus on identifying and defining system inputs for external events only and not for temporal events as well?

3-7. How are the documents and displays in an information system related to the columns of an event table? Give examples for a system with which you are familiar.

3-8. What are some of the implications for the system development process of the fact that events are independent of each other?

3-9. Why is it important to model the system's complete response to each event? Formulate a question that could be used to test whether the complete response has been shown.

3-10. Discuss the relationships between the form of event descriptions and the identification of actors, system inputs, and system outputs.

3-11. Consider the following statements related to event analysis of a banking system. Indicate if each statement describes an event in appropriate language. If the description is inappropriate, identify what characteristic of an event is missing. If the language is appropriate, identify the type of event.

    a. Amalgamated Bank is continually striving to improve service to its customers.
    b. Customer makes a deposit.
    c. Loan payments received on Saturday are credited on the next business day.
    d. Teller cashes a customer's check.
    e. It is time to produce a statement for a customer's account.

3-12. Additional cycles of system development often extend the scope of the system by identifying additional events to which users wish the system to respond. This exercise expands the scope of the student registration system.

    The Records Office still maintains students' grades and transcripts manually. The Registrar wishes to extend the current automated system to be able to record students' grades at the end of each term and produce grade reports for both students and instructors.

    In your conversation with the Registrar, you have learned that within one week after the examination period instructors submit a grade sheet containing the grades students have earned in each class. The Records Office keeps a permanent record of the grades and produces a student grade report, which is mailed to each student, and an instructor's grade report, which is distributed to each faculty member.

    a. Identify the additional events to which the automated system must now respond.
    b. Modify the event table to incorporate these events. (Use the format suggested in Figure 3.6.)

    Imagine that each system input associated with an event arrives individually. Do not assume that its data structure contains iterations unless you know that such a structure is essential.

3-13. List other events which might be included in a university registration system of extended scope. If you wish, you may add them to the event table.

FIGURE 3.7   CIOs Sure Think IT Matters

CIOs and chief technology officers beg to differ with a recent *Harvard Business Review* article titled "IT Doesn't Matter."

Does IT matter? A recent *Harvard Business Review* article titled "IT Doesn't Matter" sparked discussion among attendees at a Chief Information Officer (CIO) conference at MIT in Cambridge, Mass., this week. And not surprisingly, the CIOs and chief technology officers (CTOs) begged to differ.

General Motors Corp. CTO Tony Scott, while saying the story raised interesting points, argued with the article's premise that IT doesn't matter because it has become commoditized and provides no competitive advantage. IT that provides competitive advantages continues to be developed, Scott said, and even technology that's a commodity still provides business flexibility.

"Brakes are a commodity, but I don't think anybody would say they don't matter," Scott said, using an auto-industry analogy. Because of the rate of IT development, any company that fails to invest in IT is doomed to fall behind, he said.

CIO and executive VP Michael Harte at PFPC/PNC (part of the PNC Financial Services Group) questioned the article's argument that IT is less productive than other forms of capital. If anything, IT is becoming more productive with new generations of IT portfolio-management tools, he said. But he agreed that there's increased pressure to measure the return provided by IT investments.

Adapted from Rick Whiting, *Information Week*, May 20, 2003.

3-14. Consider the following systems with which you are familiar. Prepare an event table for each system. Make appropriate assumptions to limit the scope of each system. Some of these assumptions are suggested below.

   a. A restaurant. Limit the scope of the system to the events related to customers' dining. Ignore the purchase of food and supplies as well as what goes on in the kitchen.

   b. A library. Focus on events related to the circulation of books and other materials. Ignore the acquisition and disposal of the lendable items.

   c. A video rental store. Focus on events related to the rental of videos. Ignore the acquisition and disposal of the videos.

   d. A motel. Limit the scope of the system to the events involving interaction with the guests.

3-15. What similarities do you notice between the events in the restaurant and those in the motel? Between the events in the library and those in the video rental store?

3-16. Consider the article about whether information technology matters in Figure 3.7.

   a. Read the *Harvard Business Review* article to which it refers (Nicholas G. Carr, "IT Doesn't Matter," May 2003, 41) and summarize its major points.

   b. Summarize the response of the CIOs and CTOs mentioned in Whiting's article.

   c. Which point of view do you find more persuasive, and why?

   d. You may also wish to investigate the comments of others with respect to this controversy. See, for example, "IT Does So Matter," *Computerworld*, July 7, 2003, 36–37.

Giant Forest
INN

This section introduces two case studies — a hotel system and a car rental system — as a basis for more extensive project assignments. Suggested project tasks appear at the end of each project narrative in this chapter and in the remaining chapters which introduce tools or models for object-oriented analysis and design.

A Case Study
by Robert Stumpf

History

After World I and before the stock market crash that led to the Great Depression was a period of great prosperity in the United States. Many of the people who lived during this time say that it was even better than the prosperity of the 1990s. One of the persons who accumulated a sizable amount of capital was Fred Manger. He decided to sell all his securities before the stock market crash and build a first-class resort hotel on his mountain property.

He succeeded in every way. By 1927, he had built a 100-room hotel containing five stories, which he called Giant Forest Inn. To go with it, he had many amenities, such as tennis courts, sauna baths, stables with a covered horseback trail, boat rentals, a ballroom, five dining rooms, and both an indoor and an outdoor swimming pool. The tile work on these pools was a work of art. He also had built 25 cottages with garages in the wooded area near the Inn. These cottages provided seclusion for the guests and also security for their handcrafted automobiles. The service and food were outstanding, and his resort hotel became almost immediately one of the top hotels in the world. The prices were very expensive, but many people who prospered during this time could easily afford the high prices.

With the beginning of the Great Depression, operations had to be cut back because of the low occupancy rate. By the time World War II began, the Inn had to be shut down. Unfortunately, Fred never lived to see it open again. In 1946, after World War II was over, Fred's son Howard leased the property to Belton Hotels. Belton Hotels was a chain with hotels all over the world, and its managers supposedly had the expertise to operate such a fine hotel. Belton lowered its standards and was able to operate it with a reasonable profit. After 20 years, however, Belton Hotels discontinued the lease, leaving Howard again with an empty property.

The Beginning of the New Company

In 1967, Howard's son Bill was finishing business school and was looking for an opportunity to run a business. He asked his father for permission to create a new corporation to run the Inn. Howard liked the idea. Bill had a close friend named Roger Morris who had recently graduated from law school and who helped with obtaining additional capital to use for repairs. Bill did not re-open the cottages, as they were expensive to maintain. However, the new corporation did issue bonds in order to build a new three-story bungalow with 80 more rooms and 15 conference rooms. When the bungalow was completed in 1969, the Inn was again a stable business. Many aerospace firms booked the conference rooms for retreats. Also, many of the engineers came back to bring their families, and finally the Inn was again profitable. In the 1990s, the Inn became popular with the new Internet companies.

Major Event and Reorientation of the Inn

In September of 2000, a fire broke out in the bungalow, and it was damaged sufficiently to be condemned for further use. The only option was to have it demolished. This left Bill and Roger with some major decisions to make. After they did an analysis of the market, they realized that there was a sufficient base of customers who liked the original Inn for its charm. Also, there was a large demand for the cottages from guests who lived in foreign countries. They decided not to rebuild the bungalow but instead to renovate the cottages. They also hired a world-famous chef and began to offer fine food. The hotel they now envisioned would be a true five-star hotel.

Rooms Referred to by Name, Not by a Number

The guests the Giant Forest Inn is now dealing with want to be treated like celebrities. Fred had originally named each guest room, such as the George Washington Room or the Abraham Lincoln Room. Thus, most customers ask for their favorite room by name when they make a reservation. If the specific room is not important, this is also noted on the reservation. Most reservations, except for cottages, are charged one night's lodging as a deposit. Cottages typically require a deposit of one month's rent.

Special Check-In Services

Guests check in upon arrival when a credit card is presented or a deposit is paid. Their address and guest data are already on the check-in form. Usually, all they need to do is sign it if a reservation was made. Walk-ins (those who do not have reservations) are accepted as long as there is room. A quick reservation is made for them, and from then on, they are treated as regular guests.

Special System to Handle Receipts for Services

Guests wish to be able to charge services by using their own name and not a room number. In fact, many guests expect the Inn staff not to ask who they are. They feel the staff should remember them. The guests do not want to sign receipts for service during meals or while ordering drinks from the lounge. So Fred devised a system where all receipts at the end of the day are hand-delivered to the guest's room.

Some Rooms Leased Instead of Rented

Many guests want to stay for two months or longer. Some guests in the cottages actually want to stay for as long as a year. Thus, a lease is used instead of a simple room registration. Leased rooms are billed once a month. Ordinary rooms are charged each night. A bill for the amount due is presented the night before checkout, and it is paid before the guest leaves.

Special Check-Out Procedures

The guests expect not to have to wait in line to check out. The night before they are to leave, a bill is hand-delivered to their room. If all is okay, they do nothing; however, if there are problems, they call the Inn's bookkeeping department, and adjustments are made. Then a new copy is hand-delivered to them. Payment is done mostly by check or credit card. Figure 3.8 shows an example of a bill.

Current Inn Rates

Figure 3.9 shows current prices at the Giant Forest Inn.

Computer System Problems

The computer system which Giant Forest Inn had leased was created not for hotels serving this type of clientele but for convention hotels. After checking with other vendors of computer systems, Bill and Roger realized none of them could satisfy the unique needs of their guests. It was time to create a new custom hotel reservation and guest management system.

FIGURE 3.8 Sample bill for Giant Forest Inn

Statement		
Guest	**George Washington** **3 Old Wood Trail** **Eucalyptus, California 90000**	
Date	**Charge**	**Amount**
2/15/2004	Room	$ 262.00
	Room Tax	26.20
	Telephone	2.47
	Dining Room	122.22
2/16/2004	Room	262.00
	Room Tax	26.20
	Equestrian Adventure	195.00
	Room Service	33.50
	Dining Room	87.50
	Total	**$ 1,017.09**

The new computing system needs to:

1. Provide a web interface to make reservations, with automatic mailing (via U.S. Mail) of reservation confirmations; phone reservations are still popular.
2. Track room status (ready, occupied, under repair, not ready).
3. Track room cleaning and laundry (when to issue new sheets).
4. Track all services and present the guests with a bill at the end of each day; guests may then adjust these bills by adding tips for good service.

Your job is to complete the analysis and design for new software for Giant Forest Inn.

Assignments

1. Draw up a list of all external, internal, and temporal events that are encountered in making a reservation, checking in, charging for services, billing, and checking out of the Inn.

FIGURE 3.9 Current room types and rates at Giant Forest Inn

	NUMBER OF ROOMS	PATIO 1	PATIO 2	PATIO EXTRA	FOREST 1	FOREST 2	FOREST EXTRA
Luxury							
1 Queen bed	50	$220	$232	$22	$250	$262	$22
2 Queen beds	50	$250	$262	$22	$280	$292	$22
Two Room	15	$270	$282	$22	$300	$315	$22
Three Room	5	$320	$332		$350	$365	
Bridal	5	$270		$320	$320		
Cottage							
Two Room	10	$350	$370	$30	$380	$400	$30
Three Room	12	$380	$400	$30	$410	$430	$30
Four Room	3	$400	$420	$30	$430	$450	$30

2. Once the list of events is complete, create an event table, as in Figure 3.6.

A Case Study
by Robert Stumpf

History

Bill Parker learned to work hard at a very early age. When he was 11, his father disappeared, leaving the family unsupported financially. This forced his mother to work to care for him and his little sister. Income was meager for the Parker family at this time, so Bill had to help support the family. His first job was a paper route. Because of his ability to sell subscriptions to new customers, he became the most successful carrier of the *Riverdale Times*.

Throughout his formative years, he sold other products as well. He was always selling something, whether it was magazines, candy, or brushes. He learned to keep books, and he learned the value of selling something for more than he paid for it.

His best friend, Jim Adams, also was from a poor family. However, from the beginning, Jim was fascinated with automobiles. If it had wheels, he wanted it. To help support his family, he worked at local service stations, where he learned how to maintain cars, and picked up body and fender skills as well. He barely finished high school. If the school had had real academic standards, he would not have finished. Jim knew this, so he decided to continue his studies at a local community college.

The Impact of Business School

Bill realized he needed some formal business schooling, so he also entered the local community college. It was in the business classes that they met. Bill took advanced business classes, while Jim specialized in all the auto mechanics courses. It was during this time that they became determined to go into a business together. They knew their business had to deal with cars. Bill could sell, and Jim could repair them. They tried to open a car lot, but it failed because the banks would not lend them money with their lack of capital and experience.

In their business classes, they listened to success stories on existing businesses. One story was about a large national car rental company. Bill wondered why their prices were so high. Since most of their friends were relatively poor, they were certain that a market existed for a cheap rental car agency.

Since they could not afford new cars for rent, they decided to start Ugly Duckling Car Rental. The cost of cars was cheap, and Jim could fix them up so they were fairly reliable; he also made them look respectable. Bill would take care of renting them. Their advertising was limited to notices on bulletin boards. Their emphasis was a low rental price. They succeeded after a fashion. This went on for about 18 months. They actually made a fair profit due to the fact that that they worked hard and still did most of the work themselves.

The Discovery of a New Market

They discovered that the customers who rented most often were not business travelers, but local residents who needed a spare car. The reasons varied, but often the renters had a visitor, or their car was in the shop for mechanical or body repairs.

Then business stated to decline. Bill remembered his marketing course in college, and he called up prior customers to find out why they did not rent again. They learned that customers wanted basic but new. They were interested in price but only up to a point. Bill was discouraged because he thought his competitors charged high prices due to the high price of new cars. He thought new cars were too high-priced for them.

Assistance from Ernie Hall

One Friday night Bill and Jim decided to drown their troubles in drink at a local pub. As is typical at these establishments, other people were doing the same. Ernie Hall was drinking at the pub because his boss was really upset with him for the downward trend in car leases.

Ernie worked for one of those independent companies that leased cars of all makes. They leased popular makes and models at low monthly prices. The car leasing business works on the principle that cars cost more than most people can afford. However, the depreciation on many makes and models is fairly reasonable per year. Thus, the actual monthly cost of leasing is quite a bit cheaper than that of financing a car of the same value.

Several hours passed, and by the time the pub closed, Bill, Jim, and Ernie had become friends. Ernie got the idea of leasing cars to Bill and Jim. By leasing, Bill and Jim did not need the capital to purchase new cars. Within one week, Ernie had written up a lease for ten new basic cars. They still had air conditioning and modern radios, but they were missing the options like sunroofs and power windows.

Jim was excited, since his job just became easier. With more modern cars, he could handle more volume. If the cars were damaged, he still fixed them up in their own shop. He enjoyed his new role very much. Bill found that business was better, since the customers liked the new cars.

Bill gave each customer a gift certificate if he or she would fill out a questionnaire after returning the rental car. What he discovered from the responses was that many people who rented the newer cars had been involved in accidents. They needed a temporary car while their car was being repaired. Bill then tried to contact the insurance companies directly, but he could not get past the receptionists at the large insurance company offices.

Meanwhile Ernie had leased a fleet of 50 cars to a large insurance company for employees to use on the job. The company was the Federal Farmers Insurance Company, one of the largest in the state. He had won the bid by being the lowest bidder. Ernie approached Federal Farmers for them, and, in a short time, Federal Farmers was recommending Jim and Bill's company to its customers who needed a car. When the repair was an insurance claim, Federal Farmers paid the bill, and the customers only needed to sign the rental agreement. This made their rental agency very popular with customers. It seemed that Ernie, Bill, and Jim had found the formula for a successful business.

They decided to incorporate the company with a new name. They wanted to be listed at the beginning of the phone book's yellow pages, and Apache Rent A Car seemed to be just the name they needed.

Success Brings a Need

The business was growing substantially, and thus a new problem developed. They needed a computer system. They were using a home-built system developed by some of their classmates from the local community college. Clearly, it was not able to do the job now required. Purchasing a car rental system was an option, but these systems were geared for the more conventional car rental companies. In particular, they did not handle the payments by third parties such as insurance companies.

Car Rental System Requirements

The system needs consist of a lot more than keeping track of cars.

1. Customers want to reserve cars in advance.

2. Car rental is complicated by the following factors:

    a. The customer renting the car may not be the driver, and there could be many drivers. For each driver, the following information needs to be captured: full name, birth date, driver's license number, and state of issue of driver's license.

    b. Information about the third party who may be paying the bill also needs to be captured.

    c. Extras such as collision damage waiver, liability insurance, and personal accident insurance may be added for an additional daily charge.

    d. A rental agreement consists of an agreement number, the customer's name, type of rate (daily, weekend, or weekly), car identification (license number), and car price category. It also includes the date, time, and mileage when car leaves and the expected date and time of return.

3. Returning a car consists of dropping it off. Payment is a separate transaction. The following items need to be considered:

    a. The car is rented with a full tank of gas, and the customer is responsible for refueling the car before returning it. When a car is returned, an amount for gasoline is added if the tank is not full.

    b. The date, time, and mileage when the car is returned are recorded.

    c. The car must be inspected for damage. If the collision damage waiver is not accepted at the time of rental, the cost of repair is added to the bill.

    d. The car is also inspected to determine the need of minor maintenance. If maintenance is needed, the car is not cleaned up and returned to the rental lot. Instead, it is sent to the shop for needed repairs and maintenance.

    e. If the car passes inspection, it is sent to a car wash and then placed on the lot, ready to be rented again.

4. A bill is given to the customer if the customer is present. Otherwise, it is mailed to the customer. Often this customer is a third-party payer, such as an insurance company.

5. Payment is made by either cash or credit card. A $1,000.00 deposit is collected at the time of rental if there is no damage waiver. The deposit is either paid in cash or charged to the credit card.

6. Rates are charged as follows:

    a. A weekend is defined as the period from 6:00 P.M. Friday to 8:00 A.M. Monday.

    b. There is no mileage charge for the first 250 miles each day.

    c. Any time over one week is computed by prorating the weekly rate.

    d. The company has four price categories for cars, although more categories may be added in the future. All the cars are four-door sedans with air conditioning and automatic transmission. The four categories are:

i.	Economy (E)	Ford Focus or Toyota Tercel
ii.	Budget (B)	Ford Contour or Toyota Corolla
iii.	Midsize (M)	Ford Taurus or Toyota Camry
iv.	Full Size (F)	Ford LTD or Toyota Avalon

7. The current rates are:

Class	Daily Charge	Weekly Charge	Weekend Charge	Mileage Charge
E	$24.99	$149.99	$39.99	$0.20
B	29.99	169.99	44.99	0.22
M	34.99	189.99	49.99	0.25
F	39.99	209.99	54.99	0.27

Your job is to complete the analysis and design of new software for Apache Rent A Car.

Assignments

1. Draw up a list of all external, internal, and temporal events that the car rental company encounters in making reservations, renting, accepting returned cars, inspecting, billing, and receiving payment.

2. Once the event list is complete, create an event table, as in Figure 3.6.

ESSENTIAL USE CASES AND SYSTEM SEQUENCE DIAGRAMS

4

After mastering the material in this chapter, you will be able to

▌ Identify use cases based on prior event analysis.

▌ Derive a use case diagram from an event table.

▌ Draw a use case diagram.

▌ Discover use case scenarios.

▌ Write both high-level and expanded essential use case narratives.

▌ Define system inputs and outputs.

▌ Draw a system sequence diagram for a use case scenario.

INTRODUCTION

The technique of event analysis, introduced in Chapter 3, was used by systems analysts before object-oriented systems became widespread and is not part of the Unified Modeling Language (UML). In this chapter, we present use cases and system sequence diagrams, which are UML models for object-oriented analysis. It seems appropriate therefore to start with a brief history of the UML before continuing to explain the process for object-oriented systems analysis.

THE UNIFIED MODELING LANGUAGE (UML)

Object-oriented programming languages may be traced to Simula, a general system modeling language invented in 1965 in Norway by Ole-Johan Dahl and Kristen Nygaard. Smalltalk (developed at Xerox PARC by Alan Kay and Adele Goldberg) appeared about 1980, followed by C++ (created by Bjarne Stroustrup), and more recently by Java, developed at Sun Microsystems by James Goslin.

Object-oriented systems analysis and design had their origins much later — in the 1980s. This was a time of experimentation. The main topic of discussion into the early 1990s was comparative methods, as a variety of approaches and models were developed and applied. Practitioners became aware of the need for a common set of models as well as the desirability of widely accepted standards and methods. In 1997, under the sponsorship of the Object Management Group (OMG), an industry association, a working group published a standard for describing and modeling object-oriented systems known as the Unified Modeling Language (UML). The principal contributors to the UML were Grady Booch, Ivar Jacobson, and James Rumbaugh (often referred to as the Three Amigos). The UML specification is managed and coordinated by the OMG and may be accessed via the OMG's Web site.[1] The UML standard emphasizes simple models which are more easily understood by its users. The UML was not accepted as rapidly as object-oriented languages had been. However, industry is rapidly adopting tools which incorporate the UML.

However, the UML defines only a standard for object-oriented system description. How and when to use the UML models in an analysis and design process are left to system developers. The Unified Process, summarized in Chapter 2, provides one way to describe and organize the system development process.

CONTINUING THE OBJECT-ORIENTED ANALYSIS PROCESS

Part II of this book presents a six-step method for object-oriented analysis using the UML, as shown in Figure 4.1. Chapter 3 explained the first step in the process — identifying the business events. This chapter describes Steps 2, 3, and 4, which begin to define the response of the system to the business events identified in Step 1. They define how the system behaves when an event occurs and what actions are triggered as a result of an event.

The initial event analysis partitions the system by event. As the events occur independently of each other, the system also responds to the events independently. Thus, the analysis of the system may proceed event by event. There may, however, be information dependencies between events which must be taken into account

FIGURE 4.1	Procedure for using event analysis to develop object-oriented analysis models

Step 1. Identify the business events and make an event table.

Step 2. Identify the use cases and produce a use case diagram for the system.

Step 3. Write an essential use case narrative for the system's response to each business event.

Step 4. Draw a system sequence diagram for each use case scenario related to an external event.

Step 5. Produce a domain model showing the concepts, attributes, and associations in the problem domain of the system.

Step 6. Write a contract for each system operation.

---

[1] www.omg.org/technology/documents/formal/uml.htm.

because they imply a sequence of occurrence. For example, a payment must follow, not precede, a bill for a purchase.

OVERVIEW OF STEPS 2, 3, AND 4

Briefly, in the next three steps in object-oriented analysis, we do the following.

Step 2. Identify the use cases and produce a use case diagram for the system.

This step begins with an event table. Initially, there will be one use case for each business event listed in the event table. The use case diagram (or, for a large system, a set of use case diagrams) shows all the use cases as well as all the actors related to each use case.

Step 3. Write an essential use case narrative for the system's response to each business event.

The word **essential** emphasizes the fact that the use case narrative should describe the business requirements and not how the system is implemented. The flow of events in the use case narrative should cover the system's complete response to the business event.

Step 4. Draw a system sequence diagram for each scenario of a use case related to an external event.

A system sequence diagram shows the messages from the actors to the system, which is viewed as a black box. The messages in the system sequence diagram are ordered from top to bottom in time sequence.

USE CASES FOR OBJECT-ORIENTED SYSTEMS

The development of object-oriented methods is still evolving. Some practitioners skip right to graphical techniques to display the functionality of a computer system. The problem with this approach is that a model is developed without any clear understanding of what the true high-level business events are.

What follows is the use case method for specifying the requirements for a computer system. It is assumed that the resulting software design will be object-oriented. The use case method was originally developed by Ivar Jacobson.[2]

USE CASES

A *use case* is the sequence of actions which occur when an actor uses a system to complete a process. Use cases were originally employed to test what happens when the system responds to a message from the environment. A use case can be identified with the system's response to an event. It shows the complete response to the event. In particular, it emphasizes the value which the system produces for the actors.[3]

Practice varies in naming use cases. Some practitioners choose a noun or noun phrase; we (and others) prefer a verb phrase to emphasize the fact that a use case describes a process. The name of the use case is usually two to three words. The first

---

[2]See Ivar Jacobson, Magnus Christerson, Patrick Jonsson, and Gunnar Övergaard, *Object-Oriented Software Engineering: A Use Case Driven Approach* (Reading, Mass.: Addison-Wesley, 1992), and Ivar Jacobson, Maria Ericsson, and Agneta Jacobson, *The Object Advantage: Business Process Reengineering with Object Technology* (Reading, Mass.: Addison-Wesley, 1994).

[3]See Hans-Erik Ericksson and Magnus Penker, *UML Toolkit* (New York: John Wiley & Sons, 1998), 52, for a more detailed discussion.

is a verb and the second is a noun, often preceded by an adjective. Frequently, a preposition is inserted to make the use case name grammatically correct. We name the use case from the perspective of the actor rather than that of the system. For example, "Buy Items" takes the point of view of a Customer actor; "Sell Items" looks at the use case from the system's perspective.

It is very important to remember that a use case is not a computer process or even a model of a computer process. It is a model of a requirement. This model exists for the benefit of the users of the system. Use case diagrams specify the essential processes which handle the external business events. They also specify the processes which handle the temporal events. At this time, users are not concerned about standard system functions, such as system start-up and maintenance. They may assume that the designers will take care of these functions.

Some analysts like to remind their users that use cases do not compute. They are models to help understand what the system must do. It is not important to model everything that may potentially occur in a system.

EVENTS AND USE CASES

How do we identify the use cases of a system? In Chapter 3, the event was the critical discovery. The beauty of event analysis is that **each event corresponds to one or more use cases**.

Thus, if there are four events, there will be four (or more) use cases. We recommend that the initial use case model contain one use case per business event. Later, and in more complex situations, it may be desirable to model one event with several use cases, perhaps with the «includes» and «extends» relationships discussed later in this chapter. The role of the use case is to respond to the event by providing services to users of the system. Each use case may be viewed as a requirement for a process which will eventually be turned into a piece of software.

In the initial use case model, there is one use case for each business event. Thus, for the Public University registration system, there are four use cases:

- Submit Department Class Schedule
- Produce University Class Schedule
- Register for Classes
- Produce Class Roster

Note that the use case names follow the practice recommended above.

IDENTIFYING ACTORS

In Chapter 3, an actor was defined as a person, organization, or system which interacts with a system by sending messages to the system or receiving messages from the system. An actor may be a person (or persons) who sends messages to a system when an external business event occurs. An actor may also be a computer system or a computer device accessed via a network (including the Internet). Finally, organizations such as corporations or institutions may be actors. Examples of computer systems as actors might be accounts receivable systems, credit card verification systems, and inventory systems. The nonhuman actors in the Public University Registration System might be the grade-reporting system, class schedule maintenance system, and catalog maintenance system. An example of an organization as an actor is the Internal Revenue Service, which receives payments of income taxes withheld by an employer.

However, the most common actor is a human acting out a **role**. Thus, the concept of a role is very important. A single person can take on different roles at different times or in different systems. For example, a professor at a university can at one time act as an instructor and at another time act as a student. Other examples are employees of a company who also act as customers of the same company.

If event analysis has been the starting point for systems analysis, as described in Chapter 3, the most important actors have already been identified. These actors appear in the event table.

Otherwise, to find actors, it is helpful to ask six questions:

▌ Who initiates each external event?
▌ Who gets information from and puts information into the system as part of each event?
▌ Who updates the information in the system as part of each event?
▌ Who starts and stops the system?
▌ What computer systems does each use case communicate with?
▌ What organizations does each use case communicate with?

The most common problem in identifying the appropriate actors is understanding who is sending the system a message. This is often related to the question of where to locate the boundary of the system, as discussed later in this chapter.

Always refer to an actor in the singular. For example, the appropriate name for an actor is Customer, not Customers. Never use the proper name of an actor. Thus, it is not acceptable to name an actor — say, Louella Fernbee — instead of using Customer. To do so would specify a particular implementation. In this case, the specification would be absurd because it specifies that only one customer exists.

ACTORS IN THE PUBLIC UNIVERSITY REGISTRATION SYSTEM

Using the questions above, we identify the following candidates for actors in the use cases corresponding to the four events identified in Chapter 3:

• Who initiates the external events?	Department, Student
• Who gets information from and puts information into the system?	Department, Registrar, Professor
• Who enters information to be stored in the system?	Department
• Who starts and stops the system?	System Administrator
• What computer systems does the use case communicate with?	Grading System
• What organizations does the use case communicate with?	University (other universities which might send or receive transcripts)

Recall that Department and Student are both initiators of external business events. Professor participates in some of the use cases by receiving system outputs. Registrar, System Administrator, Grading System, and other Universities are not involved in these four use cases. They either perform maintenance functions or participate in other use cases.

TYPES OF ACTORS

Actors are usually classified as either initiating actors or participating actors. An *initiating actor* initiates a use case (by initiating an external event). A *participating actor* is involved in a use case but does not initiate it. For example, the initiating actors in the four events we have identified for the Public University Registration System are Department and Student, and the participating actors are Department, Professor, and Student. It is common for an actor to be both an initiator and a participant.

THE USE CASE MODEL

Once we have identified the use cases in a system, we can develop a use case model. The UML specification[4] describes the use case model. This model is general enough to allow for variations in its application. The model consists of two parts. The first part — a use case diagram — is graphical. The second is a description of each component of the use case diagram. In the UML, use cases are considered to be part of the User View Model.

Before building a use case model, it is important to understand each component thoroughly.

USE CASE DIAGRAMS

A *use case diagram* is a graphical model which shows the system in relation to the actors in its environment. As discussed earlier, graphical models are important because they enable us to view relationships simultaneously. A use case diagram may be produced directly from an event table. All that is necessary is to change each system-level event name into an appropriate name for the corresponding use case.

Drawing a use case diagram is Step 2 of the procedure for object-oriented systems analysis. Figure 4.2 shows a use case diagram for the Public University Registration System. Figure 4.3 shows the portion of the event table from which it is derived.

Note that a use case diagram provides less information than an event table because the lines in a use case diagram are not labeled to show system inputs or outputs.

| FIGURE 4.2 | Use case diagram for the Public University registration system |

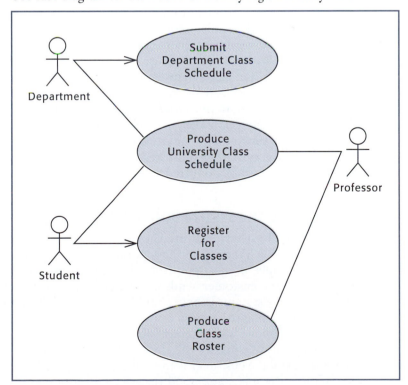

---

[4]See www.omg.org/technology/documents/formal/uml.htm for the complete UML specification.

FIGURE 4.3

Selected columns from the event table for the Public University Registration System

EVENT NUMBER	EVENT DESCRIPTION	ACTOR PROVIDING INPUT	ACTOR RECEIVING OUTPUT
1.	Department submits class schedule.	Department	
2.	Time to produce class schedule.		Student Department Professor
3.	Student registers for classes.	Student	Student
4.	Time to produce class roster.		Professor

Components of a Use Case Diagram

A use case diagram can be very simple. It contains only four types of components, each represented by an icon. They are:

1. *Use Cases.* The icon for a use case is an oval. The name of the use case appears inside the oval.
2. *Actors.* The icon for an actor is a stick figure. The stick figure is labeled with the name of the actor.
3. *Associations Between Actors and Use Cases.* A line connects each actor to a use case in which the actor participates. These lines are not labeled. Many actors may participate in each use case.

    The UML standard connects actors and use cases with straight lines. However, some practitioners identify initiating actors in the use case diagram. An arrow from an actor to a use case means that the actor is an initiating actor for the use case. Lines between participating actors and use cases have no arrowheads. In this book, we will use arrowheads to denote initiating actors.
4. *System or Subsystem Boundary.* A rectangle represents the system boundary (or a subsystem boundary), which shows what is inside and what is outside the system or subsystem. One or more use cases can be inside the rectangle representing the system or subsystem. When only one subsystem is defined, the rectangle is usually omitted.

IDENTIFYING THE SYSTEM BOUNDARY

As mentioned earlier, locating the system boundary is often a difficult decision. (Remember the "Warning of the Doorknob" in Chapter 1.)

For example, in most point-of-sale applications, there is both a customer and a clerk. First, the customer sends a message to the clerk, and then the clerk sends a message to the system. Whom should we model as the actor — the customer or the clerk? If we define the system as the point-of-sale terminal (the cash register), then the clerk is the one who interacts directly with the system. (See Figure 4.4.) On the other hand, if we consider the store to be the system, the clerk is inside the system boundary, and the customer is the actor. (See Figure 4.5.)

Unless there is some good reason to do otherwise, we recommend the more inclusive location for the system boundary. This often avoids the problem of assuming a specific technology for the use case. For example, the point-of-sale system could be implemented with automated checkout, as occurs in many libraries

FIGURE 4.4   **System boundary at a point-of-sale terminal**

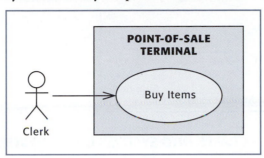

FIGURE 4.5   **System boundary at a retail store (the clerk and point-of-sale terminal are inside)**

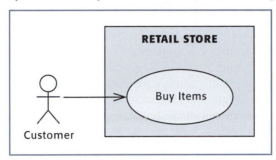

and grocery stores. Or the customer could be making a purchase using a Web interface. These alternative implementations do not even have a clerk. Modeling the clerk as an actor may make an unwarranted and perhaps critical assumption about the implementation.

This consideration forces one to model only the essentials of a system. Actors who represent only an implementation of a real system should not be modeled at this time. To do so would force a particular solution during analysis. In systems analysis, only the essential requirements should be specified. Actors who act as intermediaries should not be considered.[5]

INITIATORS FOR TEMPORAL AND INTERNAL EVENTS

How do we handle temporal events, which are initiated by time instead of a person, organization, or system? One solution might be to designate a clock or calendar as an initiating actor. This solution will work, but it adds extra complexity. Since all processors have a clock with a calendar, we can assume that a use case, which represents a process, has a clock as well. Thus, we do not show any initiating actor for a use case associated with a temporal event. In Figure 4.2, note that the use cases Produce University Class Schedule and Produce Class Roster have no initiating actors.

We also have to decide how to handle internal events. Like a temporal event, an internal event has no initiating actor. Consider the internal event "Inventory level at reorder point." The system's response to this event is to generate a purchase order. In the use case diagram, we will see the use case Reorder Inventory with the participating actor Supplier, who receives the purchase order, as shown in Figure 4.6.

---

[5]For a discussion of essential models in structured analysis, see Stephen M. McMenamin and John F. Palmer, *Essential Systems Analysis* (New York: Yourdon, 1984).

FIGURE 4.6   Use case diagram for Reorder Inventory, corresponding to an internal event

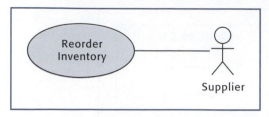

PACKAGING USE CASES INTO SYSTEMS OR SUBSYSTEMS

When there are many use cases, it is often convenient to package them. A *package* of use cases may represent a **system** or **subsystem**. If only one system is shown in the use case diagram, the rectangle representing the system boundary is unnecessary and is usually omitted. However, if more that one computer system is being specified, we might put rectangles around each group of use cases. For example, two subsystems for the Public University Registration System might be Registration Subsystem and Registration Maintenance Subsystem. The use cases which are not mainline, such as Add New Courses and Start Up Registration System, can be packaged separately as Registration Maintenance Subsystem. See Figure 4.7 for two subsystems within the Public University Registration System.

The major advantage of using subsystem notation is evident when we are considering more than one system for a user. Then we can concentrate on only a single subsystem at a time.

DESCRIBING USE CASES

Writing an essential use case narrative for the system's complete response to each business event is Step 3 of the procedure for object-oriented systems analysis.

A *use case narrative* is a narrative presenting the sequence of internal actions by which the system responds to the actions of an actor. Two levels of use case narratives — high-level and expanded — are helpful.

In writing an *essential use case narrative*, focus first on describing the expected system response when all goes well. The use case narrative may be modified later to describe exceptions and how errors in a system input are handled.

HIGH-LEVEL USE CASE NARRATIVES

A short use case narrative may consist of only two or three sentences. A template for a *high-level use case narrative* appears in Figure 4.8, with an example in Figure 4.9. These brief use case narratives are helpful early in systems analysis to provide an overview of the scope and functionality of a system.

EXPANDED USE CASE NARRATIVES

Frequently, a more complete description of the system's response to an external business event is desired. A business (or system-level) event often comprises several lower-level, or small-scale, events. These small-scale events describe the interaction between an actor and the system in greater detail.

An *expanded use case narrative* contains additional detail about the low-level events. It lists each low-level event in sentence form, followed by the system's response to it. This sequence of actions of an actor and the corresponding responses of the system is known as a *flow of events*.

A typical flow of events for a library system might be that shown in Figure 4.10.

FIGURE 4.7   Use case diagram showing two subsystems

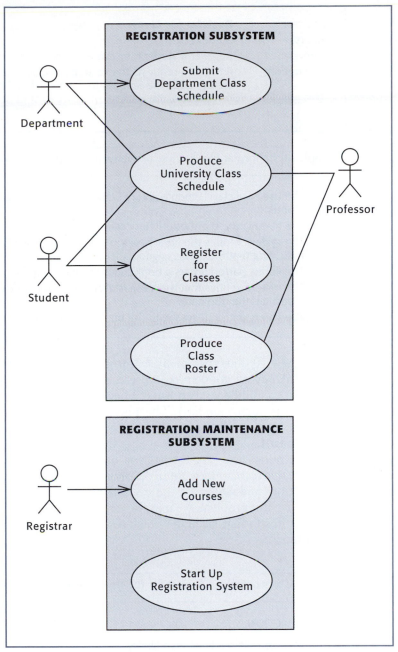

FIGURE 4.8   Template for a high-level use case narrative

Use case:	Name of the use case
Actors:	List of all actors, with the initiating actor listed first
Purpose:	Reason for the use case.
Description:	A brief but complete description of who initiates the use case, the expected system action, and the response of value to the actor.

FIGURE 4.9

Example of a high-level use case narrative

Use case:	**Register for Classes**
Actors:	Student
Purpose:	Register a student for classes and record the student's schedule.
Description:	A Student requests the sections of classes desired for a term. The system adds the Student to each section if space is available. On completion, the Student receives a list of the classes in which he or she is enrolled.

FIGURE 4.10

Example of the format for the flow of events in an expanded use case narrative

1. The use case starts when a library patron arrives at the checkout counter with a book.
2. The library patron enters a library card number.
3. The system verifies the library patron's status and then displays a message indicating that the status is good.
4. The library patron enters a book's identification number.
5. The system verifies that the book is available and records the transaction. Then it displays the due date.
6. The library patron leaves with the book and the due date.

Figure 4.10 illustrates many features used in describing the use case's low-level events. Like every good story, a use case should have a beginning ("Once upon a time . . . "), a middle, and an end ("They all lived happily ever after."). Typically, the beginning is fairly standard. The phrase "The use case starts when . . . " is very common. At the end, the words "The actor leaves with (or receives) . . . " are also fairly standard.

Most books use the format for use case narratives shown in Figure 4.10. However, this format does not make obvious which steps in the flow of events are the actor's actions and which are the system's responses.

To solve this problem, we may use a two-column format, as shown in Figure 4.11.[6] Note that this format facilitates quick recognition of the low-level events and the system's response.

FIGURE 4.11

Example of a two-column format for the flow of events in an expanded use case narrative

ACTOR ACTION	SYSTEM RESPONSE
1. The use case starts when a library patron arrives at the checkout counter with a book.	
2. The library patron enters a library card number.	3. The system verifies the library patron's status and then displays a message indicating that the status is good.
4. The library patron enters a book's identification number.	5. The system verifies that the book is available and records the transaction. Then it displays the due date.
6. The library patron leaves with the book and the due date.	

[6]Originally proposed by Rebecca Wirfs-Brock in "Designing Scenarios: Making the Case for a Use Case Framework," *Smalltalk Report* (New York: SIGS Publications, November-December 1993).

FIGURE 4.12   Expanded essential use case narrative for Register for Classes

Use case:	**Register for Classes**
Actors:	Student
Purpose:	Register a student for classes and record the student's schedule.
Overview:	A Student requests the sections of class desired for a term. The system adds the Student to each section if there is space available. On completion, the system provides the Student with a list of the classes in which he or she is enrolled.
Type:	Essential
Preconditions:	Class schedule must exist. Student is known by the system.
Postconditions:	Student was enrolled in the section.
Special Requirements:	Student must get a system response within 10 seconds.

Flow of Events

ACTOR ACTION	SYSTEM RESPONSE
1. This use case begins when a Student desires to register for classes.	
2. The Student provides the Student's identifier and a list of the department code, course number, and section number for each section desired.	3. Adds the student to the section if there are seats available.
4. On completion of entry of the section requests, the Student indicates that the request is complete.	5. Produces a student class list for the Student.
6. The Student receives the student class list.	

Alternative Flow of Events

Line 3: Invalid department code and course number entered. Indicate error. Return to Step 2.

Invalid section number entered. Indicate error. Return to Step 2.

No seats remaining. Inform the Student. Return to Step 2.

An expanded narrative for the Register for Classes use case is shown in Figure 4.12. It is an **essential** narrative of a use case. In this context, essential, as defined in Chapter 3, means that the use case narrative ignores the specifics of the technology with which the system is or will be implemented.

As the right-hand column contains only actions of the system, we will omit the words "the system" at the beginning of each system response.

Note that the descriptions of the actor actions in Figure 4.12 contain the specific pieces of information which must be supplied by the actor in order for the system to respond correctly. For example, Line 2 mentions the Student's identifier and the department code, course number, and section number for each section.

Note that Figure 4.12 shows more than the flow of events. It also lists the actors and includes a brief statement of the purpose of the use case, a somewhat longer overview (a short version of the use case narrative, similar to the description in Figures 4.8 and 4.9), a type, and an alternative flow of events section.

Other requirements, such as preconditions, postconditions, and special requirements, can be added to the use case narrative. Preconditions, postconditions, and special requirements are listed before the flow of events.

A *precondition* for a use case is a condition which must be true in order for the use case to begin and produce the desired results. For example, before a student can register for classes, a class schedule must exist. Since this is of critical importance, this requirement can be specified as a precondition. Note that this requirement is really significant; if no classes are in the system's memory, the student cannot register for them. Most preconditions refer to the prior occurrence of another use case or to the arrival of a deadline if the use case corresponds to a temporal event.

A *postcondition* for a use case is a condition which must be true after the use case has been completed. It is a way of describing what changes should occur in the system during the execution of the use case.

In addition, some of the users' requirements are so important that the system is unusable if these requirements are not met. For example, if a student does not get a system response to a request to register for a class after 10 seconds, the student might assume that the system has failed or may become impatient and discontinue the process. Thus, this *special requirement* might be specified in the use case narrative.

Preconditions, postconditions, and special requirements are optional. It is up to the analyst to decide what information to include. At a minimum, the use case diagram and the event narratives tell the user about the overall requirements. Adding the flow of events aids our understanding of the use case and makes it easy to check if various scenarios are handled correctly. Preconditions, postconditions, and special requirements will make the designer's task easier, as this information is often critical. It will have to be either understood or written down at a later time during design.

Expanded use case narratives must capture the details of the input provided by the actor. Note that in Figure 4.12, Line 2 makes explicit what data the Student enters. It also makes clear that the message describing an individual section can be repeated. The data items will be the same; their values will vary from section to section. This will be the basis for drawing the system sequence diagrams explained later in this chapter.

Figure 4.13 shows an expanded narrative for the Produce University Class Schedule use case.

Expanded use case narratives are seldom written for temporal events because (as can be seen from Figure 4.13) the flow of events always looks like this:

Action	System Response
1. This use case begins when a temporal required event triggers a system response.	2. The system produces the system output(s).

FIGURE 4.13   Expanded use case narrative for Produce University Class Schedule

Use case:	**Produce University Class Schedule**
Actors:	Student
	Department
	Professor
Purpose:	Produce a university class schedule
Overview:	In accordance with a schedule determined by the Registrar, the university class schedule for a term is produced and displayed.
Type:	Essential
Preconditions:	All department class schedules must have been entered.
Postconditions:	None
Special Requirements:	Students, professors, and departments must be able to print their own copy of the university class schedule.

Flow of Events

ACTION	SYSTEM RESPONSE
1. This use case begins when it is time to produce the university class schedule for a term.	2. Produces and displays the university class schedule.

INDICATING EXCEPTIONS, ALTERNATIVES, AND ERROR-HANDLING IN A USE CASE NARRATIVE

The flow of events in an expanded use case narrative presents what is often called a "Sunny Day narrative." That is, the low-level, small-scale events and their corresponding system responses describe an ideal interaction — one which has no problems.

If a user is to communicate the system requirements to an analyst effectively and accurately, the requirements must first be understood and presented without any complications due to errors.

Potential errors generally fall into two categories:

▮ Errors caused by the actor and
▮ Errors discovered by the system or participants of the system.

For example, actor errors might occur because:

▮ The actor provides bad data. A student enters an incorrect student identification number.
▮ The actor is unable to complete a transaction due to system or user constraints. A customer does not have sufficient funds to pay for a purchase.
▮ The actor decides not to complete a transaction. A bank customer cancels a withdrawal transaction.

Errors discovered by the system include the following:

▮ A violation of business rules occurs. A withdrawal is over the maximum amount allowed.
▮ The system is unable to obtain required information from external systems or organizations which participate in the process. An external credit-card authorization system is down.

Allowing a customer to exceed his credit limit is really a violation of a business rule. The participating actor — the authorization system — did not fail. It was only a provider of information used to apply the business rule.

The usual way of incorporating these errors and the system's response to them is to add *alternatives* to the bottom of the use case narrative. The style resembles footnotes. By locating the alternatives outside of the flow of events, the "Sunny Day scenario" is still intact. At the same time, the use case narrative captures the part of the requirements which are of critical interest to some users. In many online systems, such as banking and Web shopping carts, it is prudent to consider these factors when writing a use case narrative. This will ensure that the designers realize that these requirements are to be a part of the new system.

For example, in the Public University Registration System there are four use cases. In Line 2 of the use case Register for Classes, the Student might request a section which has reached the maximum number of students allowed. This situation requires us to add the following:

Alternative Flow of Events

Line 3: Invalid department code and course number entered. Indicate error. Return to Step 2.
Invalid section number entered. Indicate error. Return to Step 2.
No seats remaining. Inform the student. Return to Step 2.

See Figure 4.12. Note that the incorrect input occurs in Line 2, but the error is not detected until input is verified by the system in Line 3.

This is an example of an error caused by the initiating actor.

ASSOCIATIONS BETWEEN USE CASES

It is very likely that parts of many use cases will share the same narratives. For example, Purchase Item and Return Item may both require the same credit-card authorization routine. The UML specification provides for three different kinds of associations between use cases: the «includes» «extends», and «generalizes» relationships. Their purpose is to identify commonalities and take advantage of them.

The use of « » (called *guillemets*) is the UML's way of depicting a stereotype. A *stereotype* is a categorization of a concept. Stereotypes are often used to help the reader understand more completely what the author intends to convey in the models of system requirements.

The *«includes»* association between use cases means that the included use case always occurs whenever the use case which includes it occurs. The *«extends»* association augments the behavior of the use case which it extends. The occurrence of the extension is conditional and does not necessarily occur every time. The *«generalizes»* association implies that the child use case contains all the attributes, sequences of behavior, and extensions of the parent use case. The «generalizes» association is less useful than the other two and will not be discussed further in this book.

The «includes» Association

As an example of the «includes» association, the status of a hotel room must be changed during check-in and checkout. The common actions can become a separate shared use case, as shown in Figure 4.14.[7] Note that the arrows point to the included use case.

The «extends» Association

A common occurrence in modeling events is that a use case is modified by special circumstances. For example, a special discount for employees might apply at the payment step in a point-of-sale application. Or a student, when registering for classes, may be allowed to register for a class even if the class is full because the student is on

---

FIGURE 4.14   Example of the <<includes>> association

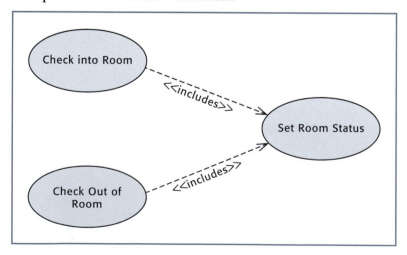

---

[7]For a fuller explanation of the associations between use cases, refer to Martin Fowler and Kendall Scott, *UML Distilled: Applying the Standard Object Modeling Language* (Reading, Mass.: Addison-Wesley, 1997).

FIGURE 4.15   Examples of the <<extends>> association

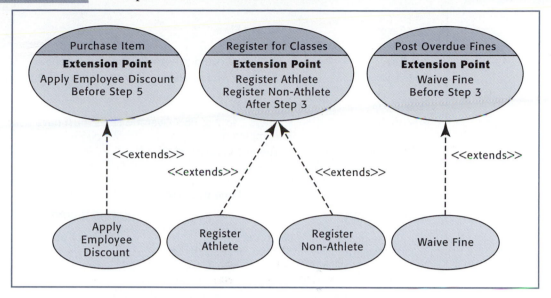

an athletic team. Or some patrons at a library may not be required to pay fines because they donate large sums of money to the library. Rather than writing a special use case for each of these exceptional situations, an extension is all we need.

The extension shows in both the flow of events and the use case diagram. Note that the arrow points from the extension to the use case which it extends, as in Figure 4.15.

The flow of events for the extension Apply Employee Discount is shown in Figure 4.16.

The flow of events for the extension Waive Fine is shown in Figure 4.17.

It is possible to model the whole extension in the flow of events using an **if** statement. However, there is no mention of this important business logic at the top level. What the extension does is bring these exceptions to the top, so even a casual reader of the use case will understand that exceptions are being made. Indeed, such exceptions are important business policy.

FIGURE 4.16   Expanded use case narrative for Apply Employee Discount

Use case:	**Apply Employee Discount**
Actors:	Employee
Purpose:	Apply a special employee discount to a purchase.
Overview:	When an Employee purchases an item, a special employee discount applies.
Type:	Essential
Preconditions:	Steps 1 to 4 of Purchase Item by an Employee must have been completed.
Postconditions:	The purchase amount was reduced by the amount of the employee discount.
Special Requirements:	None

Flow of Events

ACTOR ACTION	SYSTEM RESPONSE
1. This use case begins when the customer is an Employee.	2. Calculates and applies the special employee discount.

FIGURE 4.17   Expanded use case narrative for Waive Fine

Use Case:	**Waive Fine**
Actors:	Patron
Purpose:	Waive the overdue materials fine for a donor.
Overview:	A patron who is a donor is not charged a fine for overdue materials.
Type:	Essential
Preconditions:	Steps 1 to 2 of Post Overdue Fines must have been completed.
Postconditions:	The fine was cancelled.
Special Requirements:	None.

Flow of Events

ACTOR ACTION	SYSTEM RESPONSE
1. This use case begins when the Patron is a donor.	2. Does not post a fine.

It is important to specify with a conditional statement where in the flow of events the extension applies. The flow of events for the extension is then very short. Figure 4.18 shows the addition of the conditional statement to the Register for Classes use case narrative to select the applicable registration policy. Figures 4.19 and 4.20 show the extensions Register Athlete and Register Non-Athlete.

FIGURE 4.18   Expanded essential use case narrative for **Register for Classes**, showing the extension point

Use case:	**Register for Classes**
Actors:	Student
Purpose:	Register a student for classes and record the student's schedule.
Overview:	A Student requests the sections of class desired for a term. The system adds the Student to each section if there is space available. On completion, the system provides the Student with a list of the classes in which he or she is enrolled.
Type:	Essential
Preconditions:	Class schedule must exist.
	Student is known by the system.
Postconditions:	Student was enrolled in the section.
Special Requirements:	Student must get a system response within 10 seconds.

Flow of Events

ACTOR ACTION	SYSTEM RESPONSE
1. This use case begins when a Student desires to register for classes.	
2. The Student provides the Student's identifier.	3. The Checks to see if the Student is an athlete. If the Student is an athlete, executes the **Register Athlete** use case; otherwise, executes the **Register Non-Athlete** use case.

Alternative Flow of Events

Line 3: Invalid student identifier entered. Indicate error. The use case terminates.

FIGURE 4.19 Expanded essential use case narrative for Register Athlete

Use case:	**Register Athlete**
Actors:	Student
Purpose:	Register a student for classes and record the student's schedule.
Overview:	A Student who is an athlete requests the sections of class desired for a term. The system adds the Student to each section even if it is full.
Type:	Essential
Preconditions:	Steps 1 to 3 of Register for Classes have been completed.
Postconditions:	Student was enrolled in the section.
Special Requirements:	Student must get a system response within 10 seconds.

Flow of Events

ACTOR ACTION	SYSTEM RESPONSE
1. This use case begins when a Student desiring to register for classes has indicated that he or she is an athlete.	
2. The Student provides a list of the department code, course number, and section number for each section desired.	3. Adds the Student to the section.
4. On completion of entry of the section requests, the Student indicates that the request is complete.	5. Produces a student class list for the Student.
6. The Student receives the student class list.	

Alternative Flow of Events

Line 3: Invalid department code and course number entered. Indicate error. Return to Step 2.

Invalid section number entered. Indicate error. Return to Step 2.

USE CASE SCENARIOS

A *use case scenario* is a narrative of a single occurrence or instance of a use case. It describes a specific path through the use case when the use case is acted out in the real world. Scenarios are used to discover alternative paths through a use case. They are also used to test the completeness or correctness of a use case narrative.

For example, the following might be scenarios for the Public University use case Register for Classes:

- *Scenario 1:* Louella Fernbee registers on May 1, 2005, for the classes CIS 200 Section 2 (Systems Analysis at 2:00 P.M. on Monday and Wednesday) and ACC 208 Section 1 (Financial Accounting at 10:00 A.M. on Monday and Wednesday). Upon completion of her registration, her Student Class List is printed and given to her.

  Several things stand out. The most obvious is the use of the proper names instead of simple nouns. This means that this use case is described for a specific instance of Student, "Louella Fernbee." It also involves a selection of two specific class sections.
- *Scenario 2:* Louella Fernbee attempts to enroll in the section CIS–4–01. She is a student in good standing, and the section is not full. She enrolls successfully.

FIGURE 4.20   Expanded essential use case narrative for Register Non-Athlete

Use case:	**Register Non-Athlete**
Actors:	Student
Purpose:	Register a student for classes and record the student's schedule.
Overview:	A Student requests the sections of class desired for a term. The system adds the Student to each section if it is not full.
Type:	Essential
Preconditions:	Steps 1 to 3 of Register for Classes have been completed.
Postconditions:	Student was enrolled in the section.
Special Requirements:	Student must get a system response within 10 seconds.

Flow of Events

ACTOR ACTION	SYSTEM RESPONSE
1. This use case begins when a Student desiring to register for classes has indicated that he or she is not an athlete.	
2. The Student provides a list of the department code, course number, and section number for each section desired.	3. Adds the Student to the section if there are seats available.
4. On completion of entry of the section requests, the Student indicates that the request is complete.	5. Produces a student class list for the Student.
6. The Student receives the student class list.	

Alternative Flow of Events

Line 3: Invalid department code and course number entered. Indicate error. Return to Step 2.

Invalid section number entered. Indicate error. Return to Step 2.

No seats remaining. Inform the Student. Return to Step 2.

■ *Scenario 3:* Louella Fernbee attempts to enroll in the section ACC–2–03. She is a student in good standing, but the section is full. She is unable to enroll.
■ *Scenario 4:* Mortimer Snow attempts to enroll in the section CS–2–01. He is not a student in good standing. He is unable to enroll.

How does a scenario differ from the flow of events? Both appear to be narratives of a run-through of the process. However, the flow of events, together with the alternative flows of events, describes all possible instances of the use case. A scenario, on the other hand, describes only one of the possible paths through the use case. The objective of analysis is to develop a comprehensive flow of events and a complete set of alternatives instead of a set of scenarios. The specific scenarios help develop and test the flow of events and alternatives.

EVALUATING THE QUALITY OF A USE CASE NARRATIVE

A use case and its narrative must be evaluated according to a standard. Recall that a use case is a process which provides required functionality within a system. This statement of a use case's functionality is static in nature. It merely specifies what the requirements are. Nothing is said about how the requirements are met — that is part of system design.

A use case is best understood by beginning from the event table. There the initiating event is specified as well as the output. Producing a system output and storing data for future use are the two fundamental actions of a use case.

Ultimately, if a system produces no output, it has no reason for being — it creates nothing of value for its users. Thus, it seems clear that one measure of the quality of a use case is the production of something of value to an actor.

Often a use case is completed by providing direct output to an actor at the time of the process. This is common in external events such as "Student registers for class." When the process is finished, the student has something of value. In this case, it is the student class list.

In other situations, however, a use case cannot generate useful output for an actor at the time. For example, the event "Department submits class schedule" produces no output. The useful output is the University Class Schedule. But the complete information to generate the University Class Schedule is not available until all the Department Class Schedules have been submitted. That is, all the instances of the use case Submit Department Class Schedule must take place before the use case Produce University Class Schedule can take place. The desired output is produced only after a delay. The system memory, which is present in all processors, maintains the information in the Department Class Schedules until it is ready for use. Recall such real processors as personal computers have internal storage in the form of hard disk drives. Thus, the other measure of whether a use case produces something of value is whether it stores data for future use when it cannot generate an immediate output.[8]

Recall that we defined a use case as the sequence of actions which occur when an actor uses a system to complete a process. The actor, who models a real user, expects the use case to complete one or several functions. It follows then that the use case is not completely specified until all the expected functionality is specified. Only then can we say that the use case narrative is complete. This is equivalent to saying that a complete use case narrative states the system's complete response to an event. To do this, the user must communicate all the required functionality to the analyst who writes the use case narrative. What is then available is a "complete" functional specification of the requirements set forth by the user.

SHORTCOMINGS OF A USE CASE MODEL

There are several shortcomings of a use case diagram and the corresponding textual narratives of the use cases:

▌ No distinction between the initiating actor and the participating actor in the UML standard,
▌ No mention of the data input or output in the use case diagram — only in the use case narrative, and
▌ No clear indication of the difference between a temporal and an external event.

Fortunately, the use of event analysis overcomes the above shortcomings. It provides an event table. The event list and event table, however, are not part of the UML specification. We recommend them in order to facilitate a more complete understanding of the functional requirements. With both an event model and use cases, design is able to continue. Otherwise, many questions such as those above will still need to be answered.

COMPLETING THE USE CASE NARRATIVES FOR THE PUBLIC UNIVERSITY SYSTEM

The remaining expanded essential use case narratives appear as Figures 4.21 and 4.22. They complete the use case model for the Public University Registration System.

---

[8]See Use Cases in the *UML Specification*, Version 1.4, September 2001, 2–127.

FIGURE 4.21 Expanded use case narrative for Submit Department Class Schedule

Use case:	**Submit Department Class Schedule**
Actors:	Department
Purpose:	Record a department class schedule.
Overview:	The Department submits a schedule of the classes it will offer for the next term. Details of each section (department code, course number, section number, maximum number of seats, meeting time, meeting place, and instructor identifier) are recorded in the system.
Type:	Essential
Preconditions:	Courses and instructors are known to the system.
Postconditions:	Department class schedule was saved in the system.
Special Requirements:	Department must get a system response within 8 seconds when each section is entered.

Flow of Events

ACTOR ACTION	SYSTEM RESPONSE
1. This use case begins when a Department submits its schedule for a term.	
2. The Department provides the department code, course number, section number, maximum number of seats, meeting time, meeting place and instructor identifier for each section in the schedule.	3. Records the section schedule information.
4. On completion of entry of the schedule, the Department indicates that the schedule is complete.	

Alternative Flow of Events

Line 3: Invalid department code and course number entered. Indicate error. Return to Step 2.

Invalid meeting place entered. Indicate error. Return to Step 2.

Invalid meeting time entered. Indicate error. Return to Step 2.

Invalid instructor identifier entered. Indicate error. Return to Step 2.

FIGURE 4.22 Expanded use case narrative for Produce Class Roster

Use case:	**Produce Class Roster**
Actors:	Professor
Purpose:	Produce a class roster for each instructor.
Overview:	At the close of the registration period, a roster for each class section for a term is produced and displayed.
Type:	Essential
Preconditions:	Students have completed enrollment into sections.
Postconditions:	Class roster was made available to instructors.
Special Requirements:	Instructors must be able to print their own copy of the class roster.

Flow of Events

ACTOR ACTION	SYSTEM RESPONSE
1. This use case begins when it is time to produce the class rosters for a term.	2. Produces and displays the class rosters.

SYSTEM SEQUENCE DIAGRAMS

After the use case model is completed, the next step is to produce a set of system sequence diagrams. **Drawing a system sequence diagram is Step 4** of the procedure for object-oriented systems analysis. (See Figure 4.1.)

A *system sequence diagram* shows the interaction between an actor and a system for one use case scenario. Recall that a *use case scenario* is an instance of a use case. It describes a specific path through the use case when the use case is acted out in the real world. If the system is small and simple, several use case scenarios or use cases may be shown on a single system sequence diagram without confusing the reader.

A system sequence diagram shows:

- The initiating actor of the use case,
- The messages from the initiating actor to the system,
- Each external system which sends a message to the system,
- Messages between the system and other systems required in responding to the business event,
- The order in which these messages occur, and
- The system (as a black box).

A system sequence diagram may also show:

- Messages from the system to actors.

Because only external events result in system inputs, the only system sequence diagrams of interest deal with use cases corresponding to external events.

Figure 4.23 shows an example of a system sequence diagram for the university registration system derived from the Register for Classes use case.

A dashed vertical line (called a *lifeline*) extends downward from the symbol for each actor as well as from the rectangle representing the system. Each message from an actor to a system is regarded as a stimulus (system-level event) which triggers a system operation. A system input is shown on a system sequence diagram as an arrow from the actor who sends the message to the system, as shown in Figure 4.23. The dashed line becomes a rectangle where it is connected to a message.

| **FIGURE 4.23** | System sequence diagram for the Register for Classes use case |

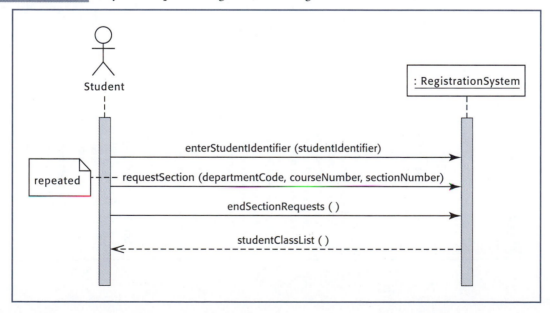

FIGURE 4.24   System sequence diagram for the **Register for Classes** use case, together with the flow of events

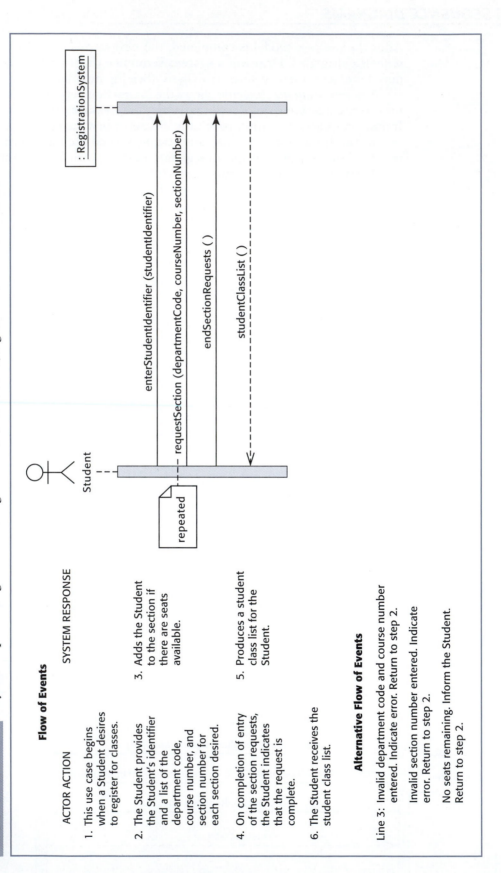

Flow of Events

ACTOR ACTION   SYSTEM RESPONSE

1. This use case begins when a Student desires to register for classes.

2. The Student provides the Student's identifier and a list of the department code, course number, and section number for each section desired.

3. Adds the Student to the section if there are seats available.

4. On completion of entry of the section requests, the Student indicates that the request is complete.

5. Produces a student class list for the Student.

6. The Student receives the student class list.

Alternative Flow of Events

Line 3: Invalid department code and course number entered. Indicate error. Return to step 2.

Invalid section number entered. Indicate error. Return to step 2.

No seats remaining. Inform the Student. Return to step 2.

Each arrow representing a system input is labeled with the name of the input. The names of system inputs are verb phrases. They begin with a lower-case letter and contain no spaces. Any additional words in the system input name have an initial capital letter. In parentheses following the input name is a list of parameters. In naming system inputs, try to keep the verb phrases free of implementation-dependent language.

The system sequence diagram should show whether any of the messages in the input occur as repetitions or as alternatives. However, the focus is on the content and structure of the system input, not on low-level design of the user interface.

A single repeated message may be preceded by an asterisk or labeled with a note (as in Figure 4.23). A repeated sequence of messages may be enclosed in a rectangle.

A system output associated with the previous message is shown as a dashed arrow. Including system outputs is optional, but we recommend it in order to show all the messages between the actors and the system. The system sequence diagram may be annotated with text from the use case. (See Figure 4.24.) However, this is difficult to do with some automated modeling tools.

Actors may be participants in a use case even when they do not initiate the use case. For example, a Credit Card Bank must be contacted before a credit card purchase may be completed. In this situation, the actor figure for the bank appears on the right in the system sequence diagram. Figure 4.25 illustrates this situation for a Credit Card Bank. Note that this message goes from the system to the Bank actor and the response comes back to the system.

DEFINING SYSTEM INPUTS AND OUTPUTS

In order to define the system inputs and outputs, we must specify both the information *content* — the constituent parts — and the information *structure* — how the parts are arranged. The content and structure of an input or output are called its *composition*.

Traditionally, the inputs and outputs are considered as flows of data. Their composition is specified using a notation for data structure.[9] In object-oriented systems, inputs are specified as messages. Outputs are specified either as messages to other information systems or as output objects.

SPECIFYING THE STRUCTURE OF INCOMING MESSAGES (SYSTEM INPUTS)

The structure of system inputs refers to how many messages are required for the actor to inform the system about the external event which triggers the system's response. Often only a single message is necessary. However, if more than one message is required, the input structure also deals with the relationship among the messages.

In the event table, a system input has a single name — for example, Registration Request. In object-oriented systems, this necessary system input will be organized as one or more messages. We need to pay attention to the sequence and structure of the incoming messages for each event.

The following questions need answering:

> **What does the system need to know first?**
>
> **Does part of the message have a repeated structure?**

If so, the repeated part should be treated as a separate message and should be followed by a message indicating to the system that there are no more repetitions.

---

[9] See Lavette C. Teague, Jr., and Christopher W. Pidgeon, *Structured Analysis Methods for Computer Information Systems* (Chicago: Science Research Associates, 1985), ch. 7.

FIGURE 4.25   System sequence diagram for the operation make Credit Card Payment

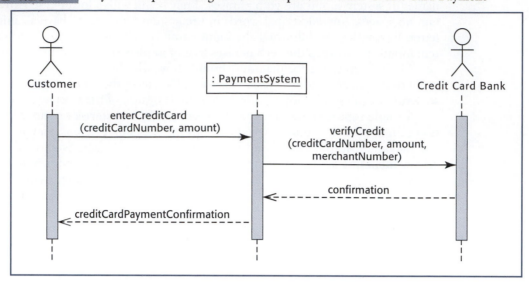

For example, a student who wishes to register for classes must provide at least the following information:

▮ Who the student is (an identifying number) and
▮ A sequence of messages specifying all the classes requested (a section identifier or a combination of department code, course number, and section number for each section).

As Figure 4.23 shows, the Register for Classes use case expects a student to request more than one section at a time. Thus, the student must send the system three messages — a single message containing the student's identifier, a repeated message specifying a particular section, and a single message signaling the end of the list of sections.

Are there alternative messages?

Sometimes a use case requires alternative messages. For example, a hotel guest may check in without a reservation if a room is available. So the Check In Guest use case could require one message for a guest with a reservation and a different message for a guest without a reservation.

SPECIFYING THE CONTENT OF INCOMING MESSAGES (SYSTEM INPUTS)

Once the structure of the incoming messages has been determined, we must define their information content. We must identify the minimum information which the system needs to know about each **external** event in order to respond completely and correctly. The goal is to specify each piece of data required by the system. **The expanded essential use case narratives should identify all these critical pieces of data.** If not, the analyst must do so before completing the system sequence diagrams.

Data Elements

Every system input (and output) is ultimately defined in terms of its data elements. We must specify completely which essential data elements are contained in each input in a system sequence diagram.

A **data element** is an item of information that does not require any decomposition in the system of which it is a part. Sometimes it makes no sense to further subdivide the data. At other times, we choose not to further subdivide the data because we are not interested in its lower-level structure.

For the purpose of data definition, a data element is the lowest, or atomic, level. It is defined in terms of the values it may take on and the meaning associated with each value. In practice, a data element may be referred to by any of several terms: data item, data primitive, or field. We will use the term "data element." A data element can be recognized because it is capable of having a value, such as a number or name.

Message Format

The format for a message is

> **messageName (parameter list)**

The data elements transmitted as part of a message are known as the *parameters* of the message. The parentheses following the message name enclose the names of the parameters of the message. Empty parentheses may mean one of three things:

▌ The message has no parameters.
▌ The parameters are not currently defined.
▌ The parameters have been omitted to simplify the presentation of the message.

Message names are verbs or verb phrases; they may emphasize either the entry of data or the action the system is requested to perform.

According to the UML standards, the initial letter of a message name is lower case. There are no spaces in the message name. Instead, the first letter of each additional word in the message name is capitalized.

For example, the incoming messages for the event "Student registers for classes" could be named

> **enterStudentIdentifier ()**
>
> **enterSectionIdentifier () (or requestSection ()), and**
>
> **endSectionIdentifiers () (or endSections ())**

As mentioned above, the message containing section identifiers would occur once for each class requested by the student. The other two messages would each occur once.

Specifying the Data Elements in a Message

Now it is time to specify the information content of a message. This is shown by listing the data elements inside the parentheses.

Parameter names follow the same UML conventions as message names. They begin with lower-case letters and contain no spaces, and additional words in a parameter name begin with a capital letter. Parameter names are separated by commas.

Now the input messages for the event "Student registers for classes" are expanded as follows:

> **enterStudentIdentifier (studentIdentifier)**
>
> **requestSection (departmentCode, courseNumber, sectionNumber)**
>
> **endSectionRequests ()**

Note that no parameters are necessary for the endSectionRequests message which terminates the list of section identifiers.

SPECIFYING OUTGOING MESSAGES (SYSTEM OUTPUTS)

In general, there are two types of outgoing messages:

- *A response of the system to complete an event.* This is a flow of data to one of the actors in the environment which requires no response from the actor. This is by far the most common type of output. A list of the classes for which the student successfully registered is an example of this type of output.
- *A message to an external system requesting action and a reply.* An example would be a request to the issuing bank to authorize a credit card purchase.

Every output must be derivable from the system input or from internally stored data. Remember that the event flows which trigger the response to temporal events contain no application-related data. Therefore, the outputs associated with temporal events must be entirely derivable from stored data.

Defining a System Output

How a system output is shown on a system sequence diagram depends on its type:

- *Show an ordinary system response by a name which describes its information content.* This will be a noun such as Student Class List.
  Or, alternatively,
- *List all the data elements in the output in the UML format for parameter names.* (See Figure 4.26.)
- *Show a message to an external system in the same message format used for system inputs.* For example, authorizePurchase (creditCardNumber, amount, merchantNumber), as shown in Figure 4.25.

Specifying the Content of System Outputs as Output Objects

When an information processing system is implemented, what we have called ordinary outputs (those which require no action on the part of the receiver) may be produced by output objects. If the system sequence diagram shows one of these ordinary outputs with a single name, we may define its information content by defining an output object. To define an output object, we will use the UML notation discussed in Chapter 5.

We may wish to define the composition of all system outputs at the time we draw the system sequence diagrams. In this way, we can check more carefully whether a system input contains everything not already stored in the system which is necessary to produce the required output. See Figure 4.27 for a detailed description of the system outputs. Only the name of the output will be listed on the system sequence diagram. However, as Figure 4.27 shows, it is important to identify all the individual data elements at this time.

FIGURE 4.26 System inputs and system operations

USE CASE	SYSTEM INPUT MESSAGES/SYSTEM OPERATIONS
Submit Department Class Schedule (Figure 4.21).	enterSection (departmentCode, courseNumber, sectionNumber, maximumNumberOfStudents, meetingTime, meetingPlace, instructorId)
2. The Department provides the **department code, course number, section number, maximum number of students, meeting time, meeting place, and instructor identifier** for each section in the schedule.	endSectionsOffered ( )
Produce University Class Schedule (Figure 4.13).	*(Use case for temporal event — no input)*
Register for Classes (Figure 4.12).	enterStudentIdentifier (studentIdentifier)
2. The Student provides the. **Student's identifier** and a list of the **department code, course number, and section number** for each section desired.	requestSection (departmentCode, courseNumber, sectionNumber) endSectionRequests ( )
Produce Class Rosters (Figure 4.22).	*(Use case for temporal event — no input)*

On the other hand, we may wish to defer the specification of the data elements in the outputs. In that case, we treat the detailed output specification as part of the user interface design. At that time, we must still confirm that the domain model (see Chapter 5) contains all the data required to produce the outputs.

FIGURE 4.27 System outputs

USE CASE	SYSTEM OUTPUTS WITH DATA ELEMENTS
Submit Department Class Schedule (Figure 4.21).	*(No output to actor)*
Produce University Class Schedule (Figure 4.13). 2. The system produces and displays the university class schedule.	University class schedule = term, year, and, for each department: Department code, course number, course title, section number, maximum number of seats, meeting time, meeting place, instructor identifier, and instructor name.
Register for Classes (Figure 4.12). 5. The system produces a student class list for the Student.	Student class list = student identifier, student name, and, for each section: Department code, course number, course title, section number, maximum number of seats, meeting time, meeting place, instructor identifier, and instructor name.
Produce Class Rosters (Figure 4.22). 2. The system produces and displays the class rosters.	Class rosters = department code, course number, course title, section number, maximum number of seats, meeting time, meeting place, instructor identifier, and instructor name, and, for each student: Student identifier and student name.

SYSTEM INPUTS AND SYSTEM OPERATIONS

A *system operation* is an operation which the system carries out in response to a system input. The system input and the corresponding system operation have the same name.

The format for a system operation (as well as the matching system input) is

messageName (parameter list)

Figure 4.26 lists the system inputs and operations for the university registration system. Compare the messages shown in Figure 4.26 with those in Figure 4.23. Figure 4.27 lists the outputs and their compositions.

CREATING A SYSTEM SEQUENCE DIAGRAM

To create a system sequence diagram for a use case:

▪ Draw a rectangle representing the system as a black box. Label the rectangle with the name of the system — e.g., :System. Below the rectangle draw a lifeline.

▪ Identify each actor who provides an input directly to the system. To the left of the system's lifeline, draw a stick figure representing the actor and label it with the actor's name. Below the stick figure, draw a lifeline for the actor.

▪ From the text of the use case, identify each system input and the corresponding actor. Draw a horizontal arrow from the actor's lifeline to the system's lifeline and label it with the name and parameters of the system input.

▪ Confirm that the sequence in which the inputs are shown from top to bottom is the expected sequence in which the inputs are provided to the system.

▪ If desired, add text from the use case narrative to the left of the diagram.

SUMMARY

The models presented in this chapter begin to describe the response of a system to events in its environment. They comprise the following deliverables:

▪ *Use case diagrams* — Diagrams showing the set of use cases within the scope of the system

▪ *Use case narratives* — Structured narratives of the system's response to an event or event scenario (an instance of an event)

▪ *System sequence diagrams* — Diagrams showing the messages between the system and the environment for a particular use case scenario

The UML defines a standard notation for use case diagrams and system sequence diagrams.

A use case is a sequence of actions which occur when an actor uses a system to complete a process. The initial analysis produces one use case for each event. An initiating actor begins a use case by sending the system a message which reports essential data about an external event. Use cases for temporal events are triggered by time. Participating actors interact with a use case but do not initiate it.

A use case diagram contains only four types of components, each represented by an icon. They are the use case, shown as an oval; the actor, shown as a stick figure;

the association, shown as a line connecting an actor and a use case; and the system or subsystem boundary, shown as a rectangle.

A use case narrative may consist of only two or three sentences. Such high-level use case narratives are helpful early in systems analysis to provide an overview of the scope and functionality of a system. An expanded use case narrative contains additional detail about the low-level events. It lists in sequence each action of an actor and the corresponding responses of the system. This sequence is known as a flow of events. The expanded narratives may also contain preconditions, postconditions, and special requirements. Expanded use case narratives are written for external business events but seldom written for temporal events.

To be concise and to minimize redundancy, use cases may include or extend other use cases. The «includes» association requires both use cases to occur. With the «extends» association, the extension is conditional.

A use case scenario describes a single specific occurrence or instance of a use case. Scenarios are used to discover alternative paths through a use case. They are also used to test the completeness or correctness of a use case.

After the use case narratives have been prepared, the next step is to produce a set of system sequence diagrams for the use cases which deal with external events. A system sequence diagram shows the messages between an actor and a system for a use case or use case scenario.

The definition of the system inputs and outputs requires a description of their information structure and content. The structure of system inputs refers to the number of required messages from an actor to inform the system as well as to the relationship among these messages. The content of system inputs and outputs is ultimately defined in terms of data elements. System inputs are defined as messages which include data elements as parameters. System outputs are defined as output objects or as messages to other systems. The UML provides a notation for defining messages and their parameters.

KEY TERMS

alternatives in a use case narrative *109*	postcondition *108*
essential use case narrative *104*	precondition *107*
expanded use case narrative *104*	system operation *124*
«extends» association *110*	system sequence diagram *117*
flow of events *104*	use case *98*
high-level use case narrative *104*	use case scenario *113*
«includes» association *110*	

REVIEW QUESTIONS

4-1. What is the Unified Modeling Language?

4-2. How many use cases are there for each business (system-level) event?

4-3. What are the components of a system sequence diagram?

4-4. What is the relationship between the number of system sequence diagrams and the number of events? The number of use cases?

4-5. Explain the difference between a use case and a use case scenario. How are they related to each other?

EXERCISES AND DISCUSSION QUESTIONS

4-1. Does every use case need a description? An expanded use case narrative? Explain the reasons for your answers.

4-2. Modify the use case narrative for Register for Classes (Figure 4.12) to require that the system check prerequisites before adding a student to a class.

4-3. Draw a system sequence diagram for the typical flow of events for the use case Enter Department Class Schedule. Why are system sequence diagrams not necessary for the use cases Produce University Class Schedule and Produce Class Roster?

4-4. Prepare expanded essential use case narratives for the additional events in the Public University Registration System discussed in Exercise 3–12.

4-5. Prepare system sequence diagrams for use cases in Exercise 4–4.

4-6. Draw a system sequence diagram for the use case Check Out Library Book, shown in Figures 4.10 and 4.11.

4-7. Consider the four systems included in Exercise 3–14 — a restaurant, a library, a video rental store, and a hotel. Prepare a use case diagram for each of these systems. Prepare expanded essential use case narratives and system sequence diagrams for at least three use cases for each of these systems. Be sure that the use cases you select correspond to external business events.

4-8. Consider the article about the PCX system at Cedars-Sinai Hospital in Figure 4.28.

    a. Who are the various types of users of the system?

    b. What are the attitudes of each type of user toward the system and its benefits?

    c. Discuss this system from the perspective of system change.

    d. How might the decision to develop custom software instead of purchasing a commercially available product have affected users' expectations of and reactions to the completed system?

    e. Was the development effort a waste of time and money?

    f. What do you think will happen next?

    g. To what extent could an early audit have prevented the difficulties with the new system at Cedars-Sinai Hospital (see Figure 2.4)?

    h. To what extent do you feel that the problems with the PCX system resulted from failure to determine system requirements, and to what extent were they due to failures in design or implementation?

FIGURE 4.28   Hospital Heeds Doctors, Suspends Use of Software

Hospital Heeds Doctors, Suspends Use of Software

Cedars-Sinai Medical Center, the largest private hospital in the West, is suspending use of a multimillion-dollar computerized system for doctors' orders after hundreds of physicians complained that it was endangering patient safety and required too much work. Ironically, the computer software was designed to do the opposite: Reduce medical errors, allow doctors to track electronically, and warn them about dangerous drug interactions and redundant laboratory work. But, from the start of its rollout in October, the Patient Care Expert program (PCX) has been plagued with problems, many doctors said.

The concept behind PCX and similar programs is simple: Instead of writing orders for medications, lab tests, therapy and dietary restrictions on paper, physicians put them into a computer system. The software compares the orders to standard dosing recommendations, checks for allergies and drug interactions, and alerts physicians to alternatives or potentials. It has been shown to reduce medication errors by 60% to 80%, and to cut the number of lost orders.

The uproar is a case study in what can happen as hospitals belatedly modernize record-keeping on a large scale. Years behind other industries, many hospitals are on the cusp of converting from paper to electronic ordering systems to increase efficiency and accuracy.

Interest in computerized physician-order entry software accelerated in 1999 after the influential Institute of Medicine concluded that up to 98,000 patients die annually in hospitals from avoidable errors. A 2000 California law requires hospitals to implement formal plans, including new technologies, to eliminate or substantially reduce medication-related errors by Jan. 1, 2005.

Hospitals and experts are watching Cedars-Sinai because it has developed a customized system they may want to emulate or purchase. Most hospitals buy a commercially available product, but Cedars-Sinai decided to create its own. Several doctors said they had been told that Cedars-Sinai spent $34 million on the electronic order system, but hospital officials said that estimate was too high.

This week, Cedars-Sinai suspended the ordering system after more than 400 physicians confronted hospital administrators at a tense staff meeting Friday. The doctors voted unanimously to urge the hospital to halt the system until the problems are fixed. Officials at Cedars-Sinai said PCX was not easy enough to use and it took too long to enter orders.

The complexity of this change "is enormous," said Jane Metzger, research director for First Consulting Group, which evaluates computer physician-order systems. "It is not uncommon for there to be delays and midcourse corrections."

More than a dozen Cedars-Sinai physicians interviewed by The Times said they experienced problems ordering medication, tests and supplies using the PCX software. Stories of delays and inconvenience abound, although none involved deaths or permanent injuries, doctors said.

But Dr. Stephen Uman, an infectious disease expert, said that although it used to take him five seconds to write an order for the powerful antibiotic Vancomycin, it now takes him up to two minutes to log on to PCX, select his patient's record, search through several screens and warnings about Vancomycin, and then justify his decision to protect against overuse of the drug. He then has to reenter his password to confirm the order. Uman said he can have 15 to 20 patients in the hospital at any given time, "If I have to add five to 10 minutes to each patient, that adds hours to my day," he said.

Dr. Jack Coburn, a nephrologist at Cedars, said the system's complexity has caused doctors to delay writing orders or to enter them imprecisely.

Dr. Donald Nortman, a nephrologist, said he hopes Cedars-Sinai's corrections will address physicians' concerns. "In science and medicine, we don't change to new treatment systems until the new system has been shown to be as good as the old system, and better in some ways," he said. "It's the overwhelming perception of people using it that this system is worse."

Adapted from *Los Angeles Times*, "Hospital Heeds Doctors, Suspends Use of Software," January 22, 2003, B1

Assignments

1. Draw a use case diagram showing the use cases in the hotel system for each of the following events:
    a. Guest reserves room
    b. Guest registers
    c. Guest incurs charge for service
    d. Guest adds tip to bill for service charges
    e. Time to produce final bill
    f. Guest checks out
    g. Guest pays bill

2. Write an expanded essential use case narrative for each use case associated with an external event.

3. Add the alternative flow of events to the above expanded use case narratives.

4. Draw a system sequence diagram for each of the use cases in the hotel system.

Assignments

1. Draw a use case diagram showing the use cases in the car rental system for each of the following events:
    a. Customer reserves car
    b. Customer rents car
    c. Customer returns car
    d. Employee inspects car
    e. Company creates bill
    f. Customer pays bill

2. Write an expanded essential use case narrative for each use case associated with an external event.

3. Add the alternative flow of events to the above expanded use case narratives.

4. Draw a system sequence diagram for each of the use cases in the car rental system.

INTRODUCTION

Use case narratives state what the system is expected to do in response to each event. They make it possible to define the content and structure of the messages between the system and its environment, as shown in a set of system sequence diagrams. The next step is to construct a model of the concepts in the problem domain of the application. It is important to emphasize that this model is an analysis model whose purpose is to specify users' requirements. This model will show all the concepts of interest in the application domain as well as their relationships. It is common for a concept to be involved in more than one use case. During design, many of these concepts will have software counterparts.

LEARNING OBJECTIVES

After mastering the material in this chapter, you will be able to

▌ Discover concepts used in the domain model.

▌ Identify attributes of concepts.

▌ Derive the associations between concepts.

▌ Distinguish an instance of a concept from a concept.

▌ Understand the use of multiplicity in associations.

▌ Know when to use whole-to-part associations such as aggregations and compositions.

▌ Find generalization-specialization hierarchies.

▌ Complete the system operation contracts.

THE DOMAIN MODEL

Producing a domain model is Step 5 of the procedure for object-oriented systems analysis. A *domain model* is a static model of the structure of a problem domain. It models real-world concepts rather than software units. A domain model is composed of:

▮ Concepts,
▮ Attributes of concepts, and
▮ Associations between concepts.

A domain model includes only attributes — not behaviors. It also does not include concepts related to the implementation of the user interface, such as screens or buttons. Deciding how the user interface will be implemented is a design activity. A domain model is a diagram which makes it easy to see the relationships among its components.

"Domain model" is the term used by the Unified Process. As far as the Unified Modeling Language (UML) is concerned, a domain model is a class diagram. The UML uses the same conventions for all class diagrams, whether they are analysis models, design models, or implementation models. Figure 5.1 shows a simple example of a domain model in order to illustrate the UML conventions.

A *concept* is an abstraction of a thing, a person, or an idea. As shown in Figure 5.1, a concept is represented as a rectangle. The name of the concept appears in the compartment at the top of the rectangle. The initial letter of each word in the concept name is capitalized.[1]

The **attributes** of a concept are listed in the rectangle in the middle compartment. An *attribute* is a named characteristic of a concept which may have a value. Attribute names begin with a lower-case letter and contain no spaces. Any additional words in an attribute name have an initial capital letter. Each attribute name may be followed by optional details, such as data type and default values.

FIGURE 5.1   Example of a domain model

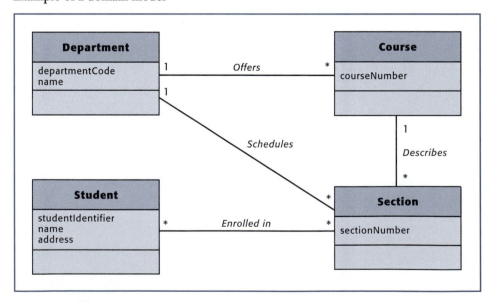

---

[1]The term "concept" has a variety of synonyms. These include "conceptual class" (a UML term), "domain object," and "analysis object." "Domain concept" would also be appropriate. We prefer to use the term "concept."

An *association* indicates a significant connection between problem-domain concepts. An association is represented as a line connecting a pair of concepts. The line may be labeled with the name of the association. Association names should be verb phrases; they are italicized and should start with a capital letter. Associations are assumed to be bi-directional — that is, capable of being understood or traversed in either direction. However, the name given to a bi-directional association applies to only one direction; the reader must supply a name for the opposite direction. The direction of a one-way association may be shown with an arrow. The ends of the associations are also labeled to show *multiplicity*, which will be defined later in the chapter.

The next several sections discuss each of these components of a domain model. They cover how to find them and when to include them in the model. In this text, how to find and add each type of component to the model is explained separately. In practice, concepts, attributes, and associations are added to the model as they are discovered. We can take advantage of event analysis to construct the domain model one use case at a time.

CONCEPTS

As defined above, a **concept** is an abstraction of a person, a thing, or an idea in the problem domain. People are modeled as roles such as guest, customer, patient, and student. Examples of things are bins, cash registers, and parts catalogs. Ideas are abstract concepts. They are often called intangible things. For example, airline flights, bank accounts, systems, and product specifications are ideas. A specification concept is a very important kind of idea. A *specification concept* provides a common description for a set of other concepts. For example, all 36-exposure rolls of 35mm ISO–200 color slide film have the same specification, even though there are 12 dozen on the shelf. All copies of a library book with the same ISBN have the same specification.[2]

FINDING CONCEPTS

There are two main strategies for finding concepts. Both are useful. They may be applied to the problem domain as a whole or may be applied to one use case at a time.

1. *Look for nouns and noun phrases describing the problem domain.* Sometimes these words and phrases may be found by referring to written descriptions of the domain, especially the expanded use cases. Sometimes they are found in discussions with users. One difficulty with this approach is that not all nouns are concept names. Some, such as date of birth, may be attribute names. Others, such as tabulation, may in fact describe actions rather than concepts.

2. *Use a checklist of concept categories.* Figure 5.2 shows a concept category checklist. Concept names should be taken from the users' vocabulary. For example, a customer of a consulting firm is known as a client; a customer of a hotel is known as a guest.

Consider the use case Register for Classes (Figure 5.3). Its description contains the following noun phrases — student, section of class, seats available, list of classes, student's identifier, department code, course number, section number, and student class list.

Comparing these phrases to the category list in Figure 5.2, we note that department is an organization and seat is a tangible object. This suggests the concepts Department and Seat.

---

[2]Sally Shlaer and Steven J. Mellor, *Object-Oriented Systems Analysis: Modeling the World in Objects* (Englewood Cliffs, N.J.: Yourdon, 1988), 15*ff*.

FIGURE 5.2 Conceptual category checklist.

CONCEPT CATEGORY	EXAMPLES
Business transactions	Sale Payment
Business transaction line items	Sale Line Item
Catalogs	Product Catalog Parts Catalog
Containers	Bin Airplane
External systems	Credit-Card Authorization System
Organizations	Sales Department Airline
Places	Store Airport
Roles of people	Student Professor
Specifications or descriptions of things	Product Specification Book Specification
Tangible objects	Cash Register Seat
Things in a container	Stock Item Passenger

Excerpted from Craig Larman, Applying UML and Patterns: An Introduction to Object-Oriented Analysis and Design and the Unified Process, 2nd ed. (Upper Saddle River, N.J.: Prentice-Hall, 2002), 134–135.

CRITERIA FOR INCLUDING CONCEPTS IN THE DOMAIN MODEL

We can use the following criteria to help decide whether to include a concept in the model.

▪ *Include a concept in the domain model when the system needs to store data about the concept in order to respond to a future event.*
In order to enroll a student in a class, the system must know the student's name, identifier, and other attributes. It needs to know which sections of each class are in the schedule for the current term and the maximum number of students in a section.

This analysis leads us to the concepts Student and Section.

▪ *There does not have to be a concept for every actor.*
Note that Student is an actor in the Register for Classes use case as well as a concept. But we should not automatically assume that there must be a concept for every actor. The test is whether the system needs to remember the attributes of the actor.

▪ *Distinguish between concepts and the attributes which describe concepts.*
Both concepts and attributes are important to the model, but they have different roles.

FIGURE 5.3	Expanded essential use case narrative for Register for Classes

Use case:	**Register for Classes**
Actors:	Student
Purpose:	Register a student for classes and record the student's schedule.
Overview:	A Student requests the sections of class desired for a term. The system adds the Student to each section if there is space available. On completion, the system provides the Student with a list of the classes in which he or she is enrolled.
Type:	Essential
Preconditions:	Class schedule must exist. Student is known by system.
Postconditions:	Student was enrolled in the section.
Special Requirements:	Student must get a system response within 10 seconds.

Flow of Events

ACTOR ACTION	SYSTEM RESPONSE
1. This use case begins when a Student desires to register for classes.	
2. The Student provides the Student's identifier and a list with the department code, course number, and section number for each section desired.	3. Adds the Student to the section if there are seats available.
4. On completion of entry of the section requests, the Student indicates that the request is complete.	5. Produces a student class list for the Student.
6. The Student receives the student class list.	

Alternative Flow of Events

Line 3: Invalid department code and course number entered. Indicate error. Return to Step2.
Invalid section number entered. Indicate error. Return to Step 2.
No seats remaining. Inform the Student. Return to Step 2.

Student identifier is an attribute, referring to the concept Student. Space available is related to the number of unfilled seats in a specific section and appears to be an attribute of the concept Section. Department code is an abbreviation for a department name, which refers to a department, so department code is an attribute of the concept Department. We have found the concept Department indirectly by finding an attribute which describes it. Similarly, course number is an attribute of the concept Course, and section number is an attribute of the concept Section.

Exclude concepts which represent system outputs unless the system needs to know about them in the future.

Student class list appears to be a synonym for a system output. As long as the domain model contains other concepts and attributes which will permit a student's list of classes to be reassembled on demand, the class list can be omitted from the model.

FIGURE 5.4   Initial set of concepts

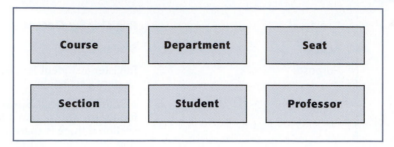

On the other hand, the Cashier's Office may send bills to students and needs to retain the identity and amount of each bill and the date on which it was sent. In this case, Tuition Bill should be a concept in the model.

System outputs cannot be ignored, however. Their attributes must be defined as a basis for user interface design. An output may be documented either in the UML form for a message or as a concept (or set of related concepts) in a domain model. Any data elements needed to produce an output in response to an event must be contained in a system input, must be an attribute in the domain model, or must be able to be calculated from inputs and attributes.

We have now identified Course, Department, Seat, Section, and Student as concepts related to the use case Register for Classes. These are shown in Figure 5.4. At this point, the concepts are not connected to each other, and no attributes are shown. Not a very interesting or useful model!

Identifying and adding concepts to the domain model may be considered as Step 5a of the procedure for object-oriented systems analysis.

ATTRIBUTES

How do we describe concepts? A concept is described or characterized by its attributes. An *attribute* of a concept is a named characteristic of the concept which may have a value.

CONCEPTS, ATTRIBUTES, AND VALUES

Different concepts have different concept names and, in most cases, different sets of attributes. Note that some concepts may have identical attribute names, e.g., identifier for Student and Professor, or name for Student and Professor, as shown in Example (5.1).

Concept:	Student	Professor	Section
Attributes:	identifier	identifier	number
	name	name	meetingTime
	address	address	meetingPlace
	major	title	maximumNumberOfSeats
	classLevel		

When we need to identify an attribute of a particular concept uniquely, we prefix the attribute name with the concept name and a period, as shown in Example (5.2). This is known as *qualifying* the attribute name.

Concept:	Student	Professor	Section
Attributes:	studentIdentifier	professorIdentifier	number
	studentName	professorName	meetingTime
	studentAddress	professorAddress	meetingPlace
	major	title	maximumNumberOfSeats
	classLevel		

Our university registration system will store information about many different students. It must be possible to refer to each student individually. A particular student is called an *instance* of the concept Student. Thus, an instance is a specific member of the collection associated with a concept.

By assigning values to attributes, we can distinguish between two instances of the same concept, as in Example (5.3).

Student Concept:	Student Instance 1:	Student Instance 2:
Attributes	*Values*	*Values*
identifier	41068	82704
name	Louella Fernbee	Mortimer Snow
address	123 Any St.	456 Some St.
major	CIS	CS
classLevel	Junior	Sophomore

Thus, assigning a value to each attribute of a concept completely determines an instance of the concept.

Notice that there are two perspectives of a concept. One is abstract — it names the concept and enumerates its attributes. The other is concrete — it assigns a specific value to each attribute to distinguish an instance of the concept.

FINDING ATTRIBUTES

In general, the search for attributes is a quest for the necessary descriptive data to be stored for each concept. As we discovered earlier, the approach of looking for noun phrases in descriptions of the problem domain usually yields attribute names as well as concept names. Thus, in our search for concepts, we found the attributes maximumNumberOfSeats, sectionNumber, departmentCode, and courseNumber.

Another strategy is to look at the data contained in each system input. We ask whether that piece of data must be kept for future use and, if so, which concept it describes.

Similarly, we may examine the required system outputs to make sure that they can be produced from the attributes contained in the domain model. If not, that is our clue that we have overlooked one or more attributes (and possibly concepts, as well). In some cases, we may even have overlooked a necessary system input or event.

CRITERIA FOR INCLUDING ATTRIBUTES IN THE DOMAIN MODEL

We can use the following criteria to help decide whether to include an attribute in the model:

- *Include an attribute in a domain model when the system needs to remember the value of the attribute in order to respond to an event.*
- *If in doubt as to whether something is an attribute or a concept, define it as a concept in the initial model.*
- *Do not use an attribute to record a connection between concepts; use an association instead.*

FIGURE 5.5   Concepts with attributes

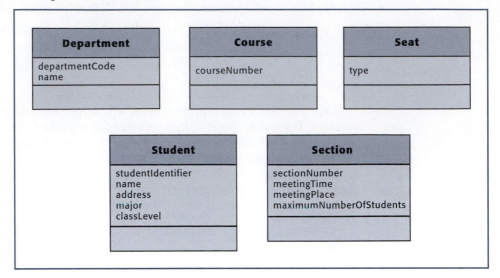

▌ *Do not include the same attribute as an attribute of more than one concept.*
▌ *Do not include an attribute if it can be derived or calculated from other attributes in the model.*

Try to find attributes whose values do not change but which can be used to calculate desired values. For example, a date of birth is a preferable attribute to a person's age. Age changes every year, but it can always be computed from the date of birth. Similarly, the maximum number of seats is a better attribute for Section than the number of available seats. The number of available seats can be calculated from the maximum number and the number of students currently registered.

Figure 5.5 adds some of the attributes discovered thus far to the domain model. **Identifying and adding attributes to the domain model may be considered as Step 5b** of the procedure for object-oriented systems analysis.

ASSOCIATIONS

Even if we add more concepts and attributes to Figure 5.5, we still have a set of disconnected concepts. The power of a domain model is in showing how the concepts in the application domain are related.

Information systems would not be very useful if they contained only data about concepts. Most interesting systems also incorporate associations, which represent relationships or interactions between concepts. Associations extend the domain model to show a broadly interconnected view of the users' problem domain.

An *association* indicates a significant connection between two problem-domain concepts. One of the concepts is logically connected to or associated with the other. Further, just as we have instances of concepts, we have *instances of associations*.

Associations are shown in a domain model by a line between the two concepts in the association. An association should be named to explain its meaning in the problem domain.

Consider an association between the concepts Student and Section, which we have called Enrolled In. An instance of the association Enrolled In exists when an instance of the concept Student is paired with an instance of the concept Section. Figure 5.6 and Example (5.4) show an instance of Student, Louella Fernbee, enrolled in an instance of Section, CIS-4-01.

FIGURE 5.6   Instance of the Enrolled In association

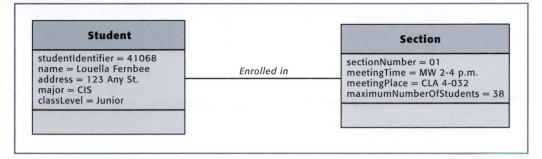

Student Concept:	Student Instance 1:	Student Instance 2:
Attributes	*Values*	*Values*
identifier	41068	82704
name	Louella Fernbee	Mortimer Snow
address	123 Any St.	456 Some St.
major	CIS	CS
classLevel	Junior	Sophomore

Association: Enrolled In
Instance: studentIdentifier = 41068 associated with sectionNumber = CIS-4-01

Most associations are bi-directional, but only one direction is explicitly labeled on the domain model. Although not required by the UML, associations are usually named so that they can be read from left to right and from top to bottom in the diagram.

Figure 5.7 shows the domain model corresponding to Figure 5.6. In Figure 5.7 the Enrolled In association goes from the Student concept to the Section concept. The association can be read in stilted English as

Student Enrolled In Section.

If necessary, a small arrowhead may be added to the association name to show the direction in which it should be read. For example, in Figure 5.8, the association reads from right to left:

Section Has Enrolled Student.

FIGURE 5.7   Association from a Student concept to a Section concept

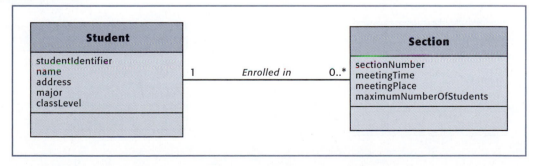

FIGURE 5.8   **Association from a Section concept to a Student concept**

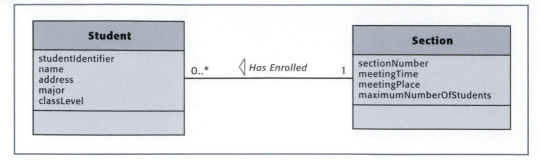

MULTIPLICITY

The *multiplicity* of an association defines how many instances of one concept can be associated with one instance of another concept. The line representing the association also shows the minimum and maximum number of instances of concepts which can be connected by the association. These multiplicity values are shown as pairs of numbers at the ends of an association — the symbol * is used for zero or more (**many**); ranges of values are shown as, for example, 1..*. The minimum value is the left number of the pair; it is usually either 0 or 1. The maximum value is the right number of the pair; it is usually either 1 or *(many; zero or more).

In Figure 5.7, the one-directional association Enrolled In (from Student to Section) is *one to many*; that is, one student may be enrolled in zero or more classes. The association Has Enrolled (from Section to Student) is also one to many, as seen in Figure 5.8. That is, a section may have many (zero or more) students enrolled.

However, a more likely scenario is that each section has many students enrolled in it and each student also has enrolled in many sections. This is shown in Figure 5.9. Note the use of two asterisks for multiplicity.

For conciseness, a one-to-many association in both directions is called a *many-to-many* association. Figure 5.9 shows the bi-directional association between Student and Section as it would appear as part of a domain model.

There are ten possible multiplicities for a bi-directional association between two concepts, A and B: There are three kinds of one-to-one, four kinds of one-to-many, and three kinds of many-to-many associations. These combinations are shown generically in Figure 5.10 and by example in Figure 5.11. Unlike in these figures, for conciseness, the multiplicity value 1..1 is usually shown as 1, and the value 0..* as *.

The astute analyst anticipates the need for a bi-directional relationship even though only a one-directional association has been identified. If only one direction turns out to be of interest, the domain model can be modified later.

FIGURE 5.9   **Association between many Student concepts and many Section concepts**

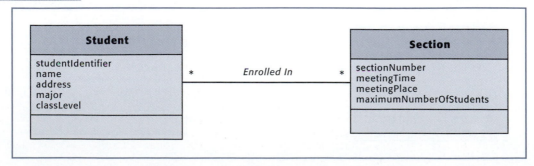

FIGURE 5.10 Possible multiplicities of an association between concepts A and B

MULTIPLICITY	CONCEPT	VALUE		VALUE	CONCEPT
One-to-one	A	0 .. 1	———	0 .. 1	B
	A	0 .. 1	———	1 .. 1	B
	A	1 .. 1	———	1 .. 1	B
One-to-many	A	0 .. 1	———	0 .. *	B
	A	0 .. 1	———	1 .. *	B
	A	1 .. 1	———	0 .. *	B
	A	1 .. 1	———	1 .. *	B
Many-to-many	A	0 .. *	———	0 .. *	B
	A	0 .. *	———	1 .. *	B
	A	1 .. *	———	1 .. *	B

We stated earlier that associations usually exist between two different concepts. However, consider the association shown in Figure 5.12. The association Prerequisite For means that a student must have passed a prerequisite course before being permitted to enroll in a subsequent course. In this case, there is an association between two instances of the same type of concept. The diagram shows the concept associated with itself, and the direction of the association may be indicated.

FINDING ASSOCIATIONS

To help find associations, Larman suggests the use of a common associations check-list, from which Figure 5.13 is excerpted. Note that the categories in the list are drawn from the types of associations discussed in this section of the chapter.

CRITERIA FOR INCLUDING ASSOCIATIONS IN THE DOMAIN MODEL

Include an association in a domain model when the system needs to remember the association in order to respond to an event. For example, in a student registration system, it is necessary to remember in which specific class sections a specific student is enrolled. However, it may not be necessary to record the name of the student's advisor, as this information is not relevant to the registration process.

Show associations explicitly instead of using an attribute to imply the association. Associations are always modeled directly; an attribute of one concept should never be embedded in a different concept. Each attribute in the domain model should be an attribute of one and only one concept.[3]

---

[3]Students who have studied relational data bases might be tempted to develop a domain model as if it were an entity-relationship (ER) diagram. In the ER model, the only way to uniquely identify an instance of an entity is with a key, a combination of attributes which take on unique values for each instance. Thus, ER models include keys. Objects, on the other hand, have unique identifiers assigned internally by the system. An association between concepts implies the association of a pair of these unique identifiers. There is no need to include keys as such (either complete composite primary keys or the foreign keys which are a means of representing associations in a set of relational tables) in a domain model.

FIGURE 5.11   Examples of possible multiplicities of an association between two concepts

| Office | 0..1 | Houses | 0..1 | Employee |

An office is empty or houses only one employee.
An employee is not assigned an office or has only one office.

| Customer | 1..1 | Has | 0..1 | Account |

A customer has no account or only one account.
An account belongs to one and only one customer

| Employee | 1..1 | Is Paid | 1..1 | Pay Rate |

An employee has one and only one pay rate.
Each pay rate applies to one and only one employee.

| Rating | 0..1 | Rates | 0..* | Movie |

A rating applies to zero or more movies.
A movie is either unrated or, if rated, has only one rating.

| Father | 0..1 | Living Father Of | 1..* | Son |

A father is the living father of one or more sons.
A son is the son of zero or only one living father.

| Club Member | 1..1 | Rents | 0..* | Video Rental |

A club member rents zero or more video rentals.
A video rental is rented by one and only one club member.

| Invoice | 1..1 | Contains | 1..* | Invoice Line |

An invoice contains one or more lines.
An invoice line is contained in one and only one invoice.

| Student | 0..* | Enrolled In | 0..* | Section |

A student is enrolled in zero or more sections.
A section has enrolled zero or more students.

| Product | 0..* | Contains | 1..* | Part |

A product contains one or more parts.
A part is contained in zero or more products.

| Book | 1..* | Written By | 1..* | Author |

A book is written by one or more authors.
An author writes one or more books.

WHOLE-TO-PART ASSOCIATIONS

Associations between concepts referring to a whole and concepts referring to its parts are commonly found in many problem domains.

A *whole-to-part association* relates a concept to other concepts of which it is composed. Examples include a university class schedule and the sections listed in it, an invoice and the line items which it contains, and a club and its members. In

FIGURE 5.12   Reflexive association

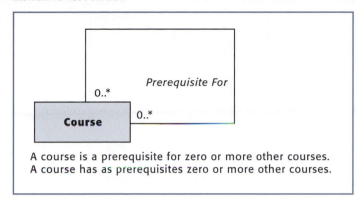

Prerequisite For

0..*

Course

0..*

A course is a prerequisite for zero or more other courses.
A course has as prerequisites zero or more other courses.

interpreting a whole-to-part association, we sometimes describe it with words such as "has a" or "contains" (from the whole to the part) or "is a part of," "is–a–member of," or "is –contained in" (from the part to the whole). The UML provides two ways to model whole-to-part associations — aggregation and composition.

Aggregation

In an *aggregation*, the concept representing the whole is called the *aggregate*; each concept representing a part is called a *constituent*. In an aggregation, the aggregate and the constituents may exist independently of each other. Moreover, a constituent may be a part of more than one whole at a time. For example, a student may simultaneously belong to more than one club.

An aggregation is shown in a domain model as follows. A small open diamond appears at the end of the association next to the concept representing the **whole**.

FIGURE 5.13   Common associations checklist.

ASSOCIATION CATEGORY	EXAMPLES
Concept A is a physical part of Concept B	Drawer — Cash Register Wing — Airplane
A is physically contained in/on B	Stock Item — Bin Passenger — Airplane
A is logically contained in B	Flight — Flight Schedule
A is a line item of a business transaction B	Sale Line Item — Sale
A is a member of B	Student — Club Pilot — Airline
A is an organizational subunit of B	Department — University Maintenance — Airline
A is related to a transaction B	Customer — Payment Passenger — Ticket

Excerpted from Larman, Craig, Applying UML and Patterns: An Introduction to Object-Triented Analysis and Design and the Unified Process, second edition, Prentice Hall, Upper Saddle River, NJ. (2002), pp. 156–157.

FIGURE 5.14   Example of aggregation (members of a group)

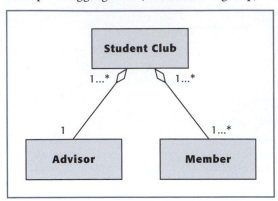

The multiplicity must be shown at both ends of an aggregation. Aggregations are customarily labeled only if necessary to clarify an unusual whole-to-part association. Figure 5.14 shows an example of an aggregation — a student club with an advisor and members.

Composition

The other type of whole-to-part association is called *composition*. The concept representing the whole is called the *composite*; each concept representing a part is called a *component*. (Note that the words "composition," "composite," and "component" all begin with "comp").

A composition is a more restrictive association than an aggregation. In a composition, the composite does not exist independently from its components. (However, components may exist without the composite.) At any given time, a component may be a part of only one composite.

When modeling a composition, there is a black diamond at the end of the association next to the concept representing the **whole.** The multiplicity must be shown at the component end. Unless otherwise indicated, the multiplicity at the composite end is assumed to be 1. Like aggregations, compositions are usually not labeled.

Figure 5.15 shows an example of a composition — a chair composed of a frame, a back, a seat, and two arm rests.

Figure 5.16 summarizes the differences between an aggregation and a composition.

FIGURE 5.15   Example of composition (assembly of parts)

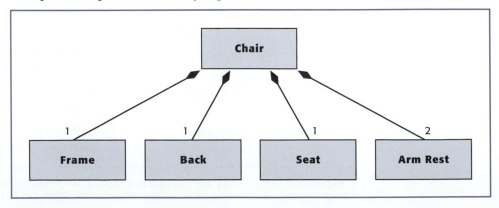

FIGURE 5.16   Aggregation and composition

	AGGREGATION	**COMPOSITION**
Name of whole	Aggregate	Composite
Name of part	Constituent	Component
Parts	May be of different types	Usually of the same type
Existence	May exist without its parts	Does not exist without its parts
Number of wholes to which a part may belong	Part may belong to more than one aggregate at a time	Part may belong to only one composite at a time

CATEGORIES OF WHOLE-TO-PART ASSOCIATIONS

Domain modelers identify three kinds of frequently occurring whole-to-part associations:[4]

- Assemblies of parts,
- Members of groups, and
- Containers and their contents.

There may be other whole-to-part associations which do not fall into any of these three categories. What is important is the fact that there is a whole-to-part association.

Assemblies of Parts

The parts of an assembly may be either physical or conceptual. Figure 5.15 shows an assembly of physical parts.

A common kind of assembly in business systems is a concept which includes a list of subordinate items. For example, the University Class Schedule is composed of a list of Department Class Schedules, and a Department Class Schedule includes a list of Sections. These assemblies are shown in Figure 5.17.

Members of Groups

This kind of aggregation refers to both organizations and more informal groups.

Figure 5.14 shows a Student Club as an organization with an Advisor and 1 or more Members.

Containers and Their Contents

Containers and contents may also be physical or conceptual. A physical example of this kind of aggregation can be found in the arrangement of items in a grocery store, as shown in Figure 5.18. As another example, Product Catalogs listing Items for sale are common aggregations in business systems.

Not every association shows a whole-to-part relationship. Certain associations are application-specific. These are often the most interesting and important associations in the problem domain. For example, the Enrolled In association is central to the university registration system but is unlikely to be useful in many other systems.

---

[4]See Peter Coad and Edward Yourdon, *Object-Oriented Analysis*, 2nd ed. (Englewood Cliffs, N.J.: Yourdon, 1991), 90 *ff.*

FIGURE 5.17   Example of assembly of parts in a business system (composition)

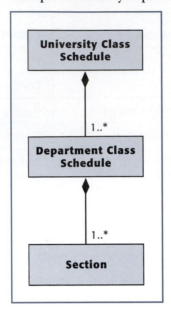

GENERALIZATION-SPECIALIZATION HIERARCHIES

We often notice that a concept may be partitioned into subclassifications. These subclassifications may be mutually exclusive or may overlap. The partitioning is based on different values of a common attribute or attributes. For example, the concept Student may be classified as either an undergraduate or a graduate student based on values of the attribute degreeLevel. We may wish to show this distinction in our domain model for the student records system, particularly if some of the courses are restricted to undergraduate students and others to graduate students.

The higher-level concept may be referred to as a **_generalization_** (or **_supertype_**) and the lower-level concepts as **_specializations_** (or **_subtypes_**). The subtypes are specializa-

FIGURE 5.18   Example of container and contents (aggregation)

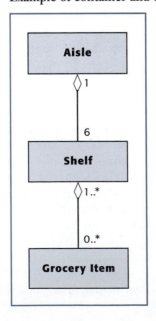

FIGURE 5.19   Example of a generalization-specialization hierarchy

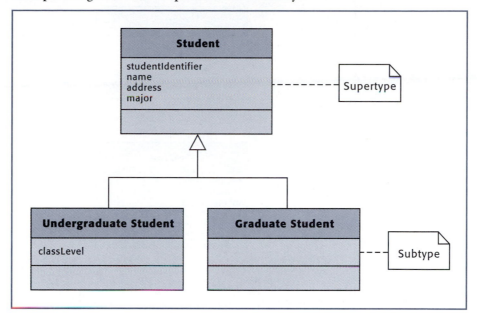

tions or refinements of the supertype. In interpreting a hierarchy, we sometimes relate a subtype to its supertype with words such as "is a," "is a kind of," and "is a type of."

A generalization-specialization hierarchy is depicted in a domain model shown in Figure 5.19. The subtypes and supertype are connected with an arrow. An open triangular arrowhead appears at the end next to the supertype. This connection is not usually named on the diagram but may be read as Graduate Student "is a" Student, or Graduate Student "is a kind of" Student, or Student "is either an" Undergraduate Student or Graduate Student.

The ability to use the words "is a" and "is a kind of" is a test for whether we have a generalization-specialization hierarchy. Can we say that a Graduate Student is a Student? If so, then we have found a generalization-specialization hierarchy. It also helps us determine which is the supertype and which is the subtype. If we can say, "Every graduate student is a student," Graduate Student is the subtype. If we cannot say, "Every student is a graduate student," Student is the supertype.

Every instance of a subtype must also be an instance of its supertype. Thus, every instance of the concept Graduate Student is also an instance of the concept Student. If this condition is *not* true of the relationship between two concepts, then the relationship is *not* that of generalization and specialization.

The generalization-specialization hierarchy permits some of the attributes to differ from one subtype to another. For example, in Figure 5.19, note that Undergraduate Student has the attribute classLevel, which does not also belong to Graduate Student. By convention, the shared attributes are shown only in the supertype, and the distinct attributes appear in the subtypes.

A second example of a generalization-specialization hierarchy is that of a Course and its Sections. (See Figure 5.20.) A Section could be a Lecture Section or a Laboratory Section. The laboratory section could have an extra fee as an attribute, while the regular section does not. Note again that the course has attributes such as number, title, and number of units. A regular section has attributes of number, meeting time, meeting place, and maximum number of students. A laboratory section has attributes of number, meeting time, meeting place, maximum number of students, and fee. The distinctive attribute is the fee. Applying the "is-a" test above, one notes that every section is also a course, but every course is not also a section.

FIGURE 5.20   Another example of a generalization-specialization hierarchy

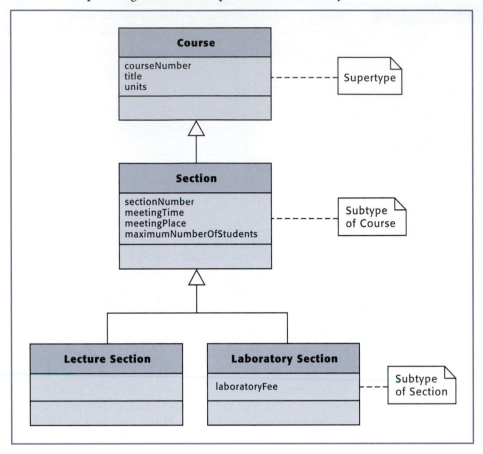

The Course/Section example cannot be modeled as a whole-to-part association. A course does not contain sections. A section is not a part of a course. A student who has taken a section of a course has completed the entire course. He or she does not have to enroll in other sections in order to obtain full credit.

GENERALIZATION VERSUS AGGREGATION

Beginning students of object-oriented systems analysis often fail to grasp the important distinction between subtype-supertype hierarchies and aggregations. Rumbaugh comments on the differences:

> Aggregation is not the same thing as generalization. Aggregation relates *instances*. Two distinct [instances] are involved: one of them is part of the other. Generalization relates [concepts] and is a way of structuring the description of a single [instance]. Both [supertype] and [subtype] refer to properties of a single [instance]. With generalization, an [instance] is simultaneously an instance of the [supertype] and an instance of the [subtype]. Confusion arises because both aggregation and generalization give rise to trees. . . .[5]

---

[5]James Rumbaugh, Michael Blaha, William Premerlani, Frederick Eddy, and William Lorensen, *Object-Oriented Modeling and Design* (Englewood Cliffs, N.J.: Prentice-Hall, 1991), 58. Emphasis added and terms changed to be consistent with the vocabulary of this chapter.

This confusion can be avoided by asking these questions: "Is this instance of a concept a part of the instance of the other concept?" and "Is an instance of this concept also an instance of the other concept?" An engine is a part of an automobile, but an engine is not a kind of automobile — hence we have aggregation. An advisor and a member are affiliated with a student club, but neither the advisor nor any of the members is a student club — also aggregation. However, a professor is a university employee, and a convertible is a kind of car — each is an example of a generalization-specialization hierarchy.

ASSOCIATION CONCEPTS

Suppose we wish to include a student's grade in the Public University domain model. To do so, we must determine the concept to which the grade belongs. But of which concept is grade an attribute? A grade is assigned to a particular student in a particular class. It cannot be an attribute of Student alone because it is also dependent on Section. Nor can it be an attribute of Section alone because it is also dependent on Student. It is really related to the association Enrolled In, in which both Student and Section participate. However, our domain modeling restrictions do not allow us to make the grade an attribute of any association. The solution is to create a new concept, Enrollment, which is allowed to have the attribute grade, as shown in Figure 5.21. Note that it takes Student.identifier together with Section.number to specify an instance of the concept Enrollment.

Such a concept is called an ***association concept*** because it corresponds to an association between other concepts. In the UML, an association concept may be represented as a rectangle connected to the association by a dashed line, as shown in Figure 5.21. Note also that the existence of a specific instance of an association concept requires a corresponding instance of the association between the concepts.

Identifying and adding associations and generalization-specialization hierarchies to the domain model may be considered as Step 5c of the procedure for object-oriented systems analysis.

| FIGURE 5.21 | **Association of the Enrollment concept to the Student and Section concepts** |

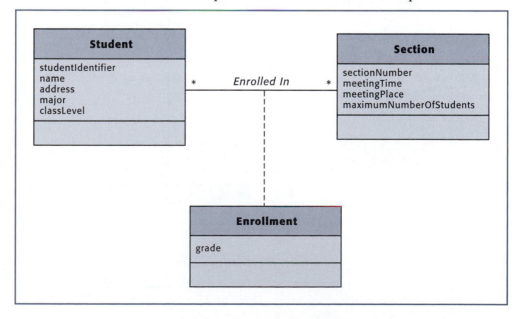

THE DOMAIN MODEL FOR THE PUBLIC UNIVERSITY REGISTRATION SYSTEM

We will now produce the domain model for the Public University registration system, generating it one event or use case at a time.

EVENT 1. DEPARTMENT SUBMITS ITS CLASS SCHEDULE.
(USE CASE: SUBMIT DEPARTMENT CLASS SCHEDULE)

This event involves the concepts Department, Department Class Schedule, Course, Section, and Professor as well as the associations among them. The Department Class Schedule concept is nothing more that a heading for the schedule with term and year and a body containing multiple listings of sections. The association is modeled as a composition, as the Department Class Schedule does not exist without the Sections. The department class schedule also lists the name of the professor who teaches each section, so we must add a Professor concept and associate it with Section. As discussed above, Section is a subtype of Course in a generalization-specialization hierarchy.

Figure 5.22 presents the domain model for the part of the problem domain affected by Event 1.

EVENT 2. TIME TO PRODUCE UNIVERSITY CLASS SCHEDULE.
(USE CASE: PRODUCE UNIVERSITY CLASS SCHEDULE)

Since the University Class Schedule is made up of all the Department Class Schedules, no new concepts are required.

FIGURE 5.22   Domain model for the problem domain affected by Event 1

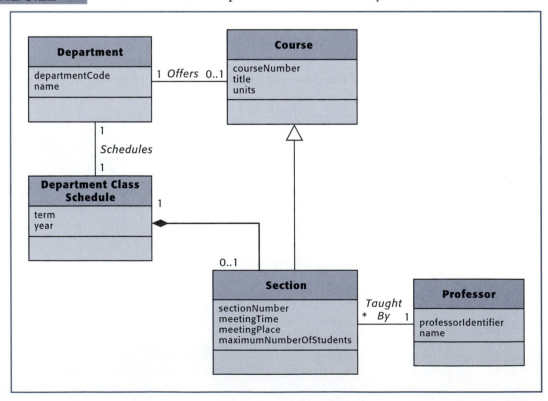

FIGURE 5.23   Domain model for the Public University Registration System

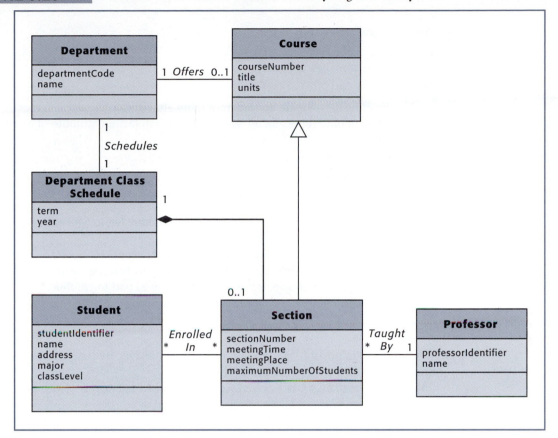

EVENT 3. STUDENT REGISTERS FOR CLASSES.
(USE CASE: REGISTER FOR CLASSES)

Registration creates an instance of an Enrolled In association between a student and a section. After adding Student and Enrolled In, the domain model looks like Figure 5.23.

EVENT 4. TIME TO PRODUCE CLASS ROSTER.
(USE CASE: PRODUCE CLASS ROSTER)

The class roster contains no new information. It can be produced from the domain model as it stands. Thus, Figure 5.23 presents the completed domain model for the Public University Registration System, the result of Steps 5a, 5b, and 5c.

CHECKING THE DOMAIN MODEL

As the domain model is developed, it is important to check it for completeness, correctness, and consistency. Figure 5.24 contains a checklist for this purpose.

CONTRACTS

The **system sequence diagrams** produced in Chapter 4 show the messages from the initiating actor to the system. Associated with each of the messages is a system operation. Writing contracts for system operations is the final step in object-oriented systems

FIGURE 5.24   Checklist for domain models

For each concept:

> Is the concept name unique?
> Are all the attributes defined?

For each attribute:

> Can the attribute value be derived from other attributes in the domain model?
> Does the attribute represent an association (Is it in fact an attribute of another concept)?

For each association:

> Is the association name unique?
> Is the multiplicity (one-to-one, one-to-many, many-to-many) shown on the domain model correct?
> Does the association name make sense when read from left to right or top to bottom?
> Is every subtype instance also an instance of its supertype?
> Is the generalization arrow next to the supertype concept?
> Is the multiplicity of the whole concept in every aggregation specified?
> If any aggregation is shown, is the association that of part to whole?
> Is the aggregation diamond next to the whole concept?

analysis and makes possible the transition to system design. In design, we will define the interactions of software objects within the system.

Writing a contract for each system operation is Step 6 of the procedure for object-oriented systems analysis.

A system operation contract describes **what** the system must do internally to respond to the message from the actor. Because the contract does not say **how** the system will do this, it is still a statement of requirements and thus part of analysis.

Contracts are the basis for an important approach to object-oriented design known as *design by contract*, an approach articulated by Bertrand Meyer.[6] A *contract* is a description of a behavior which a system component (in our case, a system operation) commits itself to carry out.[7] It emphasizes what will be accomplished rather than how it will be accomplished. A contract may be written for an individual operation of a software unit or for a system-level operation.

A contract is an agreement between the sender of a message and the receiver of the message. The metaphor of the contract implies that

1. If the sender of the message can guarantee that the precondition is true, then the target operation will guarantee that the postcondition will be true after execution.
2. If, on the other hand, the sender of this message cannot guarantee that the precondition is true, then the whole deal is off: The operation is neither obliged to execute nor to guarantee the postcondition.[8]

Contracts are commonly written in terms of pre- and postconditions. A *precondition* is a condition which must be true before an operation begins. A *postcondition* is a condition which must be true after the execution of the operation has finished.

---

[6]Bertrand Meyer, *Object-Oriented Software Construction* (Englewood Cliffs, N. J.: Prentice-Hall, 1988).
[7]Rebecca Wirfs-Brock and Alan McKean, *Object Design: Roles, Responsibilities, and Collaborations* (Boston: Addison-Wesley, 2003), 308–310.
[8]Meilir Page-Jones, *Fundamentals of Object-Oriented Design in UML* (Reading, Mass.: Addison-Wesley, 2000), 270.

FIGURE 5.25   Components of a contract

Contract	
Name:	Operation name and parameters.
Responsibilities:	A brief description of the responsibilities this operation must fulfill.
Type:	Indicates whether this is a system operation or other operation.
Exceptions:	Departures from the typical flow of events and what to do when they occur.
Output:	Messages sent to **external** systems (not to the user interface).
Preconditions:	Assumed state of the system before the operation is executed.
Postconditions:	State of the system after the operation has been executed.

We will write pre- and postconditions in terms of the effect a behavior or operation has on the state of the system, as expressed in the domain model.

SYSTEM OPERATIONS AND SYSTEM OPERATION CONTRACTS

A *system operation* is an operation which the system carries out in response to a system input. The system input and the corresponding system operation have the same name.

A system operation contract describes the changes in the state of the overall system when a system operation is carried out. Figure 5.25 defines some of the components of a contract. Other components may be added to the contract as helpful. Figure 5.26 presents an example of the contract for the **requestSection** system operation.

CREATING SYSTEM OPERATION CONTRACTS

To create contracts for the system operations in a system sequence diagram:

▌ Identify each system operation in the diagram.
▌ Following the format of Figure 5.25, name the contract and write the responsibilities of the contract. Figure 4.23 is repeated here as Figure 5.26. It is used to

FIGURE 5.26   System sequence diagram for the Register for Classes use case

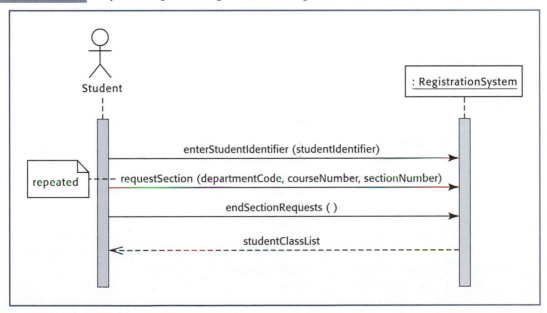

FIGURE 5.27   Contract for the requestSection system operation

Contract	
Name:	**requestSection**
	(departmentCode, courseNumber, sectionNumber)
Responsibilities:	Enroll the Student in the Section.
Type:	System
Exceptions:	If the combination of department code, course number and section number is not valid, indicate that it was an error.
	If no seats are available, inform the Student.
Output:	
Preconditions:	Department and Section are known to the system.
Postconditions:	A new instance of the Enrolled In association was created, linking the Student and the Section.

identify the system operations requiring contracts. The primary system operation is **requestSection**. However, there are two other system operations supporting this primary one. First, the student's identifier must be identified, and second, the handling of more than one request must be addressed.

▌ Write the postconditions, describing the **required changes to concepts in the domain model**.

To discover the postconditions for a system operation, first, isolate the portion of the domain model which is affected by this system operation. Then ask these questions:

What instances of which concepts must be created or deleted?

Which attributes have their values modified? To what new values?

Which instances of associations between concepts must be added or deleted?

Use the past tense and the passive voice for postconditions to emphasize the result of the operation instead of how the results were achieved.

▌ Add the preconditions and exceptions.

These check to see that the input is valid in the context of this system operation and the use case in which it appears.

Figures 5.27, 5.28, and 5.29 show the contracts for the **requestSection**, **enterStudentIdentifier** and **endSectionRequests** system operations. The remaining system operation contracts for the Public University Registration System are left as exercises.

FIGURE 5.28   Contract for the enterStudentIdentifier system operation

Contract	
Name:	**enterStudentIdentifier**
	(studentIdentifier)
Responsibilities:	Accept and validate the Student's identifier.
	Verify that the Student is eligible to register.
Type:	System
Exceptions:	If the student identifier is not valid, indicate that it was an error.
	If the Student is not eligible to register, inform the Student.
Preconditions:	Student is known to the system.
Postconditions:	None

FIGURE 5.29   **Contract for the endSectionRequests system operation**

> Contract
> Name: **endSectionRequests( )**
> Responsibilities: Produce the student class list.
> Type: System
> Exceptions: If a student registration was not under way, indicate an error.

SUMMARY

A domain model describes concepts in the problem domain with their attributes and associations. A concept refers to a person, a thing, or an idea. An attribute is a named characteristic of a concept which may have a value. An association indicates a significant connection between problem-domain concepts.

There are two main strategies for identifying concepts. One is to look for nouns and noun phrases describing the problem domain. The other is to use a checklist of concept categories. Include a concept in the domain model when the system needs to store data about the concept in order to respond to a future event.

There are two perspectives of a concept. One is abstract — it names the concept and enumerates its attributes. The other is concrete — it assigns a specific value to each attribute to distinguish an instance of the concept.

Looking for noun phrases in descriptions of the problem domain usually yields attribute names as well as concept names. This is one strategy for finding attributes of concepts. Another strategy for finding attributes is to look at the data contained in each system input and output.

Include an attribute in a domain model when the system needs to remember the value of the attribute in order to respond to an event. Do not use an attribute to record a connection between concepts; use an association instead. Do not include an attribute if it can be derived or calculated from other attributes in the model.

Just as we have instances of concepts, we have instances of associations. The multiplicity of an association defines how many instances of one concept can be associated with one instance of another concept.

Whole-to-part associations are found in many problem domains. Three common kinds of whole-to-part associations are assemblies of parts, members of groups, and containers and their contents.

There are two types of whole-to-part associations — aggregation and composition. They are modeled with a diamond at the whole end of the association. The diamond is open to indicate aggregation and black to show composition. Composition is a more restrictive association than aggregation. These associations are usually not labeled.

Include an association in a domain model when the system needs to remember the association in order to respond to an event. Show associations explicitly instead of using an attribute to imply the association.

A generalization-specialization hierarchy relates a more specialized concept (a subtype) to a more general concept (a supertype). Every instance of a subtype must also be an instance of its supertype

An association concept is a concept which corresponds to an association between other concepts.

After the domain model is complete, the next step is to produce a set of system operation contracts — one for each system operation. A system operation is an operation which the system carries out in response to a system input. There is one system operation for each system input message. The system input and the corresponding system operation have the same name.

A contract is a description of a behavior which a system component commits itself to carry out. It emphasizes what will be accomplished rather than how it will be accomplished. A system operation contract describes the changes in the state of the domain model when a system operation is carried out. It is written in terms of preconditions and postconditions.

KEY TERMS

aggregation *141*

association *131*

association concept *147*

attribute *130*

composition *142*

concept *130*

contract *150*

domain model *130*

generalization *144*

instance of an association *136*

multiplicity *131*

postcondition *150*

precondition *150*

specialization *144*

subtype *144*

supertype *144*

system operation *150*

system sequence diagram *149*

REVIEW QUESTIONS

5-1. What are the components of a domain model?

5-2. What are the two main strategies for finding concepts?

5-3. What is the principal reason for including a concept in the domain model?

5-4. If two concepts have attributes with the same name, how are the attributes distinguished from each other?

5-5. What is the difference between a concept and an instance of a concept?

5-6. State two strategies for finding attributes.

5-7. What is the principal reason for including an attribute in the domain model?

5-8. When should an attribute not be included in a domain model?

5-9. Explain the relationship between a subtype and its supertype.

5-10. Name three common categories of aggregation.

5-11. In general, what kinds of changes to a domain model can result from the execution of a system operation?

EXERCISES AND DISCUSSION QUESTIONS

5-1. In Figure 5.19, how many attributes does Graduate Student have? How many does Undergraduate Student have?

5-2. What is the difference between a system input (as shown in a system sequence diagram) and a system operation? Why do system inputs and system operations have the same names?

5-3. Write a system operation contract for each operation shown in the diagram you prepared for Exercise 4–3.

5-4. Modify the domain model for the Public University Registration System to accommodate the new events discussed in Exercise 3–10.

5-5. Write a system operation contract for each system operation shown in the diagrams you prepared for Exercise 4–5.

5-6. Draw a domain model for the use case Check Out Library Book, shown in Figures 4.10 and 4.11. Write a system operation contract for each operation shown in the system sequence diagram you prepared for Exercise 4–6.

5-7. Consider the four systems included in Exercises 3–11 and 3–14 — a restaurant, a library, a video rental store, and a hotel. Draw a domain model for one or more of these systems. Write system operation contracts for at least three use cases for each of the systems for which you prepared a domain model.

CASE STUDIES FOR PROJECT ASSIGNMENTS

Assignments

1. List all the concepts involved in the Giant Forest Inn system.

2. Draw a domain model for the Inn using the above concepts.

3. Write a contract for each system operation.

Assignments

1. List all the concepts involved in the Apache Rent A Car system.

2. Draw a domain model for the car rental company using the above concepts.

3. Write a contract for each system operation.

PART THREE

OBJECT-ORIENTED SYSTEM DESIGN

Part II of this book presented the models and techniques used in object-oriented systems analysis. In analysis, we specified users' requirements for a new system. We began by identifying business events and use cases and then producing descriptions of the typical flow of events for use cases initiated by an actor. We also produced a model of the significant concepts in the problem domain — comprising these concepts, their attributes, and their relationships. Then we defined more precisely the messages from actors which would initiate the execution of system operations. Finally, we wrote contracts for these system operations, the results of which were expressed as postconditions describing changes to the domain model.

Part III covers object-oriented system design. First, it provides an overview of system design in general as well as of the information system design process. Chapter 6 discusses fundamental concepts and principles common to all design disciplines. Chapter 7 states the goals of information system design and surveys the components used to implement an information processing system. It relates the activities of system design to the information system development process and examines the roles and skills of a system designer. It also introduces a three-tier version of layered system architecture and presents system design as comprising three subproblems — program design, user interface design, and database design.

Chapters 8 and 9 address object-oriented program design. Chapter 8 discusses critical characteristics of software objects and introduces basic design patterns used to appropriately assign responsibilities to objects. It then presents interaction diagrams — sequence diagrams and collaboration diagrams — and the essential UML conventions required to read, understand, and develop them. Chapter 9 discusses design class diagrams and concludes by addressing techniques for specifying methods.

Chapter 10 deals with issues regarding the interface between object-oriented software and object-oriented or relational databases. Design of the data base itself is outside the scope of this book.

Chapters 11 and 12 are concerned with designing the user interface — the form and structure of the messages crossing the automation boundary. We stress a basic approach and fundamental principles which can be expected to endure when devices and details change. We encourage the designer to take a broad perspective rather than being

OBJECT-ORIENTED
SYSTEM DESIGN

immediately constrained by what is familiar. Chapter 11 provides the context for user interface design, summarizes important design principles and guidelines, and applies these principles to the design of reports and displays. Chapter 12 presents state transition diagrams for modeling the interaction between user and computer. It also addresses the connection between the user interface and the application layer.

6 INTRODUCTION TO SYSTEM DESIGN

INTRODUCTION

Design is a human activity which operates in a variety of domains, including computer information systems. Designs vary from creations which are almost purely aesthetic in their aims to very practical systems in the disciplines of applied science and engineering.

The design of computer information systems is a process of inventing a solution which fulfills users' requirements for an information processing system. It involves an understanding of how information systems are structured as well as how these structures can be actualized through hardware and software to meet users' needs. Yet information system designers share many concerns with designers of other useful systems and objects, such as buildings, automobiles, advertising materials, or educational curricula. All of them need to transform users' requirements into a specification of a buildable solution. They must capture the requirements, state the design problem, develop a method for solving the problem, describe a solution which can be made real, and evaluate alternative solutions.

Information system designers are not the only professionals to face these issues — certainly, they are not the first. They have much to learn, if they will, from the experience of those in other design disciplines throughout human history.

The specific decisions to be made by designers in different disciplines vary with the domain, and the criteria used in decision making depend on the aims of the designers. Yet the process of design can be understood at a general level — independently of the specific domain in which it operates.

To establish a context for understanding information system design, this chapter provides an introductory overview of system design in general. It discusses fundamental concepts and principles common to all design disciplines. Thus, many of the examples in this chapter are intentionally drawn from other systems. Chapter 7 will apply some of these principles to the design of computer information systems.

This chapter looks at the nature of design from a variety of perspectives, leading to a definition of design. It then examines why we design instead of trying to construct a solution directly from the requirements. It describes the roles and goals of a design method and presents several strategies for generating a design solution as well as strategies for simplifying the decision process. It addresses ways of evaluating alternative designs and of terminating the search for more alternatives. It also introduces the use of patterns as a technique. It concludes with a brief discussion of the important place of models in design.

LEARNING OBJECTIVES

After mastering the material in this chapter, you will be able to

- Identify similarities in the concerns of all designers regardless of their specific discipline.
- Summarize some differing perspectives on the nature of design.
- Explain how design differs from requirements analysis and construction.
- Give some reasons for design.
- Define design as used in this book.
- Discuss why it is important to have a design method when developing systems.
- Name and explain some strategies for generating design solutions, simplifying design decisions, evluating designs, and terminating the search for alternatives.
- Discuss the purpose of design models and the principal categories of design models.

THE THEORY AND CONTEXT OF DESIGN

Humans have an amazing capacity for inventiveness. Early humans showed their creative ability by making cave paintings and bone tools. Today we design the intricate microtechnology of computer components and create genetically engineered pharmaceuticals. The Industrial Revolution brought new technology and unprecedented problems to civilization, and with them the need for a new self-awareness in the design process. Over the past several decades, developers of general systems theory and of design theory have illuminated our understanding of the interrelated activities of design, problem solving, and decision making.

This section, based on current views, considers design in general, without regard for the specific domain in which the designer works.

WHAT IS DESIGN?

Design is a complex and multifaceted activity involving a variety of skills. Although our understanding of it has increased in recent years, there is still much to be learned.

Design as Innovation and Creativity

One of the most common notions of design is that it requires innovation or creativity. This perspective stresses the intuitive in design, in contrast to the systematic, and tends to highlight and recognize the contributions of individuals rather than groups. This familiar way of thinking about design is valid, yet incomplete. Design has other important facets as well.

Design as Concerned with the Artificial

According to Herbert A. Simon, winner of the 1978 Nobel Prize for Economics:

> Design . . . is concerned with how things ought to be, with devising artifacts to attain goals.[1]

An *artifact* is something that does not occur in nature.[2] It has been created by human beings to serve human purposes. Thus, design is a quintessentially human activity. The story of civilization is to a large extent the story of the creation of artifacts and of the purposes leading to and fulfilled by those artifacts. From this perspective, an artifact is not simply an object; it may also be any kind of system, including the social, political, and economic structures by which our common life is organized and maintained.

Design as a Source of Change

New artifacts are needed because our existing world is unsatisfactory in some respect. As William Newman states:

> We design in order to produce a change in the environment. The typical design exercise begins when someone decides that things are not as satisfactory as they could be. He or she realizes that a particular technology can be configured to bring about an improvement. With this as a starting point a design exercise is undertaken: the chosen technology is gradually refined into a precise specification of a solution to the problem.

---

[1] Herbert A. Simon, *The Sciences of the Artificial*, 2nd ed (Cambridge: MIT Press, 1981), 133.
[2] This is a more general definition of an artifact than that of a work product of the development process.

Suppose, for example, we decide that the layout of furniture in our office is unsatisfactory. The filing cabinet by the door gets in the way of people entering and leaving, and there is no room for more than two people to sit and have a meeting; also, the view from the window is mostly blocked by a cupboard. To solve these problems, we must design a new layout. We may decide to work with existing furniture, looking for ways to improve access and increase seating space; or we may decide to replace the furniture with something new and more compact. Whatever we do, our aim is to change the office. The choice of technology — old furniture or new — has a strong bearing on the final design and on the degree of change brought about.

This view of design as an activity aimed at producing change owes much to Herbert Simon, who has described it in some detail in his book *The Sciences of the Artificial*. Simon makes the fundamental points that, when we design,

1. There is an *inner environment*, or technology, that we select as a means of bringing about change.
2. There is an *outer environment* in which the change is to be produced.
3. The inner environment operates on the outer environment across an *interface* that protects the latter from the complexities of the former.[3]

Design as Problem Solving

Design is often regarded as a problem-solving activity. It is initiated by the statement of a problem. A complete problem statement incorporates a set of tests used to determine whether a solution has been found.

Each of these tests is a question or condition with a binary answer: true or false. It is known as a *constraint*. A tentative solution which satisfies all the constraints is said to be *feasible*. If a single constraint is violated, the tentative solution is *infeasible*. If the constraints are inconsistent, a solution is impossible, and the problem is said to be *overconstrained*. If there are few constraints, the designer is left with many possibilities to consider.

It is customary to classify constraints into four broad groups: economic, technological, political (organizational), and sociological (cultural). Economic constraints deal with the resources consumed by the designs — money, time, materials, labor, and other human or natural resources. Technological constraints deal with the means by which the design is constructed or realized. Political constraints are concerned with power relationships, the legal environment, and organizational factors. Cultural constraints incorporate societal values and concerns.

For the design process to result in a useful artifact, the constraints contained in the problem statement must be related to the users' requirements. The objectives of the object or system are also made as explicit as possible to help evaluate alternative solutions. The design process ends when an acceptable solution to the problem has been found.

Design as Decision Making

Design may also be regarded as a decision-making process. From a systems perspective, a solution is a system with components and a structure. Thus, a designer must decide what the structure will be as well as what components will form that structure. Ultimately, each detail is the result of a design decision, whether it has been selected from available components or newly created.

Design decisions, like decisions in general, are usually improved if several alternatives are compared and the best selected. To compare feasible solutions, a designer uses *criteria* which are related to and derived from the purposes or objectives for

---

[3]William M. Newman, *Designing Integrated Systems for the Office Environment* (New York: McGraw-Hill, 1987), 6–7.

which the problem is being solved or the decisions made. To apply these criteria to the alternatives, the designer must develop explicit performance measures as well as overall measures of the relative desirability of each alternative.

Design as Modeling

Designers often model an artifact or system. Some *models* — such as three-dimensional scale models — are physical. Others — such as two-dimensional diagrams or sketches — are graphic. Mathematical models also play an important role, especially in the design of complex systems.

The significant role of modeling in design is implied by the etymology of the word itself. The verb "design" is derived from the Latin verb *designare*, with the roots *de* (down) + *signare* (to sign or mark) — to mark out or make a sign. Thus, the verb came to mean to draw or sketch, and the related noun to denote a drawing or sketch. A drawing is a relatively easy way of recording and visualizing a possible solution. Before the development of algebra, even mathematical models were likely to be geometric and constructed graphically.

Charles Eastman stresses the importance of modeling in commenting on his definition of *design*:

> "Design is the specification of an artifact that both achieves desired performances and is realizable with high degrees of confidence." Design involves both prediction of future performances with its attendant uncertainties and requires knowledge of technology and production so as to guarantee realization of the specified artifact.
>
> . . . I will distinguish between a performance model, that projects from some limited description of the artifact to its performances (such as a beam's bending moment, a circuit's delay , or the flow capacity of a piping system), as distinct from a specification that is an attribute description of the artifact being designed. While the purpose of models in design is to predict the performances of an artifact and to guide the selection of attributes that will achieve them, the purpose of the specification is to relate the individual attributes together so as to guarantee that they are realizable, e.g., are not logically contradictory and can be associated with available materials and components. Thus models and specifications correspond to the two kinds of criteria applied to design: performance and realizability.[4]

Every model is an abstraction from reality — a selection of characteristics of the artifact which are relevant to the decisions the designer must make and which depend on the designer's goals. Graphical or physical means of displaying a model are called *representations*. Sometimes a model may be represented in more than one way.

Design models are discussed further later in this chapter.

Design as Planning

Design models serve as an aid to planning for the artifacts being devised. Performance models estimate or predict the future behavior of the artifact, allowing the designer to anticipate how the artifact will function. A design specification facilitates the artifact's construction by becoming the basis for detailed planning of construction activities as well as their sequence and resource requirements.

Design as Learning

The activity of designing usually turns out to be an occasion for learning. A design problem is rarely exactly like one the designers have solved before. The greater the

---

[4]Charles M. Eastman, *Recent Developments in Representation in the Science of Design*, Institute of Building Sciences Research Report no. 17 (Pittsburgh: Department of Architecture, Carnegie-Mellon University, April 1981), 1.

CHAPTER SIX | INTRODUCTION TO SYSTEM DESIGN

differences from the designers' previous experience are, the more applicable is, Jones's remark: "If we'd known at the start what we've learnt while designing it, we'd never have done it like this."[5]

Failures during the design process and failures of the completed artifact are the source of valuable, though sometimes painful, lessons.

> Because man is fallible, so are his constructions. . . . [T]he history of engineering . . . may be told in its failures as well as in its triumphs. Success may be grand, but disappointment can often teach us more.[6]

Design as an Intermediary Between Requirements and Construction

The process of design stands as an intermediate step between a statement of requirements and construction of the artifact. When the design is completed, designers are confident that the design problem has been solved and the users' requirements satisfied. Usually, alternatives have been compared so that the best design decisions possible under the circumstances have been made. Yet the product of design is not the new artifact itself; it is only a description of what is to be constructed. Although the artifact or system has not yet been realized, its construction is known to be feasible and, as mentioned above, the description resulting from design is an adequate basis for constructing it.

A DEFINITION OF DESIGN — PROCESS AND PRODUCT

As a consequence of the above discussion, we define design as follows:

Design is a process which creates descriptions of a newly devised artifact. The product of the design process is a description which is sufficiently complete and detailed to assure that the artifact can be built.

We use the word "design" to refer to both the process and the description(s) it produces.

WHY DESIGN?

The preceding discussion of the nature of design has implied why we design — why we engage in producing mere descriptions of not-as-yet-existent artifacts. It may be worthwhile to make explicit some of these reasons.

Designers plan, sketch, model, evaluate, and compare proposed solutions because

- *The desired artifact or system does not exist.* Thus, it must be devised. The primary motivation for design is an unsatisfied need. Satisfying the need is the underlying purpose of design. From the designer's perspective, stating the problem completely, clearly, and accurately is an essential prerequisite, but merely formulating requirements does not satisfy them. At the end of the design process, the solution has been found, even though it must still be realized in order to meet the need.

  In many cases, the desired artifact or system is not entirely new; rather, what already exists must be improved or modified.

- *People cannot wait for gradual evolution.* Traditionally, the creation of new artifacts has been a slow, evolutionary response to slowly changing human needs. Traditional solutions to human needs were handed down from generation to generation. Because the pace of change was slow, artifacts could slowly

[5]J. Christopher Jones, *Essays in Design* (Chichester, England: John Wiley & Sons, 1984), 207.
[6]Henry Petroski, *To Engineer Is Human: The Role of Failure in Successful Design* (New York: St. Martin's Press, 1985), 9.

adapt to changed requirements and changing technology. First, the Industrial Revolution and, more recently, the Computer Revolution produced drastic shifts in technology and dramatically accelerated the rate of change. Entirely new systems of industrial production, transportation, communication, and energy production were developed. The new artifacts associated with these new systems were largely without historical precedent. There was no time for gradual evolution — and no traditional cultural basis for it. Design had to become a self-conscious, explicit process.[7]

■ *Complex systems require multidisciplinary teams and explicit, shared design processes.* At the same time, the size and complexity of human artifacts have increased significantly. Airplanes, hospitals, and application software, for example, require the knowledge and skills of multiple disciplines; their details exceed the expertise of any one person. Moreover, it would take one person too long to design these system alone. As a result, invention has become a deliberate human enterprise, and design is now an activity consciously pursued and a process explicitly taught. This means that the design process itself is also consciously designed.[8]

■ *It is risky and expensive to construct without a plan.* Why not proceed directly from a perceived need or statement of requirements to the construction of an artifact? We feel intuitively that even building an object directly entails a conceptual model or image of what will be constructed — an implicit plan. In all but the simplest cases, there are too many things that can go wrong without an explicit plan. Such a plan reduces the risk that the desired artifact will fail to fulfill its purpose or will have serious defects. It is better to plan ahead than to "build one to throw away."

■ *There is an opportunity to model and predict performance.* Design models permit the behavior of the future artifact or system to be estimated or predicted. Changes to the model allow designers to understand the impact of changes in the design on system performance. This insight is a valuable contribution of the design process.

■ *Alternatives can be compared in order to select the best.* During design, a variety of alternatives can be described, modeled, and compared. Otherwise, the only way to compare alternatives is to build them and measure their performance. This approach requires realizing multiple solutions to a problem.

■ *It is less expensive to test, predict, and evaluate during design than after construction.* It is usually cheaper and faster to build a model than to construct an artifact or system itself. Models are easier to manipulate and modify than what they model; they have been deliberately simplified to focus on significant attributes and relationships. It is easier to move lines on a floor plan than to shift a wall in a completed building. In modeling, time and distance can be compressed. Multiple sets of operating and environmental conditions can be simulated. Models can be subjected to extreme conditions which are impossible or prohibitively expensive to achieve in reality. Even if a model must be destroyed to test it, destroying the real system is likely to be even costlier.

■ *The cost of detecting and correcting errors increases as the process of creating an artifact unfolds.* To the extent that models of an artifact become more complex as the process moves from conception to completion, detecting problems also becomes more complex. If portions of the artifact have to be redesigned or rebuilt, the direct cost of doing so is incurred twice or more. In addition, there is the cost of managing the change process.

---

[7]Christopher Alexander, *Notes on the Synthesis of Form* (Cambridge: Harvard University Press, 1964).
[8]Jones, *Essays in Design*, 136 *ff*.

GOALS OF DESIGN

Designers strive to accomplish a variety of goals during design. Some of these goals are those of the users of the artifacts. Others are objectives of the designers and are related to the activity of design.

The fundamental goals of design arise from the fact that designers are given a problem to solve.

Satisfaction of Requirements

One basic goal of design is to satisfy the requirements which define the problem and the constraints which define what is an acceptable solution. At the very least, this means providing effective, essential functionality.

Performance

Along with essential functionality, system requirements specify the acceptable levels of performance. Where possible, designers seek either to attain performance beyond the merely acceptable or to achieve the required performance with the greatest overall system efficiency.

Constructability

It must be feasible to construct the new artifact or system. Designers must ensure that the description they produce is sufficiently complete and detailed for construction. Architects and engineers make detailed construction drawings supplemented by extensive descriptions of the materials and techniques to be used in construction. Composers convert their musical sketches into a full score containing every note played by every instrument as well as indications of how the music is to be performed.

Efficient Design Process

Designers may have goals related to the design process itself, such as maximizing the efficiency of the process for the project at hand or for a series of projects.

Personal Preferences and Objectives

The design process may incorporate personal preferences of the designer among its objectives. What is perceived as a designer's style arises largely from design decisions based on these personal goals. In fashion design as well as in the fine arts, style may be an important factor in the selection of the designer and may have a major effect on the resulting artifact.

EMPHASES OF GOOD DESIGN

In achieving its goals, good design emphasizes the following:

▌ *A design whose structure fits the structure of the problem.* The architect Louis Sullivan's dictum that "form ever follows function"[9] is regarded by many as a requisite for good design. A correspondence between the structure of the design and that of the requirements models is important. Object-oriented design derives program structures from the models of the problem domain which express the system requirements. This approach helps achieve the desirable structural correspondence between problem and solution.

---

[9]Louis H. Sullivan, "The Tall Office Building Artistically Considered," in *Kindergarten Chats and Other Writings* (New York: George Wittenborn, 1947), 208. See also the two essays on "Function and Form," ibid, *42 ff.*

■ *A system which is easy to understand, modify, and maintain.* New information processing systems not only introduce change, but also must continue to change in response to users' needs and changes in the system's environment. Flexibility and ease of modification are an appropriate response to the fact of continuing change. People are relatively expensive resources; computer hardware is cheap. System structures which facilitate efficient development and future flexibility are preferred, even if the software requires more memory or other hardware and takes longer to execute.

■ *Models which use graphic representations.* Graphic models are the most effective means of communicating complex relationships to humans. The human eye receives a high volume of information at a rapid rate. It is also capable of fine discrimination. Visual information processing permits relationships to be grasped simultaneously rather than serially because they are presented in a spatial medium.

■ *Explicit criteria for refining and improving an initial design.* Currently, in comparison with designers in many other disciplines, information system designers lack an adequate repertory of models for many aspects of system performance. In this situation, it is important for the designer to have criteria to guide the refinement and improvement of an initial design.

DESIGN METHOD

A *method* is an organized procedure for accomplishing a task. It is formulated so that it can be taught and shared by groups of people. It may be general or focused on some particular class of tasks. It may incorporate specific models, techniques, processes, or subprocedures as well as specialized tools and training.

Thus, a *design method* is an organized procedure for carrying out the design process. It marshals the resources of participants in the process in order to achieve an effective result.

Design methods may be described in a three-level hierarchy. At the highest level are the concepts, principles, and strategies shared by all the design-oriented disciplines which devise artificial systems for human use. The middle level is concerned with what is common to a broad class of artifacts or systems. The third level deals with the characteristics of specific domains of application within the broader class. The discussion in this chapter begins with design concepts and continues to the domain of computer information systems.

Roles and Goals of a Design Method

Following are some important roles of a design method.[10]

Role 1. To provide a conceptual framework for understanding the design process and for communicating that understanding to the participants. This role often involves partitioning the design process into a sequence of steps.

Role 2. To guide the design process to a successful outcome for a single design project. The process, and therefore the guidance, has both a technical dimension and a management dimension. A method provides a set of models and techniques for carrying out the design process. These models support technical decisions about the system being designed as well as decisions for managing the design process. The technical and managerial models are coordinated with the overview of the process provided by

---

[10]These general roles apply (with appropriate modifications in references to the process) to nearly all methods. This section on design method is based in part on Lavette C. Teague, Jr., "Development Methods for Information Systems: Retrospective and Evaluation," *Sistemas de Informática*, no. 5, año I, October 1985 (paper presented at XVII Congresso Nacional de Informática, São Paulo, Brazil, September 26, 1985).

the conceptual framework. This coordination allows the conceptual and decision-oriented aspects of the process (and its supporting techniques) to reinforce each other. Nevertheless, any design method must be general enough to encompass a domain and thus must always be tailored to the circumstances and characteristics of each specific project.

Role 3. In some cases, to provide a strategy for selecting, sequencing, and coordinating multiple projects. The more specific goals of a design method adopt the overall goals of design and add goals related to the design process. They include the following:

> **Goal 1. An acceptable result.** What constitutes an acceptable result is stated by the constraints, notably those incorporating the users' requirements.
>
> **Goal 2. A product of adequate quality.** Minimum adequate quality is defined by the constraints; enhancements are associated with the criteria.
>
> **Goal 3. Specific steps or procedures which allocate appropriate models and techniques to the activities and decisions of the design process.** These steps in fact define or specify a design method concretely, as it guides a project to a successful outcome.
>
> **Goal 4. Well-defined roles and tasks for the participants in design — both technical and managerial.**
>
> **Goal 5. Compatibility of the design with the goals of the using organization.** This may occur within a more inclusive strategy at a higher level than that of the project.

A General Design Method

A general method for design is described below. As discussed earlier, it may also be regarded as a general problem-solving process.

> 1. *Define the objectives of the design.* Determine what purpose the solution will serve and what underlying needs it will fulfill.
> 2. *State the problem, defining its constraints.* Formulate the set of tests which will determine whether or not the problem has been solved and, at the same time, define precisely what is meant by a solution.
>   **Repeat until a solution is found:**
> 3. *Generate a tentative solution.*
> 4. *Test the tentative solution for feasibility.* Apply each constraint to see if the tentative solution in fact satisfies the entire set.

If the problem is overconstrained, it may be impossible to find a feasible solution. Or, after finding a solution to the problem as stated, the designer may find the solution undesirable. In either case, it may be necessary to restate the problem by modifying the objectives or constraints until there is a satisfactory solution.

PHASES OF DESIGN

Some methods for the design of complex systems organize the design process into a sequence of phases or steps. Usually there are two or three major phases with varying names, depending on the method. Each phase addresses certain design issues and the related design decisions. The description of the system increases in size and detail at each step.

A fairly common three-phase design process consists of conceptual, preliminary, and detailed design phases.

Conceptual Design

During *conceptual design*, the focus is on the overall system structure and the interrelationships of the major subsystems. Designers are concerned with the generic type of system and subsystems. The viewpoint is primarily qualitative, supplemented by quantitative analysis if there are concerns about feasibility. Conceptual design is sometimes called architectural design. In the Unified Process, described in Chapter 2, much of the conceptual design in this sense takes place during the Inception phase.

Preliminary Design

Preliminary design emphasizes feasibility. Major subsystems are defined and modeled in sufficient detail to permit designers to predict performance and feel confident that the design constraints are satisfied. In the Unified Process, preliminary design is mostly complete by the end of Elaboration.

Detailed Design

Detailed design (sometimes called final design) concentrates on constructability. Details of the artifact are described sufficiently for it to be built. In the Unified Process, detailed design is completed during the iterations of the Construction phase.

A two-phase design process combines conceptual and preliminary design, adopting either name or calling it general design.

STRATEGIES FOR GENERATING A DESIGN SOLUTION

Strategy, originally a military term,[11] refers to planning at the highest level within a domain. Thus, a strategy is a high-level or overall approach or plan for accomplishing some goal or objective. There are a number of strategies for generating a solution to a design problem. They include reuse of an existing design, modification of an existing design, synthesis, and direct design.

Reuse of an Existing Design

It is sometimes possible to solve a design problem by using an existing design. In principle, this strategy requires no design activity at all because a new artifact is not being devised. In practice, the design problem is solved with a minimum expenditure of resources. No one wants to "reinvent the wheel."

Modification of an Existing Design

More often, no existing design precisely satisfies the problem requirements. But with an existing solution as a starting point, some changes will lead to an acceptable design. This strategy takes an evolutionary approach.

Synthesis

Synthesis is a general design strategy which defines components and aggregates or assembles them into an appropriate structure. It is sometimes called **bottom-up design**.

One specialized approach to synthesis is the **morphological approach**.[12] It analyzes the structure of a possible design in order to identify the requisite components. All possible selections for each component are systematically combined with the available choices for the others. This strategy is usually impractical due to the resulting combinatorial explosion but may aid a designer's imagination when applied informally.

---

[11]From the Greek *strategos:* a general officer.
[12]From the Greek *morphe:* form or shape. See, for example, Thomas H. Athey, *Systematic Systems Approach: An Integrated Method for Solving Systems Problems* (Englewood Cliffs, N.J.: Prentice-Hall, 1982), 74–79, for a discussion of the morphological approach.

Direct Design

For some specialized design problems, notably in engineering domains, a design (or at least significant portions of it) may be generated directly by computation. Problems of this sort involve a system which is required to respond with a prescribed performance to one or more sets of demands. The designer's task is to determine an overall structure for the system and to proportion the components so as to achieve the required behavior.

For example, in designing a bridge, a structural engineer determines the type of truss or girder to use and must make the structure the right size to carry the weight of the bridge, the load from the traffic on the bridge, the force of high winds, and the movements induced by an earthquake. In conventional design, the engineer will specify the size of the structural elements and then analyze the structure to compute the forces, stresses, and deflections in the bridge under the specified loads.

In *direct design,* the procedure is inverted. The loads and performance are specified, and the required sizes of the structural components are calculated.

STRATEGIES FOR SIMPLIFYING DESIGN DECISIONS

The two strategies described below are among those used to simplify design decision making by establishing priorities for decisions, with the more important decisions made first. The early decisions create a context which makes subsequent decisions more effective.

Stepwise refinement is a **top-down** design strategy that focuses on system-level decisions first, leaving detailed decisions until later. This strategy is implicit in a design process organized into conceptual, preliminary, and detailed phases. Stepwise refinement also takes advantage of the fact that in many systems, the overall system structure has a greater effect on system performance than do the details of the component subsystems. Because of trade-offs, a design which combines optimized subsystems can result in worse overall performance than does a design in which optimization has occurred at the level of the system as a whole.

One way of thinking about stepwise refinement is that it moves from a situation in which most design decisions — those about details — are implicit to a situation in which most decisions have become explicit. The design specification is an explicit and nearly complete description of the system, but early in design those details are left implicit and imprecise. The designer depends on a knowledge of the design domain for confidence that neither performance nor realizability will be compromised by subsequent explicit decisions.

Another common strategy for coping with a complex design is to **partition the system at critical interfaces**, specifying precise standards for the interface.

A familiar example of such an interface is a grounded 110-volt electrical outlet with three holes — one round and two rectangular — and a compatible plug. A variety of different electrical devices (lamps, appliances, computers, etc.) may be connected to the power source at the outlet as long as they are designed to operate at 110 volts and do not overload the circuit. Standard lamp sockets allow bulbs of different styles and wattages to be interchangeable.

Consistent entrance requirements for different campuses in a state university system permit students to prepare for college at many secondary schools and know they will be qualified to attend any campus.

Computer programming languages specify the syntax for transfer of control and data between program units in a consistent way.

An *interface* partitions a design into *subsystems*. It specifies the form and content of the interaction among the subsystems. Thus, an interface constrains the interaction among subsystems. The use of an interface between two subsystems limits the effect of changes to one subsystem on the other. It permits a designer to hide the internal details of a subsystem from the rest of the system, permitting that subsystem to be viewed from the outside as a black box. Creating an interface of this sort is often called encapsulation.

By identifying critical interfaces first, designers isolate and attend to critical design decisions first. Well-chosen interfaces partially decouple the subsystems from one another and limit the impact of decisions within each subsystem.

STRATEGIES FOR EVALUATING DESIGNS

The need to compare alternative designs was mentioned earlier in this chapter. This section looks more closely at design criteria, some issues which arise from the use of multiple criteria, and the impact of comparative evaluation on the design process.

Design Criteria

A *design criterion* is a characteristic of a solution used to measure or evaluate its performance. It provides an explicit, objective measure of performance. A set of design criteria allows alternative solutions to be compared in consistent terms across a variety of performance characteristics.

It is customary to classify criteria as economic, technological, political (organizational), and sociological (cultural), just as is done with the constraints used in a feasibility analysis.

The Value of a Design and Utility Theory

In making design decisions, designers attempt to increase the value of a design beyond the minima required by the constraints — to enhance its advantages and diminish its disadvantages. How is it possible to assess the value of a design? And whose values are to be used? In practice, the dominant values are those of the decision makers — the designers and those who control the design process politically or economically. Responsible design decision making gives priority to the values of the users, with designers acting as surrogates for the users. A process which makes values explicit and objectively measurable furthers this aim.

Each design criterion states a value from which one or more measurements of desirability can be derived. In mathematical optimization problems, there is a single criterion (called the *objective function*) whose value is to be optimized. The objective function is expressed as a cost to be minimized or as some other value to be maximized.

More generally, there are multiple criteria; hence, there are a variety of measures of desirability. Usually, not all criteria are of equal importance. In addition, the various measurements for the different criteria are incommensurable. Thus, there needs to be a way of determining the relative desirability of the criteria, as well as a way of combining the different measures of value into an overall assessment of the entire design, so that alternatives can be readily but fairly compared.

These issues are dealt with by *utility theory*, which addresses the problem of making valid comparisons of alternatives where the criteria are multidimensional and incommensurable. Utility theory has limited value if designers expect it to lead directly to the best solution to the kinds of problems many of them face. On the other hand, the concepts of utility theory may provide a helpful framework for a systematic comparison and discussion of design alternatives. One application of utility theory to evaluation and decision making is presented by Thomas H. Athey in his *Systematic Systems Approach: An Integrated Method for Solving Systems Problems*.[13]

---

[13]Ibid.

DESIGN TRADE-OFFS

Whether seeking to achieve feasibility by satisfying minimum performance requirements or attempting to enhance the overall value of a design in terms of the criteria, designers frequently face **trade-offs**. Improving performance in one respect may degrade it in another.

For example, in designing a crystal goblet, thinner glass may result in a more elegant shape; it will probably also make the goblet more fragile. Using less metal in an automobile will reduce the weight and improve the gas mileage but may make the car easier to damage. A unitary body and frame will increase the strength for a given weight and reduce the rattles because there are no connections to come loose, but repairs are more expensive, since body panels cannot be unbolted for replacement. Vegetables bred for resistance to disease may have less flavor. In families, there is conflict among increased income and career advancement, time for child care, community service, and leisure activities with friends.

More generally, the quality of materials or construction, size of the system, performance, functionality, and construction cost are interdependent — often in rather complex ways. A designer cannot arbitrarily control all these aspects of a system simultaneously.

Figure 6.1 shows the broad aspects of a design which are involved in trade-offs made while reaching design decisions and reflected when assessing the costs and benefits of alternatives during the transition from analysis to design as well as during design. These aspects are functionality, technology, and performance.

Functionality

The functionality of the system is determined by the scope and complexity of the system — by the number of essential transformations and the complexity of each, as well as by the amount of essential information to be stored and transported. In general, both costs and benefits increase with increasing functionality.

Technology

The technology of the system is the hardware and software it comprises. Hardware costs have declined with time, accompanied by increasing sophistication. Software costs may increase when the complexity of transformation increases as well as when the complexity of the program structures increases.

FIGURE 6.1 Design trade-offs

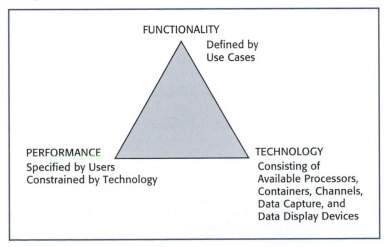

Performance

Minimum levels of performance are specified as part of the users' requirements. The more stringent the performance constraints are, the higher the costs are expected to be. For a given functionality, the choice of technology affects the performance of the completed system.

Thus, functionality, technology, and performance are interdependent; together they determine the system's costs and benefits. If costs must be limited, all three cannot be improved without limit. Trade-offs and compromises are inevitable. The objective of designers and other system developers is to maximize the cost/benefit ratio as measured by the amount of functionality and performance provided with respect to the life-cycle cost of the system.[14]

FRAMEWORK FOR DESIGN TRADE-OFFS

A formal procedure for the cost/benefit analysis of alternatives requires an explicit statement of the criteria for comparison. These criteria are derived from the value system of the decision makers.

Users' Value System

The users' values depend on their role in the organization and the degree and kind of contact they have with the automated system, as reviewed in Chapter 2. Most important to users are effectiveness, convenience, reliability, freedom from defects, ease of use, capacity for growth and enhancement, security and integrity of the database, and quality of the user interface.

Designers' Value System

Important to designers are understandability, ease of modification and change, freedom from defects, and use of current technology.

STRATEGIES FOR TERMINATING THE SEARCH FOR ALTERNATIVES

What determines when we will continue to examine more alternatives and when we will accept as our design one of the solutions already found? Three strategies for guiding this decision are satisficing, optimizing, and adaptive searching.

Satisficing

Satisficing[15] is a strategy which accepts the first feasible solution found.

Optimizing

In certain restricted cases, which can be formulated mathematically, it is possible to find a single solution or set of solutions with a higher value, as measured by one or more criteria, than all other feasible solutions. That solution is an **optimum**; it is better than or at least equal to the best of all possible solutions to the stated problem.

Adaptive Searching (Adaptivizing)

This strategy, sometimes known as *adaptivizing*,[16] recognizes that there is a cost to generate each additional solution. It continues to generate improved solutions until the estimated cost of producing another solution exceeds the estimated improvement in value.

---

[14]Tom DeMarco, *Controlling Software Projects: Management, Measurement, and Estimation* (Englewood Cliffs, N.J.: Yourdon, 1982), 60.

[15]The term was introduced by Herbert Simon in *The New Science of Management Decision* (New York: Harper and Row, 1960).

[16]The term is attributed to Russell L. Ackoff. See *A Concept of Corporate Planning* (New York: John Wiley & Sons, 1970), 15*ff.*

A GENERAL DESIGN METHOD REVISED

Unless designers are content to satisfice, the general design method described previously must be extended to incorporate the generation and comparison of several designs. As presented in Chapter 1, one way of describing the steps in an extended method for problem solving and design decision making is as follows:

1. *Identify the problem.* Examine the situation to state clearly what the problem is. As part of the formal problem statement, define explicitly the constraints implied by the informal problem statement.
2. *Generate possible solutions.* Describe each solution in sufficient detail to carry out the remaining steps in the process.
3. *Eliminate infeasible proposed solutions.* Check each proposal to see whether it satisfies all constraints. If not, reject it or modify it until it becomes acceptable.
4. *Define quantitative and qualitative criteria* for comparing alternative solutions.
5. *Evaluate the expected performance* or behavior of each proposed solution, using the criteria.
6. *Compare the alternatives to select the best solution.* The relative advantages and disadvantages of each alternative are now known as a result of the previous step.

PATTERNS AS A DESIGN TECHNIQUE

Recent practice in program design (see Chapter 8) makes extensive use of patterns. **A *pattern* is a statement of a design problem together with an appropriate solution to that problem.** A designer approaches a new problem with a repertory of patterns — tried-and-true predefined solutions for that specific design domain. Ideally, a pattern has a name for ease of reference and provides guidance about when and how to apply it in new contexts.

This conception of a pattern originated with the architect Christopher Alexander. For Alexander, a pattern provides a local solution to a relatively low-level design problem, such as where to locate a window or how to arrange an eating area. The designer integrates these local solutions into the overall design.[17]

DESIGN AND AESTHETICS

A discussion of design would seem to be incomplete without some mention of aesthetics. Both designers and users bring their personal and cultural aesthetic values to the evaluation of designs as a part of or in addition to the stated constraints and criteria.

As mentioned in Chapter 2, the Unified Process regards software architecture as "concerned with not only structure and behavior but also context: usage, functionality, performance, resilience, reuse, comprehensibility, economic and technological constraints and trade-offs, and aesthetics." Even in software design, there is freedom to make many decisions on the basis of aesthetics, as there is more than one way to satisfy the system requirements.

If you wish to explore this aspect of design further, you may find that Stephen Pepper's *The Basis of Criticism in the Arts*[18] provides a helpful framework. Pepper outlines four predominant approaches to aesthetic value — each derived from a more general world view. They are formism, mechanism, organicism and contextualism.

---

[17]See Christopher Alexander, S. Ishikawa, and M. Silverstein, *A Pattern Language — Towns-Buildings-Construction* (New York: Oxford University Press, 1977).
[18]Stephen Coburn Pepper, *The Basis of Criticism in the Arts* (Cambridge: Harvard University Press, 1945).

▌ *Formism* is based on the concept of natural norms — states of equilibrium and the properties associated with them. It finds aesthetic value to the degree that a work approximates an ideal.[19] It emphasizes a balance, a golden mean. A formist approach might emphasize similarity of a system design to models accepted as good.

▌ *Mechanism* views the universe as an aggregation of individual, atomic primitives. Aesthetic values are "things liked or disliked for themselves" and "lie in the feelings of pleasure or displeasure."[20] Mechanism might emphasize the system components and their connections.

▌ *Organicism* stresses coherence or internal relatedness; it values integration in all domains of existence. It stresses "the degree of integration and the amount of material integrated."[21] Organicism would perhaps stress the scope of the system and the quality of the system interfaces.

▌ *Contextualism* stresses the whole environmental context or situation as the basis of value. Intensity and depth of experience are the standard of beauty. "The more vivid the experience and the more extensive and rich its quality, the greater its aesthetic value."[22] Contextualist aesthetics stresses the appropriateness of artifact to context, the fit between technology and environment.

MODELING AND REPRESENTATION

As we have indicated, designers employ a variety of types of models to serve a variety of purposes.

PURPOSES AND USES OF MODELS

The most basic purpose of a model is to facilitate an understanding of what is modeled. Not only can a model aid designers' understandings, but also it can help communicate those understandings to others. The more clearly we understand, the better we can communicate, and clearer communication can result in improved understanding. Design models are used to satisfy the following important needs of the design process.

The need to simplify complexity. Models allow designers to cope with complexity through abstraction and simplification. A complex system can be regarded as a group of interacting subsystems. Each subsystem is modeled independently, selecting a subset of relevant attributes and relationships. In modeling a building, an interior designer will be interested in the color and surface texture of a wall, a lighting engineer in its ability to transmit or reflect light, an air conditioning engineer in its thermal conductivity, and a structural engineer in its weight and the load it can carry.

The need for a way to calculate or simulate the expected performance of the artifact or system. Many of the constraints on a design problem establish acceptable limits on the performance of systems or subsystems, preferably in quantitative terms which can be measured objectively. Performance models permit the future behavior of a system to be estimated or predicted from the behavior of the model. What is modeled is dependent on which aspects of performance the designer wishes to study and evaluate.

The need for a way to manipulate and alter the relationships between the components of the system. By changing a model, a designer can investigate the effects of specific changes on the performance of the model. These may be changes in the design or

---

[19]Ibid., 109.
[20]Ibid., 44.
[21]Ibid., 79.
[22]Ibid., 57.

changes in the environment of the new artifact. Design is usually a highly interactive process, so design models must be easy to manipulate, modify, and discard. The kinds of changes to be studied and the number of variations to be examined may affect the designer's choice of representations or modeling techniques.

MODELING TECHNIQUES

System models may be classified by the principal modeling technique used.

Physical: Measurable

Of course, all explicit models require some physical medium for representation and communication. But one class of models relies primarily on building a physical replica of some sort. The most straightforward are three-dimensional scale models, such as those an architect may use to study proportions and relationships among building masses. Instrumented scale models of airplanes or automobiles may be placed in a wind tunnel for aerodynamic studies. Structural engineers use photoelastic models made of plastic to investigate stress patterns. Drawings, which are two-dimensional, also belong to this category. Common to physical models is the fact that they are measurable. The relevant aspects of performance (or constructability) can be measured from the model.

Mathematical: Calculable

Mathematical models permit and facilitate the calculation of properties of a system. They may be used to model systems which are apparently orderly or those which are apparently chaotic. They may be deterministic or probabilistic. The advent of digital computers has significantly enhanced our practical ability to use mathematical models in design. Those design disciplines whose mathematical models predated computers were able to automate their computations relatively quickly. Because of computers, new mathematical models have been developed which are impractical to compute manually, such as finite element models of buildings, aircraft, machines, and other physical structures.

Simulations: Experimental or Observable

Simulations may be either quantitative or qualitative, permitting designers (and users) to study systems through experiment and observation.

Mathematical simulations are used to obtain quantitative estimates of system performance when direct calculation using the previous class of models is not possible. Again, computers have made mathematical simulation a practical modeling technique. General-purpose simulation languages are available as well as software for specialized applications.

Other types of simulation provide direct observation of a model. These are valuable where qualitative or subjective evaluation is important. Drawings allow people to evaluate the appearance of a design. Design prototypes allow designers or users to observe or operate selected features of a new artifact. They may also help answer questions about constructability.

Analogies and Other Conceptual Abstractions

A final category of modeling techniques is primarily conceptual, although the model may be communicated verbally or through some other physical medium. It uses *analogy* to focus on similarities between the object of design and other known objects or systems. Or it may depend on some vivid image or central concept to guide a designer's understanding or evaluation. For example, Leonardo da Vinci drew on his knowledge of birds and bats when he sketched ideas for ways in which humans might fly. Personal computers use the metaphor of the desktop as a way of organizing the "look and feel" of the user interface. Perhaps an insect which skates on the surface of a pond will inspire the design of a new type of watercraft.

EVALUATING MODELS

Designers must be concerned with the quality and adequacy of the models they build. They must consider the applicability of a model to its basic purpose and the relative accuracy with which it will measure the desired aspects of performance or realizability.

Designers use four factors — consistency, completeness, correctness, and communicability — to help them review design models as they are being constructed.

1. *Consistency.* Consistency assures that all parts of the model are compatible, that there are no internal contradictions, and that the interface to the environment at the system boundary is also consistent.

2. *Completeness.* Completeness assures that all components of the model are present and all their required attributes have been defined and given values. The issue of whether the scope of the model completely covers the system or domain being modeled is also addressed.

3. *Correctness.* Correctness addresses the applicability and adequacy of the model. It tries to determine whether the model was built properly. It looks for errors in the process of abstracting from reality or transforming it as well as in the result.

4. *Communicability.* Because models are so critical to communicating a design so that it can be understood, they need to be reviewed for their effectiveness at communication and their ability to be understood. Sometimes this is merely a matter of neatness and good graphic and written presentation. Sometimes the need for good communication will affect the type of model selected or the way in which it is represented.

SUMMARY

Design refers to both a process and a product. It is a process which creates descriptions of a newly devised artifact. It is also a product of the design process — a description which is sufficiently complete and detailed to assure that the artifact can be built. The process of design stands as an intermediate step between a statement of requirements and construction of the artifact. Yet the product of design is not the new artifact, only its description.

We design because a desired artifact or system does not exist and people cannot wait for gradual evolution. It is also risky and expensive to construct without a plan. Design provides an opportunity to model and predict performance. Alternative designs can be compared in order to select the best. Moreover, it is less expensive to test, predict, and evaluate during design than after construction.

One basic goal of design is to satisfy the requirements which define the problem — the constraints which define what an acceptable solution is. Designers must ensure that the description they produce is sufficiently complete and detailed for construction.

A design method is an organized procedure for the design process. It marshals the resources of participants in the process to achieve an effective result. Some important roles of a design method are:

1. To provide a conceptual framework for the design process;
2. To guide a single design project to a successful outcome; and
3. In some cases, to provide a strategy for selecting, sequencing, and coordinating multiple projects.

Specific steps or procedures which allocate appropriate models and techniques to the activities and decisions of the design process define or specify a design method concretely.

Strategies for generating a solution to a design problem include reuse of an existing design, modification of an existing design, synthesis, and direct design.

In making design decisions, there are usually trade-offs: A decision that improves one aspect of performance may cause degradation of another aspect. Functionality, technology, and performance are interdependent aspects of a design which are involved in trade-offs during design. The system developers' objective is to maximize the amount of functionality and performance provided with respect to the life-cycle cost of the system.

A design process which incorporates the comparison of alternatives has the following steps:

1. Identify the problem, defining the constraints explicitly.
2. Generate possible solutions.
3. Apply the constraints to eliminate infeasible designs.
4. Define quantitative and qualitative criteria for comparing alternative solutions.
5. Evaluate the expected performance or behavior of each proposed solution, using the criteria.
6. Compare the alternatives to select the best solution.

According to best recent practice, a designer approaches a new problem with a repertory of patterns — tried-and-true predefined solutions for a specific design domain with guidance about when and how to apply them.

A model may serve a variety of purposes. The most basic of these is to facilitate an understanding of what is modeled. Models also selectively simplify complexity, provide a way to calculate or simulate expected performance, and permit designers to manipulate and alter relationships between the components of the system. System models may be classified by the principal modeling technique used — physical, in which performance is measured; mathematical, in which performance is calculated; simulation, in which performance is observed; and conceptual or analogical models. Models are evaluated for consistency, completeness, correctness, and communicability.

Design criteria permit alternative solutions to be compared in consistent terms. These criteria are derived from the value systems of the decision makers, both users and designers. A formal procedure for the evaluation and comparison of alternatives requires an explicit statement of the criteria for comparison as well as objective measures of the performance of each alternative.

KEY TERMS

analogy *175*

artifact *160*

conceptual design phase *168*

constraint *161*

criteria *161*

design *162*

design method *166*

detailed design phase *168*

feasible *161*

infeasible *161*

method *166*

model *162*

objective function *170*

overconstrained *161*

preliminary design phase *168*

trade-off *171*

utility theory *170*

REVIEW QUESTIONS

6-1. State Herbert Simon's definition of design. Define or explain his use of the following terms:
   a. inner environment
   b. outer environment

6-2. Name four groups of design constraints and describe the domain of each group.

6-3. Why, according to Eastman, is modeling important in design? State his distinction between a model and a specification.

6-4. State seven reasons for design.

6-5. State some important design goals.

6-6. State three roles of a design method.

6-7. What are the steps in a general method for design or problem solving?

6-8. Name four strategies for generating a design.

6-9. Name two strategies for simplifying design decisions.

6-10. Name three strategies for determining when to stop the search for alternatives.

6-11. What modifications must be made to the design process to incorporate the comparison of alternatives?

6-12. State three purposes of design models.

6-13. Name four general categories of techniques for modeling.

6-14. State four factors used to evaluate design models.

EXERCISES AND DISCUSSION QUESTIONS

6-1. Design produces change in the environment. What are some of the consequences of this fact for information system development?

6-2. According to Simon, an interface (at the system boundary) protects the environment from the complexities of the technology used to bring about the change. Give some examples of interfaces and discuss how they hide the complexities of the implementing technology.

6-3. What is the difference between a statement of requirements and a design specification?

6-4. Christopher Alexander contrasts un-self-conscious cultures, in which people learn to design informally, with self-conscious cultures, in which design is taught academically. Why are design methods important in our culture?

6-5. What are some of the difficulties of constructing a solution to a problem without first designing one or more solutions? What if the tentative solution must be tested to determine whether it satisfies the problem requirements?

6-6. How could the strategies of reuse of an existing design, modification of an existing design, and synthesis be used to generate a design for an automated accounts receivable system?

6-7. Discuss the meaning of the phrase "black box" in terms of concepts presented in this chapter.

6-8. Give an example of a linear programming problem. Identify the problem, the constraints, the objective function, and the criteria. What strategy for terminating the search for additional solutions is followed in solving this problem?

6-9. Give examples of situations in which trade-offs are required or implicit.

6-10. What are the advantages of using patterns in design?

6-11. According to the quotation from Newman in this chapter, design introduces change within organizations. In the article in Figure 6.2, Schwartz refers to new technologies as disruptive.

a. Schwartz states as a widely held assumption that if people in business organizations have perfect information, they can never make a mistake. Do you agree with this assumption? Why or why not?

b. How does Schwartz define a "disruptive technology"? Does he regard this sort of disruption as desirable? Why?

c. Choose one of the ten disruptive technologies mentioned in the article and comment on its potential for improving how business is done.

d. How is Schwartz's position related to Newman's idea that design is a deliberate attempt to cause change?

e. Newman refers to choosing a technology in order to solve a problem. On the other hand, many criticize the application of new information technology for its own sake rather than in response to specific problems. Yet Schwartz sees information technology as a driver of changes in the way we work. What are some of the strengths and weaknesses of each position? Should information technology be used to force change on workers?

f. What does Schwartz think is the most serious threat to the survival of a company or industry in the global economy?

FIGURE 6.2   Disruptive Technologies — Defining Disruption

Disruptive Technologies — Defining Disruption

Technologies bring change to IT, business worlds

The goal of IT since its inception has been the timely delivery of information to those who need it. Behind this goal is an unspoken belief in technology: If IT could deliver to its internal enterprise customers all of the information all of the time, it would be impossible for them to make a mistake.

If a product manager had available at his or her fingertips all the relevant pieces of data, so the belief goes, there could be only one possible answer.

Take for example a company that sells high-end widgets. If the widget inventory is running low at the warehouse, should you tie up millions of dollars and order more?

Now imagine that 10,000 retail outlets that sell your widgets are submitting hourly sales reports. These reports have been created as a Web service and feed into your enterprise resource planning (ERP) system. These retailers use Wi-Fi to get real-time inventory levels from every store and regional warehouse around globe.

Imagine that the factories that make your widgets are using self-service customer relationship management (CRM) with their raw-materials suppliers to update schedules and submit production projections that go beyond a good guess. Imagine a business intelligence system that analyzes not only the structured data streaming into your enterprise but also the unstructured data from Weblogs, Office 11 XML (extended mark-up language) documents, widget-related news stories, and weather reports and road conditions that might affect everything from production and delivery schedules to consumer demand.

Wi-Fi, 10-Gigabit Ethernet, digital identity technologies, Web services, and virtualization are just some of the technologies that will disrupt the status quo.

But are they really disruptive? The 10 technologies listed below should ease — not impede — the flow of information. Such technologies are called disruptive because they bring change.

That change is not at the cost, we hope, of IT departments' tearing out their collective hair. However, disruptive technologies will force us to re-examine the way we work. In one form or another, each of these technologies attempts to increase the flow of data and make information more accessible to more of the people who need it by reducing its complexity and cost.

It is obvious that this is the case in eight of the 10 technologies: Wi-Fi, Weblogs, Office 11 XML, digital identity, 10GbE, virtualization, Web services, and self-service CRM. And it could be argued that open source/open standards and Mac OS X, the two technology areas that don't quite fit the "accessibility" profile, also help gather and proliferate information: Open source certainly makes information about itself — the source code — available, and Mac OS X gives the enterprise another choice as to how information can be shared.

Change can shift the balance of power and leap over generations of business evolution. Disruptive technologies seed the growth of change in the same way that the automobile changed the very nature of what a business is.

The difference between a dairy farmer delivering milk with a horse and cart at 5 mph to a local market and a tanker truck rolling across the country at 75 mph meant the difference between family farms and corporate farms, between mom-and-pop and the enterprise. Changing just one variable of the formula — in this case speed — turned the entire economy upside down.

It is safe to say that over the long haul these disruptive technologies that both speed up the delivery and increase the amount of relevant data will also have a dramatic impact on the evolution of business and, in the end, on the economy itself.

As technology proliferates, the U. S. economy will feel the disruption in the form of far more sophisticated global competitors. For example, the broadcasting industry has enjoyed a 50-year near-monopoly on programming — thanks to its ability to offer polished television shows (from I Love Lucy to CSI: Crime Scene Investigation) that garner No. 1 ratings worldwide. Now this industry is suddenly changing. The dispersal of technology and knowledge means global and local broadcasters are reaching the same level of production quality and savvy and are pushing American programs out of prime time, according to a recent New York Times article.

And this trend is destined to reach farther, across more industries. Thanks to the expanding reach of technology and better access to information, more companies can gain the sophistication to compete on the same level as the traditional, often larger players in the same market.

As global competition increases, the truth is that complacency — not cheap labor — is what will bring down a company or an industry. The impact is already being seen, for example, as vendors grapple with the challenges of adjusting business models to the disruptions caused by Web services.

Refusing to address or even explore technology that might change the way business gets done will only hamstring a company's ability to roll with the punches in an already punch-drunk business world.

Consider this for the short term: If the inability to have the right information has a negative impact on business decisions and ultimately a company's survival, then those who use technology to improve the flow of information and thus the decision-making process will be the winners. Becoming one of those winners requires faith in the capability of technology to deliver on its promise. Over time, it will require a dollar investment, too.

If we had absolutely all the relevant data, would it be impossible to make a mistake? These technologies are out to prove the point.

Adapted from Ephraim Schwartz, "Disruptive Technologies — Defining Disruption." *InfoWorld*, January 6, 2003, 1

7 INFORMATION SYSTEM DESIGN

INTRODUCTION

Chapter 6 discussed the nature of design. It explored what is common to design in general and what is shared by a variety of design methods. This chapter looks at the design of computer information systems. It states the goals of information system design. It describes the abstract structures and principal types of information processing systems. It discusses the kinds of components currently used to implement or realize a system. It provides an overview of the information system design process and its constituent activities. It describes the participants in system design. It then addresses the transition from information systems analysis, particularly object-oriented analysis, to system design.

The information system design process takes the essential system description from analysis and defines a technology for its implementation. The designer defines an overall structure for the real system, partitions it into subsystems, and designs each subsystem in detail. Current best practice organizes the system architecture in layers or tiers — containing at least a user interface layer, an application layer, and a data storage layer.

The chapter provides an overview of information system hardware and software before describing a design process for the system as a whole. First, however, we present a brief history of object-oriented software systems.

After mastering the material in this chapter, you will be able to

- Describe how analysts and designers view system requirements from different perspectives.
- Explain why analysts and designers view the boundary between analysis and design differently than managers do.
- State some goals of information system design.
- Distinguish among batch, online, interactive, and real-time systems.
- Name and state the purpose of each of the layers of a three-tier system architecture.
- Give examples of each of the three generic types of hardware components of a computer information system.
- Discuss why it is important to have a design method when developing systems.
- Explain the function of infrastructure and administration components in a real information processing system.
- Discuss what additional design decisions and system components are required in distributed systems.
- Describe the principal subsystems into which a computer information system is partitioned.

OBJECT-ORIENTED SYSTEMS — A BRIEF HISTORY

As we shall see in the next several chapters, object-oriented systems are composed of software **objects**, which encapsulate behavior and the information needed to carry it out; **classes**, which describe sets of objects; and **messages**, by which objects communicate and coordinate their behaviors.

Object-oriented programming languages and techniques for object-oriented analysis and design have evolved since the 1970s. Norwegians Ole-Johan Dahl and Kristen Nygaard introduced these concepts in 1966 in Simula, a programming language intended for simulation and system modeling.[1] Alan Kay, Adele Goldberg, and their colleagues at the Xerox Palo Alto Research Center (Xerox PARC) began to develop Smalltalk around 1970. Smalltalk–80 was the first language to consist entirely of objects and classes and to use messagepassing as the only way to invoke actions and share information.[2] Bjarne Stroustrup extended the C programming language to provide object orientation in C++ .

Among the conceptual contributors to object-oriented software design were Edsger Dijkstra, who proposed constructing software in layers; David Parnas, who stated principles of modular software construction and information hiding; and Barbara Liskow, who wrote about the theory and implementation of abstract data types. Ivar Jacobson developed the techniques of use case analysis, applicable to business process analysis as well as requirements analysis for object-oriented systems.[3] Numerous methods for object-oriented analysis and design competed for adoption during the mid–1980s and early 1990s. Finally, Grady Booch, Ivar Jacobson, and James Rumbaugh (known as the Three Amigos) collaborated in the late 1990s to develop a common notation for object-oriented analysis and design, known as the Unified Modeling Language (UML).[4] The UML has become the standard notation for object-oriented software development.

RELATION OF SYSTEM DESIGN TO THE SYSTEM DEVELOPMENT PROCESS

The design of a computer information system occurs within the more comprehensive context of the system development process.

THE RATIONAL UNIFIED PROCESS

The Rational Unified Process for software development was presented and described in Chapter 2. It assumes a system development process involving detailed requirements analysis and custom software design and construction. This is the most complete and extensive system development situation; other situations may be considered as modifications or abridgments of this basic process. The Unified Process recognizes the need for iterations within this overall framework as well as

---

[1]Ole-Johan Dahl and Kristen Nygaard, "SIMULA — An Algol-Based Simulation Language," *Communications of the ACM* 9, no. 9 (September 1966): 23–42; O-J. Dahl, B. Myhrhaug, and K. Nygaard, *Simula 67, Common Base Language*, Technical Publication no. S–2 (Oslo: Norwegian Computing Center, 1968).
[2]Alan Kay, *The Reactive Engine* (Salt Lake City: University of Utah, Department of Computer Science, 1969); Adele Goldberg and D. Robson, *Smalltalk–80: The Language and Its Implementation* (Reading, Mass.: Addison-Wesley, 1983), revised as Adele Goldberg and D. Robson, *Smalltalk–80: The Language* (Reading, Mass.: Addison-Wesley, 1989).
[3]Ivar Jacobson, M. Christerson, P. Jonsson, and G. Overgaard, *Object-Oriented Software Engineering: A Use Case-Driven Approach* (Reading, Mass.: ACM Press, 1992).
[4]The current UML specification may be found at www.omg.org/technology/documents/formal/uml.htm.

the importance of developing the system incrementally. It is intended as a basis for understanding the system development process and not as a universal method directly applicable to any specific system development project.

Figure 7.1 summarizes the four-phase process presented in Chapter 2[5] The principal tasks accomplished during each phase are as follows:

1. Inception (Make the Business Case)

The goals of the Inception phase are to develop a vision of the system, define its scope, and make a business case for it.

2. Elaboration (Define the System Architecture)

The goals of this phase are to define a system architecture which can serve as the basis for subsequent system development and to produce a more reliable project plan and cost estimate. The *system architecture* is the set of significant decisions about what the

---

FIGURE 7.1   Phases, core disciplines, and iterations in the Rational Unified Process

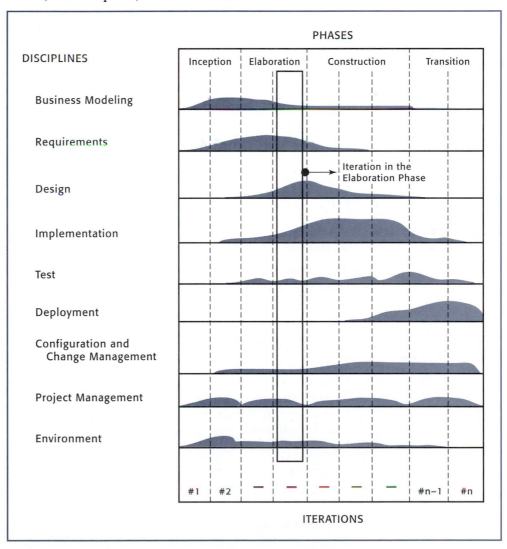

---

[5]Also refer to Figure 2.9 for a table presenting the participants, products, and principal decisions for each phase of the information system life cycle.

software components are and how they are to be organized. It specifies the most critical subsystems and defines their relationships with each other. The Elaboration phase incorporates the design and initial implementation of the most important portions of the system, as shown in Figure 7.1.

3. Construction (Construct the System)

Following the Elaboration phase, the system is constructed. The Construction phase produces an operational system ready for beta testing. During construction, the development proceeds in a series of build cycles. The most important core disciplines are the remaining analysis, the final design, the implementation, and the test of the code.

Transition (Integrate with the Using Organization)

The Unified Process provides for a Transition phase, in which the product of the latest build cycle is released for beta testing (or acceptance testing). After the documented and tested software has been delivered by the developers and accepted by the users, it must be integrated into the using organization. This requires training the users, delivering and installing any additional hardware, converting or creating the files or database for the system, and possibly operating both the old and the new systems in parallel for a period of time. The Transition phase also includes a postimplementation review and modifications and minor enhancements to the system.

Quality assurance is a continuing activity throughout system development, with reviews during as well as at the end of each phase.

THE SCOPE OF SYSTEM DESIGN

Three of the four phases in the Unified Process — Initiation, Elaboration, and Construction — involve decisions about the system architecture and the technology needed to satisfy users' requirements. Depending on the system development project, the choice of part or all of the hardware/software environment may be left to the designers or not. However, the scope of system design always includes specifying the structure of the software as well as its interface to the selected hardware/software environment.

ACTIVITIES OF DESIGN

The detailed activities of the system design depend on the system development method and the design method used. A process for the design of object-oriented systems is presented later in this chapter (see Figure 7.9).

PARTICIPANTS IN SYSTEM DESIGN

Chapter 2 described the participants in system development as well as their roles. That discussion is summarized below. Although designers are the primary participants in system design, analysts, users, and programmers may play supporting roles from time to time.

ROLES AND FUNCTIONS OF DESIGNERS

Important responsibilities of designers are shown in Figure 7.2.

Required Design Skills

Among the skills most valuable to a system designer are:

1. Facility with the tools and techniques of design,
2. Working knowledge of several design methods with expertise in at least one,

FIGURE 7.2   Responsibilities of designers

1. Reviewing the requirements specification to verify its completeness and consistency.
2. Notifying users and analysts of any deficiencies found in the requirements specification.
3. Ensuring the technical quality of the products and procedures of system design.
4. Facilitating communication and understanding among the participants in design.
5. Defining design alternatives and selecting the best.
6. Assuring that the design can comply with the performance standards of the requirements specification as well as those of the system acceptance tests.
7. Coordinating the design with decisions about the hardware and system software environment.
8. Determining the implications of their designs for system performance and construction.
9. Assuring that the system as designed is still technically, economically, and operationally feasible.

3. The ability to master complexity and to sense the key issues in a design problem,
4. Familiarity with the best current design practice, Creative imagination,
5. Creative imagination,
6. The ability to defer decisions to an appropriate time in the design process, and
7. The ability to reach closure on design decisions.

ROLES OF USERS AND ANALYSTS DURING DESIGN

During design, users and analysts may be called on to help plan the continued system development. They may be asked to set priorities for delivering various portions of the automated system. Analysts and users may also help clarify and interpret the system requirements to the designers. This role is essential when ambiguities, omissions, or errors remain in the statement of requirements despite everyone's best efforts. These discrepancies must be corrected as they are discovered.

The interface between the manual and automated parts of the system is critical. Responsibility for designing this interface is often given to the members of the development team who design the manual part of the system. Since this is such a critical interface, all the designers, the users, and the analysts must agree on its design. Recently, this has become such an important consideration that some analysts include a specification of the style or format of the man-machine interface as part of the statement of requirements.

Other aspects of the design of the manual system involving both users and analysts include restructuring the users' organization, reassigning tasks to personnel, reorganizing work and document flow, and developing documentation and training aids.

ROLES OF PROGRAMMERS DURING DESIGN

Programmers may aid designers by assessing the realizability of a design in differing hardware or software environments. They may also contribute a knowledge of system performance in areas where good performance models are lacking.

THE TRANSITION FROM ANALYSIS TO DESIGN

Where does analysis end and design begin? In part, the answer to this question depends on whether we take a technical or a management perspective. The technical criteria for moving from analysis to design differ from the managerial criteria. Analysts are concerned with whether all the users' requirements have been adequately defined; managers are concerned with whether the project is worth continuing. Consequently, activities which, from a technical standpoint, are early design activities may have to be carried out during analysis, at least in a preliminary manner, to produce reliable cost estimates for the management decision.

THE TRANSITION FROM OBJECT-ORIENTED ANALYSIS TO OBJECT-ORIENTED DESIGN

The location of the boundary between analysis and design also depends on whose approach to object-oriented system development is followed.[6] We regard analysis as modeling the problem domain and design as modeling the software objects. Thus, we make a clear conceptual distinction between analysis and design. (Others blur this separation by producing an evolving system model which progresses from requirements definition to software design.)

The domain model shows only concepts, attributes, and associations. In analysis, only the interaction at the system boundary between actors and the system is modeled. The modeling of messages internal to the system is a design activity. Thus, as we shall see in subsequent chapters, when we add behaviors to the domain model of the system, we have moved from analysis to design.

RETROSPECTIVE: A DESIGNER LOOKS AT ANALYSIS

When the analyst breathes a sigh of relief upon completing the requirements specification, the designer's work is just beginning. Each of them views the product of analysis from a different direction. How do their perspectives differ?

Mutual Concerns for the Requirements Specification

Before considering their differences, let us remember that analyst and designer have a common interest in the quality of the system requirements specification. Both are aware that a successful outcome of the entire system development project is much more likely if the specification:

▮ Is complete, containing all the requirements critical to the users' acceptance of the constructed system;
▮ Is correct, free of inaccuracies and ambiguities;
▮ Is consistent, so that its description of what the new system must do is without internal conflicts, and so that the stated requirements are compatible with the objectives and policies of the using organization; and
▮ Communicates the essential information processing requirements clearly, precisely, and understandably to users and system developers alike.

Analysts and designers know that defects in early work products can become costlier and more time-consuming to remedy the longer they remain undetected.

The Analyst's Viewpoint: Defining a Problem

The activities during analysis are directed toward defining a problem — stating the problem and specifying the constraints which must be satisfied by any proposed solution. Analysts view the future system from the users' perspective, trying to understand and communicate the users' requirements.

---

[6]Unlike most earlier views of system development, the Rational Unified Process, presented in Chapter 2, sees analysis and design as core disciplines working together during every phase of system development rather than as successive phases. The discussion of analysis and design in this chapter is generally consistent with that perspective.

The analysts' first concern is functionality — what the information processing system must do to support the users. In developing the use case descriptions, the problem domain model, and the system sequence diagrams, analysts view the system qualitatively in order to identify all the components and specify them accurately and nonredundantly. They also specify quantitative aspects of the performance requirements.

The use case descriptions and system operation contracts produced during analysis are **essential** — that is, independent of the technology with which the completed system will be implemented. These descriptions depict a system with perfect internal technology. The only imperfections taken into account are those arising in the environment, which is not controllable from within the system.

In many system development projects, the implementation is constrained because specific hardware and operating system environments are mandated. There may be real or perceived economic benefits from using hardware which exists or is compatible with existing hardware and from using existing system software. These constraints may have been defined during the feasibility analysis and incorporated in the requirements statement. Even so, the essential system description may ignore these constraints; they can be introduced when the new system's implementation is described.

The Designer's Viewpoint: Clues to a Solution

Designers must solve the problem posed by the requirements specification. Design models describe an information processing system which, when successfully constructed, will satisfy all the specified functional, environmental, and performance requirements.

Designers scrutinize the requirements for clues which will lead them to a satisfactory design as well as for tests which will tell them that their design is satisfactory. They need to know what tests will measure their success in satisfying the specific system requirements for each development project.

Design decisions determine the technology of the constructed system. During analysis, essential system capabilities are independent of the volume of inputs and outputs, the volume of stored data, and the number of times a process is to be executed. In contrast, in order to assure adequate performance, the size of the system, the quantity of stored and moving data, and the frequency of execution of operations are critical to appropriate design decisions. Thus, designers pay particular attention to quantitative details in the requirements specification.

Designers also hope that experienced analysts familiar with object-oriented software have not trespassed on the designers' and territory that analysts have not done "hidden design" under the guise of analysis, describing a solution rather than the requirements or otherwise biasing the designers' decisions.

Designers pay close attention to the system-specific constraints stated in requirements. These constraints, such as the use of specific hardware or system software or programming languages, are in fact prescribed design decisions, not subject to change by the designers. Are these predetermined decisions truly necessary requirements, critical to system acceptance and effective operation? Or did they result from conscious bias, unwarranted assumptions, or lack of serious attention and thought?

Other questions with which designers approach the statement of requirements include the following:

▎ Has the rationale for important requirements been recorded? Did the analysts state why they located the system boundary or the automation boundary as shown? Is the location of these boundaries expected to change?

▎ Can requirements stated in the specification be traced back to written sources such as system objectives, company policy, records of management decisions, or legal or industry requirements?

TECHNICAL VERSUS MANAGEMENT CONCERNS IN THE TRANSITION

Page-Jones remarks that the location of the analysis/design boundary from a conceptual perspective (as discussed above) can conflict with the needs of managing a system development project.[7] That is, the technical and managerial criteria for moving from analysis to design are different:

▮ The technical criterion for exiting analysis is "Have all the users' requirements been adequately defined?"
▮ The managerial exit criterion is "Is the project worth continuing?"

In some cases, tentative design decisions must be made or assumed in order to estimate schedules, costs, or benefits for subsequent phases of system development. Consequently, activities which, from a technical standpoint, are early design activities may have to be carried out during analysis, at least in a preliminary manner, to produce more reliable estimates.

Technical Issues in the Transition

The technical issues in this transition from analysis to design support the management decisions concerning the continuation of the project. They are the same issues dealt with in designing the overall system structure and discussed in detail later in this chapter. From a technical purist's point of view, these are design issues.

Use Case to Processor Mapping. Which essential use cases will be allocated to which processors? What type of processor will each one be?

Data Storage Strategy. Which portions of the essential stored data should be allocated to which storage devices? Where should the database be located? Should it be centralized or local to each processor? How much redundant stored data is appropriate? What additional transforms are necessary to provide access to the data?

Communication Channel Sharing. How should the major information flows be grouped to share communication channels, based on the allocation of processors and stored data?

Answers to these technical questions inform the important managerial decisions.

Management Issues in the Transition

At the end of each iteration in system development, the manager needs to decide whether a project is still worth pursuing or should be terminated and advise the users accordingly. The anticipated costs and benefits of the new system must be reevaluated based on current information about the partially completed system and its environment.

Detailed costs and schedules are prepared for the next iteration of development, and the overall project plan is revised as necessary. These schedules and cost estimates require assumptions which inherently anticipate the decisions to be made in subsequent iterations. Those assumptions will in fact be confirmed or proved incorrect as system development continues.

Even if the costs are still within earlier estimates, the expected benefits may have changed due to economic and other changes in the environment. Changes in the organization's strategic plan may have rendered the application far less attractive. Changes in the competitive environment may have shifted the priorities for the use of corporate resources. Constraints on the availability or cost of labor, capital, or computing resources may make continued development impossible.

---

[7]Meilir Page-Jones, *The Practical Guide to Structured Systems Design*, 2nd ed. (Englewood Cliffs, N.J.: Yourdon, 1988), 310.

COMPUTER INFORMATION SYSTEM DESIGN

This section moves our discussion of design to the domain of computer information systems. It relates the general principles applicable to all design-oriented disciplines (as discussed in Chapter 6) to information system design. It provides an overview of design issues and technology specific to software. It surveys the goals of computer information system design; the structure of information systems; and the hardware, software, database, and user interface, which are the principal subsystems to be designed.

GOALS OF COMPUTER INFORMATION SYSTEM DESIGN

The general design goals described in Chapter 6 may now be restated in terms of the design of computer information systems:

1. *Solving the problem posed in the requirements specification.* The design problem is to define an automated information processing system (with related manual procedures) which will carry out the required functions.
2. *Satisfying the performance requirements determined during systems analysis.* The requirements statement includes all the constraints which are critical to users' acceptance of the new information processing system. In some cases, these constraints may prescribe design decisions; in others, the designers are left free to determine how to satisfy the requirements.
3. *Deriving an automated system whose structure fits the structure of the problem* and which is integrated smoothly with the people who use it and the organization whose business it supports. This goal recognizes that change is inherent in design and seeks to minimize its adverse or disruptive impact on the people and organization using the system. It also tries to maximize the compatibility between problem and solution.
4. *Considering alternative system designs to select the one most suitable for the organization* within the limits of the time, resources, and information available. This goal is directed toward a system of maximum value for the users over the life of the system.
5. *Matching the application software design to the hardware and system software environment in which it will operate.* Depending on the circumstances, the hardware or the system software environment may be prescribed as design constraints, or they may be subject to the designers' decision.
6. *Creating a system whose structure makes it easy to understand, construct, and modify,* even if it requires more hardware and takes somewhat longer to operate. This goal reflects the current economic environment, in which custom software is considerably more costly than hardware, and an organizational environment in which frequent change is to be expected over the life of the system.

THE SYSTEM DESIGN SPECIFICATION

As we indicated above, the principal goal of information system design is to specify a realizable information processing system which satisfies the users' requirements.

The *system design specification* must describe the new information processing system in a way which is adequate for the system to be constructed or realized. It must also enable those who will use it to understand the system design. A specification which cannot communicate its content clearly will be useless in practice. The primary users of the design specification are the system's constructors, but parts may also be read by users and analysts.

Like a good statement of requirements, a realizable system design specification is graphic, partitioned, and accurate. It is also:

- *Explicit.* It spells out whatever is critical to building the new system and achieving the required system performance.
- *Complete* in scope and in significant concrete detail. It defines the system boundaries and the interfaces to the environment. Critical details of the system are the responsibility of its designers; they are not to be left to the programmers or other system builders by default or omission.
- *Unambiguous.* It is not subject to multiple interpretations. If the designers wish to leave options to the discretion of programmers, the acceptable options should be explicit.
- *Consistent.* It contains no internal conflicts, which would make portions of the system incompatible — and the entire system unrealizable.
- *Accurate.* There are no mistakes requiring subsequent correction. Errors lead to confusion and waste the time of designers and constructors alike. Some errors may result in inadequate system performance or problems in construction.
- *Minimally redundant.* Minimal redundancy facilitates revisions to the design during the iterations of design and construction and after the system is in operation.

INFORMATION SYSTEMS AND THEIR STRUCTURE

To solve the information system design problem, it is necessary to specify a realizable technology which will carry out the processing stated in the requirements specification. The next few sections provide a high-level overview of current information processing technology.

SYSTEM TYPES AND THEIR CHARACTERISTICS

There are at present two principal types of automated information processing systems — knowledge-based systems and data-based systems.

Expert systems are the most familiar examples of knowledge-based systems. Successful applications of expert systems include medical diagnosis, computer system configuration, retail credit screening and approval, investment portfolio management, and software code generation. Expert systems and other types of knowledge-based systems are expected to be increasingly significant aids in the complex decisions which business organizations make. However, the focus of this book is the development of data-based systems.

Data-based systems include business data processing systems as well as systems for scientific applications. Figure 7.3 shows a block diagram of a typical data-based system. The major components are an application database, an application program, and a user interface.

The *application database* stores application-specific data, often comprising one or more *application-related models*. Database management software stores information as the data base is built or modified and retrieves information for display or analysis.

The *application program* builds, modifies, manipulates, or analyzes the application models in the data base. It accesses the data base through a database management system (DBMS).

The *program structure* for a data-based system has traditionally been hierarchical. Such systems have been written in procedural programming languages such as COBOL, Pascal, and FORTRAN. Much new software is object-oriented, written in languages such as Smalltalk, C++, and Java.

The *user interface* manages communication between the user and the computer. Through it, the user tells the computer what actions to perform, and the computer

FIGURE 7.3   Structure of a data-based system

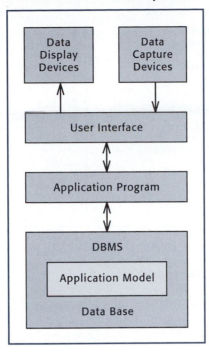

informs the user of what is happening and displays the results of the actions requested by the user.

BATCH, INTERACTIVE, AND REAL-TIME SYSTEMS

It has been traditional to speak of batch, interactive, and real-time systems. However, this distinction may be of limited use to the designer, as most application software developed today is interactive to some degree. (From the designer's perspective, it is probably more useful to think of the time it takes the automated system to respond to a user's request.)

Batch Systems

A *batch system* may be defined as one in which essential system inputs are stored at or near the automation boundary. This batch data store delays the incoming data to accommodate differences between the speed with which data is entered and the speed with which it is processed. The batch data store also collects data which must be processed as a group. Figure 7.4 illustrates the defining structure of a batch system.

Following are some of the characteristic features of a batch system:

- Information entering the computer is processed in groups or "batches." This grouping of input may result from an inherent requirement to process the entire collection of data at once.
- The batch data store may introduce a delay to match a time cycle imposed by organizational policies or procedures. For example, employees' hours are recorded in detail by date and work category for cost distribution purposes, but paychecks are issued biweekly or monthly.
- Error detection and correction continue until the entire batch is error-free; only then is the batch released to the automated system for processing.
- Response time ranges from minutes to overnight or longer.

Batch processing may also produce output, such as a set of paychecks or bank account statements. Batch output is often associated with a temporal event.

FIGURE 7.4   Structure of a batch system

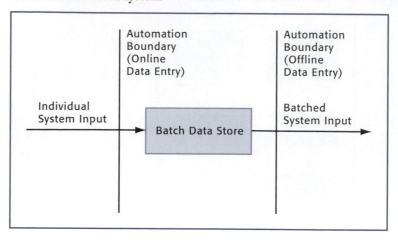

Interactive Systems

In contrast, in an *interactive system*:

▌ Essential system inputs enter the computer one at a time. Time delays or requirements for collections of data are handled with internal data storage.
▌ As a consequence, error detection and correction also applies to a single input, although it may be checked for consistency with the internally stored data.
▌ Response time ranges from milliseconds to a few minutes, depending on the task.

In current usage, interactive also implies that there is interaction between an automated system and a human user.

Interactive systems are often further described as **on line**. Originally, online meant that there was a direct electronic connection between the input-output devices and the central processing unit and that transmission of input and output took place without delay. In offline systems, on the other hand, there were separate devices for coding input in machine-readable form or decoding output to human-readable form. These devices were not connected to the computer. In the 1960s, a keypunch and verifier were typically used to encode cards for input via a card reader. Output might be another card deck, a listing on an electronic accounting machine or a magnetic tape, or a document printed via a separate peripheral computer so as not to slow down the main central processor. Today off-line input devices are more likely to be hand-held product code readers for inventory and shelf-stocking applications or recorders for utility meters.

By this definition, **all interactive systems are online systems**. For historical reasons, the term "online" suggests interaction via a terminal or remote workstation, often as part of a multiuser system.

Real-Time Systems

A *real-time system* is one which responds rapidly enough for its output to affect or control events in its environment. A real-time system can eliminate interaction with a human user by using input from instruments to monitor its environment. Some systems are inherently or essentially real-time; in these systems, the time at which a stimulus arrives is significant information. Other systems are real-time in their implementation; in these systems, timeliness may require that the response to a later, higher-priority event be completed before the system has completed its response to an earlier, lower-priority event. Examples of real-time systems include industrial process control, vehicle guidance and navigation, and automated execution of trades in the securities markets.[8]

---

[8]See the discussion in Meilir Page-Jones, *The Practical Guide to Structured Systems Design*, 2nd ed., (Englewood Cliffs, N.J.: Yourdon Press), 1988, p. 193ff.

FIGURE 7.5   Three-tier model of system architecture

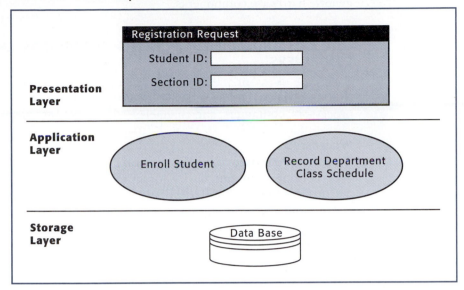

LAYERED SYSTEM ARCHITECTURE — THE THREE-TIER MODEL

In Chapter 6, we discussed the strategy of simplifying system complexity by creating well-defined interfaces between subsystems. For software systems, this principle results in a *layered system architecture*.

The best system design practice organizes a system into at least three layers (or *tiers*), as implied by Figure 7.3 and illustrated in Figure 7.5.

The layers of this *three-tier model of system architecture* are:

▌ The *presentation* (or *user interface*) *layer*,
▌ The *application* (or *business*) *layer*, and
▌ The *storage* (or *database*) *layer*.

The sole purpose of the user interface is to capture and display data. It is responsible only for user interface tasks, such as updating the display. The presentation layer should forward all requests for application-domain-oriented tasks to the business layer. The logic related to the business processes is contained entirely within that layer. As a consequence, business rules may be changed without changes to the user interface, and the user interface may be modified without affecting the underlying business procedures.

Sometimes the application layer itself is further subdivided into separate layers for domain logic and for services such as database interaction, report generation, communications, and security.

FUNDAMENTAL TECHNOLOGY OF AN INFORMATION PROCESSING SYSTEM

In specifying users' requirements for an information processing system, analysts describe the new system using abstractions which are independent of the technology which will be used to construct it. These abstract components are essential data flows, essential data stores (memory), and essential operations or transformations.

Designers specify a technology — inherently imperfect — through which the essential information processing system will be realized. The design specifies physical components — the hardware and software through which the requirements will be actualized or realized. During the early stages of system design, designers find it convenient to describe the implementation technology in terms of abstract or generic hardware components.

GENERIC HARDWARE COMPONENTS: PROCESSORS, CHANNELS, AND CONTAINERS

Each type of essential component in an information processing system has a corresponding type of component in a constructed system. In generic terms, they are processors, containers, and channels.[9]

Processors

A *processor* **transforms information** — changing inputs into outputs. It is the generic implementation device for an operation or process. It contains circuitry for performing Boolean and arithmetic operations on its input. In addition, there are instructions for changing the flow of control or sequence of execution. Together these built-in operations permit the implementation of processes incorporating the three basic control structures of structured programming — sequence, selection, and iteration. A program controls the actions performed by a processor.

Containers

A *container* **stores data.** It is the generic implementation device for storing data. It provides a medium on which information can be recorded for storage and subsequently read.

CHANNELS

A *channel* **transports information,** connecting processors, channels, and external information sources or destinations. It is the generic implementation device for an information flow. It provides a path along which a signal containing the coded information can move.

Channels, containers, and processors appear as a variety of devices used in both manual and automated information processing systems. Figure 7.6 lists some of these devices. **Appropriately allocating channels, containers, and processors to each of the layers of the three-tier architecture is the fundamental design problem at the system level.**

TECHNOLOGY OF A REAL INFORMATION PROCESSING SYSTEM

An essential system description assumes perfect internal technology:

▌ No processor ever fails to carry out an operation correctly and completely.
▌ No container ever loses, destroys, or alters the data stored in it. The ability to access and retrieve data correctly does not diminish with the passage of time.
▌ No channel ever loses, destroys, or alters the data it transports. Data is always delivered to the receiver in the order in which it is transmitted.

Because real-world technology is imperfect, the implementation model must incorporate not only the essential components, but also the additional components needed to compensate for the imperfections.

These additional functions of a real information processing system require additional components — implying additional channels and containers, and possibly even additional processors. Using the terms introduced by McMenamin and Palmer,

---

[9]This usage is attributable to Stephen M. McMenamin and John F. Palmer, *Essential Systems Analysis* (New York: Yourdon, 1984).

FIGURE 7.6   Representative channels, containers, and processors

	MANUAL SYSTEM	**AUTOMATED SYSTEM**
Channel	Mail clerk Pneumatic tube Telephone network	Network cable Printer cable Local area network
Container	File folder Spindle of tickets Microfiche Catalog	Fixed hard disk Magnetic tape reel Random access memory Removable disk (zip or CD)
Processor	Human brain Abacus Hand-held calculator	Central processing unit (chip) Communications processor Database processor

Note in these examples that the components themselves are typically organized in hierarchies. The hand-held calculator (a processor) contains channels, memory, and a processing unit. Local area networks and telephone networks (channels) contain both containers to store data and processors to manage the information flow.

these technology-dependent components are organized into infrastructure and administration.[10]

Infrastructure

The term *infrastructure* comes from the vocabulary of urban planning. In general, an infrastructure is a collection of secondary systems or subsystems which provide services or utilities to support the functions of a principal system or systems. Thus, the infrastructure of a city or subdivision comprises the transportation network; the distribution systems for water, gas, and electricity; and the collection systems for storm water, sewage, and garbage. In computer information systems, the infrastructure comprises the components which provide communication within the system (or between the system and its environment). It may incorporate channels, processors, or data stores. Within a processor, the infrastructure moves data between where it is stored and where it is used. The infrastructure also moves data between processors and synchronizes the communication between processors.

Administration

The *administration* provides additional components for quality control and coordination. It includes processors which monitor a processor's own output for correctness, processors which check for errors, and processors which save the current state of the system in order to facilitate recovery from system errors, system failure, environmental disaster, or sabotage.

Both human and automated processors incorporate these characteristic components.

DISTRIBUTED SYSTEMS

Information systems often support multiple users in multiple locations. Systems with processors or data bases in more than one location are called *distributed systems*. These systems are usually organized as client/server systems.

---

[10]Ibid., Chapter 12.

CLIENT/SERVER SYSTEMS

A *client/server system* comprises three components:

- *Client machine.* This is the hardware and software which request a service from another machine in the system.
- *Server machine.* This is the hardware and software which carry out the client's request and return the results to the client.
- *Communications network.* This is the hardware and software which transmit the message(s) in the request from the client to the server and transmit the message(s) in the response from the server to the client.

Various configurations of client/server systems can be defined in terms of the three-tier model of system architecture. Among these, Martin and Leben[11] list the following:

- **The user interface distribution model**, in which the client houses the user interface;
- The **file server database model**, in which the client houses the database software and the server houses the database; and
- The **client/server database model**, in which the database software is split between the client and the server, which also houses the database.

These three configurations are illustrated in Figure 7.7.

COMMUNICATIONS NETWORKS

The channels which interconnect components of a distributed system form a *communications* (or *telecommunications*) *network*. The major types of communications networks and their components are summarized below. Refer to a telecommunications textbook for additional details and an understanding of network design.

Types of Networks

Networks are often classified as local area, metropolitan area, and wide area networks. *Local area networks* (LANs) have their components within a single building or a group of nearby buildings. A *metropolitan area network* (MAN) typically serves a central business district. *Wide area networks* (WANs) span the planet.

Networks may also be described by the type of information they carry — usually *voice, data*, or *video*. High-capacity MANs and WANs increasingly carry a mixture of types of information.

A network is analog or digital, depending on the form of the signal it carries. *Analog* networks were originally developed for telephone systems and transmit information in the form of sine waves. *Digital* networks transmit information represented as bits.

The communication links in a network are either *wireless* or *wired*. Wireless links include *microwave* signals and signals relayed via *satellite*. Transmission media for wired links include pairs of *copper wire, coaxial cable*, and *optical fiber*.

Network Protocols

A *protocol* is a specification of the formats of messages which are exchanged by two or more communicating processes, as well as a specification of the rules which govern those exchanges. Some important protocols are TCP/IP (the Internet protocol), Netware IPX/SPX, Ethernet, and Open Systems Interconnection (OSI).

---

[11]James Martin and Joe Leben, *Client/Server Databases: Enterprise Computing* (Upper Saddle River, N. J.: Prentice-Hall, 1995), chs. 7 and 8.

FIGURE 7.7   Three configurations of client/server systems

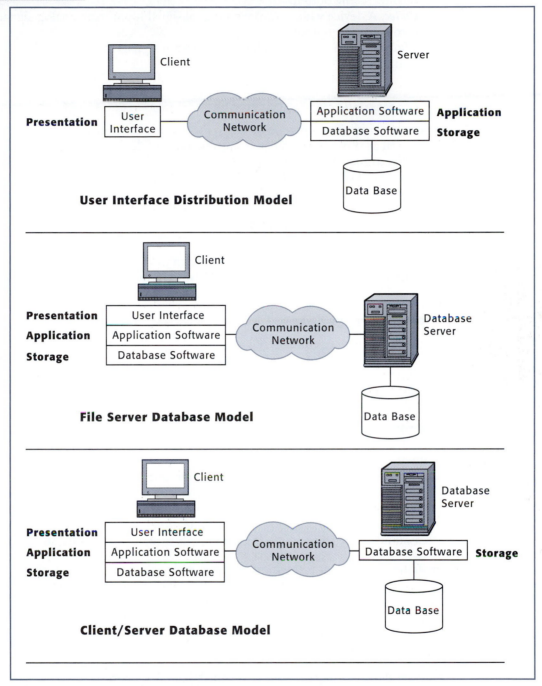

James Martin and Joe Leben, *Client Server Databases: Enterprising Consulting,* Prentice Hall,
Upper Saddle River, NJ, Figure 7.3, p. 98; Figure 8.2, p. 111; Figure 8.4, p. 112.

Network Components

Important components of a network include the following:

- *Router.* An intelligent device which connects networks (which may or may not
  be similar).
- *Switch.* An intelligent device which directs a signal over one of a choice of paths.
- *Hub.* An unintelligent device which allows sharing of a signal.

▌ *Modem.* A device which converts an analog signal input to a digital signal and reconverts the output.

▌ *Codec.* A device which converts a digital signal input to an analog signal and reconverts the output.

▌ *Multiplexer.* A device which permits several signals to be carried by a single channel.

TELECOMMUNICATIONS SOFTWARE

Telecommunications software manages the communication in distributed systems — from local area networks to data transmission via telephone, microwave, satellite, or other electronic linkage. This software must be matched to the processors in the system, the speed of transmission, and the host operating system.

OTHER COMPONENTS OF AN IMPLEMENTATION

Other important components of an implementation include the application software, its system software environment, its database environment, and the user interface.

APPLICATION SOFTWARE

Application software controls the operation of a general-purpose computer so that it functions as a special-purpose processor, carrying out application-specific transformations. Some application software can be purchased as a package as a stand-alone system, as a special-purpose program, or as a library of predefined modules.

Program Structures

Software structures vary in detail with the processor, the operating system environment, and the programming language used. Much existing application software written with conventional procedural programming languages has a hierarchical or vertical structure. Other structures are horizontal, as in concurrent software or a UNIX pipeline. Still others may be employed in parallel processing or object-oriented software.

Following are some of the important constituents of software structures.

Programs. A *program* is the most comprehensive and general software unit. It is executed on a single processor (or on a configuration of cooperating processors managed by a single operating system). The most common program structure is a hierarchy of lower-level program units called *modules*. The top module (main program) is invoked by the operating system. That module in turn may invoke others, transferring data as well as flow of control.

Program Units. A *program unit* is a named, bounded contiguous set of program statements. It is the smallest unit of software visible to the operating system and may contain executable code defining operations as well as space for the storage of data. The program units for procedural languages are *modules* and, for object-oriented languages, *classes*. Within a program unit, algorithms for its operations may employ the constructs of sequence, selection, and iteration.

Tasks. A *task* is a unit of software which can operate concurrently with other tasks. On a single processor, concurrency is simulated. Tasks which cooperate to carry out processing require some mechanism for *synchronization*. Synchronization is supported by constructs in the programming language and compatible capabilities in the operating system.

THE SYSTEM SOFTWARE ENVIRONMENT

The hardware environment comprises the processors on which the application programs will be executed, the data storage devices, and the communication channels connecting the automated devices to each other and to the user interface. System software supports the application-specific software by providing general and special-purpose services.

Even in an automated system for which custom software is developed, there are many functions common to a variety of applications. System-level software often provides these functions in order to increase the efficiency of software development. Thus, application software developers can focus on the unique requirements of their application domain. As a consequence, application software may invoke system software. Interfaces between the application software and the system software are prescribed as a part of the system software. The system software and the prescribed interfaces then become important constraints on the design of the application software.

This section briefly describes the major types of system-level software which constitute the environment for the application software. System-level software includes operating systems, data management software, user interface software, programming language translators, and software libraries.

Operating Systems

An operating system controls the use of a system's resources — its processors, channels, and containers. It loads program units, invokes and coordinates their execution, allocates storage for programs and data, and manages the channels which communicate with peripheral devices. Some operating systems support multiprogramming, multiprocessing, or time sharing.

Data and Storage Management Software

This software provides access to stored data. It can vary in capability and complexity from methods which provide access at the record level to a sophisticated database management system. A database management system (DBMS) provides independence of the data from the application programs by hiding lower-level data storage structures. It controls redundancy of stored information, enforces integrity constraints to maintain consistency within the database, and discourages unauthorized access to the data. Associated with the DBMS is data dictionary software, which maintains a global description of the data for an organization or application, thus supporting consistent data names and compatible formats throughout the database.

User Interface Support

Other system-level software supports input and output for the user interface. It includes the device drivers for data capture and display hardware, as discussed below. An interface employing computer graphics hardware introduces additional complexity. Special graphics software facilitates management of graphical input and display devices.

Programming Language Translators

Language translators convert a high-level programming language into a form executable by a processor. Although a translator is not normally part of the application software,[12] higher-level languages greatly facilitate the construction of software.

---

[12]Unless the language is executed interpretively.

Software Libraries

This category of system-level software refers to libraries of predefined program units intended for incorporation into other application-related software. Examples include class libraries, statistical libraries, and graphics routines.

THE DATABASE ENVIRONMENT

Most application software operates within a database environment. The most common database structure is relational, in which stored data is organized as tables. Older data bases had hierarchical or network structures. Object data bases are still evolving and are currently tied to specific object-oriented programming languages. Important database design issues for object-oriented systems are surveyed in Chapter 10.

Database Management Systems

Database management systems (DBMS) assume the responsibility for controlling access to the data base while maintaining the security and integrity of the data stored in it. Normally, the data base is accessed by a commercially available database management system rather than a custom DBMS. Choice of the DBMS is based on the type of storage structures supported, compatibility with the host operating system, the availability of adequate interfaces to the programming languages to be used for construction, portability, compatibility with other data bases maintained by the organization, and vendor support. The selection of a DBMS interacts with the design of the data base. During design, the database structure must eventually be defined using the language required by the chosen DBMS.

THE USER INTERFACE

The user interface is the portion of an information processing system which permits human beings and computers to communicate with each other. Chapters 11 and 12 describe the user interface and its structure in greater detail.

The Automation Boundary

When an electronic processor is used to automate information processing, it requires electronic media for information flow, storage, and transformation. Humans, on the other hand, require their information in a different, human-readable and -processible form. An *automation boundary* divides human processing from electronic processing. As information crosses the automation boundary, it must be changed to the form appropriate to the processor on the other side. Thus, there is a need for devices at the boundary to accomplish the change.

Hardware for Data Capture and Display

We call the input/output devices at the automation boundary data capture and data display devices. A *data capture device* transforms inputs to an automated system into machine-readable and -processible form from human-readable and -processible form. A *data display device* transforms outputs from an automated system into human-readable and -processible form from machine-readable and -processible form.

Figure 7.8 lists some familiar data capture and data display devices. They are discussed in greater detail in Chapter 11.

Software for Managing User-Computer Interaction

Software for managing the dialogue between user and computer must control the data capture and data display devices as well as transmit to the automated system the actions requested by the user. Some or all of this software is often provided as a system-level utility.

FIGURE 7.8	Representative data capture and data display devices

DATA CAPTURE DEVICES	DATA DISPLAY DEVICES
(translators of data from human-processible to machine-processible form)	(translators of data from machine-processible to human-processible form)
Keyboard	Line printer
Mouse	Character printer
Function button	Laser printer
Lightpen	Ink-jet printer
Voice input	Video display
Bar code scanner	Plasma display
Optical character reader	Light emitting diode display
Magnetic code reader	Liquid crystal display
Touch-sensitive screen	Voice synthesizer
Digitizer	

DESIGN ACTIVITIES IN SYSTEM DEVELOPMENT

Figure 7.9 shows the activities of the system design process. The circles show the activities, and the arrows show the information flows between activities. For the most part, at this high level, the process shown is independent of whether or not the software is object-oriented. Nevertheless, the most detailed activities of system design will depend on both the software structure and the information system development method.

Each activity of system design is summarized below. More detailed discussion of the activities within the scope of this book is contained in Chapters 8 through 12.

Computer information system design may be viewed as a sequence of decisions about how the users' requirements will be implemented. The first of these decisions — which portions of the system will be automated — is made during analysis. Each subsequent decision defines the implementation in further detail. Thus, the system description changes from one which is almost entirely implementation-independent to one which specifies the details of the implementation.

1. Design the Overall System Structure

The central problem of information processing system design is finding an appropriate system structure — a good relationship among the major subsystems and among the major components of each subsystem. The overall system structure has a greater impact on satisfying the system objectives than the constituent program units. In practice, this means that a top-down strategy is likely to be the most fruitful, especially in the case of complex systems. Such an approach addresses the most important system interfaces first.

This activity involves partitioning the system into its three major subsystems — the programs, the user interface, and the data base. This partitioning corresponds to the three-tier (or three-level) system architecture introduced above. It determines the processor boundaries and the data flows across them. If the processors are distributed, a telecommunications network will be necessary. This activity also determines the location of the essential stored data — centralized or distributed. Additional components may be required to cope with the imperfections in the technology with which the system will be implemented.

FIGURE 7.9   Activities of system design

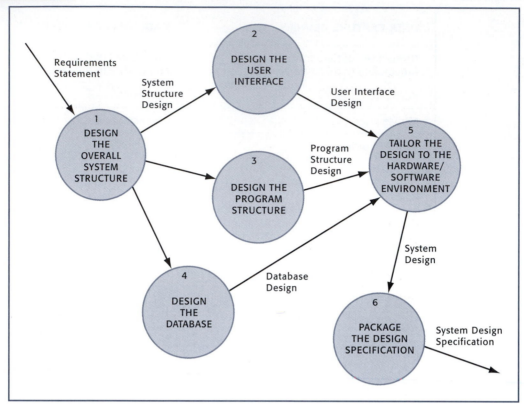

Adapted from Lavette C. Teague, Jr., and Christopher W. Pidgeon, *Structured Analysis Methods for Computer Information Systems* (Chicago: Science Research Associates, 1985), 357.

After the system-level partitioning is complete, the design of the three subsystems can proceed in parallel. There are now three mostly independent design problems with the interfaces between them relatively well defined.

2. Design the Program Structure

This activity organizes the operations to be executed on each processor into tasks and programs. It defines the structure of each program — the constituent program units (objects) and the interfaces between them. It also specifies the data structures and the algorithm for each operation in a program unit. A preliminary version of a reference manual for the application is produced.

3. Design the User Interface

This activity specifies the content and format of all the system inputs and outputs, including the layouts of all source documents, reports, and displays. Some of these may have been defined as part of the requirements analysis. For interactive systems, user interface design includes the detailed procedures for entering the data, requesting output, and initiating other system functions. It may also include manual procedures for collecting input and distributing output. A preliminary version of a users' manual is produced.

4. Design the Data Base

This activity defines physical storage structures based on the conceptual database description produced during systems analysis. It also involves identifying a method of implementing the required accesses to the data base. In most cases, the file access software will be part of a database management system. If so, database design is primarily a matter of providing interfaces to the system software environment. Database design is also concerned with achieving the required level of performance for operations on the data base.

5. Tailor the Design to the Hardware/System Software Environment

This activity addresses compatibility between the application software and its computing environment. It is concerned with the interfaces to the operating system, the database management system, and graphics or other user interface software. The design is adjusted as the computing environment becomes better defined. The program structure may also be adapted to the constraints of a specific programming language.

6. Package the Design Specification

In this activity, the design models are collected in final form into a document from which the system can be constructed.

DESIGN IN RELATION TO THE SYSTEM ENVIRONMENT AND TESTING

Decisions about the hardware and system software environment interact with and may affect design decisions about the application software. Significant features of the hardware and system software environment were discussed earlier in this chapter. The design of the system and its subsystems must be tailored to the environment before the design is complete.

The system acceptance tests provide the detailed performance measures for the system as designed and constructed. Thus, they may affect which critical aspects of system performance must be modeled during design. Awareness of these issues will facilitate making compatible design decisions in all these areas.

The System Acceptance Tests

The system requirements state definitively what performance standards the new system must meet. However, these performance requirements must be expressed as a specific set of tests. If the system passes all these tests, it is considered to be acceptable by the users. The acceptance tests establish measurable standards of system performance. In principle, they are passed or failed as a whole, although in practice some tests may be considered as less important, and therefore the acceptance standards may be relaxed somewhat if the system does not meet them exactly.

The acceptance tests may be generated before system design or in parallel with system design. The designers' task is to anticipate and achieve the required system performance. It is important that the designers know what the tests will be because the tests provide standards for evaluating the system design.

Acceptance tests make an important contribution to quality control in system development. As we have seen, to be effective, quality control must begin in the early stages of system development. Quality control involves a continuing critique of the system requirements and of what is being produced in response to those requirements.

Ideally, people who have no analysis, design, or construction responsibilities for a system should define the acceptance tests for that system. In this way, there is an independent interpretation of the system requirements as stated by the analysts. In addition, system designers and constructors are prevented from setting the standards by which their own work will be evaluated. If the organization is large, a team not otherwise involved in the system development project can do the test design.

FIGURE 7.10   Characteristics of dependent and independent acceptance test designers

DEPENDENT TEST DESIGNERS	INDEPENDENT TEST DESIGNERS
Emphasize system structure: reliable, robust, bug-free.	Emphasize functions the user explicitly asked for.
Can thus ignore real user needs.	Can thus ignore real user needs.
Assure good coverage of the system.	Provide less and less thorough coverage of the system.
Are vulnerable to pressure to get the system certified.	Are vulnerable to deception by worthless fixes.
Understand the application and software details better.	Understand users' operational realities better.

In many situations, however, analysts prepare or help prepare the acceptance tests because they are most familiar with the users' requirements. Users are consulted if necessary to clarify the requirements statements.

In practice, the tests can be designed by the system designers themselves, by an independent quality assurance group in the developers' organization, by the users, or by a consultant representing the users. The value of the test design depends on how much independence the test designers have and what the trade-off is for that degree of independence. The impacts of dependent and independent test designers are summarized in Figure 7.10.[13]

The plan for the system acceptance tests identifies the specific tests to be performed, grouping them by major categories of requirements. For each test, the following are specified: objectives, initial conditions and setup, references to the database and hardware configuration, references to the relevant portions of the requirements or design specification, operating instructions, specification of the input, specification of the outcomes, and method of verifying the outcomes.[14]

DESIGNING THE SYSTEM STRUCTURE

Designing the system structure transforms an essential system description into a description oriented toward the technology for its realization. It defines the high-level partitioning of the system, locating the interfaces between the major components.

As we would expect from our knowledge of general systems theory and of complex systems in other domains, decisions at the system level will have a greater impact on the system's performance than subsequent, more detailed decisions.

Since decisions about partitions and interfaces are interdependent, the location of the automation boundary has the most significant impact. Yet, in a sense, the physical description of the new system is complete only when the entire system-level structure is defined. That is why it is important to address the system architecture during the Inception and Elaboration phases. A stable design for the system structure is the principal work product of the Elaboration phase of the Unified Process.

---

[13]Boris Beizer, *Software Testing and Quality Assurance* (New York: Van Nostrand Reinhold, 1984), 181–182. See pages 182–192 for his discussion of acceptance test design.
[14]Ibid., 189.

FIGURE 7.11   Activities of designing the system structure

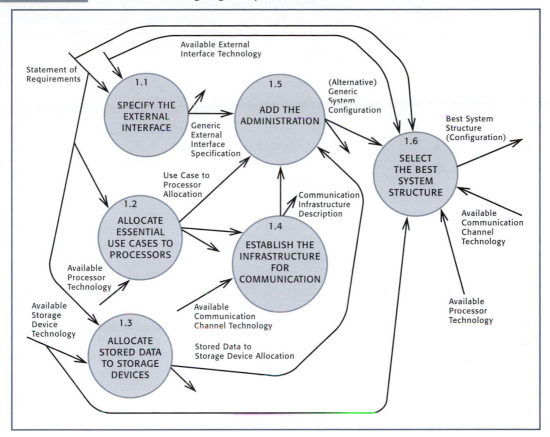

DESIGNING THE OVERALL SYSTEM STRUCTURE

This section gives an overview of designing the system structure, based on the approach presented by McMenamin and Palmer in *Essential Systems Analysis*.[15] Figure 7.11 shows the activities involved. This figure has been simplified by omitting any interactions with the parallel activity in which the hardware and system software environment is determined. Prior constraints on the design are assumed to be part of the statement of requirements. The activities shown in Figure 7.11 comprise the high-level mapping from an essential system description to a model of its implementation.

The activities of designing the system structure may use any modeling notation which can represent processors, channels, and containers and their contents. We have used UML symbols where appropriate.

It should be obvious that the decisions involved in these activities are highly interdependent. The activities are tightly coupled because they all involve various aspects of what is really a single system-level decision: Where should the interfaces at this level be located? Once these interfaces are fixed, the subsystems can be defined with considerably greater independence. Detailed decisions about each subsystem belong to subsequent activities.

Several alternatives at the system level may be considered. Within each, there may be variants at the subsystem level. Thus, the first five activities will be required (perhaps in varying detail) for every alternative. The selection of the best alternative will occur by considering and eliminating possibilities throughout the process as well as at the end of system-level design.

---

[15]McMenamin and Palmer, *Essential Systems Analysis*, ch. 26. We have adapted this approach to the design of object-oriented systems.

1: Specify the External Interface

This activity defines generically how the interface between the system and its environment will be realized. It begins with the essential data flows which cross the system boundary, as shown in the system interaction diagrams produced during analysis. It determines:

▮ The form of the system inputs. This defines the data-carrying medium, how the incoming messages will be grouped (if they do not enter the system individually), and how the data elements will be coded externally. The starting point is the input messages from the system sequence diagrams.

▮ The amount of time required for the system to carry out each preplanned response. Critical minima for the application should be contained in the special requirements for each use case or for the system as a whole.

▮ The form of the system outputs. The means by which the system transmits its responses to the outside world are defined in terms similar to those for the inputs: medium of transport, grouping of messages, and external coding.

2: Allocate Essential Use Cases to Processors

The automation boundary is located, or the location determined during analysis is reviewed and perhaps adjusted. This decision determines which portions of the use cases are to be performed manually and which by a computer. The zone around the automation boundary is elaborated. The use cases to be automated may be allocated to one or more processors.

Designers may also divide one essential use case among several processors. The allocation is shown by drawing boundaries on the use case diagrams. Use cases may be partitioned until processor boundaries enclose entire use case ovals instead of cutting through the middle of them. This makes the messages across each processor boundary visible.

These decisions are affected by the available processor technologies, the geographic location of the users of the application, the kinds of skills required by each process, the required processing capacity, and the desired response time. The choices will affect the cost and quality of service provided by the system.

3: Allocate Stored Data to Storage Devices

In this activity, the essential stored data is allocated to storage devices (containers). Stored data that is accessed only by a single processor can occupy a storage device local to that processor. However, if several processors must share stored data, as, for example, in a data base, there is a spectrum of alternatives.

At one extreme of this spectrum is a single container for all the shared data; at the other is a private data store for each processor. The latter option necessitates a redundant copy of the shared data for each additional processor.

This allocation may be shown by drawing boundaries on the domain model and making appropriate annotations. Where data is to be stored redundantly, it may be necessary to modify the diagram accordingly.

4: Establish the Infrastructure for Communication

As defined above, the infrastructure supports communication among processors (or among use cases in a single processor) to provide access to shared stored data and to send intermediate results from one fragment of an essential use case to another.

If there is a single data base, it may be necessary to add transporter processes to move data from their containers to the processors and translator processes to transform the data to the format suitable for the each processor. If there is redundant data storage, each copy of the data will need its own transforms to update its contents.

The communication channels between processors must be specified, along with the medium of transmission and the associated transporter and translator processes.

There may also be a need for buffers or batch data stores to hold the results of one processor until the other is ready to receive it.

Note that the above activities — specification of the user interface, allocation of essential use cases to processors, and allocation of stored data to storage devices, as well as allocation of channels to essential information flows — would be required even if the internal technology of the system were perfect. These allocations may have been defined as part of the statement of requirements, with alternatives considered in a preliminary way during the initial analysis.

5: Add the Intra- and Interprocessor Administration

This activity involves adding the administrative processes defined above.

6: Select the Best System Structure

The preceding five activities produce alternative designs for the system structure. Each of these generic system configurations incorporates the devices necessary for implementing the system as well as the operations required to cope with imperfect internal technology. Now these alternatives may be compared qualitatively and quantitatively using cost/benefit analysis techniques.

The hardware costs over the life of the system may be reduced by looking for excess capacity which is not shared with or used by other applications. Some slack (perhaps as much as one-third) is desirable at this stage of design to compensate for the margin of error in the estimates of required capacity. Nevertheless, a configuration in which devices are loaded to only 10 or 20 percent of capacity ought to be examined to see if an acceptable alternative can be found with greater utilization of its capacity.

Consider these options:

- Consolidating use cases into fewer or smaller processors.
- Combining multiple data bases into a single container.
- Combining the channels for incoming and outgoing data flows. The volume and timing of the flows will affect the required capacity of the channels.
- Batch processing if the response times will still be acceptable. This can spread processor utilization over a greater portion of the day or reduce peak loadings by shifting the time of demand.

PARTITIONING A SYSTEM FURTHER (OPTIONAL)

Activities 2, 3, and 4 partition the use cases, stored data, and information flows into manual and automated processors and by hardware boundary within the automated portion of the system. For each processor in the system, further partitioning identifies which portions of the application software will be implemented as batch, online, and real-time.

Within each of these implementation types, the processes or objects are organized into sets which will be invoked by the operating system as distinct executable units. Yourdon and Constantine refer to one of these units generically as a **load unit** and to the process of partitioning as packaging.[16] Packaging decisions are shown initially by drawing additional boundaries on the domain models. Subsequent packaging decisions may be depicted by drawing boundaries on design class diagrams (introduced in Chapter 12). In general, there will be one design class diagram for each load unit.[17]

---

[16]See Edward Yourdon and Larry L. Constantine, *Structured Design: Fundamentals of a Discipline of Computer Program and Systems Design* (Englewood Cliffs, N.J.: Prentice-Hall, 1979), for the seminal treatment of packaging issues.

[17]The UML permits use cases, objects, and other UML elements to be grouped into packages.

Partitioning the Batch Portion

Batch software is often partitioned into jobs and job steps. A job is a sequence of job steps, and a job step consists of one main program (invoked by the operating system), which in turn may activate subordinate program units. Preliminary packaging into jobs may already have been done as part of the transition from analysis to design. This partitioning is based on qualitative characteristics of the operation of the system.

Partitioning into Jobs. Job boundaries may be based on the need for processes which are executed on different time cycles.

Partitioning into Job Steps. An important reason for packaging into job steps is related to controls or administrative issues. The administrative concerns leading to additional steps include:

- *Audit.* This permits the separation of special audit statements or calculations from normal routine processing.
- *Security.* This permits isolation of processes with special security needs, such as payroll checks or tax statements or other sensitive business information.
- *Backup.* This permits periodic copying of programs and data for backup.
- *Recovery.* This restores the state of the system so that processing can be resumed after errors or failures in the hardware or software or interruption of the power supply.
- *Checkpoint and restart capabilities.* These allow very long running programs to suspend execution periodically or at the end of major steps in the computation. The state of the process is saved so that if there is a subsequent error, execution can be resumed from the last checkpoint rather than having to go back to the beginning.

Another reason for packaging is insufficient resources. This may be the result of either a limitation on the number of data storage devices which can be accessed simultaneously or a constraint on processor memory. Packaging to accommodate memory limitations should be deferred until the end of program design.

In any event, the number of job steps should be minimized, as each job step imposes additional overhead. Figure 7.12 shows questions to be asked if additional interfaces are contemplated when packaging for implementation.

| **FIGURE 7.12** | Factors for assessing the penalty for an additional interface |

> What is the rate at which data crosses the interface (both average and peak)?
>
> If several types of data share the same interface, what is the typical distribution of those types?
>
> Does the interface introduce redundancy (such as extra files) into the system?
>
> What in the interface (if anything) has to be shared by the components of the system on either side of the interface?
>
> What processing is required to carry data across the interface?
>
> What processing is required to take data off the interface?
>
> Which users will be affected? How?
>
> What is the value to the corporation of the data crossing the interface? What security is needed?
>
> What technology should be allocated to the interface?

From Meilir Page-Jones, *The Practical Guide to Structured Systems Design*, 2nd ed. (Englewood Cliffs, N.J.: Yourdon, 1988), 204.

Partitioning the On-LinePortion

On-line software is typically packaged into transactions or related groups of transactions. When the system requirements have been developed using event analysis, the event list is the basis for this packaging.[18] Note, however, that when software packages are used for transaction processing, the transactions are not necessarily identical to those identified in event analysis.

Administrative operations might also be added to log the incoming transactions and the successfully completed transactions, both to permit recovery if the system goes down and to provide an audit trail.

DESIGNING THE USER INTERFACE AND DATA BASE

In addition to defining the overall system structure and the program structure, system design involves designing the user interface and the data base. Designing the user interface is the subject of Chapters 11 and 12. Detailed methods for database design are outside the scope of this book, but Chapter 10 does discuss the design of the interface between the application layer and the storage layer in accordance with the three-tier system architecture.

PUBLIC UNIVERSITY — SYSTEM ALTERNATIVES

The approach to information system design described in this chapter will be illustrated for the Public University Registration System. The starting point for designing the system structure of the Public University Registration System is the essential system description produced in Chapters 3 through 5. It contains four use cases.

DEFINING ALTERNATIVE SYSTEM STRUCTURES

Three alternatives for the system structure are introduced here. They illustrate the beginning of the system design process described in this chapter. More detailed comparison and discussion are deferred until after the presentation of program design in Chapters 8 and 9.

The chief characteristics of these alternatives may be summarized as follows:

- Alternative A is a centralized, single-processor system.
- Alternative B is a distributed system with a department database server and a local microcomputer in each department office.
- Alternative C is a two-processor system, with one of the processors serving as a database machine.

Alternative A

Alternative A:

- Allocates all the essential use cases to a single automated processor.
- Allocates the entire data base to that automated processor.

This alternative is shown in Figure 7.13. Note that the humans who interact with the automated system are depicted as actors. They could also be shown as processors inside the system in order to emphasize their role as information processors.

---

[18]A similar approach is followed when a real-time system is packaged into tasks. See Stephen J. Mellor and Paul T. Ward, *Structured Development for Real-time Systems*, vol. 3, *Implementation Modeling Techniques* (New York: Yourdon, 1986).

FIGURE 7.13   Alternative A

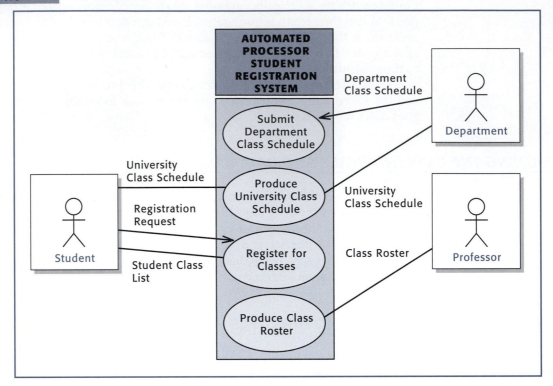

Alternative B
Alternative B:

∎ Allocates the essential use cases to two types of automated processors:

The use case Submit Department Class Schedule is allocated to a series of processors located in the department offices.

The remaining use cases are allocated to a centralized processor.

∎ Allocates the data base to the automated processors as follows:

To each departmental processor — the instances of concepts and associations related to that department, the sections it schedules, and the professors who teach them.

To the other processor — the remaining concepts and associations needed for student registration.

This alternative is shown in Figure 7.14.[19]

Alternative C
Alternative C:

∎ Allocates all the essential use cases to a single automated processor, as in Alternative A.
∎ Allocates the entire data base to a dedicated database processor.

This alternative is shown in Figure 7.15.

---

[19]The discussion of partitioning the objects in the data base among the containers for each processor is deferred until Chapter 10. The rationale for this partitioning is discussed in Exercise 10–6.

FIGURE 7.14 Alternative B

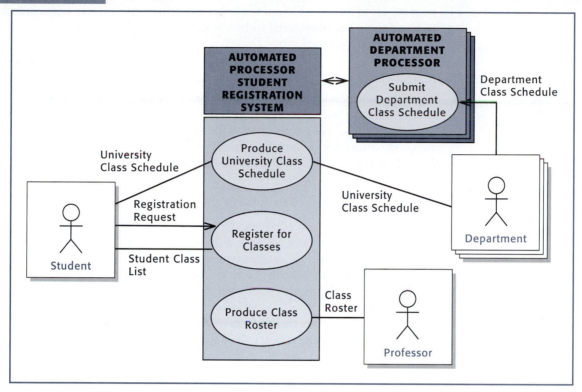

FIGURE 7.15 Alternative C

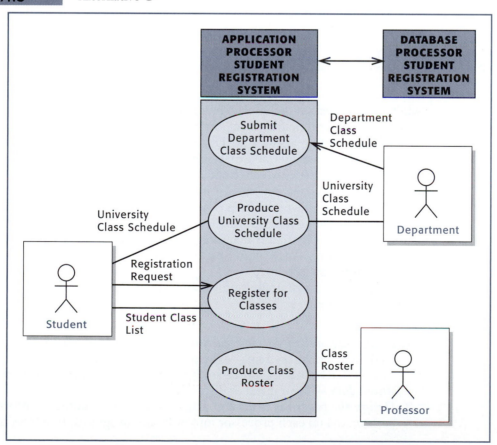

PARTITIONING THE SYSTEM INTO BATCH AND ON-LINE PORTIONS

The next step is to define which of the processes will be interactive and which will be batch. The decision is considered to be the same for all alternatives.

For the four use cases defined above:

▌ Student registration will be interactive via touch-tone telephone.

▌ Department secretaries will enter department schedules interactively.

▌ Batch processes will print the university schedule, student class lists, class rosters, fee bills, and grade reports for students and faculty. In Alternative B, the class rosters for department faculty will be printed at the departments; the remaining outputs will be printed centrally.

If we expand the scope of the system with additional use cases:

▌ The posting of grades can be done either interactively or in batch mode, depending on whether professors enter grades on line or fill out grade sheets for scanning by a mark-sense reader or handwriting scanner.

▌ In Alternative B, the grade reports for department faculty can be printed at the departments.

▌ Withdrawals from class can be interactive. Students can drop via touch-tone telephone until a deadline; after that, withdrawals will be handled by the Registrar's Office.

▌ Personnel in the Cashier's Office can record the payment of fee bills interactively.

We will defer further discussion of the system design alternatives until Chapter 10. At that point, the student will be familiar with the models and techniques of object-oriented program design as well as some important database design issues.

SUMMARY

Analysis defines users' requirements for a new information processing system, while design specifies the implementation of the new system. However, the technical and managerial criteria for moving from analysis to design are different. The technical criterion for exiting analysis is "Have all the users' requirements been adequately defined?" The managerial exit criterion is "Is the project worth continuing?" Consequently, activities which, from a technical standpoint, are early design activities may have to be carried out, at least in a preliminary manner, to inform the management decision about whether to proceed from analysis to design.

The principal goal of information system design is to specify a realizable information processing system which satisfies the performance standards of the requirements specification. An accurate and understandable specification of the design is the necessary principal product.

The design of a computer information system is an iterative process, comprising six major activities:

1. **Design the overall system structure.** This involves partitioning the system into its three major subsystems — the programs, the user interface, and the data base. It determines the processor boundaries as well as the location of the stored data — centralized or distributed.

2. **Design the program structure.** This activity organizes the transformations to be executed on each processor into tasks and programs. It defines the program

units and the form and content of the messages from one program unit to another. It also specifies the algorithms for each program unit.

3. ***Design the user interface.*** This defines the content and formats of all system inputs and outputs, the layouts of all source documents, and all other details of the interaction between the user and the manual and automated portions of the system. A preliminary version of a users' manual is produced.

4. ***Design the data base.*** This defines the physical storage structures for the data and provides the required access paths to the data base. It is also concerned with achieving the required level of performance for operations on the data base.

5. ***Tailor the design to the hardware and software environment.*** The design is then adjusted to the hardware and system software environment in which the system will be executing. It may also adapt the program structure to the constraints of a specific programming language.

6. ***Package the design specification.*** In this activity, the design model is collected in a document from which the system can be constructed.

Designing the system structure transforms the essential system description into a description which specifies the technology for its realization. It consists of six highly interdependent activities:

1. Specify the external interface.
2. Allocate the essential use cases to processors.
3. Allocate stored data to storage devices.
4. Establish the infrastructure for communication.
5. Add the intra- and interprocessor administration.
6. Select the best system structure.

The first five activities produce alternative system designs. The sixth compares alternatives to select the best system design.

The physical components of an information processing system — channels, containers, and processors — must not only realize the essential information flows, stored data, and use cases of the system, but also compensate for imperfect technology. For this purpose, components constituting the infrastructure and administration must be added to the essential system.

The interprocessor infrastructure provides communication between processors within the system, between processors and shared memory, and between the system and its environment. This infrastructure incorporates processes to transport data across processor boundaries, translate it into the appropriate format, and create batch data stores at processor interfaces to synchronize communication between processors.

The administration comprises processes which monitor the system to detect errors introduced by the processors or the infrastructure as well as coordinate the operation of processors.

When the system-level design decisions are made, the automated system may be partitioned into load units. Boundaries are defined to separate the batch, online, and real-time portions. Batch portions may be packaged further into jobs and job steps. Different time cycles also establish partitioning into jobs. Online portions are organized by transactions. Packaging because memory is limited should be deferred until the end of detailed design.

The design of the user interface and the data base complete the design of the system.

Before the end of design, the design must be made consistent with the decisions about the hardware and system software environment and with the specific system acceptance tests being defined in parallel.

KEY TERMS

administration *195*

application layer *193*

automation boundary *200*

batch system *191*

channel *194*

communications network *196*

container *194*

data capture device *200*

data display device *200*

distributed system *196*

infrastructure *195*

interactive system *192*

online system *192*

presentation layer *193*

processor *194*

real-time system *192*

storage layer *193*

three-tier system architecture *193*

REVIEW QUESTIONS

7-1. What is the technical criterion for exiting systems analysis and entering system design? The managerial criterion?

7-2. State six goals of computer information system design.

7-3. Name and briefly describe the major activities of information system design.

7-4. Name the three types of generic hardware components and give some examples of each.

7-5. What is the purpose of the infrastructure in an implementation of a computer information system? What is the purpose of the administration?

7-6. Name the activities of designing the system structure and describe each briefly.

7-7. How can designers depict the partitioning of an automated system into processors, jobs, and job steps?

7-8. Summarize what happens in determining the hardware and system software environment and in developing the system acceptance tests. How are these activities related to design?

EXERCISES AND DISCUSSION QUESTIONS

7-1. Is system design limited to program design? Why?

7-2. Compare and contrast the respective viewpoints of analysts and designers with regard to the statement of system requirements.

7-3. Summarize some of the technical issues involved in the location of the analysis/design boundary and in the transition from analysis to design.

7-4. Summarize some of the management issues involved in the location of the analysis/design boundary. Why are there differences, even tensions, between the technical and managerial perspectives?

7-5. Why is it important for the analysis models of a system to be kept distinct from the models developed during system design?

7-6. Why is it important for a system design specification to be explicit, complete, unambiguous, consistent, accurate, and minimally redundant?

7-7. Discuss the contribution of event analysis to system design and to program design.

7-8. What assumptions are made when we say that an essential system description has perfect internal technology? Why don't we assume that the technology outside the system is perfect also?

7-9. Why is a layered system architecture considered a best practice in system design? Explain the advantages of this architecture in terms of general systems concepts presented in Chapter 1.

7-10. What additional design decisions are necessary in a distributed system as compared to a centralized system?

7-11. Consider the article about predicting the future of technology in Figure 7.16:

    a. Schwartz (see Figure 6.2) confidently identifies ten information technologies which he expects to change the way companies and industries will work in the future. How do you think Gomes would react?

    b. What is Gomes's view of how new technologies lead to dramatic change in the way we live and work?

    c. What does Gomes think is the chief reason for the failure of attempts to make radical changes in the way businesses operate?

FIGURE 7.16   Future of Technology Is Hardly What Anyone Has Ever Predicted

Future of Technology Is Hardly What Anyone Has Ever Predicted

When Apple computer introduced its first laser printer in the 1980's, its sales material made the strongest case the company could for the device. Put the laser printer in your office, said the brochures, and it will be a lot quieter than the daisy-wheel or dot-matrix printers you are probably using now.

The new Apple printers did indeed print very quietly. But they did something else, too, that ended up being vastly more important. Unlike existing printers, which were essentially computer-powered typewriters, the laser device could print both text and graphics, and in any layout imaginable. Someone soon wrote a program called PageMaker and the field of desktop publishing was born. Apple prospered.

Technology companies are often described as "inventing the future." Maybe they do. But they aren't very good at predicting it. That's how it is with the future: You never quite see it coming.

Last week on this page, Larry Ellison, chief executive of Oracle, made his predictions for Silicon Valley. He saw a mature industry in a dreary state of monopoly maintenance, marked by meager innovation and tepid growth.

I don't disagree with the outlook: the notion that Silicon Valley's rah-rah days are behind it has been something of an organizing principle of this column. But let's not discount out of hand the idea that something unforeseen might appear on the scene to change things. Just don't expect to recognize it for what it is right away.

People in the technology world are forever searching for the killer "app" — the must-have sure thing that the whole world will want to buy. You wake up one day and realize that you can't remember how you ever got along without, say, search engines.

That's one irony of Silicon Valley: The more hype something gets, the less likely it is to amount to anything.

Several themes run through such famous letdowns as the Apple Newton hand-held gizmo of a dozen years ago, the "data superhighway" of the mid–1990's, Mr. Ellison's own anti-PC "thin client" computer and Microsoft's recent ".Net" reworking of on-line commerce. All involved wishful thinking passed off as prognostication. All involved the assumption that the most important new technologies are handed down fully formed to us mortals from Olympian heights. All got a lot of attention, but not much use.

It's a problem for technology companies. Most of the really transforming technologies bubble up in unexpected ways. More often than not, they require some sort of existing infrastructure, which they gently nudge in the direction of additional usefulness. The Internet, for instance, would never have happened without a vast and efficient telephone network, not to mention tens of millions of powerful PCs.

And these technologies are almost never envisioned in advance, but instead are appreciated after the fact, like the laser printer. Name your favorite technology. I'll bet it wasn't introduced with a big product launch. The typical pattern is that by doing something useful, simple, and slightly new, it attracted customers and programmers who then began investing it with ever more uses, many of them utterly unforeseen.

Wireless networking, for example, started as something of a hobbyist's experiment to find a use for a deserted part of the computer spectrum. Now, people are talking about using Wi-Fi to solve cheaply the "final mile" problem of bringing fast Internet access to every home. There was a time when people thought broadband access to every home would take billions of dollars worth of fiber-optic cable laid everywhere. In the end, we might get it free.

While all predictions are problematic, we should be especially wary of those that don't contain a healthy sense of respect for the way people do things now. Consider the business-to-business Internet craze of a few years ago. These were dot-commers who wanted to set up on-line exchanges to replace the way Detroit auto makers ordered their supplies, for example, or the way the steel industry unloaded its surplus capacity. They mocked the nonwired state of Old Economy enterprises and promised all manner of stunning new efficiencies through the simple addition of a few Internet browsers.

In the end, the exchanges went nowhere, largely because most businesses were already managing their affairs pretty well; after all, they had been at it for years. "Beware of all enterprises that require new clothes," said Thoreau. If he were alive today, he might have added "or new software."

People who believe the stock market is largely unpredictable are called "random walkers." They say that nothing in the history of a stock price is of any use in estimating its future value. It would be hard to be so rigorously agnostic about the future of technology, if only because it's so much fun crystal-balling about which new gizmo will be hot. The trouble starts in taking the predictions too seriously.

Adapted from Lee Gomes, "Future of Technology Is Hardly What Anyone Has Ever Predicted," *Wall Street Journal*, April 14, 2003, C1

**CASE STUDIES
FOR
PROJECT
ASSIGNMENTS**

Assignments

1. Define three alternative system structures for the Giant Forest Inn system. (See Figures 7.13, 7.14, and 7.15 for the university registration system.)

2. Discuss qualitatively the advantages and disadvantages of each alternative.

Assignments

1. Define three alternative system structures for the Apache Rent A Car system. (See Figures 7.13, 7.14, and 7.15 for the university registration system.)

2. Discuss qualitatively the advantages and disadvantages of each alternative.

PROGRAM DESIGN — INTERACTION DIAGRAMS

8

INTRODUCTION

As described in Chapter 7, designing an information system requires critical decisions about the structure of the system. These decisions allocate use cases to processors and stored data to containers. Communication channels transmit information as required among the processors and the containers. After the system structure (or architecture) has been defined, the design of the data base, the user interface, and the programs can proceed in parallel within this overall structure.

In Chapter 8, we begin our presentation of object-oriented program design. For the first time, we are concerned with design models — models which represent object-oriented software. Therefore, we first define fundamental concepts of object-oriented software, for the benefit of those who do not already know an object-oriented programming language. The chapter continues with an overview of the process for object-oriented program design. It describes the structure of object-oriented software and introduces the Unified Modeling Language (UML) models which describe that structure. It presents patterns which guide the design of object-oriented software and introduces the steps in the program design process. It continues with an explanation of the first two steps in this process — defining a façade object and producing an interaction diagram for each system operation.

After mastering the material in this chapter, you will be able to

▌ Explain fundamental object-oriented concepts.

▌ Understand what patterns are and how they are used.

▌ Learn how to assign responsibilities to classes using the façade, creator, and expert patterns.

▌ Understand the differences between collaboration and sequence diagrams.

▌ Create interaction diagrams.

FUNDAMENTAL CONCEPTS – OBJECTS, CLASSES, AND MESSAGES

Object-oriented software is made up of objects which cooperate to carry out the work of the system. In order to design object-oriented systems, it is necessary to understand objects and how they function as part of a system. This section discusses some fundamental concepts of object-oriented systems which analysts and designers must understand.

Object oriented analysis focuses on the response of a system as a whole to messages from actors in the environment. It also identifies and models relationships among significant concepts in the problem domain. In object-oriented design, the focus shifts to the objects, classes, and messages which form the software structure of the system.

Three concepts — objects, classes, and messages — are fundamental to object-oriented systems. *Objects* are the basic structural components of object-oriented software. They are organized into *classes* and communicate with each other by *messages*.

OBJECTS

An object may be considered from two perspectives. During analysis, it may be regarded as an abstraction of someone or something in the real world which is significant to the system. During design, it is viewed as a unit of software.[1]

Components of an Object

Each object has three components:

- A unique *identity* by which it may be referenced,
- A set of *attributes*, and
- A set of *behaviors*.

An object's unique identity enables other objects to direct messages to it. From the perspective of analysis, an attribute is a descriptor of an object, and (for those who identify behaviors during analysis) a behavior is a responsibility of an object. From the viewpoint of design, an attribute is internal data of an object, and a behavior is an operation.

Encapsulation

An object is *encapsulated* when its internal attributes and behaviors are protected from external access by an interface. Only those behaviors defined as *public* may be requested by other objects. The value of an attribute of an object may be modified or retrieved by other objects only if the object provides them with a public behavior to do this. An object's attributes are usually *private*, available only from within the object. Thus, the encapsulation of behaviors serves the important function of protecting the attributes from being changed by other objects in the system. This ability helps maintain a more stable system.

Persistence

Many objects which belong to the application domain (often known as business objects) are *persistent*. They have relatively long lives. A person may be a customer

---

[1]In our discussion of object-oriented analysis, we avoided the use of the term "object" in order to reinforce the distinction between analysis and design. Instead, we referred to concepts in the problem domain and, if necessary, instances of those concepts.

of a bank for many years and maintain accounts over that period. During that time, the banking system must remember the attributes of the customer and the accounts and must process transactions for the accounts. In the real world, instances of many concepts are inherently persistent. In software, permanent data storage devices and data bases implement persistence. The way this is done is typically discussed in a database or advanced systems course.

CLASSES

Every object is a member of a class. **A class is a group of objects having an identical set of attributes and an identical set of behaviors.** The value of an attribute may vary from one object in a class to another. The algorithm for a behavior is the same for each object in a class; thus, all objects in the class can share the code for the algorithm.

These attributes and behaviors may be regarded as a template for creating a new object in the class. The relationship of a class to an object is parallel to the relationship of a mold to a product. A class may create new objects belonging to it.

In the early days of object-oriented software development, many authors referred to objects as **instances** in order to emphasize the relationship of an object to its class. At present, the word "instance" is merely a synonym for "object."

Class Hierarchies and Inheritance

Classes may also be organized as generalization-specialization hierarchies, with *subclasses* and *superclasses* (as discussed in Chapter 5). Within such a hierarchy, each subclass *inherits* the attributes, behaviors, and associations of its superclass. That is, **every object in a subclass has:**

- **All the attributes of its superclass** (and may have additional attributes),
- **All the operations of its superclass** (and may have additional operations), **and**
- **All the associations of its superclass** (and may have additional associations).

Furthermore, the algorithm for an operation in a subclass may differ from that of the operation of the same name in the superclass. This permits the behavior defined for the subclass to override that of the superclass. It is a way to implement polymorphism (discussed below) within an inheritance hierarchy.

This ability to inherit from another class allows the designer to extend the attributes and behaviors of a class easily. This capability is heavily used in object-oriented design.

In the Public University Registration System, the university catalog lists the members of the class Course. A student who wishes to know the title and number of units[2] for the course CIS 235 would look in the university catalog. The university class schedule lists all the sections offered in a given term. A student who wishes to find out how many sections of CIS 235 are being offered and when they meet would look in the class schedule. Then the student might attempt to register for one of these sections.

The left-hand side of Figure 8.1 shows a design class diagram in which Course and Section are modeled independently. Their relationship is shown as a one-to-many association. Note that Course has the attributes **courseNumber**, **title**, and **units** and the behavior **associateDepartment**. Section has the attributes **courseNumber**, **sectionNumber**, **title**, **units**, **maximumNumberOfStudents**, **meetingTime**, and

---

[2]As well as other attributes such as the course description and mode of instruction, which are not shown in Figure 8.1.

FIGURE 8.1   Modeling the relationship between Course and Section with and without a generalization-specialization hierarchy

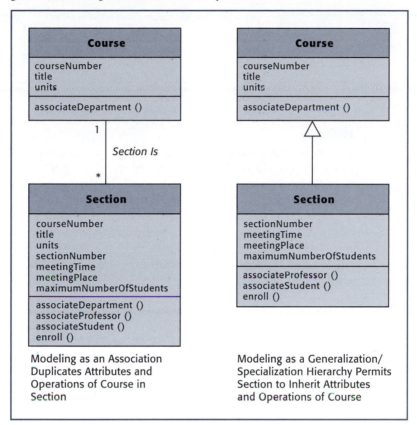

meetingPlace. Section is a subclass of Course. The right-hand side of Figure 8.1 models Section as a subclass of Course in a generalization-specialization hierarchy. Now Section inherits the attributes **courseNumber**, **title**, and **units** from Course. Section has the additional attributes **sectionNumber**, **maximumNumberOfStudents**, **meetingTime**, and **meetingPlace** and has the behaviors **associateDepartment** (inherited from Course) as well as **associateProfessor**, **associateStudent**, and **enroll**.

MESSAGES

All communication in an object-oriented system takes place via messages. **A message is a request from one object to a second object to carry out a behavior belonging to the second object.** The object sending a message is referred to as a *client* object; the receiving object is referred to as a *server* object.

Objects cooperate to carry out the work of the system by exchanging messages. A message specifies

▌ The **identity of the object** to which it is sent,
▌ The **name of the behavior** and, possibly,
▌ The **parameters** associated with the message.

In an object-oriented programming language, the identity of an object is referenced by a variable. This variable is a pointer to the object; some people think of it as the address of the object.

FIGURE 8.2   Example of the need for visibility

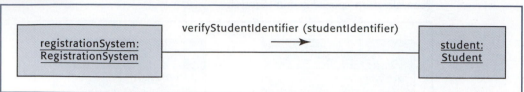

Visibility

If one object needs to send a message to another object, the receiving object must be *visible* to the sending object. In Figure 8.2, in order for the object **registrationSystem** to be able to send the message **verifyStudentIdentifier** to the object **student**, the object **student** must be visible to the object **registrationSystem**. The implementation of visibility requires the sending object to know the identity of the receiving object. This is usually done with a variable which points to the receiving object. Thus, in Figure 8.2, the **registrationSystem** object must know the identity of the **student** object. Chapter 9 discusses visibility and the techniques for implementing it.

Polymorphism

Another characteristic of object-oriented software is that objects in different classes may respond differently to messages of the same name. This characteristic is known as *polymorphism* (from the Greek *poly* (many) + *morphe* (form)). As a common example, objects in many classes have behaviors which cause them to print or display themselves. What is printed or displayed depends on the object. A display of a rectangle will be different from a display of a circle. Polymorphism is often referred to as an important basic strategy in object-oriented design.

OBJECT-ORIENTED PROGRAM DESIGN

The principal task of object-oriented program design is to assign responsibilities to classes.

RESPONSIBILITIES

A *responsibility* is an obligation of an object to other objects. There are two types of responsibilities — knowing and doing.

What an object may be responsible for knowing includes:

- **What it knows** — its attributes,
- **Who it knows** — the objects associated with it, and
- **What it knows how to do** — its behaviors (the operations it can perform).

What an object may be responsible for doing includes:

- **Doing something itself,**
- **Requesting services** from other objects, and
- **Controlling and coordinating** the activities of other objects.

An object may fulfill its responsibilities by carrying them out itself or by collaborating with other objects, sending them messages to request their services.

METHODS AND OPERATIONS

Informally, an operation is a behavior used to fulfill part or all of a responsibility. More precisely, in the UML, an *operation* is a service which can be requested from an object. An operation has a *signature,* consisting of the operation's name, its parameters, and the type of what it returns. An operation is invoked by a message with the same name as that of the operation. In the languages Java and Visual Basic.Net, operations are called *methods.* Unfortunately, as noted below, the UML has a different definition of method.

> **What are the differences among a responsibility, a behavior, a method, and an operation?**

These four terms are closely related conceptually. In practice, their usage tends to be somewhat informal, and they often appear to be synonyms. Here are some comments on the differences and our working definitions for them, from the most general to the most specific. Only two are formally defined in the UML.

Responsibility is perhaps the most general term. It emphasizes the obligation or commitment of a class to provide services to objects in the system. As noted above, an object may carry out a responsibility directly or may collaborate with objects of other classes to fulfill the responsibility indirectly.

A **behavior** is a task carried out by an operation. This term focuses on what the operation must do rather than on the algorithm accomplishing the task.

An **operation** is defined in the UML as a service which an object can be requested to perform.

Method is often used informally to mean the actions an object takes in response to a message. Formally, the UML defines a **method** as the specific implementation of an operation of a class.

MODELS FOR OBJECT-ORIENTED ANALYSIS AND DESIGN

Figure 8.3 summarizes the principal models and techniques used in object-oriented analysis and program design. As the products of analysis and design, these models are also the major deliverables of the analysis and design process.

PATTERNS FOR OBJECT-ORIENTED SOFTWARE DESIGN

As we have noted, the assignment of responsibilities to objects is the primary task of object-oriented software design. But on what basis do we decide which responsibilities to give to which object? A basic strategy for object-oriented program design is the use of a set of patterns. These patterns codify what object-oriented designers have learned through experience. They represent fundamental principles and best practices of object-oriented design.

A *pattern* is a named statement of a design problem together with its solution. The pattern also provides guidance about when and how to apply it. A pattern consists of a pattern name, the problem, the solution, and comments about the consequences of using it.

FIGURE 8.3   Models and techniques of object-oriented analysis and program design

Object-Oriented Analysis

Event analysis

Use case diagram
Essential use case narrative
Domain model
System sequence diagram
System operation contract

Report layouts
Screen layouts
State transition diagrams

Object-Oriented Program Design

Class diagram
Interaction diagrams
   Collaboration diagram
   Sequence diagram
Contract

Patterns, including
   Creator
   Expert
   Façade
   Singleton

Primary design criteria
   Coupling
   Cohesion
   Law of Demeter

Many patterns for object-oriented software design have been identified.[3] (It often appears as if there are as many patterns as there are authors, with names and details varying from author to author.) Figure 8.4 contains the patterns presented in this book. The first three of these patterns are illustrated in this chapter. The Singleton pattern is illustrated in Chapter 10.

The four patterns discussed in this chapter are fundamental to the process of object-oriented design. They provide the rationale for deciding which operations are assigned to which classes. They also lead to improved program design. Although the explanations appear now, their use will not be fully understood until they are discussed later in the chapter as a part of the Public University Registration System.

THE FAÇADE PATTERN

Application software contains many classes. As we saw in Chapter 7, the software is typically organized in layers. In a three-tier architecture, the first tier — the presentation layer — must communicate with many objects in the middle tier — the

---

[3]See, for example, Erich Gamma, Richard Helm, Ralph Johnson, and John Vlissides, *Design Patterns: Elements of Reusable Object-Oriented Software* (Reading, Mass.: Addison-Wesley, 1995) — considered by many to be the definitive work.

| FIGURE 8.4 | Common patterns for object-oriented software design |

Pattern Name:	**Façade**
Problem:	Who should be responsible for handling a system operation message from an actor?
Solution:	Assign this responsibility to an object representing the system as a whole.
Comments:	The façade pattern provides an interface between two layers (or tiers) of a system.
Pattern Name:	**Creator**
Problem:	Who should be responsible for requesting the creation of a new object?
Solution:	Assign a class B the responsibility of requesting the creation of an object in class A if any of the following is true: • B has the initializing data which will be passed to A when it is created (i.e., B is an expert with respect to creating A). • B contains objects of class A. • B records instances of objects of class A. • B closely uses objects of class A. • Objects of class A are part of objects of class B.
Comments:	Since all objects must be created at some point in the process, this pattern guides the designer on where to locate the **create** message.
Pattern Name:	**Expert**
Problem:	What is the most basic principle for assigning responsibilities to objects?
Solution:	Assign a responsibility to the class that has the information needed to fulfill it.
Comments:	By assigning behavior to classes on the basis of where the data is located, the design is improved and the program is simpler to understand.
Pattern Name:	**Singleton**
Problem:	How can global visibility be provided? How can a single access point to an interface be provided?
Solution:	Define a class which refers to only one instance (the "singleton").
Comments:	The singleton pattern provides a single place to obtain visibility to another part of the system.

application layer. The more the first tier knows about the second tier, the more complex it will become. This adds to the complexity of the whole system. A better approach is to create a "unified front-end" or a façade to the middle tier. The major advantage of using a façade is that it enforces the integrity of the three-tier architecture. It simplifies the connection between the top two tiers. The presentation layer needs to understand only the behavior in the façade object but not that of the rest of the model. From another perspective, a façade object extends the principle of encapsulation from the level of an object to that of an entire tier of architecture.

THE CREATOR PATTERN

Every software object must be created at some point during program execution. Some objects are created when the system starts up. For example, the **system** object, shown in a system sequence diagram, falls into this category. Other objects already exist; they are created outside the operations currently being designed. For example, in the Public University Registration System, objects such as **department, student**, and **professor** fall into this category. Every object which must be instantiated requires a design decision about which object will request its creation. The Creator pattern guides the designer in this most important decision. It assigns the **create** message to an object closely related to the new object.

THE EXPERT PATTERN

The Creator and Façade patterns cover special situations — instantiation and the interface from the presentation to the business layer. The Expert pattern provides guidance for more general design decisions. Since all processes work with data, it makes sense to use the location of data as a basis for assigning behavior. The Expert pattern states that a responsibility should be assigned to an object which itself contains most of the data required to carry out the responsibility or which can communicate with other objects having the data. The reason is that an operation should not have to search extensively for its essential data.

THE SINGLETON PATTERN

The Singleton pattern makes it easy to obtain access to or global visibility to another part of the system. It is frequently used to manage communication between the application layer and the storage layer (or data base). Access to the Public University data base via a Singleton object is illustrated in Chapter 10.

MODELS FOR OBJECT-ORIENTED PROGRAM DESIGN

Among the UML models for object-oriented program design are interaction diagrams and class diagrams. These diagrams are created and completed as responsibilities are assigned to objects. The domain models used in analysis emphasize associations and attributes. The interaction diagrams and class diagrams used in design emphasize messages and behaviors.

INTERACTION DIAGRAMS

An *interaction diagram* depicts the messages between objects or classes in a program. It shows the *collaborations* between objects. There are two types of interaction diagrams in the UML — collaboration diagrams and sequence diagrams. Both types of diagrams are explained in this chapter. Either type of diagram can be used to show the messages from one object or class to another.

The UML provides annotations to show elaborate details of the interactions if required. The presentation in this book is limited to the basic components of interaction diagrams.

Collaboration Diagrams

A *collaboration diagram* is a network model of the messages between interacting objects and classes. Figure 8.5 shows an example of a collaboration diagram. Note that it contains lines representing messages between objects. A collaboration diagram can also show messages from an actor to the system. A straight line represents a message to an object from an actor or from another object.

FIGURE 8.5   Example of a collaboration diagram

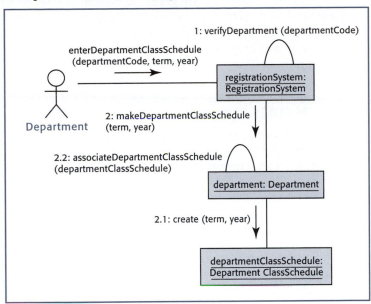

A loop represents a message from an object to itself. Messages are numbered to show the sequence in which they occur. The parameters of a message may also be shown.

Sequence Diagrams

A *sequence diagram* shows interactions in a fence format. Recall that system sequence diagrams (see Figure 5.26) are used in object-oriented analysis to show interactions between actors and a system. Figure 8.6 shows an example of a sequence diagram for objects within a system.

Note that the same information is shown in a sequence diagram as in a collaboration diagram. The difference is that the messages in a sequence diagram appear

FIGURE 8.6   Example of a sequence diagram

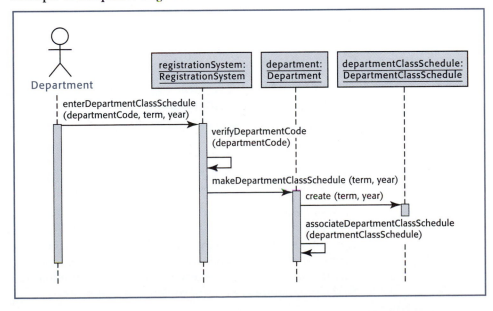

from top to bottom in time sequence. This makes it possible to omit the message numbers in a sequence diagram. A system sequence diagram, as introduced in Chapter 4, is merely a special case of a sequence diagram.

We recommend collaboration diagrams for beginning program designers because these diagrams make it easy to show more detail than sequence diagrams. In addition, only the messages required need to be shown.

DESIGN CLASS DIAGRAMS

A design class diagram follows the same graphic conventions as a domain model. However, a design class diagram also shows operations. The names of the operations for a class are located within the class rectangle in a separate section below the class's attributes. (See Figure 8.7 for an example of a design class diagram.) (As far as the UML is concerned, a domain model and a design class diagram are both class diagrams. We use different names for them to clearly distinguish analysis from design and the analysis model from the design model.) Design class diagrams are discussed in Chapter 9.

AN OBJECT-ORIENTED PROGRAM DESIGN PROCESS

We can expect methods for object-oriented program design to differ in detail, even though all may use the UML for modeling the design. In the presentation in this book, we follow the eight-step approach below.

STEP 1. PRODUCE AN INTERACTION DIAGRAM FOR EACH SYSTEM OPERATION IDENTIFIED DURING ANALYSIS.

Each system operation corresponds to a high-level system event. This step involves allocating responsibilities to classes, guided by a set of patterns for object-oriented design. Using the postconditions shown in the contract for each system operation, determine which objects should perform each responsibility. Create operations to complete each responsibility and place them in the appropriate class.

At this time, the concepts in the domain model become classes in the class diagram. Add a *façade* object to act as a *controller* for the system. This façade object is in fact the System concept shown on the system sequence diagram. This means that the messages from actors to the system in the system sequence diagram become the operations of the façade object. Make sure that there is a chain of messages linking the façade class to the objects which collaborate with it to carry out the system operation.

STEP 2. PRODUCE A DESIGN CLASS DIAGRAM SHOWING THE OPERATIONS FROM THE INTERACTION DIAGRAMS.

At this time, the designer has an initial model of the system.

STEP 3. SPECIFY THE SIGNATURE AND THE ALGORITHM FOR EACH OPERATION.

A *signature* is a complete definition of the message associated with an operation. It includes all the parameters with their names and data types or classes. Also, it includes the visibility of the operation and the data type or class returned by the operation. If the operation contains business rules, some type of pseudocode is recommended to specify them. A signature provides a standard way to communicate the definition of a message to the programmers who will construct the software.

FIGURE 8.7   Example of a design class diagram

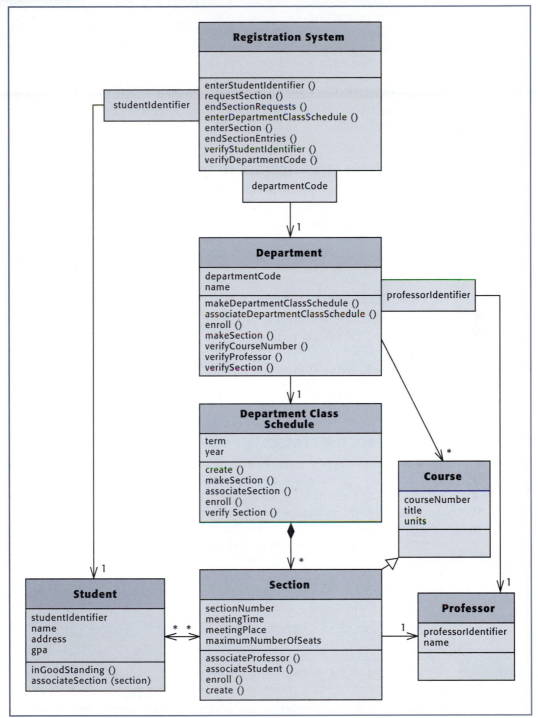

STEP 4. DESIGN THE GRAPHICAL USER INTERFACE.[4]

A good way to start is to sketch the layout of an input screen with a command button for each business event. Avoid extraneous data and fancy graphical user interface components such as list boxes for now. Just include text boxes for all data submitted

---

[4]For the purpose of this discussion, we assume a graphical user interface (GUI), the most common mode of user interaction.

and returned. These should match the essential use case narratives and system sequence diagrams created earlier. This sketch will serve as a visual reminder of the steps in the interaction.

Then enhance this sketch of the graphical user interface by providing all the required data the user wants to aid the data entry. Convert all data inputs which can be selected from a list box to either a conventional list box or a drop-down list box. Then build a mock-up using any available tool. Microsoft Access or an Integrated Development Environment which can create a mock-up in Java or Visual Basic is ideal for this purpose. User interface design is discussed further in Chapters 11 and 12.

STEP 5. DEFINE THE INTERFACE TO THE PRESENTATION LAYER.

Create an object or objects for each screen in the graphical user interface. Add the physical interface operations to each of these objects. Also add operations, other attributes, and significant details consistent with the logical model required to support the graphical user interface. This can be extensive, as each list box requires the production of an iterative list. This completes the design for an implementation.

STEP 6. DEFINE THE INTERFACE TO THE STORAGE LAYER.

Add objects with operations, other attributes, and significant details consistent with the logical model required to support the persistence of the objects in the problem domain.

Typically, this includes using a relational or other data base to contain the persistent data. It also could include updating the data base or capturing the database transactions in a file.

STEP 7. PLACE THE CLASSES IN PACKAGES.

Group related sets of classes in packages. In the UML, a *package* is a rather arbitrary grouping of constituents of a system model. A package has a name by which it may be identified. The choice of elements to be placed in a package is up to the designer. Packages are sometimes used to organize a model into subsystems. We will not discuss packages further in this book due to the great variety of purposes for which they can be used. This step completes the design specification of the system.

In practice, Steps 1 through 4 are likely to be carried out in parallel. To simplify the presentation, we will discuss them sequentially. This chapter discusses Step 1; Chapter 9, Steps 2 and 3; Chapter 10, Step 6; and Chapters 11 and 12, Steps 4 and 5.

Figure 8.8 summarizes the process for object-oriented program design.

FIGURE 8.8   Procedure for object-oriented program design

> Step 1. Produce an interaction diagram for each system operation identified during analysis.
> Step 2. Produce a design class diagram showing the operations from the interaction diagrams.
> Step 3. Specify the signature and the algorithm for each operation.
> Step 4. Design the graphical user interface.
> Step 5. Define the interface to the presentation layer.
> Step 6. Define the interface to the storage layer.
> Step 7. Place the classes in packages.

The most important activity of object-oriented software design is assigning responsibilities to objects. Our design decisions are guided by the patterns listed in Figure 8.4. We create interaction diagrams — especially collaboration diagrams — to investigate alternative assignments of responsibilities and to record our design decisions.

COLLABORATION DIAGRAMS

As defined above, a ***collaboration diagram*** is a network model of the messages between interacting objects or classes.[5] A class is represented in a collaboration diagram by a rectangle containing the name of the class, as illustrated in Figure 8.9. To represent an object, the class name is underlined and preceded by a colon. The object's name may optionally be included to the left of the colon.

A ***link*** is an instance of an association. It represents a path of navigation along which a message may be sent from one object or class (the client) to the associated object or class (the server). If an object sends a message to itself, the link has the shape of an arch (see message 3.1.3, **associateSection (section)**, in Figure 8.9).

FIGURE 8.9   **Example of a collaboration diagram**

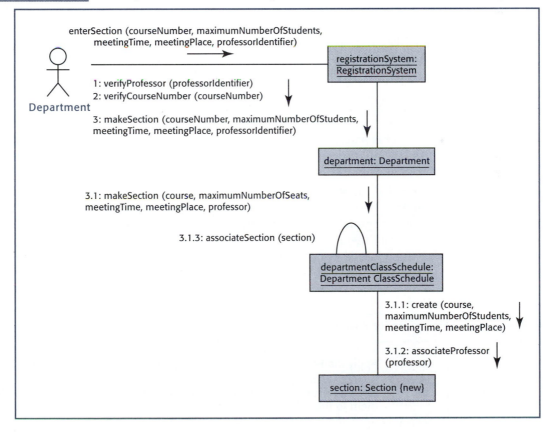

---

[5]In *Structured Design: Fundamentals of a Discipline of Computer Program and Systems Design* (Englewood Cliffs, N.J.: Prentice-Hall, 1979), Edward Yourdon and Larry L. Constantine defined a structure chart generally as a model of the structure of reference of a set of program units. According to this definition, collaboration diagrams and sequence diagrams are structure charts for object-oriented software.

A message is shown as a labeled arrow above or beside the link along which it flows. The UML has a standard syntax for messages:

> **message name (in *parameter : parameterType*, out *parameter : parameterType*)**

Only the message name is required. The other message components may be present or not as desired. In the list of parameters, the word "**in**" (in boldface) precedes the input parameters. The word "**out**" precedes the output parameters. The word "**in**" may be omitted if there are no output parameters. The word "**inout**" signifies a parameter which is used for both input and output. The examples in this text use only input parameters, in keeping with good programming practice.

The order of messages is shown with sequence numbers in a hierarchical scheme.

▌ The first message in the sequence is not numbered.
▌ Messages from the object receiving the initial message are numbered 1, 2, etc.
▌ Messages from the object receiving message 1 are numbered 1.1, 1.2, etc.

In Figure 8.9, the parameters of the messages are shown next to the links.

CREATING COLLABORATION DIAGRAMS

In Step 1 of our program design process, we create a separate collaboration diagram for each system operation shown in the system sequence diagrams. To create this collaboration diagram, we carry out five substeps, as summarized in Figure 8.10:

Step 1.1. Apply the Façade pattern. Choose a façade object to direct the messages from the presentation layer to appropriate objects in the application layer.

This pattern is applied only once. The same façade object appears in all the collaboration diagrams. Make the system input the starting message of each collaboration diagram. The façade object is its receiver.

Step 1.2. Apply the Creator pattern. Using the postconditions of the system operation contracts, identify all objects which must be created. Then using the domain model, determine which objects should send the message to their class to create them.

Include these **create** operations in the second iteration of the collaboration diagram. This will specify what objects should be some of the clients.

FIGURE 8.10	Procedure for creating a collaboration diagram

Step 1.1. Apply the Façade pattern. Choose a façade object for the system.

Step 1.2. Apply the Creator pattern. Identify all objects which must be created, together with the objects which should request their creation, and add them to the collaboration diagram.

Step 1.3. Apply the Expert pattern. Assign every behavior to the object which is the information expert. Show all the server objects and the messages to them from an unknown client object.

Step 1.4. Paying attention to information flow, fill in the rest of the clients until there is a path of messages connecting all the objects.

Step 1.5. Refine the collaboration diagrams, taking into account coupling, cohesion, and the Law of Demeter.

Step 1.3. Apply the Expert pattern. Using the use case definitions and contracts, assign every behavior to the object which is the logical expert.

Be sure to fulfill the responsibilities required by the use case narratives. Verify all the preconditions and achieve all the postconditions stated in the system operation contracts. Summarize the responsibilities of each concept. Draw mini-interaction diagrams to illustrate your decisions. Show all the server objects. Then show the messages to them from an unknown client object. To begin with, the only known clients are the initiating actors from the system sequence diagram.

Step 1.4. While paying attention to information flow, fill in the rest of the clients until there is a path of messages connecting all the objects.

Step 1.5. Refine the collaboration diagrams, taking into account coupling, cohesion, and the Law of Demeter. (The definitions and discussion of coupling, cohesion, and the Law of Demeter are deferred until Chapter 9, after the initial set of collaboration diagrams and design class diagrams has been developed.)

If the diagram gets too complex, split it into smaller diagrams.

PUBLIC UNIVERSITY — OBJECT-ORIENTED PROGRAM DESIGN

We now continue the design of the Public University Registration System, applying the procedures listed in Figures 8.3 and 8.10. We assume that Alternative A, the single-processor alternative defined in Chapter 7, was chosen for the overall system. The focus here is on the program design of the software objects in the application layer of the three-tier program architecture. Connecting the application layer to the data base in the storage layer is discussed in Chapter 10. Connecting the business layer to the user interface is dealt with briefly in Chapter 12.

INTERACTION DIAGRAMS FOR THE OBJECTS IN THE APPLICATION LAYER

The first step in designing the software for the Public University Registration System results in interaction diagrams. We use the Façade, Creator and Expert patterns shown in Figure 8.4. The product is a set of collaboration diagrams for the objects in the application layer. We discuss each use case separately.

STEP 1 — COLLABORATION DIAGRAMS FOR THE USE CASE SUBMIT DEPARTMENT CLASS SCHEDULE

We will now develop collaboration diagrams for the three system operations necessary for the system to respond to the use case Submit Department Class Schedule — **enterDepartmentClassSchedule**, **enterSection**, and **endSectionEntries**.

Step 1.1. Apply the Façade pattern. Choose a façade object to direct the messages from the presentation layer to appropriate objects in the application layer. The Façade pattern determines which object acts as a controller or director for the application layer. This façade object provides an interface to the presentation layer, which in turn manages the interaction with the user, most likely via a GUI.

A façade also can provide access to objects. For example, a façade can be assigned the responsibility for locating a department object knowing only its department code. This means that if one knows the department code "CIS," it is possible to locate the CIS object containing the department code and title ("CIS, Computer Information Systems").

FIGURE 8.11   System sequence diagram for the use case Submit Department Class Schedule

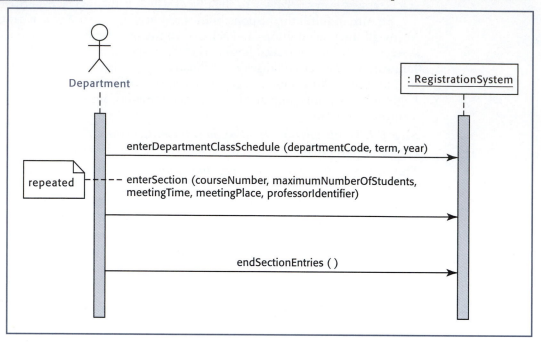

At this time, it is not essential to determine how this will be done. In fact, there are many different ways this responsibility can be implemented. For example, some techniques use a dictionary-like structure for the objects, and other techniques use a database management system.

Figure 8.11 shows the system sequence diagram for the use case Submit Department Class Schedule. This diagram ignores the presentation layer. It shows only the form and information content of the messages from the user to the business layer. It represents the business layer as a single object called **registrationSystem**. Using the Façade pattern, **registrationSystem** becomes our façade object.

Figure 8.12 shows the description of a façade object for the student registration system. The three system operations shown are its responsibilities for the Submit Department Class Schedule use case. These operations match the messages the registration system receives from the user (via the presentation layer). We will add other responsibilities to **registrationSystem** when we create collaborations for other use cases.

FIGURE 8.12   Responsibilities assigned to the registrationSystem façade for the Submit Department Class Schedule use case

FAÇADE OBJECT	SYSTEM OPERATIONS
registrationSystem	enterDepartmetClassSchedule (department code, term, year) enterSection (course number, section number, maximum number of students, meeting time, meeting place, professor identifier) endSectionEntries()

THE COLLABORATION DIAGRAM FOR enterDepartmentClassSchedule

Now it is time to create the collaboration diagram for **enterDepartmentClass-Schedule**. To do so, we refer to the use case narrative and system sequence diagram for the use case Submit Department Class Schedule and to the contract for each related system operation. These were shown in Chapter 6 for the Public University Registration System. The domain model and the use case narrative for Submit Department Class Schedule are repeated here as Figures 8.13 and 8.14. The contract for the system operation **enterDepartmentClassSchedule** appears as Figure 8.15.

Step 1.2. Apply the Creator pattern. Identify all objects which must be created. Then determine which objects should request their creation. The contract has a postcondition stating that the Department Class Schedule was created. This requires Department Class Schedule to have an operation to create itself. All object-oriented programming languages expect objects to be created by their own class. Recall that the class is a template for the object. We will use the UML notation **create**, followed by the attributes of the new object as parameters.

But which object should send this **create** message to Department Class Schedule? The Creator pattern states that the request to create an object should come from an object which closely uses the newly created object. Referring to the domain model (Figure 8.13), we note that the only class associated with the Department Class Schedule is the Department. (At this stage in the use case, the new sections have not been created.) This means that the object **department** is an excellent candidate to request the creation of its new **departmentClassSchedule** object.

FIGURE 8.13　　Domain model for the Public University Registration System

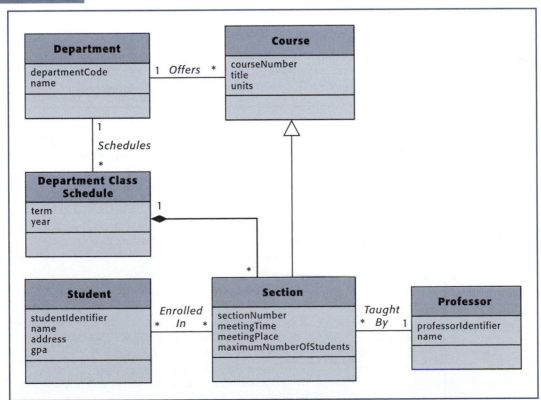

FIGURE 8.14   Use case narrative for Submit Department Class Schedule

Use case:	**Submit Department Class Schedule**
Actors:	Department
Purpose:	To enter each section to be taught by the department into the registration system so that students may register for them.
Overview:	A Department representative enters its department, term, and year, and a department schedule is created. Then each section is entered into the system. This includes all the data about the section, including the professor who is teaching the section.
Type:	Essential
Preconditions:	Courses and instructors are known to the system.
Postconditions:	Department class schedule was saved in the system.
Special Requirements:	Each Department must have access to the system.

Flow of Events

ACTOR ACTION	SYSTEM RESPONSE
1. This use case begins when a Department representative desires to enter the sections to be offered.	
2. The Department representative provides the department's code, term, and year.	3. Verifies that the department is valid. Then it creates a department class schedule.
4. For each section entered, the representative provides the department code, course number, and section number. In addition, the attributes maximum number of seats, meeting time, meeting place, and professor identifier are entered.	5. Creates a section and then adds this section to the department class schedule.
6. The Department representative indicates that there are no more sections and leaves the system.	

Alternative Flow of Events

Line 3: Invalid department code entered.	Inform the user. Return to Line 2.
Line 5: Invalid course number entered.	Inform the user. Return to Line 2.
Line 5: Invalid professor identifier entered.	Inform the user. Return to Line 2.

Step 1.3. Apply the Expert pattern. Using the use case definitions and contracts, assign every behavior to the object which is the logical expert. In a perfect world, there is no need to verify that the department code entered by the user is valid. However, in an imperfect world, we must verify the department code. The contract for **enterDepartmentClassSchedule** states this as a responsibility of

FIGURE 8.15   Contract for the system operation *enterDepartment ClassSchedule*

Contract Name:	**enterDepartmentClassSchedule** (departmentCode, term, year)
Use Case:	Submit Department Class Schedule
Responsibilities:	Create a new department class schedule for the department.
Exceptions:	If the department code is not valid, inform the user.
Preconditions:	Department is known to the system.
Postconditions:	Department Class Schedule was created. The association between Department and Department Class Schedule was created.

the system. Note the exception: "If the department's code is not valid, inform the user."

Who should carry out this responsibility? To answer this question using the expert pattern, the responsibility goes to the object who has the information — who knows the department code. This appears to be the **department** object. There is a problem, however. That is, each department object knows only one department code — its own. We somehow need an object who knows all the department codes. This sounds like a job for the façade object **registrationSystem**, which knows all the departments, as discussed earlier. Note that the precondition, "Department is known to the system," suggests this. Thus, we will assign the operation **verifyDepartment** to **registrationSystem**.

One of the postconditions in the contract requires that the association between Department and Department Class Schedule be created. Thus, we add an association operation to make that association possible. Since Department needs to be associated with Department Class Schedule and not the other way around, the expert for this operation is the **department** object. Another way to look at this is that the Department needs to see its Department Class Schedule. Thus, we will place **associateDepartmentClassSchedule** in the object **department**. The chart in Figure 8.16 summarizes the responsibilities assigned by the expert pattern.

Applying the Expert pattern has caused us to identify several incomplete collaborations. The server objects are always known, as these are the expert objects. However, the client objects are seldom known at this time.

Figure 8.17 shows the first-cut collaboration diagram for the system operation **enterDepartmentClassSchedule** after assigning responsibilities to the objects that will request the creation of new objects, as well as to the objects which are experts. Note that one client object is not yet identified. The client actor Department is known from the system sequence diagram, as determined in Chapter 5.

The next task in this step is to identify the unknown client object. Generally, the object which creates an objects, should also create its associations. Thus, unknownClient1 is **department**. It should be responsible for creating its association to **departmentClassSchedule**. The reason for this is that the task of creating an object is not complete until all its associations are also created.

We now number the messages based on what we know so far. According to the UML hierarchical numbering scheme, the first message, **enterDepartmentClass-Schedule**, has no number. We assign the number 1 to **verifyDepartment**, as it is the first message sent by **registrationSystem**. We partially number the remaining messages as ?.1, as they are both the first messages sent by their clients.

Note that there still is a big gap between the objects **registrationSystem** and **department**.

Step 1.4. While paying attention to information flow, fill in the rest of the clients until there is a path of messages connecting all objects. The next task is to fill in any missing links. Referring to the collaboration diagram in Figure 8.17, it appears that there is still one

---

FIGURE 8.16   Responsibilities assigned to expert objects for the system operation

enterDepartmentClassSchedule

EXPERT OBJECT	RESPONSIBILITIES
registrationSystem	Verify department (department code)
department	Associate department class schedule (department class schedule)

FIGURE 8.17   Initial collaboration diagram for the system operation *enterDepartmentClassSchedule*. Note that the UML permits the object receiving a *create* message to be annotated with the property {new}.

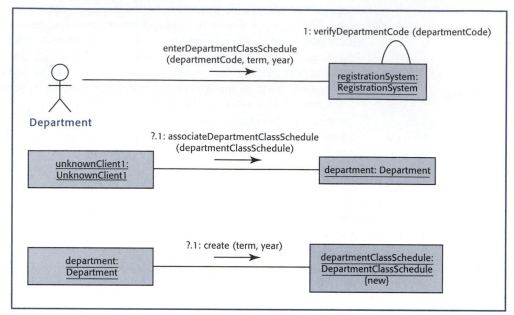

missing link. There needs to be a collaboration between **registrationSystem** and **department**. However, the message name must still be decided. It should reflect what **registrationSystem** is attempting to do. In this case, it is telling **department** to create a new **departmentClassSchedule** and associate it with **department**. The name "**create**" comes to mind, but that is reserved for a message sent to the class to which the new object will belong. A good compromise is **makeDepartmentClassSchedule**. After all, that is what the **department** is trying to do.

At this point, the collaboration diagram is done. The series of collaborations necessary to ensure the postcondition seems complete. See Figure 8.18 for the final collaboration diagram for the system operation **enterDepartmentClassSchedule**.

We can now assign the remaining message numbers. First, **makeDepartmentClassSchedule** becomes 2 because it is the second message generated by **registrationSystem** after it receives the message from the Department actor. Finally, **create** and **associateDepartmentClassSchedule** become 2.1 and 2.2, respectively, as in Figure 8.18, because they result from **department**'s receipt of message 2.

The discussion of coupling, cohesion, and the Law of Demeter (Step 1.5) will be deferred until Chapter 9, when the design class diagram has been developed and is ready to be refined.

THE COLLABORATION DIAGRAM FOR enterSection

Using the domain model in Figure 8.13, the use case narrative in Figure 8.14, and the contract for the system operation **enterSection**, shown here as Figure 8.19, we begin the analysis of the necessary operations.

Step 1.1. Apply the Façade pattern. Choose a façade object to direct the messages from the presentation layer to appropriate objects in the application layer. This decision was made for the entire system when we used the Façade pattern to select **registrationSystem** as the façade object.

FIGURE 8.18   Completed collaboration diagram for the system operation
enterDepartmentClassSchedule

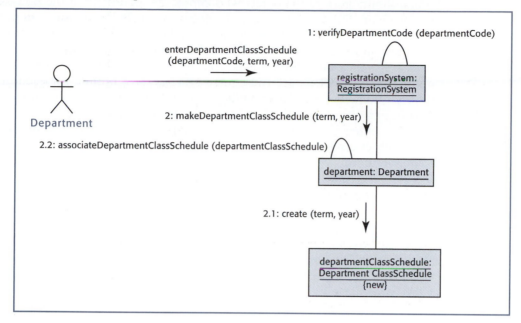

Step 1.2. Apply the Creator pattern. Identify all objects which must be created. Then determine which objects should request their creation. Since there is a whole-to-part association between Department Class Schedule and Section, the Creator pattern states that **departmentClassSchedule** should create the new **section**. Note that the Creator pattern answers the question "Who sends the **create** message to a class?" (Clearly, each class is responsible for creating its own objects.) This pattern states that the parent object in an aggregation or composition should create the child objects.

Step 1.3. Apply the Expert pattern. Using the use case definitions and contracts, assign every behavior to the object which is the logical expert. In a perfect world, the system's entire response to the message **enterSection** is to create an instance of **section** and then build

FIGURE 8.19   Contract for the system operation *enterSection*

Contract Name:	**enterSection** (courseNumber, sectionNumber, maximumNumberOfStudents, meetingTime, meetingPlace, professorIdentifier)
Use Case:	Submit Department Class Schedule
Responsibilities:	Add a new section to the department class schedule.
Exceptions:	If the course number is not valid, inform the user. If the professor identifier is not valid, inform the user.
Preconditions:	Entry of department class schedule is under way. Course is known to the system. Professor is known to the system.
Postconditions:	A Section was created. The association between Department Class Schedule and Section was created. The association between Section and Professor was created.

two associations. In the real world, we must also validate the professor identifier and the course number.

Who should verify the professor identifier? Using the expert pattern, the responsibility goes to the object who knows the identifiers of the professors in the Department. Thus, we will assign the operation **verifyProfessor** to **department**.

To determine who should verify the course number using the Expert pattern becomes more complicated. When we study the domain model, a problem emerges — the **department** object appears to be associated with each of the course numbers. This is because the course numbers are unique for each department (but not unique across departments). For example, it is possible for there to be an Accounting 101 and a CIS 101. Thus, some of the information needed to verify the course number is in the object **department**. This makes **department** the expert on which courses it offers, and we assign the operation **verifyCourseNumber** to **department**.

Now it is time to create a **section** object and then build its two associations. This requires **section** to have an operation to create itself. As before, the class Section will contain a **create** operation. Its arguments are the attributes of Section, including those attributes inherited from Course.

Next two associations need to be created. One is the association from Section to Professor, and the other is from Department Class Schedule to Section. Thus, we will insert **associateProfessor** in Section and **associateSection** in Department Class Schedule.

Figure 8.20 shows these objects with their corresponding responsibilities.

Figure 8.21 shows the first-cut collaboration diagram for the system operation **enterSection**. The client actor Department is known from the system sequence diagram. Note that there are three unknown client objects: unknownClient1 sends two messages, and unknownClient2 and unknownClient3 send one each, as shown in Figure 8.21.

It seems reasonable to assign to a single client the complete responsibility for creating a new instance of **section**, including the association of the new **section** to **departmentClassSchedule** and **professor**. Thus, unknownClient2 turns out to be **departmentClassSchedule**. This also means that an operation called **makeSection** should exist in **departmentClassSchedule**, as shown in Figure 8.22.

However, a new unknown client (unknownClient4) must be introduced to send the **makeSection** message to **departmentClassSchedule**. We can now expand the numbers for messages sent by unknownClient4 and **departmentClassSchedule**. See Figure 8.23 for the updated collaboration diagram.

Step 1.4. While paying attention to information flow, fill in the rest of the clients until there is a path of messages connecting all objects. The first task is to identify the unknownClient1 object. Referring to the domain model (Figure 8.13), we note

---

FIGURE 8.20   Responsibilities assigned to the expert objects for the system operation *enterSection*

EXPERT OBJECT	RESPONSIBILITIES
department	Verify professor (professor identifier) verify course number (course number)
section	Create section (course number, title, section number, maximum umber of students, meeting time, meeting place) associate professor (professor)
departmentClassSchedule	Associate section (section)

FIGURE 8.21   Initial collaboration diagram for the system operation *enterSection*

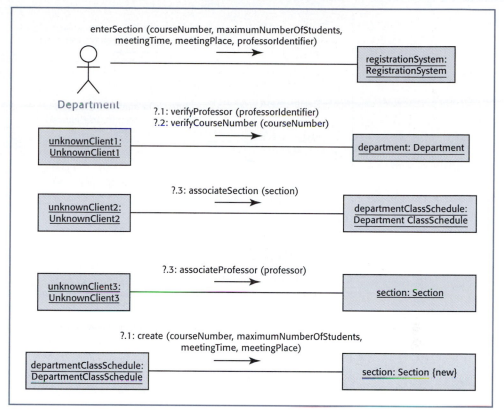

that the only class associated to **departmentClassSchedule** is the **department**. Since **department** is also associated to **registrationSystem**, **registrationSystem** would be a logical choice. Any other choice would entail more links.

The **departmentClassSchedule** object is the logical choice for unknownClient2, as it is already sending a message to **section**.

Now, if we substitute **department** for unknownClient4, we have a path connecting all the objects.

There is still a problem, however. No object has requested **department** to send the **makeSection** message. The **department** object must send **departmentClassSchedule** the message **makeSection (courseNumber, maximumNumberOfSeats, meetingTime, meetingPlace, professor)**. But **courseNumber** is the only one of these parameters which **department** can possibly know (from the **verifyCourseNumber** message). Who knows all the attributes of the new **section**? The **registrationSystem**.

We must therefore place a message on the link from **registrationSystem** to **department** to provide **department** with the data which **departmentClassSchedule**

FIGURE 8.22   Responsibilities assigned to the creator object for the system operation *enterSection*

CREATOR OBJECT	RESPONSIBILITIES
departmentClassSchedule	Make section (course number, section number, maximum number of seats, meeting time, meeting place, professor identifier)

FIGURE 8.23   Updated collaboration diagram for the system operation *enterSection*

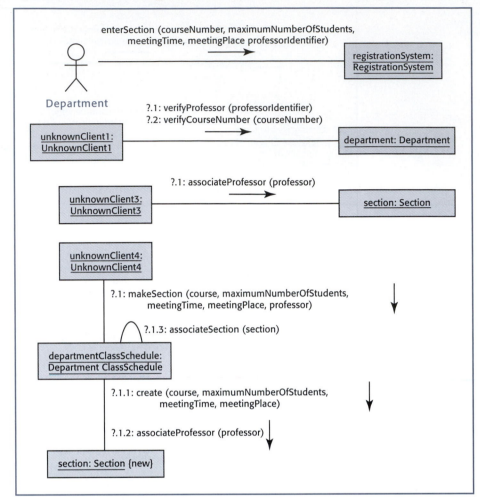

will need to create the new **section**. A choice of names for this message now confronts us. Since all it is doing is transferring data to **departmentClassSchedule**, a name reflecting this process would be appropriate. We could choose **transmitSection**, **sendSection**, or **makeSection**. We will choose **makeSection** arbitrarily. This ensures that there is a path of messages connecting **registrationSystem** to **department** and **departmentClassSchedule**. See Figure 8.24 for this assignment.

The only task left is to complete numbering the messages. The number of **verifyProfessor** remains 1. Then **verifyCourseNumber** becomes 2, and **makeSection** becomes 3; these are the messages out of **registrationSystem**. Then **makeSection** from **department** to **departmentClassSchedule** becomes

FIGURE 8.24   Additional responsibilities assigned to the department object for the system operation
enter Section

OBJECT	RESPONSIBILITIES
department	Make section (course number, section number, maximum number of students meeting time, meeting place, professor identifier)

FIGURE 8.25   **Completed collaboration diagram for the system operation *enterSection***

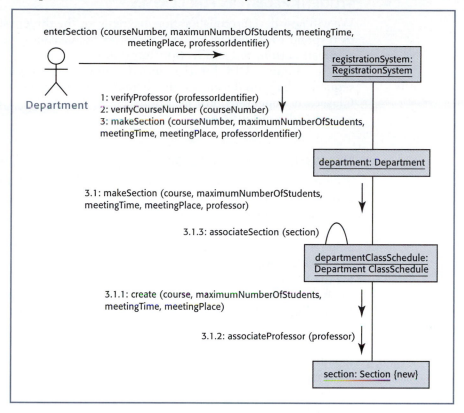

3.1. Finally, **create** and **associateProfessor** become 3.1.1 and 3.1.2, respectively. The remaining message, **associateSection** in **departmentClassSchedule**, becomes 3.1.3. Figure 8.25 shows the completed collaboration diagram for **enterSection**.

THE COLLABORATION DIAGRAM FOR endSectionEntries

Figure 8.26 shows the contract for the system operation **endSectionEntries**, which completes the system's response to the submission of a department schedule. The only remaining concern is saving the transaction. Because we have not discussed how to save data to a data base, this collaboration diagram will be delayed to Chapter 10, which talks about the interface to the storage layer.

FIGURE 8.26   **Contract for the system operation *endSectionEntries***

Contract Name:	**endSectionEntries ()**
Use Case:	Submit Department Class Schedule
Responsibilities:	Save the Department Class Schedule and Section in a data base.
Exceptions:	None
Preconditions:	Entry of sections must be under way.
Postconditions:	The instances of **section** and their associations to Professor and Department were saved in the data base.

STEP 1 — COLLABORATION DIAGRAMS FOR THE EVENT STUDENT REGISTERS FOR CLASSES

We will now develop collaboration diagrams for the three system operations necessary to respond to the event Student Registers for Classes — **enterStudentIdentifier**, **requestSection**, and **endSectionRequests**.

See Figure 8.13 for the domain model and Figure 8.27 for the system sequence diagram developed in Chapter 4. The use case narrative for Register for Classes is repeated here as Figure 8.28. We begin with the first operation, **enterStudentIdentifier**.

THE COLLABORATION DIAGRAM FOR enterStudentIdentifier

To build the collaboration diagram for **enterStudentIdentifier**, we first study the system operation contract. The contract for **enterStudentIdentifier** is repeated here for convenience as Figure 8.29.

Step 1.1. Apply the Façade pattern. Choose a façade object to direct the messages from the presentation layer to appropriate objects in the application layer. This decision was made for the entire system when we used the façade pattern to select **registrationSystem** as the façade object. Figure 8.30 shows the responsibilities added to **registrationSystem** for the Register for Classes use case.

Step 1.2. Apply the Creator pattern. Identify all objects which must be created. Then determine which objects should request their creation. Since no objects are created in this system operation, this step is unnecessary.

Step 1.3. Apply the Expert pattern. Using the use case definitions and contracts, assign every behavior to the object which is the logical expert. The system's entire essential response to the message **enterStudentIdentifier** is to verify that the student is eligible to enroll. In addition, we must find out whether the student identifier is valid. Who knows whether the student is eligible to enroll? In the Public University, eligibility to enroll requires that the student be in good standing.[6]

FIGURE 8.27	System sequence diagram for the use case Register for Classes

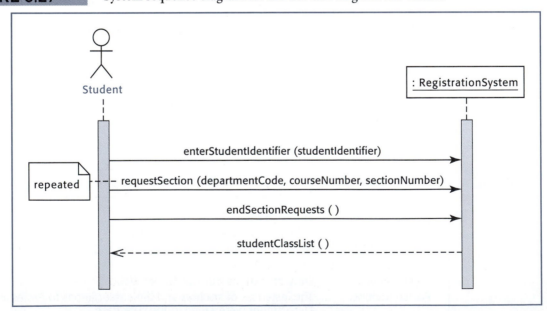

---

[6]If this is not clear from the contract or from information gathered in analysis, the designer may need to consult the user.

FIGURE 8.28   Use case narrative for the use case Register for Classes

Use case: **Register for Classes**
Actors: Student
Purpose: Register a student for classes and record the student's
                           schedule.
Overview: A Student requests the sections of class desired for a term.
                           The system adds the Student to each section if there is space
                           available. On completion, the system provides the Student
                           with a list of the classes in which he or she is enrolled.
Type: Essential
Preconditions: Class schedule must exist.
                           Student is known by the system.
Postconditions: Student was enrolled in the section.
Special Requirements: Student must get a system response within 10 seconds.

Flow of Events

ACTOR ACTION	**SYSTEM RESPONSE**
1. This use case begins when a Student desires to register for classes.	
2. The Student provides the Student's identifier.	3. Verifies that the Student is eligible to enroll.
4. For each section desired the Student provides the department code, course number, and section number.	5. Verifies there is room in the section.
6. The Student indicates there are no more sections.	7. Produces a student class list for the Student.
8. The Student receives the student class List.	

Alternative Flow of Events

Line 3: Invalid student identifier entered.	Inform the student. Return to Step 2.
Student is not eligible to enroll.	Inform the student. Return to Step 2.
Line 5: Invalid department code, course number, or section number entered.	Inform the student. Return to Step 4.
No seats remaining:	Inform the student. Return to Step 4.

By the Expert pattern, the responsibility goes to the object who knows about the student, which is, of course, **student**. Note the responsibility **inGoodStanding** in the **student** object in Figure 8.31.

As before, we assign the responsibility for knowing all the students and their identifiers to the façade object. Thus, we add the operation **verifyStudentIdentifier** to **registrationSystem**. Figure 8.31 shows this behavior as well.

FIGURE 8.29   Contract for the system operation *enterStudentIdentifier*

Contract Name: **enterStudentIdentifier** (studentIdentifier)
Use Case: Register for Classes
Responsibilities: Accept and validate the student's identifier.
                     Verify that the student is eligible to enroll.
Exceptions: If the student identifier is not valid, inform the user.
                     If the student is not eligible to register, inform the user.
Preconditions: Student identifier is known to the system.
Postconditions: None

FIGURE 8.30   Responsibilities assigned to the *registrationSystem* façade object

FAÇADE OBJECT	RESPONSIBILITIES
registrationSystem	Enter department schedule (department code, term, year)
	enter section (course number, section number, maximum number of students, meeting time, meeting place, professor identifier)
	end section entries ()
	enter student identifier (student identifier)
	request section (department code, course number, section number)
	end section requests ()

FIGURE 8.31   Responsibilities assigned to the expert objects for the system operation
enterStudentIdentifier

EXPERT OBJECT	RESPONSIBILITIES
student	In good standing ()
registrationSystem	Verify student identifier (student identifier)

Figure 8.32 shows the first-cut collaboration diagram for the system operation **enterStudentIdentifier**. Note that it requires two steps. The first one is to validate the student identifier using **verifyStudentIdentifier**. The second is to verify that the student is eligible to enroll using **inGoodStanding**. In this situation, there is one unknown client. The client for **verifyStudentIdentifier** must be **registrationSystem**, as there can be no other clients before the façade.

Step 1.4. While paying attention to information flow, fill in the rest of the clients until there is a path of messages connecting all objects. The first task is to identify the unknown client object. In the domain model in Figure 8.13, we see that Section is associated to Student. However, this association has not yet been created (it will be created as part of the **requestSection** operation). That leaves the façade as the only object with current visibility to the **student** object. Thus, we will assign unknownClient1 to **registrationSystem**. See Figure 8.33 for the final collaboration diagram for **enterStudentIdentifier**.

FIGURE 8.32   Initial collaboration diagram for the system operation *enterStudentIdentifier*

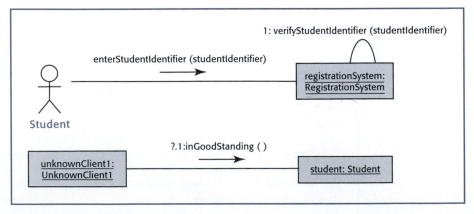

FIGURE 8.33   Completed collaboration diagram for the system operation *enterStudentIdentifier*

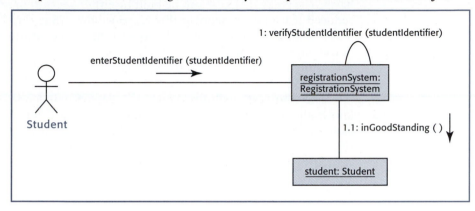

THE COLLABORATION DIAGRAM FOR requestSection

The system operation contract for **requestSection** is repeated here for convenience as Figure 8.34.

Step 1.1. Apply the Façade pattern. Choose a façade object to direct the messages from the presentation layer to appropriate objects in the application layer. This decision was made for the entire system when we used the façade pattern to select **registrationSystem** as the façade object.

Step 1.2. Apply the Creator pattern. Identify all objects which must be created. Then determine which objects should request their creation. Since no objects are created in this system operation, this step is unnecessary.

Step 1.3. Apply the Expert pattern. Using the use case definitions and contracts, assign every behavior to the object which is the logical expert. The system's essential response to the message **requestSection** is to verify that the section has seats available and then enroll the student in the section by building two associations. However, we must first find out whether the department code, course number, and section number are valid in order to ensure that the other preconditions are satisfied.

Who knows if the section has space available? By the Expert pattern, the responsibility goes to **section**. We will call the operation **enroll**. Note that we could have used the name **verifySpaceAvailable**. The name **enroll** is preferable because it describes the action expected when space is available. The name **verifySpaceAvailable** implies a request to return only a value of **true** or **false**.

FIGURE 8.34   Contract for the system operation *requestSection*

Contract Name:	**requestSection** (departmentCode, courseNumber, sectionNumber)
Use Case:	Register for Classes
Responsibilities:	Enroll the Student in the Section
Exceptions:	If the department code is not valid, inform the user. If the section is not valid, inform the user. If no seats are available, inform the user.
Preconditions:	Department is known to the system. Section is known to the system.
Postconditions:	An association was created between Student and Section. An association was created between Section and Student.

If there is space available, the two associations between **student** and **section** also have to be created. These can be built by either **section** or **student**. Coupling can be reduced if we assign **section** this responsibility. (See the discussion in Chapter 9.) These operations are **associateSection** in the object **student** and **associateStudent** in the object **section**.

Applying the Expert pattern, there are two additional responsibilities. (See Figure 8.35.)

The first responsibility, verify the department code, goes to the object who knows all the departments. This operation is already in the façade as a part of the use case Submit Department Class Schedule. The verification of the section should be the responsibility of **departmentClassSchedule**, which knows all the sections it contains. Verifying the section will require the combination of the course number and section number.

We will continue as before by building a collaboration diagram with all unknown clients. Figure 8.36 shows the first-cut collaboration diagram. Note that four clients are not identified and many links are missing.

Then we begin to identify the unknown clients. The object **departmentClass-Schedule** seems like a good candidate for unknownClient2 and unknownClient4, as it contains all the sections. We have given unknownClient3 the responsibility for seeing that the association from **student** to **section** is established. It is almost certain that unknownClient3 is probably **section**, as it has the behavior **enroll**. We identify **section** as unknownClient3 and give it the job of requesting the association from **section** to **student** as well. Thus, unknownClient4 is also **section**. See Figure 8.37 for these changes to the collaboration diagram.

Step 1.4. While paying attention to information flow, fill in the rest of the clients until there is a path of messages connecting all objects. As Figure 8.37 shows, the requests to **departmentClassSchedule** to verify the section and enroll the student must ultimately come from **registrationSystem**. However, the domain model shows that **departmentClassSchedule** is not directly connected to **registrationSystem**. Looking at the domain model, we see that the message path from **registrationSystem** should go through **department**. This implies that unknownClient1 is **department** and that it should receive the messages **verifySection** and **enroll** from **registrationSystem**.

The only task remaining is adding the sequence numbers to each collaboration. The numbers 1 and 2 can be assigned to **verifyDepartmentCode** and **verifySection**. The object **registrationSystem** can now invoke the operation **enroll** (message number 3). The chain for 3 can now be completed. The numbers 3.1 and 3.1.1 are assigned to the **enroll** messages from **department** to **departmentClassSchedule** and from **departmentClassSchedule** to **section**,

---

| **FIGURE 8.35** | Responsibilities assigned to the expert objects for the system operation *requestSection* |

EXPERT OBJECT	RESPONSIBILITIES
student	Associate section (section)
registrationSystem	Verify department code (department code)
departmentClassSchedule	Verify section (course number, section number)
section	enroll (student) associate student (student)

FIGURE 8.36   Collaboration diagram for the system operation *requestSection*

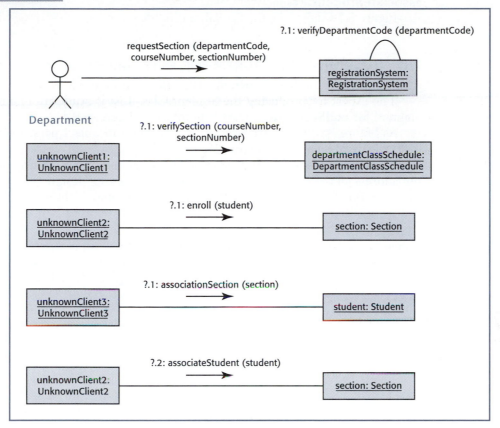

FIGURE 8.37   Intermediate collaboration diagram for the system operation *requestSection*

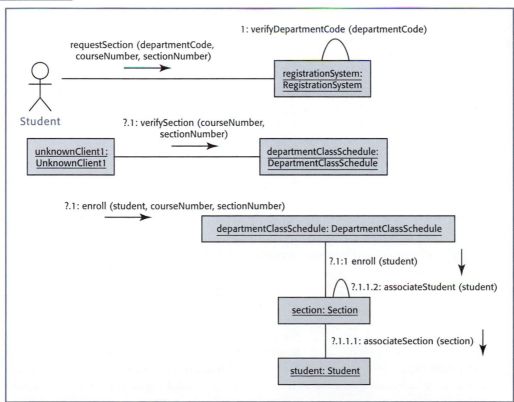

respectively. The numbers 3.1.1.1 and 3.1.1.2 go to **associateSection** and **associateStudent,** respectively.

Figure 8.38 shows the final collaboration diagram.

THE COLLABORATION DIAGRAM FOR endSectionRequests

The contract for **endSectionRequests** is shown in Figure 8.39.

The expert for producing the Student Class List is **student**. The collaboration diagram for **endSectionRequests** is prepared in Exercise 8.4.

As before, saving the transaction is a problem in object persistence. Thus, we defer the discussion until Chapter 10.

The collaboration diagrams developed thus far are only a starting point; they do not address all the issues involved in a complete working design. This design will be further refined through the use of design class diagrams, as discussed in Chapter 9.

| FIGURE 8.38 | Completed collaboration diagram for the system operation *requestSection* |

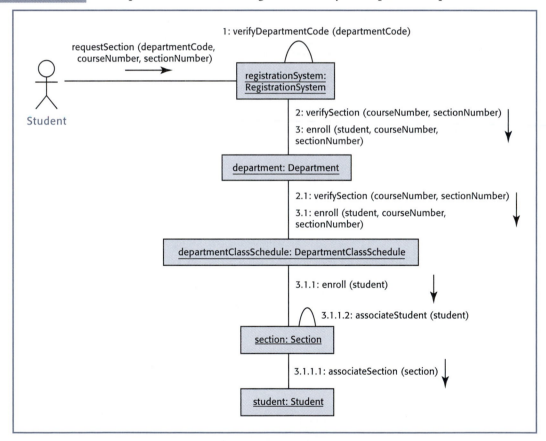

| FIGURE 8.39 | Contract for the system operation *endSectionRequests* |

Contract Name:	**endSectionRequests ( )**
Use Case:	Register for Classes
Responsibilities:	Produce the Student Class List.
Exceptions:	None
Preconditions:	Registration is under way.
Postconditions:	The Student Class List was produced.

CREATING DESIGN SEQUENCE DIAGRAMS

Recall that collaboration diagrams and sequence diagrams present interactions between objects in two different formats. Collaboration diagrams use a network format and typically show a single sequence of messages involved in carrying out a responsibility. Sequence diagrams use a fence format. It may be convenient to show several message sequences on one diagram unless the diagram becomes too complex.

To create a design sequence diagram from a collaboration diagram, draw a rectangle at the top of the sequence diagram for each object in the collaboration diagram. Then transfer the messages from the collaboration diagram to the sequence diagram. The messages appear from top to bottom in the sequence shown on the collaboration diagram. Follow the hierarchical numbering scheme in the collaboration diagram. The lifeline for each object becomes thicker during the time it is executing an operation — from the time a server object receives a message until the requested operation is completed and the result of the operation is returned to the client object.

In an integrated development environment such as Rational Rose by Rational Corporation or Together from Borland Software Corporation, it is easy to create interaction diagrams as well as to transform a collaboration diagram into a sequence diagram and vice versa. Typically, building the sequence diagrams is a matter of dragging and dropping icons representing objects onto the diagram area. The behaviors of the classes have already been defined, so the messages can be labeled merely by selecting the appropriate behavior from a list. No additional typing is usually required in most tool sets.

We are often able to show all the system operations for an entire use case on one design sequence diagram. Figures 8.40 and 8.41 repeat the collaboration diagrams shown earlier in this chapter for the use case Submit Department Class Schedule. Figure 8.42 shows an equivalent sequence diagram for this use case.

Likewise Figures 8.33 and 8.38 can be used to develop a sequence diagram for the use case Register for Classes.

FIGURE 8.40   Collaboration diagram for the system operation *enterDepartmentClassSchedule*

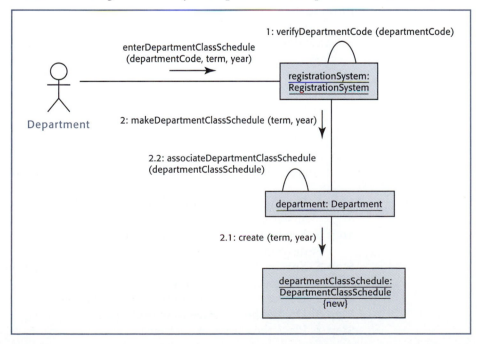

FIGURE 8.41   Collaboration diagram for the system operation *enterSection*

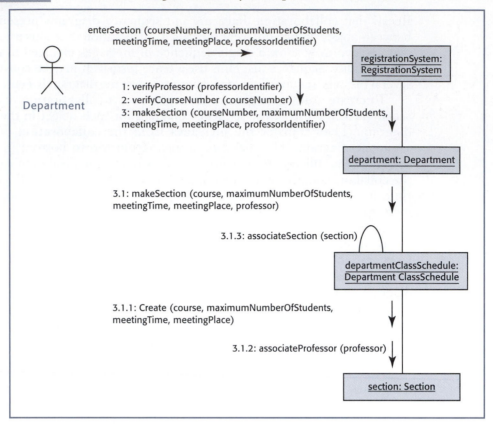

SUMMARY

In object-oriented design, the focus is on the required objects, classes, and messages forming the software structure for the system

The assignment of responsibilities to objects is the primary task of object-oriented software design. A responsibility is an obligation of an object to provide behaviors or services to other objects. An object may fulfill its responsibilities by carrying them out itself or by collaborating with other objects, sending them messages to request their services. An object knows its attributes, its behaviors, and the objects with which it is associated.

A pattern is a named statement of a design problem together with its solution. Patterns help decide which responsibilities should be given to which objects. They also promote better design quality.

Program design for the application layer consists of the following steps:

Step 1. Produce an interaction diagram for each system operation identified during analysis.

Step 2. Produce a design class diagram showing the operations from the interaction diagrams.

Step 3. Specify the signature and the algorithm for each operation.

Step 4. Design the graphical user interface.

Step 5. Define the interface to the presentation layer.

Step 6. Define the interface to the storage layer.

Step 7. Place the classes in packages.

FIGURE 8.42   Sequence diagram for the use case Submit Department Class Schedule

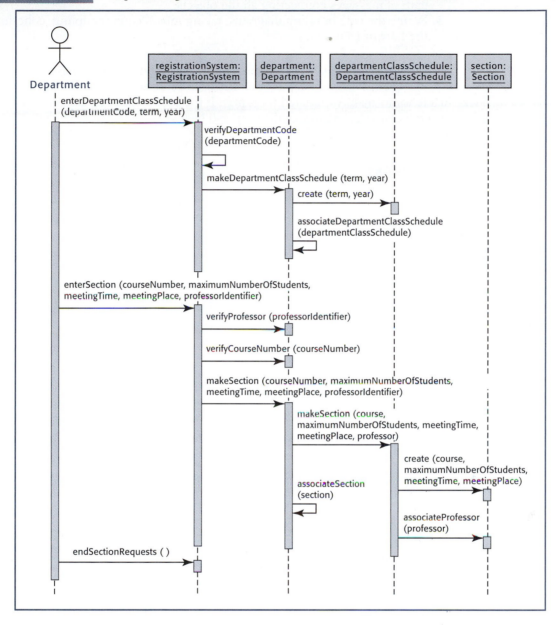

Models used in object-oriented program design include interaction diagrams — collaboration diagrams and sequence diagrams — and class diagrams.

A collaboration diagram depicts the messages between interacting objects and classes in a network format. To create a collaboration diagram for each system operation:

1. Apply the Façade pattern. Choose a façade object for the system.
2. Apply the Creator pattern. Identify all objects which must be created together with the objects which should request their creation and add them to the collaboration diagram.
3. Apply the Expert pattern. Assign every behavior to the object which is the information expert. Show all the server objects and the messages to them from an unknown client object.

4. Paying attention to information flow, fill in the rest of the clients until there is a path of messages connecting all the objects.

5. Refine the collaboration diagrams, taking into account coupling, cohesion, and the Law of Demeter.

If the diagram gets too complex, split it into smaller diagrams.

A sequence diagram depicts the messages between interacting objects and classes in a fence format. Automated tools permit the conversion of a collaboration diagram into the equivalent sequence diagram and back.

KEY TERMS

class *219*	object *219*
client *221*	operation *223*
collaboration *226*	pattern *223*
collaboration diagram *226*	persistence *219*
controller *228*	polymorphism *222*
encapsulation *219*	responsibility *222*
façade *228*	sequence diagram *227*
inheritance *220*	server *221*
interaction diagram *226*	subclass *220*
link *231*	superclass *220*
message *219*	visibility *222*
method *223*	

REVIEW QUESTIONS

8-1. What is the primary task of object-oriented program design?

8-2. Distinguish among the terms responsibility, behavior, method, and operation.

8-3. What are the two types of interaction diagrams? How do they differ?

8-4. What is the difference between the class diagram used in analysis (the domain model) and the class diagram used in design?

8-5. Explain each of the following patterns used in object-oriented design:
   a. Façade
   b. Expert
   c. Creator

8-6. Why are collaboration diagrams preferred over sequence diagrams?

8-7. How is each of the following components of a collaboration diagram represented?
   a. Class
   b. Object
   c. Link
   d. Message

8-8. What is the form of the standard UML syntax for messages?

8-9. Describe the UML numbering scheme for messages in a collaboration diagram.

8-10. What models from analysis are used in developing collaboration diagrams?

8-11. State five steps in developing a collaboration diagram.

EXERCISES AND DISCUSSION QUESTIONS

8-1. Why is the message **makeSection** from **department** to **departmentClassSchedule** in Figure 8.18 necessary?

8-2. Consider the event Professor Submits Grade Report. (See Exercises 3–12, 4–4, and 4–5). Draw collaboration diagrams for the system operations associated with this event.

8-3. Discuss what modifications to the use case Enroll Student would be required to check whether a student had passed all the prerequisite courses before being allowed to enroll. Who would be the expert(s) for the additional required information? How would this affect the domain model?

8-4. Draw a collaboration diagram showing how **endSectionRequests** fulfills its responsibility to produce the student class list.

8-5. In order for **endSectionRequests** to produce the student class list, some object must calculate the total number of units for which that student has registered. Who is the expert for this responsibility? Draw a collaboration diagram showing how this object responds when it receives the message **totalUnits ()**.

8-6. Draw a system sequence diagram for the use case Submit Department Class Schedule. Compare this diagram to the design sequence diagram shown in Figure 8.41 and the collaboration diagrams in Figures 8.39 and 8.40.

8-7. Consider the article in Figure 8.43 about the challenge of viruses to software makers:

   a. Why does Guth say that the vulnerability of software to viruses is a "wake-up call"?

   b. What are some of the reasons that much commercial software is susceptible to attacks?

   c. Are you surprised that code is written without being designed? How can software design improve software quality?

   d. What are some of the obstacles to improving the system development process?

FIGURE 8.43   Welter of Viruses Is a Wake-up Call for Software Industry

Welter of Viruses Is a Wake-Up Call for Software Industry

Hidden in the Blaster "worm" that crippled computers earlier this month was a two-sentence message taunting Microsoft Corp.'s famous founder and chairman: "Billy Gates why do you make this possible? Stop making money and fix your software!"

The recent rash of destructive computer programs — the two most prominent being Blaster and the SoBig Virus —is prompting others to ask the same question. If software makers wrote better software in the first place, the thinking goes, computers would be les susceptible to attacks.

The problem extends far beyond Microsoft and has some in high tech calling for big changes in the way commercial software is created. The rapid growth of the computer industry during the past 30 years, combined with a programming culture that rewards speed over perfection, has helped foster an industry that pumps out products first, then fixes them later. Security is a feature tacked onto software after it is made and not built into the software's original design.

The costs are high. The U. S. National Institute of Standards and Technology in May 2002 estimated that fixing "inadequate" software in the U. S. costs software makers and users between $22.2 billion and $59.5 billion annually. That figure doesn't include losses where flawed software leads to bigger problems, such as the trains that freight railroad CSX Corp. halted last week after an attack from the Blaster worm, or the delays and cancellations at Air Canada after Blaster shut down the carrier's phone-reservation system.

In some ways, today's software makers are like U. S. car makers in the early 1970s. They have ridden decades of growth from mass adoption of their products. But, like the car makers of 30 years ago, software companies haven't always mastered the fine details. Detroit's wake-up call came in the form of better-built, more fuel-efficient cars from Japan. The recent spate of computer attacks may serve the same purpose for software makers.

Revamping the industry is a big challenge. The Windows programs from Microsoft that Blaster exploits include tens of millions of lines of code and may include the work of thousands of different programmers, each with different habits, styles and experience.

But the individual programmers tend to work by intuition, with little documentation, says Watts Humphrey, a fellow at Carnegie-Mellon University's Software Engineering Institute in Pittsburgh. Programmers, Mr. Humphrey says, tend to jump right into writing code, without a clear overall design for the final product. This is kind of like a carpenter trying to build a house without a good blueprint, says Gary McGraw, chief technology officer of Cigital Inc., a Dulles, Va., software-writing consultant.

Executives at Microsoft say the company's development practices have changed sharply since last year, when Mr. Gates wrote a companywide memo calling for Microsoft to build more secure and "trustworthy" products.

Microsoft supervisors press programmers to create better designs before they start writing, and to more rigorously document what they have done. In addition, individual Microsoft programmers are more accountable for their work. Each component of software is tied to the individual who wrote it.

But critics say Microsoft, like many software makers, must struggle with programmers who see rigorous processes as restricting their creative freedom. "Microsoft has a cultural problem" with making the change, says Adam Kolawa, chief executive of Parasoft Corp., Monrovia, Calif., a maker of tools used to prevent errors in software.

Adapted from Robert A. Guth, "Welter of Viruses Is a Wake-Up Call for Software Industry," *The Wall Street Journal*, August 26, 2003, B1

Assignment

Develop a separate set of interaction diagrams (either collaboration or sequence diagrams) for each of the use cases in the Giant Forest Inn system.

Be sure that the interaction diagram for each use case demonstrates how you verify the preconditions and satisfy the postconditions for each of the system operation contracts prepared for the Chapter 5 assignments. Show an explicit **create** operation for each new object. Also show an explicit **associate** operation for each newly established link. Be sure that each object knows all the arguments for any message it sends.

Suggestion: Sketch the interaction diagrams following the method described in Chapter 8 before you use any software tool to prepare the diagrams.

Assignment

Develop a separate set of interaction diagrams (either collaboration or sequence diagrams) for each of the use cases in the Apache Rent A Car system.

Be sure that the interaction diagram for each use case demonstrates how you verify the preconditions and satisfy the postconditions for each of the system operation contracts prepared for the Chapter 5 assignments. Show an explicit **create** operation for each new object. Also show an explicit **associate** operation for each newly established link. Be sure that each object knows all the arguments for any message it sends.

Suggestion: Sketch the interaction diagrams following the method described in Chapter 8 before you use any software tool to prepare the diagrams.

PROGRAM DESIGN — DESIGN CLASS DIAGRAMS

9

INTRODUCTION

The previous chapter explained how to assign to objects the responsibilities required for the system to respond to each of the system operations. Now we create a design class diagram to present a unified view of these assignments for the entire program or system. This chapter describes how to create design class diagrams. It also discusses completing the program design by specifying a signature for every operation.

COMPONENTS OF DESIGN CLASS DIAGRAMS

A *design class diagram* follows the same graphic conventions as a domain model. (As far as the Unified Modeling Language (UML) is concerned, they are both class diagrams.) However, a design class diagram contains some components not found in a domain model. It may also omit components shown in a domain model.

CLASSES, ATTRIBUTES, AND OPERATIONS

Most important, a design class diagram shows operation names as well as attributes. The operation names for a class are located within the class rectangle in a separate compartment below the class's attributes. (Figure 9.1.)

ASSOCIATIONS AND QUALIFIED ASSOCIATIONS

Whole-to-part associations (*aggregations* and *compositions*) are shown on a design class diagram in the same way as on a domain model. Multiplicity also follows the same rules as for the domain model.

In addition to the associations introduced in Chapter 5, a UML class diagram provides a *qualified association*, which associates two objects by employing a *qualifier* to select one or a subset of instances on the other end. **A qualifier is an attribute of a class which has a unique value for each object in the class**. A qualifier may also be a set of attributes of a class for which the combination of attribute values is unique for each object in the class. If the client object knows the value of the qualifier, it can locate the server object quickly and efficiently. For example, if **registrationSystem** knows the **studentIdentifier**, it is intended that the **student** object with that identifier can be easily found. (See Figure 9.2.)

| **FIGURE 9.1** | Representation of a class in a class diagram |

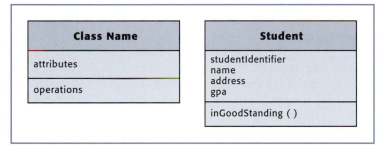

| **FIGURE 9.2** | A qualified association from Registration System to Student |

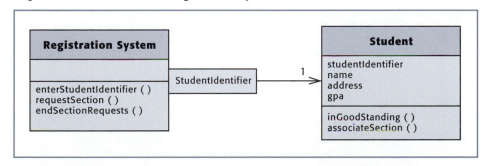

VISIBILITY

Visibility is the ability of one object to have a reference to (to "see") another object. In order for an object to send another object a message, the receiving object must be visible to the sending object. In Figure 9.2, a **student** object must be visible to the **registrationSystem** object.

There are four classical ways to obtain visibility in an object-oriented system. They are (in order of frequency of use)

1. *Reference visibility.* The client object has a pointer or reference to the server object.
2. *Parameter visibility.* An object is provided by a message as a parameter.
3. *Local visibility.* An object obtains visibility to a second object by declaring it inside one of its own methods. This is usually accomplished by capturing an object returned from a message.
4. *Global visibility.* An object is obtained from a class by the object requiring visibility to it.

Reference visibility is also known as *navigability*. It is shown in a class diagram with a stick arrowhead at one end of an association. The arrow points in the direction of visibility and navigability. If there is visibility in both directions, there are arrowheads at both ends of the link. The other types of visibility may be shown as *dependency relationships*. They are depicted as a dotted line with a stick arrowhead showing the direction of visibility.

The UML permits an association without arrowheads to be interpreted in either of two ways. One is that the visibilities are unspecified; the other is that there is two-way visibility. We prefer to show visibility explicitly. If there are no arrowheads, the visibility has not yet been determined.

All four of these techniques for visibility are commonly used. However, reference visibility is the most important to model. In object-oriented languages, pointers to (or addresses of) objects are saved in variables. In terms of implementation, there is no difference between a reference to an object and an attribute of an object. There can be many references to the same object. Even if several variables refer to the same object, there is only one object. This is one of the major benefits of a true object-oriented language.

Figure 9.3 shows examples of the implementation in Java and Visual Basic.Net of the four types of visibility. The operation **checkSection** shown in these examples returns the value **true** if a **section** is already full. In the first example, **section** is visible to the sender of the message. In the second, third, and fourth examples, **section** is obtained when needed.

The major point is that without visibility between objects, it is impossible for one object to send a message to another object. Any of these four techniques allows you to capture a reference to an object. This can also be referred to as obtaining knowledge of an object. Once this knowledge is captured, messages can then be sent to that object.

CREATING DESIGN CLASS DIAGRAMS

Creating a design class diagram is Step 2 of the procedure for object-oriented design.

A class diagram is based on the:

1. Domain model (see Chapter 5),
2. Collaboration diagrams (see Chapter 8), and
3. System operation contracts (see Chapter 5).

FIGURE 9.3 Examples of the four types of visibilities in Java and Visual Basic.Net

TYPE OF VISIBILITY	JAVA	VISUAL BASIC.NET

Reference Visibility
An example of sending a message to the reference object **section**:
	Public boolean checkStudent ()
	{
	  boolean flag = this.section.sectionFilled ( );
	  return flag;
	}
		Public Function CheckStudent ()
		        As Boolean
		Dim flag As Boolean =
		    Me.section.SectionFilled ( )
		return flag
		End Function

Parameter Visibility
An example of obtaining the object **section** as a parameter:
	Public boolean checkStudent (Section section)
	{
	  boolean flag =
	    section.sectionFilled ( );
	  return flag;
	}
		Public Function CheckStudent
		    (ByVal Section section)
		        As Boolean
		Dim flag As Boolean =
		    section.SectionFilled ( )
		return flag
		End Function

Local Visibility
An example of a return of the object **section** from a message:
	Public boolean checkStudent ()
	{
	  Section section =
	    departmentClassSchedule. GetSection
	    (courseNumber, sectionNumber).
	  Boolean flag = section.sectionFilled ( );
	  return flag;
	}
		Public Function CheckStudent ()
		        As Boolean
		Dim Section section =
		    departmentClassSchedule.
		    GetSection (courseNumber,
		    sectionNumber)
		Dim flag As Boolean =
		    section.SectionFilled ( )
		return flag
		End Function

Global Visibility
An example of obtaining the object **section** from the class Section:
	Public boolean checkStudent ()
	{
	  boolean flag =
	    DepartmentClassSchedule.
	     GetSection (). SectionFilled ( );
	  return flag;
	}
		Public Function CheckStudent ()
		        As Boolean
		Dim flag As Boolean =
		    DepartmentClassSchedule.
		    GetSection ().
		    SectionFilled ( )
		return flag
		End Function

We create a design class diagram in four steps:

1. Identify classes with their behavior.
2. Add inheritance due to generalizations in the domain model.
3. Identify associations.
4. Add qualified associations.

At this point in the design, many practitioners also create a set of sequence diagrams, incorporating any changes made to the initial set of interaction diagrams. Other practitioners prefer to use sequence diagrams instead of collaboration diagrams as the primary model for working out the initial assignment of operations to objects.

Note that the above procedure for creating a design class diagram builds the diagram from the set of collaboration diagrams. Instead, we could have started with the domain model and modified that. Why did we choose to start with a blank slate when constructing the design class diagram? We want to make sure that the design class diagram shows only the links which serve as paths for messages to objects or classes. It is possible for the domain model to include concepts or associations which will not correspond to software objects or message paths.

FIGURE 9.4   Example of a list of classes with their behaviors

SYSTEM OPERATION AND SOURCE	CLASSES WITH BEHAVIORS
enterStudentIdentifier Use Case: Register for Classes (see Figure 8.30)	Registration System enterStudentIdentifier verifyStudentIdentifier Student inGoodStanding

STEP 2.1. IDENTIFY CLASSES WITH THEIR BEHAVIORS

Using the collaboration diagrams as a basis, identify the classes in the software solution. The easiest way to do this is to list all objects from the collaboration diagrams. Each time an object appears in a collaboration diagram, it will be included in the list and subsequently in the class diagram. When listing the class names, include their behaviors from the collaboration diagrams as well. This list serves as a checklist for the initial class diagram. See Figure 9.4 for an example. Note that there is one more class than concept. This is because the façade controller **registrationSystem** did not appear in the domain model.

Next place a class symbol for each class in the list in the new design class diagram. Be sure to obtain all the attributes of each class from the domain model. The operations from the collaboration diagrams (as seen in the example in Figure 9.1) should appear in the third partition in each class rectangle. (An experienced designer would probably omit the **create** operations — and perhaps most of the **associate** operations — from the class diagram because these operations were specified in the postconditions for the contracts. We have shown them here for complete consistency with the interaction diagrams.) Omit all associations at this time. Figure 9.5 illustrates a possible initial class diagram.

STEP 2.2. ADD INHERITANCE TO THE CLASS DIAGRAM

In this step, the generalizations from the domain model are carried over into the design class diagram. This shows the attributes of superclasses that are inherited by their subclasses. Similarly, operations of superclasses are inherited by their subclasses. In the Public University Registration System, Section is a specialization of Course. That means all of the attributes of Course, such as **courseNumber** and **title**, are also attributes of every **section** object. There is no need to redefine these attributes in Section because they are inherited.

Inheritance is one of the major benefits of object-oriented software. It facilitates re-use of prior designs. The important thing is to recognize when inheritance occurs. If every instance of a **section** is also an instance of a **course**, then inheritance makes sense. See Figure 9.6 for a portion of a class diagram illustrating this idea.

STEP 2.3. ADD ASSOCIATIONS TO THE CLASS DIAGRAM

Next add the associations from the sequence diagrams or collaboration diagrams to the class diagram. Be sure to include an arrow in the direction of the message to show visibility. Also include the multiplicities from the domain model at this time.

Remember that associations include aggregations and compositions as well as ordinary associations. This step is also facilitated by using a list. Since this step can be the most complicated, it requires the most explanation. Basically, each operation is studied for its visibility requirements. One such requirement is found in the postconditions of the contract for the system operations. For example, an outcome of

FIGURE 9.5   Initial class diagram

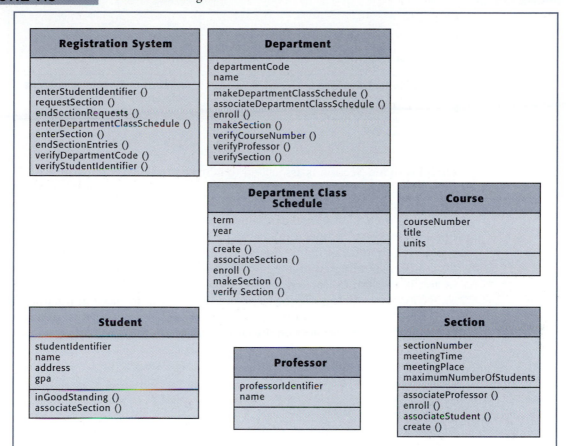

FIGURE 9.6   Inheritance from superclass to subclass

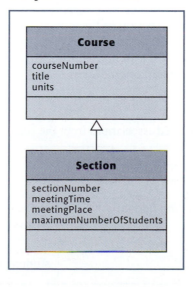

FIGURE 9.7

Identifying associations

SYSTEM OPERATION	ASSOCIATIONS REQUIRED BY CONTRACTS	VISIBILITY REQUIRED BY COLLABORATIONS
enterStudentIdentifier		**registrationSystem** to **student** (reference)

enroll is that a Section is associated to a Student. This is an example of an association being created. Another requirement is identifying how the visibility to the server object is obtained.

Using the collaboration diagrams again, determine what objects send messages. For each message or operation, list in a table the associations created by the operation or required for visibility. Figure 9.7 is an example of such a table.

Since one of the requirements is to check if a student is in good standing, visibility to the **student** object is required.

Notice that the associations may not be identical to those in the domain model. This is because an association in a domain model represents the users' analysis of the relationships in the application domain. The links in the class diagram now represent visibility only.

Figure 9.13, appearing later in the chapter, shows the class diagram with all attributes, operations, and associations.

STEP 2.4. CREATE A FINAL CLASS DIAGRAM WITH QUALIFIED ASSOCIATIONS

Recall that a qualified association in UML is used to associate two objects by employing a qualifier to select one or a subset of instances at the server end. The qualifier must be one or more attributes, each with a single value. The value must be unique for each object in the server class. A qualified association makes it very easy to provide visibility. Figure 9.2 illustrates how qualified associations are shown in a class diagram.

What needs to be done is to determine all the one-to-many multiplicities shown in the class diagram. It may be simplest to list them in a table such as Figure 9.8 in order to keep track of them. Then decide which ones are required in the class diagram.

At this point, it may be desirable to produce a set of design sequence diagrams based on the final version of the collaboration diagrams. Chapter 8 discussed how to create sequence diagrams. If the diagrams are not too complex, a single sequence diagram for each use case may suffice. It would show the system's complete response to each of the system operation messages for the use case.

FIGURE 9.8

Identifying qualified associations from the collaboration diagrams

BEHAVIOR SUGGESTING A QUALIFIED ASSOCIATION	POSSIBLE QUALIFIED ASSOCIATION
inGoodStanding (identifier)	**registrationSystem** to **student** (The **registrationSystem** object needs to retrieve a **student** object before sending the message **inGoodStanding** to the **student** object.)

CREATING A DESIGN CLASS DIAGRAM — THE PUBLIC UNIVERSITY REGISTRATION SYSTEM

At this time, an example of creating a design class diagram is in order. We will create a class diagram for the Public University Registration System. We will consider only the use cases associated with external events. The temporal events involve output and outputs must be designed as part of the user interface, which will be discussed in Chapter 12.

It may be a good idea to refer to the domain model and the collaboration diagrams indicated.

STEP 2.1. IDENTIFY CLASSES WITH THEIR BEHAVIOR

Based on the collaboration diagrams, we identify the classes in the software solution. We list all objects from the collaboration diagrams. See Figure 9.9 for a table of objects and their operations. Each object in a collaboration diagram will be included in the

FIGURE 9.9 Identifying classes and their behaviors

SYSTEM OPERATION AND SOURCE	CLASSES WITH BEHAVIORS
enterDepartmentClassSchedule Use Case: Enter Department Class Schedule (see Figure 8.17)	Registration System enterDepartmentClassSchedule verifyDepartmentCode Department makeDepartmentClassSchedule associateDepartmentClassSchedule Department Class Schedule create
enterSection Use Case: Submit Department Class Schedule (see Figure 8.24)	Registration System enterSection Department verifyCourseNumber verifyProfessor makeSection Department Class Schedule makeSection associateSection Section create associateProfessor
enterStudentIdentifier Use Case: Register for Classes (see Figure 8.30)	Registration System enterStudentIdentifier verifyStudentIdentifier Student inGoodStanding
requestSection Use Case: Register for Classes (see Figure 8.35)	Registration System requestSection Department verifySection verifyProfessor Department Class Schedule verifySection enroll Section enroll associateStudent Student associateSection

class diagram. Note the inclusion of the façade controller **registrationSystem,** which did not appear in the domain model. It is also possible, although not in our example, to have concepts which do not become classes. We want a minimum set of classes which have the necessary behaviors.

With the list obtained from Figure 9.9, we place a class symbol on a diagram page for each class. In the first row, place the name of the class. In row two, include the attributes from the domain model. In row three, add the operations from Figure 9.9.

Figure 9.10 shows an initial class diagram. For the sake of clarity, we use **studentIdentifier, professorIdentifier**, etc., for attribute names in the class diagram rather than the more customary unqualified **identifier**. Notice that there are no associations.

STEP 2.2. ADD INHERITANCE TO THE CLASS DIAGRAM

In the discussion above, we pointed out that Section is a subclass of Course. This is the only example of generalization in the registration system. A Department Class Schedule is not a special kind of Department. Similarly, Students and Professors are not subclasses of anything else in the class diagram. Also, nothing is a subclass of Registration System. See Figure 9.11 for the revised class diagram.

STEP 2.3. ADD ASSOCIATIONS TO THE CLASS DIAGRAM

This step starts with building a table. We use the four collaboration diagrams to determine what objects create associations and what objects send messages to other

---

FIGURE 9.10   Initial class diagram without associations

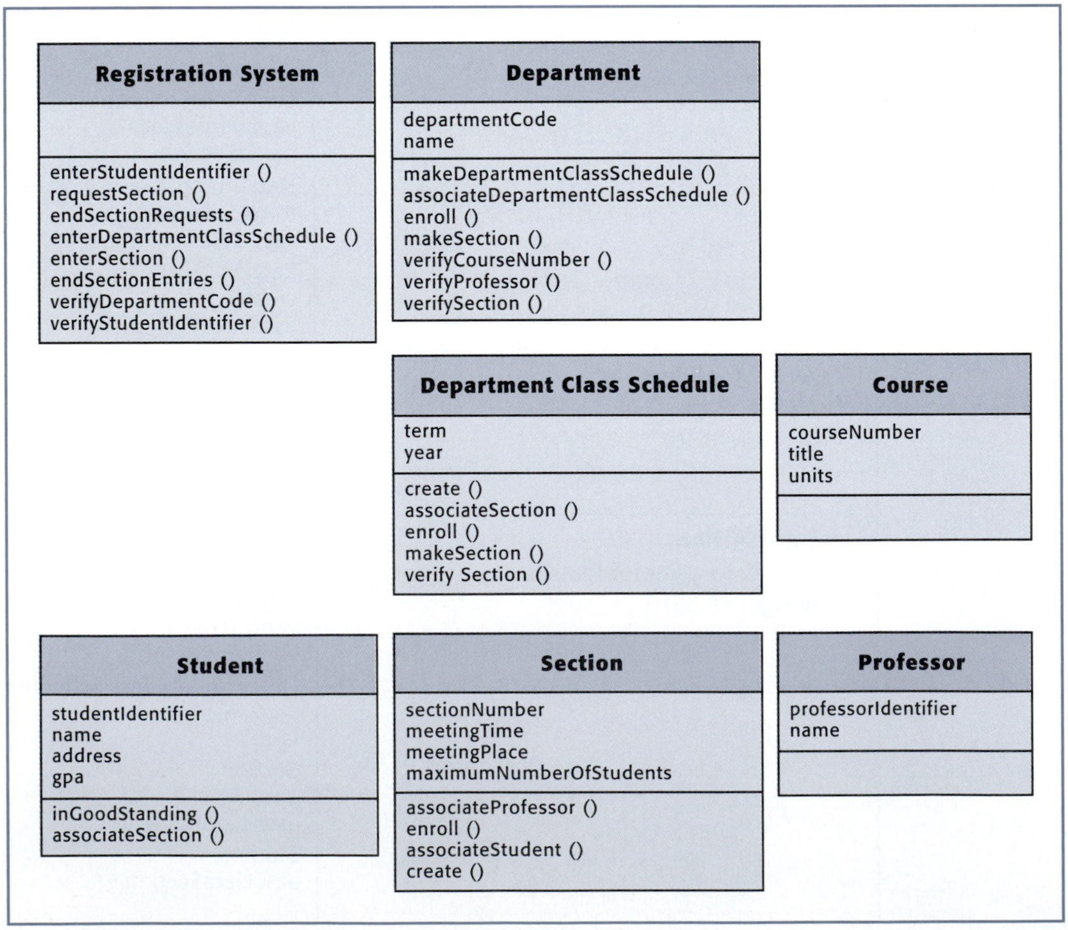

FIGURE 9.11   Revised class diagram with inheritance

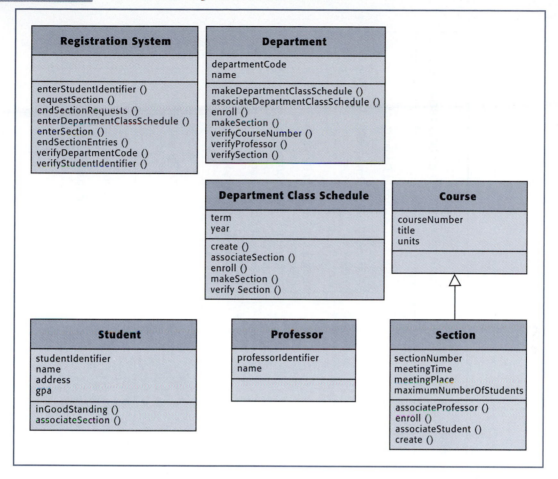

objects. Figure 9.12 shows an association list taken from the collaboration diagrams. A discussion of each operation illustrates the technique.

Associations formed is one of the easiest places to start. This is because they will all provide reference visibility. By going through each collaboration diagram, we can see that only one association is created in Figure 8.18, which shows the system operation **enterDepartmentClassSchedule**. It creates the association from **department** to **departmentClassSchedule**. In Figure 8.25, for the system operation **enterSection**, two associations are created. They are from **departmentClassSchedule** to **section** and from **section** to **professor**.

Since **course** was created previously, we will assume that the association from **department** to **course** has already been done elsewhere in the system.

In Figure 8.33, which diagrams the system operation **enterStudentIdentifier**, no associations are created. However, in the collaboration diagram, shown in Figure 8.38, for the system operation **requestSection**, two associations are created: **student** is associated to **section**, and **section** is associated to **student**.

Next let us look at visibility requirements. In Figure 8.18, for **enterDepartmentClassSchedule**, the only messages are from **registrationSystem** to **department** and from **department** to **departmentClassSchedule**. Both of these are critical, and we will select reference visibility for them.

For **enterSection** in Figure 8.25, there are three linkages: **registrationSystem** to **department**, **department** to **departmentClassSchedule**, and **departmentClassSchedule** to **section**.

Note that collaboration diagrams will seldom show local visibility, as visibility is entirely internal to a method of the client object. The use of global visibility is reserved

FIGURE 9.12   Identifying associations

SYSTEM OPERATIONS	ASSOCIATIONS FORMED IN CONTRACTS	VISIBILITY REQUIRED BY COLLABORATIONS
enterDepartmentClassSchedule Use Case: Create Department Class Schedule (See Figures 8.15 and 8.18 for contract and collaboration)	Department to Department Class Schedule (reference)	Registration System to Department (reference) Department to Department Class Schedule (reference)
enterSection Use Case: Create Department Class Schedule (See Figures 8.19 and 8.25 for contract and collaboration)	Department Class Schedule to Section (reference) Section to Professor (reference) Department to Course (reference)	Registration System to Department (reference) Department to Department Class Schedule (reference) Department Class Schedule to Section (reference) Department to Professor (parameter)
enterStudentIdentifier Use Case: Register for Classes (See Figures 8.28 and 8.32 for contract and collaboration)		Registration System to Student (reference)
requestSection Use Case: Register for Classes (See Figures 8.33 and 8.37 for contract and collaboration)	Student to Section (reference) Section to Student (reference)	Registration System to Section (redundant) Section to Student (parameter)

for situations where an object must be called from many different objects, as with a database call. This will be illustrated in Chapter 10.

For **enterStudentIdentifier** in Figure 8.33, there is only one collaboration. It is the collaboration from **registrationSystem** to **student**. Again, this will use reference visibility.

Finally, **requestSection** in Figure 8.38 shows four collaborations: **registrationSystem** to **department**, **department** to **departmentClassSchedule**, **departmentClassSchedule** to **section**, and **section** to **student**.

How do we achieve visibility from **section** to **student**? Here we find a need for parameter visibility. Note that a message from **section** to **student** is required before the association of **section** to **student** is created. Since **section** is not yet connected to **student**, it makes sense to use parameter visibility in order to make **section** visible to **student**. After **section** has sent the message **associateSection** to **student**, **student** has obtained reference visibility to **section**.

The task is almost completed. Referring to the domain model, note that there is one natural composition — a Department Schedule is made up of Sections. That association should be carried over to the class diagram as well. Although the UML models aggregation, composition, and ordinary one-to-many associations differently, the code for their implementation is usually the same. Then the multiplicities from the domain model can be copied to the class diagram. The result can be seen in Figure 9.13. Note that Figure 9.13 shows only the visibilities required by the use cases Submit Department Class Schedule and Register for Classes.

STEP 2.4. CREATE A FINAL CLASS DIAGRAM WITH QUALIFIED ASSOCIATIONS

Now we add qualified associations to the class diagram. Recall from the definitions that the qualified association in UML associates two objects using a qualifier to select one or a subset of instances from the server class. This means that all one-to-many associations need to be analyzed. We must see if a message is sent from an object at the "one" end of the association to an object at the "many" end. In particular, those which require an object to look up another object using a qualifier are best modeled as qualified associations.

All one-to-many associations are analyzed in Figure 9.14. This figure lists all the one-to-many multiplicities shown in the class diagram. It tells us that there could be four qualified associations — **registrationSystem** to **department**, **registrationSystem** to **student**, **departmentClassSchedule** to **section**, and **department** to **professor**. We decide to leave the association from **departmentClassSchedule** to **section** as a composition. We model the others as qualified associations because the operations **enterStudentIdentifier** and **verifyDepartmentCode** and the need to associate a **section** with a specific **professor** all involve accessing a single object.

Figure 9.15 shows the final class diagram with the qualified associations. In drawing a design class diagram, it is common practice to show multiplicity only at the end of a link where the navigability arrow appears. Figure 9.15 is worth studying because the class diagram is a critical model for the construction of the system. Much of the code can be produced from this model alone.

MEASURES OF OBJECT-ORIENTED DESIGN QUALITY

The Expert and Creator patterns help the designer achieve a quality design. Thus, the design presented above for the Public University Registration System is of high quality. This section discusses design principles for obtaining quality.

FIGURE 9.13   Class diagram with associations

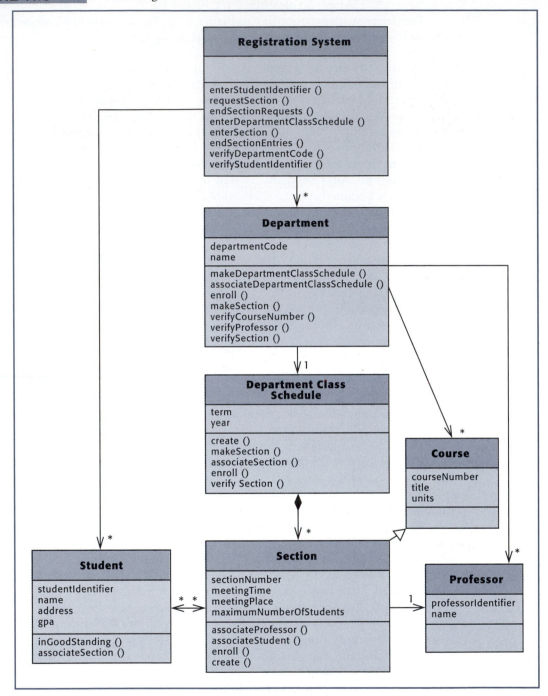

There are three common guidelines for assessing and improving the quality of program design:

■ Cohesion,
■ Coupling, and
■ The Law of Demeter.

All have the purpose of reducing system maintenance.
   We will illustrate each with examples.

FIGURE 9.14 Identifying the potential qualified associations

	BEHAVIOR SUGGESTING A QUALIFIED ASSOCIATION	POSSIBLE QUALIFIED ASSOCIATION USING ONE-TO-MANY ASSOCIATIONS
1.	**makeDepartmentClassSchedule** (term, year) **makeSection** (courseNumber, sectionNumber, maximumNumberOfStudents, meetingTime, meetingPlace, professor) **Residing in Department**	**Registration System to Department** The Registration System needs to retrieve Department before sending these messages. Thus, Registration System to Department could be qualified using the qualifier departmentCode.
2.	**inGoodStanding** (studentIdentifier) **Residing in Student**	**Registration System to Student** The Registration System needs to retrieve Student before sending this message to student. Thus, Registration System to Student could be qualified using the qualifier **studentIdentifier.**
3.	**enroll** (student) **Residing in Section**	**Department Class Schedule to Section** Department Class Schedule needs to retrieve Section before sending this message to section. Thus, Department Class Schedule to Section could be qualified using the qualifiers **courseNumber** and **sectionNumber.**
4.	**makeSection** (courseNumber, sectionNumber, maximumNumberOfStudents, meetingTime, meetingPlace, professor) **Residing in Department Class Schedule**	**Department to Professor** Department needs to retrieve Professor before sending this message to Department Class Schedule. Note that **professor** is a required parameter. Thus, Department to Professor could be qualified using the qualifier **professorIdentifier.**
5.	No behavior	**Student to Section** Since there is no behavior, a qualified association is not required.
6.	No behavior	**Section to Student** Since there is no behavior, a qualified association is not required.

COHESION

Cohesion measures how strongly related and focused the responsibilities of a class are. It is desirable to have objects with high cohesion. Generally, a class with high cohesion has relatively few closely related methods and collaborates with other objects to carry out large or complex responsibilities. This makes maintenance easier, as programmers know what to expect an object's features to be.

Another way to think about cohesion is as a measure of how diverse an object's features (attributes and operations) are. Most of the time the features of concern are an object's behaviors. When a class exhibits low cohesion, its operations are often dissimilar. For example, the **section** object has such behaviors as **create, associateProfessor, enroll,** and **associateStudent.** If the **section** object were to also have the behavior **inGoodStanding**, it would require unnecessary communication with other objects to achieve this responsibility. This is because **section** is not an expert about **student.**

Using the Expert pattern helps avoid building an object with poor cohesion. Figure 9.16 illustrates this lack of cohesion.

FIGURE 9.15   Final class diagram with qualified associations

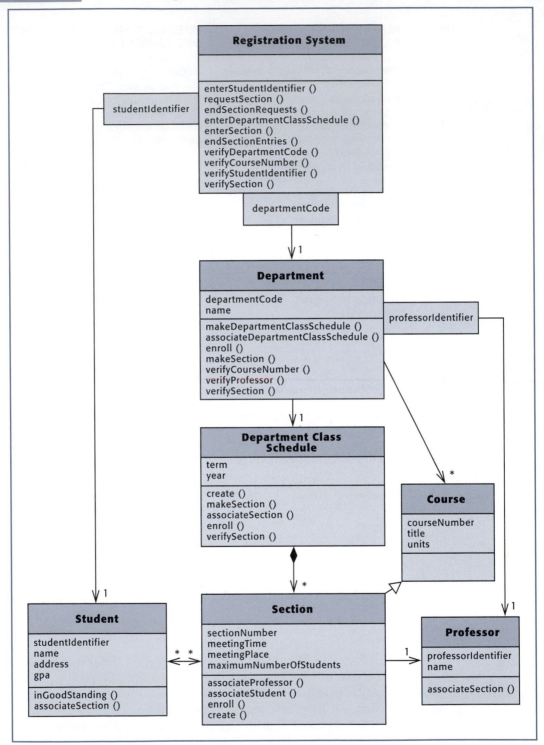

COUPLING

Coupling is a measure of how strongly one class is connected to, has knowledge of, or relies on other classes.

Any time an object depends on another object, coupling exists. Every time a message is sent, coupling increases between the client and the server. This means

FIGURE 9.16 Example of an object with poor cohesion

EXPERT OBJECT	RESPONSIBILITIES
section	create ( ) associate professor ( ) associate student ( ) **in good standing ( ) – nothing to do with section**

there must be at least some coupling. Without collaboration, objects cannot carry out the work of the system.

Each time there is coupling, one object must know about another object's interior. However, too much coupling can cause a ripple effect during system maintenance when a change in one object may affect other objects.

Thus, the objective is to reduce coupling if at all possible. Since work gets done in object-oriented design by collaborations, this appears to be a challenge.

As we might expect, subclasses are strongly coupled to their superclasses. As a consequence, a subclass inherits any coupling in which its superclass is involved.

Other sources of coupling in object-oriented software include the following:

▌ A class has reference to another class or to an object in the other class.
▌ A class has a method which references another class or an object in the other class.
▌ A class has an association with another class.

One of the primary examples of poor coupling is to give too much responsibility to the façade controller (the "bloated" controller). For example, in Figure 8.18, if **registrationSystem** were to have **departmentClassSchedule** created and then pass it down to **department**, the coupling would increase. This is because **registrationSystem** is now coupled to **departmentClassSchedule**, as shown in Figure 9.17, whereas before it was not. Figure 9.17 includes only the operations and visibilities related to the system operation **enterDepartmentClassSchedule**. Note that there is now another message in

FIGURE 9.17 Example of increased coupling

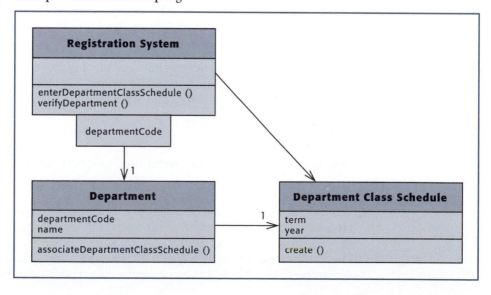

the interaction diagrams — adding to the complexity. Some designers would state that **registrationSystem** has no business knowing about **departmentClassSchedule**.

The point is that the Creator pattern prevented us from making this design error. Recall that this is the purpose of patterns. They provide a good solution to a problem. In this case, the solutions yield a best practice result — coupling is reduced, and cohesion increased.

THE LAW OF DEMETER

The *Law of Demeter* states that a client should give its server the responsibility for collaborating with other objects. This principle is also known as "Don't Talk to Strangers." It limits the objects to which messages should be sent from within an object. It reduces coupling by having an object avoid knowledge of the internal structure of its server or of indirect objects.

A object should send messages only to:

- Itself,
- An object to which it contains a reference,
- A parameter of one of its methods,
- One of its local objects, or
- A class.

However, it is possible, but undesirable, to get an object's reference and then use that object's reference to obtain another object. Thus, it is possible to send a message to an indirect object, as seen in Figure 9.18. Again, Figure 9.18 shows only the operations involved in the use case Register for Classes. In this case, the indirect object is **section**. The **registrationSystem** sends the message **getDepartmentClassSchedule** to **department**. Then **departmentClassSchedule** sends the message **getSection** to **section**. This means that **registrationSystem** now knows about **section**, which should be none of its business. It is better for **registrationSystem** to send the message **enroll** to **department** and then for **department** to send **enroll** to **departmentClassSchedule**, which can send the final **enroll** message to **section**, as was shown in Figure 8.36.

Cohesion, coupling, and the Law of Demeter all improve the quality of a design. In general, when one of these guidelines is broken, another is also broken. The patterns introduced in Chapter 8 are important because they help minimize violations of these design guidelines.

SPECIFYING SIGNATURES, OBJECTS, AND DATA TYPES

Several tasks remain in order to complete the design of the business application software. They include specifying the data type of each attribute of an object. They also include specifying the signature and algorithm for each operation.

DEFINITIONS

First, it is useful to define key terms used to specify signatures and operations.

Primitive Data Type

A *primitive data type* is a data type which can be directly represented in computer hardware. Since the inception of binary computers, there have been only three basic ways of interpreting bit patterns, each with its own set of hardware instructions. These are *integers* (_1, 0, +1, 2, . . .), *floating point numbers* (2.5, 5.004E12), and *characters* ("A", "2", "b"). The primitive data types in all computer languages utilize

FIGURE 9.18   Example of violation of the Law of Demeter

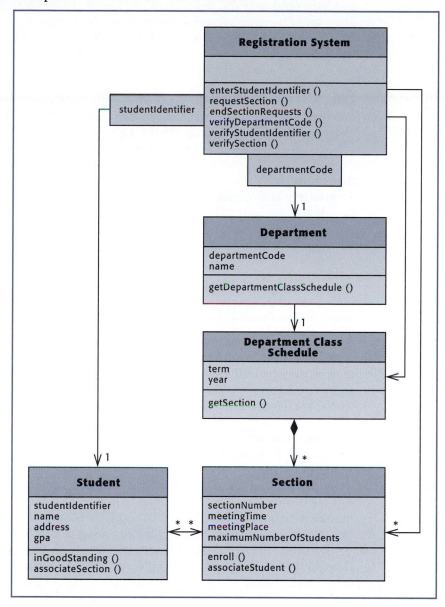

these three data types in some way. Normally, the major differences among the primitive data types lie in the size of the numbers or in the size of the character set which can be represented.

Value Object

A *value object* is an object whose unique identity is not meaningful. For example, the string of characters "Systems Analysis" is not meaningful as a unique object. If two operations require this string of characters, the string can be shared by both operations. Other examples of value objects are date, time, telephone number, social security number, and address. The point is that they exist for the purposes of presentation, and their identity is not of interest.

Reference Object

A *reference object* is an object whose unique identity is meaningful. For example, the identity of an object representing a customer is important. If there are two customers with the same name and address, they are different individuals. For example, a father and son could have the same name and live at the same address. They will have the same set of instance variables, but some of the values of those variables are likely to be different. A reference object is distinguished by the object's identifier. (This identifier is assigned internally and need not be an externally known attribute.)

Data Type

Data type is the UML term for the description of an attribute of a class. Data types are always either primitive data types or value objects. This helps form a rule for assigning data types to each attribute. This also means that reference objects are never modeled as attributes in a class diagram, since they are modeled as associations.

Signature

A *signature* is a specification of an operation which describes completely the interface of the operation. This means that the name of the operation, as well as all its inputs and outputs, must be specified in its entirety, including the specification of the data type of each input or output.

CHOOSING DATA TYPES

As far as the UML is concerned, choosing a data type implies an implementation language. This is because tools which are used to model in the UML usually generate code. For the generation of code to be successful, the data types must be present in the target language. It is therefore important to know which data types are available in the target language. We have chosen Java to illustrate data types. Java is widely used for applications; applets for web pages; and servlets, beans, and Enterprise Java Beans (EJBs) on web servers.

Data Types in Java

Java has eight primitive data types: *byte, short, int, long, float, double, char,* and *boolean.*

The first four are all integers. The only difference is the number of bits used to represent the value. For most purposes in business, only the **int** is used. It will hold numbers from –2,147,483,648 to 2,147,483,647. The data type **long** has an extremely large capacity, which is seldom necessary in business applications.

The next two are floating point numbers. The data type **double** is preferred to **float**, as it has more precision than **float**. Note that a floating point number is stored in two parts. One is a power of two, and the other is the precision. The power is usually displayed as a power of ten, which can be as high as ±308. The precision can be ±1.79769313486231570. The reason the larger capacity is chosen is that **double** is commonly used to store monetary amounts. Java can also format **double** values with proper rounding to appear as a currency in any modern computer operating system (e.g., Windows). Java asks the web browser or control panel of the hardware for the location of the system and adapts to all major currencies in the world.

The **char** primitive in Java is actually a 16-bit entity. This is twice as large as the ASCII characters in common use in the United States today. The extra capacity allows representations of many alphabets, making it possible to encode many more languages of the world. It holds hundreds of characters, both printable and nonprintable.

The last primitive data type is **boolean**. It interprets an integer as having one of two values — **true** or **false** — and can be directly interrogated by any operation.

Two commonly used value objects are Date and String. Both of these are composite objects with extensive behavior. However, their identity is not important in their use. Other value objects are the multimedia objects. Examples of multimedia objects are image maps, JPEGs, and GIFs. The list of multimedia objects is very extensive if sound and video are included.

In summary, most data types are chosen from these five — int, double, String, Date, and boolean. In the world of commerce, almost all transactions have a reference number (an integer), a monetary amount (represented differently in different languages), and a transaction date. This is because a business transaction involves money either debited or credited at a particular time. The reason for the reference number is to offer a clear audit trail.

SPECIFYING ATTRIBUTES AND OPERATIONS

Before assigning data types to the attributes and operations, the notation requirements of the UML need to be explained.

UML Notation for Specifying Attributes

Attributes are described as

> **- name : data type**

Because objects are encapsulated, the attributes of an object can be made accessible to other objects or can be kept private. The first symbol in the UML specification of an attribute represents the **visibility** of the attribute (− for **private**, + for **public**). (The UML also defines *protected* access (indicated by a **#**), which is not discussed here.)

An example of a UML definition of an attribute with its visibility is

> **- title : String   (UML)**

Note that this is different from definitions of visibility in most programming languages, including Java. Java defines attributes as

> **private *data type name***

The attribute's visibility (private or public) is spelled out, as in the following example:

> **private *String title;*   (Java)**

The reason that the UML reverses the name and data type is that the user is often not interested in the data type. Thus, it is of secondary importance in a UML model.

On the other hand, some programmers consider the data type of prime importance. Thus, Java allows us to define each data type as applying to more than one variable name. For example:

> **private *String name, address***

Visual Basic.Net is much closer to the UML. It defines attributes as

> **Dim Private Title As String**

UML Notation for Specifying Operations

Operations are described as

> **+ operation name (in *parameter name : parameter type . . . ,***
>
> **out *parameter name : parameter type . . . ,***
>
> **inout *parameter name : parameter type . . .) : return type***

The sequence is operation visibility, operation name, parameter list in parentheses (first the list of input parameter names and types, then the list of output parameter names and types, and finally the list of names and types of parameters which are for both input and output), and the type returned by the operation. Portions not applicable to a particular specification are omitted. The default parameter direction is **in**.

This is similar to the Java definition:

> ***public return type operation name (data type parameter, . . .)***

and the Visual Basic.Net definition:

> ***Public operation name (parameter : As data type, . . .) As return type***

Thus, operations are specified in the UML much as in the target language except for the visibility, the return type, and the explicit use of **in, out,** and **inout**. In Java, the data type of the return precedes the operation name. Visual Basic.Net is closer to the UML in that the data type follows the data name. As before, the operation's visibility is spelled out, and the type precedes the operation name. Both Java and Visual Basic.Net spell out the visibility clearly using the word "public." Also, it must be noted that the return type is not limited to a data primitive or value object but may also be a reference object. This is also true for the parameters. Finally, a return is omitted when there is none.

To better understand UML operations, it may be useful to show the equivalent forms in both Java and Visual Basic.Net. Figure 9.19 illustrates the equivalent forms for both functions and procedures.

FIGURE 9.19   Examples of functions and procedures in UML, Java, and Visual Basic.Net

	FUNCTION	PROCEDURE
UML	+ getCustomer (customerIdentifier : int) : Customer	+ getCustomer (**in** customerIdentifier : int, **out** customer : Customer)
Java	public Customer getCustomer (int customerIdentifier)	public void getCustomer (int customerIdentifier, Customer customer)
Visual Basic.Net	Public Function GetCustomer (customerIdentifier As Integer) As Customer	Public Sub GetCustomer (customerIdentifier As Integer, customer As Customer)

FIGURE 9.20　　Example of assignment of data types for attributes and operations

Student	Attribute	- identifier : int - name : String - gpa : double
	Operation	+ inGoodStanding ( ) : boolean + associateSection (section : Section)

The Process of Specifying Attributes

The process of specifying attributes and operations is pretty straightforward. Figure 9.20 is a table showing an example in which the attributes and operations of objects in the Student class are specified. The first operation has a return, while the second operation does not. Also, the first operation has no parameters, while the second operation does.

Algorithms for Business Rules

The specification of the business rules used in each operation is the last step in the specification of operations. The UML is not very specific on how this should be done.

One technique is to use a constraint on each attribute.[1] We, however, prefer to specify business rules in the operation specification. For example, the operation **inGoodStanding** must implement a business rule describing when the student is or is not in good standing. The rule specifies what the system produces of value to the user or to the system memory. In this example, the response is to the user in the form of a simple answer to the question posed. The response is true or false, depending on the business rule. The response is always shown in the postcondition. See Figure 9.21 for an example of this operation specification.

More complex algorithms may require some form of pseudocode.

At this point, all typing of data and descriptions of operations has been completed. It is now possible to give these specifications to a programmer who will construct the system's application layer. What remains is the design of the user interface and the database interface.

FIGURE 9.21　　Specification for the operation *inGoodStanding*

Contract Name:	**+ inGoodStanding ( ) : boolean**
Class:	Student
Use Case:	Register for Classes
Responsibilities:	Verify that the student is in good standing (the student's gpa has a value equal to or greater than a 2.0).
Exceptions:	None
Preconditions:	Student is known to the system.
Postconditions:	If the student is in good standing, true was returned; else, false was returned.

---

[1]The Object Constraint Language is one attempt at this type of solution. See Jos Warmer and Anneke Kleppe, *The Object Constraint Language: Precise Modeling with UML* (Reading, Mass.: Addison-Wesley, 1999).

FIGURE 9.22   Complete specification of attributes and operations

Student	Attributes	- studentIdentifier : int - name : String - gpa : double
	Operations	+ inGoodStanding ( ) : boolean + associateSection (section : Section)
Professor	Attributes	- professorIdentifier : String - name : String
	Operations	None
Registration System	Attributes	None

	Operations	+ enterStudentIdentifier (studentIdentifier : int) : Student
		+ requestSection (departmentCode : String,
		   courseNumber : int, sectionNumber : int)
		+ endSectionRequests ( )
		+ enterDepartmentClassSchedule (departmentCode : String,
		   term : int, year : int)
		+ enterSection (departmentCode : String,
		   courseNumber : int, sectionNumber : int,
		   meetingTime : String, meetingPlace : String)
		+ endSectionEntries ( )
		+ verifyDepartment (departmentCode : String) : boolean
		+ verifyStudentIdentifier (studentIdentifier : int) : boolean
		+ verifyDepartmentCode (departmentCode : String) : boolean

Department	Attributes	- departmentCode : String - name : String

	Operations	+ verifyCourseNumber (courseNumber : int) : boolean
		+ verifySection (courseNumber : int, sectionNumber : int) : boolean
		+ makeDepartmentClassSchedule (term : int, year : int)
		+ enroll (student : Student, courseNumber : int,
		   sectionNumber : int) : boolean
		+ makeSection (courseNumber : int, sectionNumber : int,
		   maximumNumberOfStudents : int ,
		   meetingTime : String, meetingPlace : String,
		   professorIdentifier : String)
		+ associateDepartmentClassSchedule
		   (departmentClassSchedule DepartmentClassSchedule)
		+ verifyProfessor (professorIdentifier) : boolean

Department Class Schedule	Attributes	- term : int - year : int

	Operations	+ verifySection (courseNumber : int, sectionNumber : int) : boolean
		+ makeSection (courseNumber : int, sectionNumber : int,
		   maximumNumberOfStudents : int ,
		   meetingTime : String, meetingPlace : String, professor : Professor)
		+ enroll (section : Section, student : Student) : boolean
		+ associateSection (section : Section)

Section (Course subclass)	Attributes	- sectionNumber : int - maximumNumberOfStudents : int - meetingTime : String - meetingPlace : String

(continued)

FIGURE 9.22	Continued		
	Operations	+ associateStudent (student : Student) + associateProfessor (professor : Professor) + enroll (student : Student) : boolean	
Course	Attributes	- courseNumber : int - title : String	
	Operations	None	

SIGNATURES FOR THE PUBLIC UNIVERSITY REGISTRATION SYSTEM

Figure 9.22 shows all the operations and attributes with the data types filled in. All the visibilities are shown for the sake of completeness. Normally, it is assumed that attributes are private and that operations are public. Thus, visibilities are usually made explicit only if they vary from these assumptions. Note that only int, double, and String are used for data types. There are no dates in this system. Also, the transactions are not recorded.[2]

Note also that many of the parameters and returns are reference objects. For example: **associateSection (section : Section)** has a section as a reference object in its parameter list. Also, **enterStudentIdentifier (studentIdentifier : int) : Student** returns a reference object.

This completes the signatures and the attribute definitions.[3] All that is left is the specification of the body of the operations.

Algorithms for Business Rules

The specification of the business rules for the Public University case study follows. The operation **inGoodStanding** is not repeated here, as it was shown in the previous section.

The next operation to be considered is **enroll**. This operation appears in three classes — Department, Department Class Schedule, and Section. This is because **registrationSystem** communicates directly only with **department**. It has no knowledge of how **department** accomplishes this task. In this case, **department** collaborates with **departmentClassSchedule** to do this task. Since **departmentClassSchedule** contains **section**, which has the information necessary for enrolling the **student**, another collaboration occurs. In this case, there are two collaborations beyond **department**.

This is often the case, as collaborations occur until a class is reached that has the knowledge necessary. Note that the same operation name is used. This facilitates finding the trail of collaborations.

The specification for **enroll** is shown in Figure 9.23. Because the specification is expressed in terms of a contract, it is the same for all three classes. However, as the collaboration diagram in Figure 9.24 shows, the implementation of **enroll** will be different in each of these classes. When **department** receives the **enroll** message from **registrationSystem**, it sends an identical message to **departmentClassSchedule**. The **departmentClassSchedule** in turn sends the message **enroll** to **section**, which will send **associateSection** to **student** and then will associate the **student** with itself.

---

[2]In the Public University Registration System, the transaction of enrolling in a class has not been saved. In a real system. it is likely that the transaction would be saved. Including this feature in the system is left as an exercise.

[3]Programmers should note that constructors, accessors (getters), and mutators (setters) are not included. All programmers and designers know that these operations are usually required; including them in class diagram clutters it visually.

FIGURE 9.23   Specification for the *enroll* operation

Contract Name:	**+ enroll (studentIdentifier : int, courseNumber : int, sectionNumber : int) : boolean**
Class:	Department
Use Case:	Register for Classes
Responsibilities:	Enroll the student if the section is not filled.
Exceptions:	None
Preconditions:	Student is known to the system and in good standing. Section is known to the system.
Postconditions:	If the student was enrolled, the association between Student and Section was saved and true was returned; else, false was returned.

FIGURE 9.24   Collaboration diagram for the *requestSection* system operation

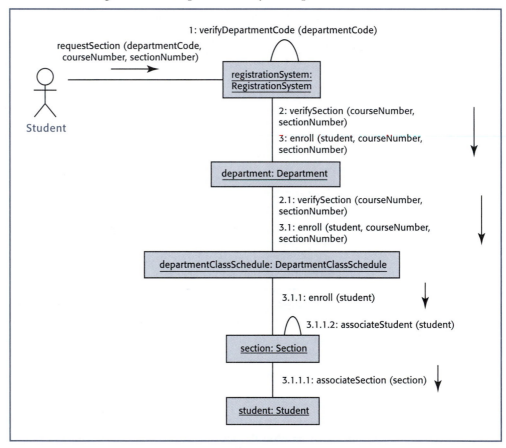

Thus, **department** delegates the responsibility of enrolling **student** to **department-ClassSchedule,** which collaborates with **section** to record the enrollment.

The next operation to be considered is creating the new **section** object by **makeSection** in **departmentClassSchedule.** (See Figure 9.25.) Note that there are two steps. One is to create the new instance of **section,** and the other is to create the association of **student** to **section.** By specifying the association as well, there is assurance that the association will not be overlooked.

It is also illustrative to show the definition of one of the **verify** operations. For our example, **verifyDepartmentCode** in **registrationSystem** will be used. (See Figure 9.26.)

FIGURE 9.25   Specification for the *makeSection* operation in Department Class Schedule

Contract Name:	**+ makeSection (courseNumber : int, maximumNumberOfStudents : int, meetingTime : String, meetingPlace : String, professor : Professor) : Section**
Class:	Department Class Schedule
Use Case:	Submit Department Class Schedule
Responsibilities:	Add a new Section to Department Class Schedule.
Exceptions:	None
Preconditions:	Department Class Schedule is known to the system.
Postconditions:	The instance of **section** was saved. The association between Section and Department Class Schedule was saved.

FIGURE 9.26   Specification for the *verifyDepartmentCode* operation

Contract Name:	**-verifyDepartmentCode (departmentCode : String) : boolean**
Class:	Registration System
Use Case:	Submit Department Class Schedule
Responsibilities:	Verify that the department code is valid.
Exceptions:	None
Preconditions:	All departments are known to the system.
Postconditions:	If the department code is valid, true was returned. Else, false was returned.

Note that how **registrationSystem** will accomplish this is still not specified. All that is required is that it be able to perform that task. Whether the departments are obtained from an external data base at system start-up, placed in a collection object, and then saved for searching, or whether the data base is searched for a department "on the fly" is not important. All that is required is that the departments be known to the system memory somehow.

This completes the specification of the signatures and operations for the Public University case study.

ERROR DETECTION AND REPORTING

The precondition for **verifyDepartmentCode** (see Figure 9.26) requires that the department be known to the system before the **makeDepartmentSchedule** message is sent to **department**. The **verify** operation, shown in Figure 9.26, makes sure that this precondition is satisfied.

Operations such as **verifyDepartmentCode** raise the issue of how much an operation should depend on previous operations. The question is "Can an operation assume that a previous operation executed successfully?" The answer is that all modules except those whose purpose is to detect errors should be written assuming they will be called with correct inputs.

Jackson outlines the basics as follows:

Is it not a principle of good design that every program component should check its own input? . . .

If the writer of an operation module cannot trust the error detection by the rest of the program, every operation will have to duplicate the error detection in a regress of redundancy. Instead, the error-detecting operations should be placed non-redundantly where they are required.

The short answer is no, no and no again.

Certainly, any component which receives its input data directly from a human agent, or from an unreliable machine source, should be designed so that all input data is valid and hence the operation is always specified. . . . But components which receive their input data from other components of the same system must be able rely on the correct functioning of other components. . . .

. . . The only consistent rule is:

> every component specification must define precisely what data is valid for the component;
> every component must be designed and coded on the assumption that its input is valid.[4]

Thus, if object A is a client of object B, then A is responsible for ensuring that any message sent to B (including its parameters) is valid for B.

Where should operations which handle errors be located? In general, they should be placed in the sequence of execution at the first point where an error is expected to be detectable.

SUMMARY

A design class diagram presents a unified view of all the collaborations in an entire program or system. It follows the same graphic conventions as a domain model. A design class diagram shows operation names as well as attributes. In addition to associations, compositions, and aggregations, it may show qualified associations, in which a client object uses a qualifier to select a specific server object or set of objects from a server class.

The most critical addition to a design class diagram is visibility. In order for an object to send another object a message, the receiving object must be visible to the sending object.

There are four ways to obtain visibility in an object-oriented system:

1. Reference visibility. The client object has a pointer or reference to the server object.
2. Parameter visibility. An object is provided by a message as a parameter.
3. Local visibility. An object is obtained locally by capturing an object returned from a message.
4. Global visibility. An object is obtained from a class by the object requiring visibility to it.

Reference visibility, also known as navigability, is shown in a class diagram with a stick arrowhead at one end of an association. The arrow points in the direction of visibility. If there is visibility in both directions, there are arrowheads at both ends of the link. The other types of visibility may be shown as dependency relationships. They are depicted as a dotted line with a stick arrowhead showing the direction of visibility.

---

[4]Michael A. Jackson, *Principles of Program Design* (New York: Academic Press, 1975), 106, 107.

A design class diagram is based on the domain model, collaboration diagrams, and contracts. Creating a design class diagram requires four steps:

Step 1. Identify classes with their behavior.

Step 2. Add inheritance due to generalizations in the domain model.

Step 3. Identify associations.

Step 4. Add qualified associations.

After the design class diagram is complete, it is usually desirable to produce revised interaction diagrams — either collaborations or sequence diagrams — which incorporate all the collaborations. It is often possible to show all the system operations for an entire use case on one design sequence diagram. Automated tools facilitate the generation of these interaction diagrams.

Coupling is a measure of how strongly one class is connected to, has knowledge of, or relies on other classes. Subclasses are strongly coupled to their superclasses. As a consequence, a subclass inherits any coupling in which its superclass is involved.

Cohesion measures how strongly related and focused the responsibilities of a class are. Generally, a class with high cohesion has relatively few closely related methods and collaborates with other objects to carry out large or complex responsibilities.

The Law of Demeter states that a client should give its server the responsibility for collaborating with other objects.

Coupling, cohesion, and the Law of Demeter provide guidelines for improving design quality. Adherence to them helps localize and minimize the effect of changes when the program must be modified.

Completing the design of the application layer requires specification of the attributes of each class as well as the signatures and algorithms of all the operations. A full specification of an attribute includes a definition of the access to the attribute (public or private) and of the data type of the attribute. A data type is either a primitive data type or the name of a value object. Primitive data types include integers of various lengths, floating-point numbers of varying lengths and precision, booleans, and characters. The implementation of data types is affected by the choice of object-oriented programming language.

The signature of an operation is a specification of the visibility of the operation (public or private), the data type of each parameter of the operation, and the data type of whatever is returned by the operation. The parameters and output of an operation may be reference objects as well as primitive data types and value objects.

Algorithms for operations may be specified in contracts for the operations. Simple algorithms may be expressed as postconditions and exceptions. More complex algorithms may require some form of pseudocode or its equivalent.

KEY TERMS

access (to an attribute or operation) *277*

cohesion *271*

coupling *272*

data type (in the UML) *276*

dependency relationship *260*

design class diagram *259*

global visibility *260*

Law of Demeter *274*

local visibility *260*

navigability *260*

parameter visibility *260*

primitive data type *274*

qualified association *259*

qualifier *259*

reference object *275*

reference visibility *260*

signature *276*

value object *275*

visibility *260*

REVIEW QUESTIONS

9-1. How is reference visibility shown in a class diagram?

9-2. How may the other types of visibility be shown in a class diagram?

9-3. Why is visibility necessary in object-oriented software?

9-4. What work products of object-oriented analysis and design provide the information on which a class diagram is based?

9-5. Name the four steps in creating a class diagram.

9-6. What is the purpose of maximizing cohesion, minimizing coupling, and adhering to the Law of Demeter?

9-7. Name some sources of coupling in object-oriented software.

9-8. State the Law of Demeter.

9-9. Name the primitive data types in Java. Classify each of them as integer, floating-point, or string.

9-10. What is the syntax of the UML notation for specifying attributes — i.e., what are the components of an attribute specification, and in what order do they occur?

9-11. What is the syntax of the UML notation for specifying operations?

9-12. How can the business rules for an operation be specified?

EXERCISES AND DISCUSSION QUESTIONS

9-1. What are some of the benefits of producing a sequence diagram for each use case or system operation?

9-2. Draw a design sequence diagram for the use case Register for Classes.

9-3. Write contracts for **verifyCourseNumber** and **verifyStudent**.

9-4. Explain the differences in what the **makeSection** operations do in the classes Department and Department Class Schedule. (See Figure 8.25.)

9-5. Modify the program design to permit the recording of an enrollment transaction. The transaction data should include the identifier of the student, the department code, the course number and section number, and the date on which the student enrolled. Do not be concerned with writing the transaction to the data base; this issue will be discussed in Chapter 10. Consider these questions: Who should be responsible for recording the enrollment transaction? To which class will each of the attributes of the transaction belong? What operations should be added, and to which class(es)? Modify the class diagram and collaboration diagrams as necessary, and write contracts for any new operations.

9-6. Michael Jackson was quoted in this chapter as writing:

> Certainly, any component which receives its input data directly from a human agent, or from an unreliable machine source, should be designed so that all input data is valid and hence the operation is always specified.

What does it mean to say "all input data is valid"? Does it means that only correct values of data can be entered?

*CASE STUDIES
FOR
PROJECT
ASSIGNMENTS*

Assignments

1. Develop a design class diagram for the Giant Forest Inn system.

   Pay particular attention to appropriate use of the aggregation and composition symbols, which are used when an association between classes relates parts to wholes, members to groups, or contents to containers. Show class hierarchies. Also be sure to indicate on the diagram navigability from one class to another.

2. Revise and refine the interaction diagrams developed for the Chapter 8 assignment. Correct any violations of the Law of Demeter, reduce the coupling, and increase the cohesion. Modify the design class diagram to be consistent with these improvements.

Assignments

1. Develop a design class diagram for the Apache Rent A Car system.

   Pay particular attention to appropriate use of the aggregation and composition symbols, which are used when an association between classes relates parts to wholes, members to groups, or contents to containers. Show class hierarchies. Also be sure to indicate on the diagram navigability from one class to another.

2. Revise and refine the interaction diagrams developed for the Chapter 8 assignment. Correct any violations of the Law of Demeter, reduce the coupling, and increase the cohesion. Modify the design class diagram to be consistent with these improvements.

DESIGNING THE DATABASE INTERFACE

10

INTRODUCTION

LEARNING OBJECTIVES

After mastering the material in this chapter, you will be able to

▌ Understand the need for persistent objects.

▌ Learn why the third tier of the three-tier architecture is kept separate.

▌ Know the types of data bases that are available.

▌ Use the singleton pattern to access the third tier.

▌ Define relational database tables and write the Structured Query Language (SQL) statements required (optional).

▌ Determine how to assign the three tiers to a processor.

Chapters 6 and 7 provided an overview of the design process. Chapter 7 also introduced the three-tier model of system architecture, which is considered a best design practice. Chapters 8 and 9 discussed the design of software in the application layer of the three-tier system architecture. (See Figure 10.1.) In particular, Chapter 8 introduced the Controller pattern, which gives a controller object the responsibility for managing the messages to the business layer from the presentation layer.

This chapter discusses the design of the interface between the application layer and the storage layer, which contains the data base. The storage layer ensures that the data residing in the objects persists in the implementation of the system for the same length of time that it does in the business world.

Chapter 11 deals with the design of the user interface, which is supported by the presentation layer. Chapter 12 discusses the connection of the graphical user interface to the business layer. The software design is not complete until all three of the tiers have been defined.

FIGURE 10.1 Three-tier system architecture

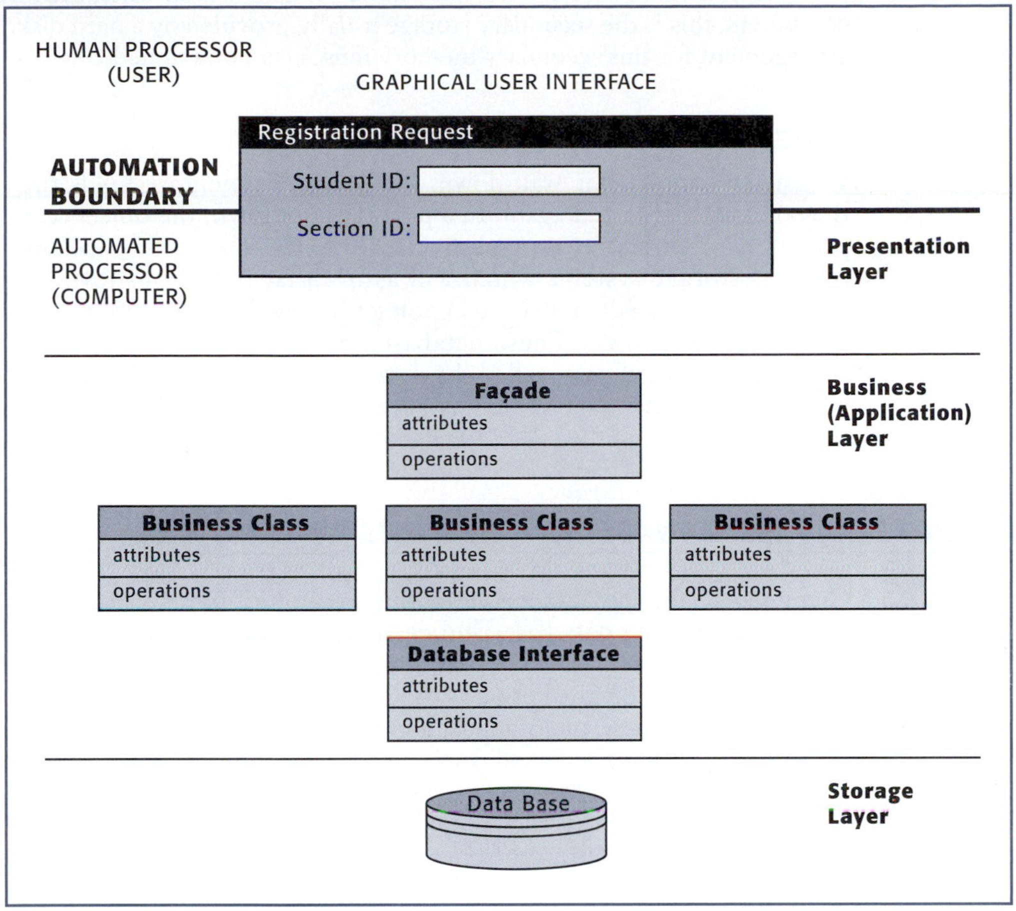

HUMAN PROCESSOR
(USER)

GRAPHICAL USER INTERFACE

AUTOMATION BOUNDARY

Registration Request

Student ID: [   ]

Section ID: [   ]

AUTOMATED
PROCESSOR
(COMPUTER)

Presentation Layer

Façade
- attributes
- operations

Business (Application) Layer

Business Class
- attributes
- operations

Business Class
- attributes
- operations

Business Class
- attributes
- operations

Database Interface
- attributes
- operations

Data Base

Storage Layer

THE NEED FOR PERSISTENT OBJECTS

Data is important to every business. The business must remember the essential facts about its customers, its employees, its vendors, and — most importantly — its transactions. When we model the business domain, we model customers, employees, products, and vendors as objects and the critical data about them as their attributes. Many of these objects are inherently *persistent* — that is, they have a relatively long existence in relation to the business. For example, banks sometimes have customers who have held their accounts for 30 or 40 or 50 years or more. Many corporations have products and vendor relationships which have lasted for a whole century. One such example is Levi's jeans. Another is an automobile company and its supplier of tires.

When we implement objects in the business domain in computer software, we need a way to implement persistence as well so that the objects with their attributes and behaviors will not be lost while the system is at rest. This is the primary function of the storage layer of the three-tier model. The interface between the application and storage layers permits either layer to be changed with relatively little effect on the other.

SYSTEM PERSISTENCE

Objects are implemented as software components inside the system memory. In practice, this memory is the random access memory (RAM) used in computer systems. This memory persists as long as it is supplied with uninterrupted power. In theory, this is not a problem, but in real life, uninterrupted power is not a given. Also, systems must be shut down for upgrades and maintenance. Because the objects must be maintained in a persistent memory, they must be stored on a different computer device where the information will be persistent even when the power is off. In computers, this is the secondary storage usually provided by a hard disk. The storage arrangement for this secondary memory must also be designed.

SYSTEM SHUTDOWNS

When the computer is shut down, the persistent memory holds the objects until the computer is started again. In a planned shutdown, the objects can be copied to persistent memory in an orderly fashion. However, an unplanned shutdown requires storage systems which will assure that nothing is lost. Over the years, highly sophisticated database technology has evolved to solve the problems of an unplanned shutdown. These database systems consist of two parts. One is the stored collection of data, called the data base. The other is the software which provides access to the data as well as backup and recovery in the case of unplanned shutdowns. This part is called the database management system (DBMS).

DATA BASES AND DATABASE MANAGEMENT SYSTEMS

Computer technology has answered the question of how to store data reliably over time by developing data bases and database management systems. A ***data base*** is a systematically partitioned, reusable, integrated collection of data which can be shared by many individual users as well as by multiple software applications.

In this multi-user, multi-application environment, a software interface to the data is needed. This interface should selectively access the data required by each user or application program. The interface should provide ***logical independence*** of the data — permitting us to alter data required by one user without affecting the others' data. The interface should insulate users from the constraints and peculiarities of storage devices, providing ***physical independence***. That is, we should be able to change storage devices or recording methods without affecting access to the data. Accomplishing this interface is a primary function of the database management system. The computer system software and hardware which manage a collection of information and provide for logical and physical data independence are called a ***database management system***. The DBMS provides logical and physical data independence while controlling the redundancy of stored information. Other major roles of a database management system are to enforce ***integrity constraints*** — restrictions that maintain consistency within a data base — and ***security*** — restrictions that prevent unauthorized access to the data.

DATABASE STRUCTURES

In the past, data bases have had a variety of structures. At present, the most likely organization for a data base in an object-oriented system is either object-oriented or relational.

Object Data Bases

Ideally, the best way to organize a data base of objects would be to directly store objects along with their attributes, behaviors, and associations. Such data bases are called ***object*** (or ***object-oriented***) ***data bases***. Object database management systems (ODBMSs) are commercially available but still have relatively limited usefulness. More development is needed before this software is widely used.

Part of the problem is that older-style data bases have become extremely reliable. Company managers are not yet willing to take a chance with one of their most valuable resources. If failure were to occur, resulting in the loss of the information central to the business, the financial consequences could ruin the company. Very few companies are willing to take this risk.

Relational Data Bases

In practice, the most common way of organizing a data base is as a collection of tables. The rows of a table represent things or concepts in the real world, and the columns represent the attributes of these things or concepts. Associations between concepts in the tables are represented by extra columns or extra tables. A data base organized as a set of tables is called a ***relational data base***. (The name "relational data base" is derived from ***relation***, which is the formal term for a table.)

Relational data bases have been in use since the mid-1980s. The cost of replacing their predecessors was very high. Most managers are unwilling to undergo another expensive conversion.

However, there are difficulties in storing objects in tables. Although the attributes and associations of the objects can be accommodated in the tables, the behaviors cannot. Some other way must be found to store the objects' behaviors. This involves a way to connect objects to their classes during system start-up and to disconnect them upon system shutdown.[1]

BUILDING AN INTERFACE TO A DATA BASE

What is needed is an interface to the data base from the objects in the business layer. This interface must invoke the capabilities provided by the DBMS to operate on the objects and their associations. At the conceptual level, these operations are independent of the database structure. At the design and implementation levels, they must be adapted to the database structure and the operations provided by the DBMS.

Software for an interface to the data base can be purchased or written by the using organization.

OPERATIONS ON OBJECTS AND ASSOCIATIONS

Four operations apply to all objects; two operations apply to all associations. These operations are independent of the organization of the data base.

The generic operations on an object are:[2]

1. ***Create:*** Establish a new object
2. ***Remove:*** Delete an existing object
3. ***Store:*** Update the value of one or more attributes of an existing object
4. ***Load:*** Read the attribute data for one object

The generic operations on an association are:

1. ***Create:*** Establish a new link (instance of an association)
2. ***Remove:*** Delete an existing link

OPERATIONS REQUIRED DURING SYSTEM START-UP

In practice, the data base is usually relational for the reasons mentioned above. Therefore, the more detailed discussion of the design of the interface to the storage will make the assumption that the data base is relational.

---

[1] A discussion of these issues is beyond the scope of this book. For a discussion of these topics, see Michael Blaha and William Premerlani, *Object-Oriented Modeling and Design for Database Applications* (Upper Saddle River, N.J.: Prentice Hall, 1998).

[2] These operation names were chosen to be consistent with the nomenclature used in the Enterprise Java Bean implementation. See Richard Monsan-Haefel, *Enterprise Java Beans* (Sebastopol, Calif.: O'Reilly and Associates, 2001).

The first major design step is to create a procedure for system start-up. In doing so, one important issue to address is the fact that relational data bases hold only data and not objects. Thus, the class templates cannot be stored. During system start-up, the objects must be reassembled using the class templates. First, new objects must be created in the volatile system memory using the class templates. Then the attributes must be read from the data base. When an object is instantiated, the data from the data base is used to populate its attributes. This process is commonly called a *load operation*. Thus, data from each table is loaded into its corresponding object. The operation may be named to reflect its corresponding object's name, as in "**loadEmployee.**" This technique assumes that there is a one-to-one correspondence between tables in the data base and objects in the business model. As it turns out, this assumption is entirely reasonable.

A second important design issue is to determine when objects are to be loaded. It is possible to load all objects in the data base into a container during system start-up in order to increase the access efficiency for qualified associations. The Unified Modeling Language (UML) does not specify how a qualified association is implemented. That is an implementation decision. We will assume that the object is instantiated and populated with its attribute values when required. For this reason, all **load** operations will require an identifier to specify the object to be loaded.

OPERATIONS REQUIRED DURING SYSTEM SHUTDOWN

The second major design step is to create a corresponding procedure for system shutdown. Such an operation could be called a **store all** operation. For example, an operation called "**storeEmployee**" might be created to save attributes of all the employees in the data base. Although this technique works in theory, it does not provide for storage after an unplanned shutdown. This type of shutdown could be due to power failures, system failures, or human failures. In any event, waiting until shutdown time to store objects in the data base is not a good idea. Once the system has shut down, no more operations may be performed. In an unplanned shutdown, there is no time to execute these store operations. Thus, a better solution is to execute **storeEmployee** for a single employee as soon as that employee's data has changed.

OPERATIONS REQUIRED BECAUSE OF SYSTEM FAILURES

Since one does not know when to expect system failures, the **store** operations must be done after each business transaction. In this way, the data base on secondary storage is always up to date. In general, there may be **create**, **store**, and **remove** operations for each individual transaction. If a transaction affects more than one object, then the operations must also be performed on all the affected objects at the same time.

An example of a transaction with more than one operation is a deposit to a bank account. First, a permanent record of the deposit must be created. Second, a balance must be changed to reflect the deposit. Third, an association from the account to the deposit must be created. Fourth, all other transactions relating to this customer and account must be suspended to prevent interference with this transaction. Fortunately, the DBMS takes care of this last part seamlessly.

INTERFACE DESIGN ISSUES

Several issues arise in the design of the interface to the data base. The first one is that most objects in the business model are persistent. This means that almost all objects in the application layer require visibility to the data base and need to use the operations of the DBMS. That is, the database operations require global visibility.

One solution to this problem is the Singleton pattern. Recall that the Singleton pattern was developed to provide global visibility. If it were not for the Singleton pattern, database access would require extensive parameter-passing. The Singleton pattern provides a single access point to the DBMS via a single interface object.

FIGURE 10.2	Singleton pattern

Pattern Name:	**Singleton**
Problem:	How can global visibility be provided? How can a single access point to an interface be provided?
Solution:	Define a class which refers to only one instance (the "singleton").
Comments:	The Singleton pattern provides a single place to obtain visibility to another part of the system.

This works fine because there is only one DBMS. Part of Figure 8.4, illustrating common patterns for object-oriented software design, is reproduced here as Figure 10.2. This approach wraps the DBMS into a singleton object which provides operations for each of the functions required to make the data persistent.

Other issues arise in the case of a relational data base. One problem is that a table must be "flat." This means each cell of the table may contain only one value of an attribute. No repetition of data is allowed. All rows in the table have the same number of attributes, and each attribute is of a single data type.

Although objects have no such restriction, the simplest solution to this problem is to maintain this restriction when modeling the attributes of objects. An object purist might object to this restriction, but in practice, it both makes sense and is often the natural solution. For example, the portions of the Public University Registration System model presented in this book satisfy this requirement.

In summary, if one makes all objects in a class have the same number of attributes and each attribute is of a single data type, the mapping of an object model to a relational model is very straightforward.[3] Also, if one uses the Singleton pattern to create an object which interfaces to the database management system, the implementation is greatly simplified. All of the discussion here makes this assumption.

The next section, on defining the data to support persistence, requires knowledge of relational database systems. For those of you without this background, all you need to know is that, in the example of the Public University Registration System, a new class called RegistrationSystemDBMS must be created. It will contain the **load, create, store**, and **remove** operations which are necessary to support system start-up and unplanned system shutdowns. In the Public University Registration System, the **load** operations are called from the **registrationSystem** and **department** objects. The operations which create **student** to **section** and **section** to **student** associations are called from the **student** and **section** objects. Thus, the need for the Singleton pattern has been justified in this example. Figure 10.3 shows the class diagram from Chapter 9 with the singleton object added.

DEFINING THE DATA BASE TO SUPPORT PERSISTENCE[4]

Defining the content and structure of the data base requires knowledge of database design. For this reason, this section is optional. To fully understand it, you must understand the principles of relational database design and Structured Query Language (SQL).

---

[3]This assumption is called **data normalization**. For an explanation, see James Martin and Joe Leben, *Client/Server Databases: Enterprise Computing* (Upper Saddle River, N.J.: Prentice-Hall, 1995), or any database text.

[4]This section is optional. For those of you who have a knowledge of relational data bases, relational DBMS, and Structured Query Language, it fills in the techniques used to map the objects to a relational data base.

FIGURE 10.3   Class diagram showing the singleton object registrationSystemDBMS

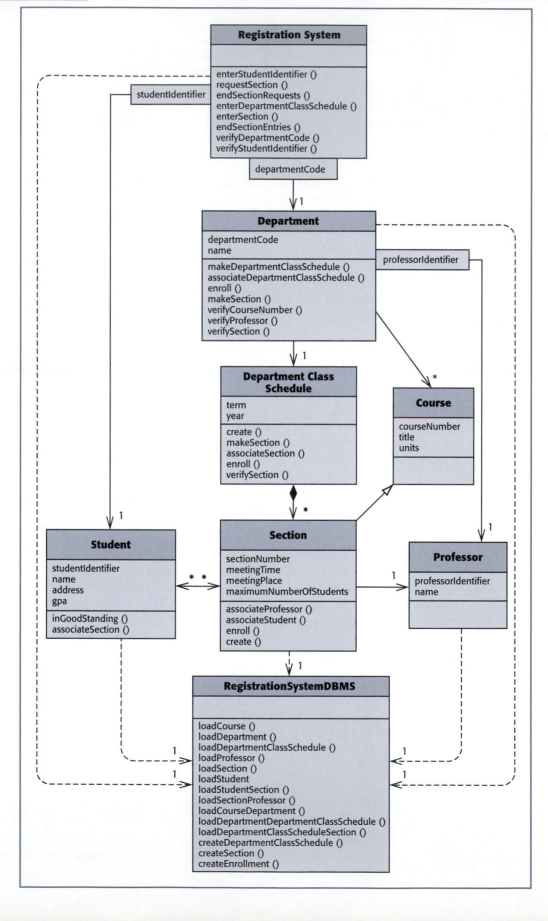

EXTRACTING THE DATABASE REQUIREMENTS FROM AN OBJECT MODEL

The first step in the data analysis is to build a table of all the objects and their essential data in order to obtain the data requirements. The table shown in Figure 10.4 contains the data requirements for all the objects in the class diagram for the Public University Registration System. For each object, the persistent data is identified.

The second step is to add the associations to the design model. This is done using a unique attribute or combination of attributes of each object as an explicit pointer to that object. In database parlance, these pointers are called *foreign keys*.

For example, the association from Section to Professor can be created if the Section knows about the attribute **professorIdentifier**. Another foreign key is **departmentCode** in Course. This foreign key is inherited by Section as well. In addition, **departmentCode** is in Professor. The most complicated association is the many-to-many association between Student and Section. The only way this association can be modeled is to record the associations in a separate table called Student/Section. That way each association has enough information to link the two objects. For example, if student number 12345 enrolls in section 6789, these two numbers provide all the information necessary to find their corresponding objects.

Figure 10.5 shows a table containing the objects and associations from the class diagram in Figure 10.3.

The third step is to create the object to represent the storage tier. This object is created using the interface Singleton pattern, as mentioned above. Recall that in the previous section we determined that almost all objects in the model need global visibility to this singleton object. This object encapsulates the data base by enclosing all the internal operations of the DBMS inside the operations of the singleton interface object. For this reason, this process is called *wrapping the data base* in an object.

| FIGURE 10.4 | Objects and their essential data for the Public University Registration System |

OBJECT	ATTRIBUTES
Course	number title units
Department	name code
Department Class Schedule	term year
Professor	identifier name
Section	courseNumber title units sectionNumber meetingTime meetingPlace maximumNumberOfStudents
Student	identifier name address gpa

FIGURE 10.5   Objects and associations for the Public University Registration System

OBJECT	ASSOCIATIONS
Course	None
Department	Department Class Schedule Course
Department Class Schedule	Section
Professor	None
Section	Professor Student
Student	Section

Figure 10.6 shows all the objects and the corresponding persistence operations in **registrationSystemDBMS**.

Since the objects are not updated during system shutdown, it will also be necessary to insert attributes and associations from the data base at the time of their instantiation. In this example, one object and one set of links are created at system start-up. Thus, there are three create operations — **createDepartmentClassSchedule**, **createSection**, and **createEnrollment** — in **registrationSystemDBMS**, as shown in Figure 10.7. The client for each **create** operation is indicated.

Note that in our Public University Registration System example no objects are updated or removed in the use cases we have modeled. Thus, there is no requirement for **update** or **remove** operations.

DEFINING THE RELATIONAL DATABASE TABLES

The next step is to define the tables in the relational data base.

The logic of transforming the data from the implementation language to SQL[5] is dependent on the implementation language. There are a number of books that describe this process in depth.[6]

Vendors provide many tools which automate all of these functions for the developer. This frees the designer from having to deal with these concerns. However, there are cases where developers may wish to write these methods manually. One reason is that they wish not to be dependent on vendor software. Another is that they wish to be in complete control. In practice, the process is not very difficult for a knowledgeable computer programmer to implement. The techniques are standard, and we have tested this application using Java with a modern relational DBMS. All that most designers need to do is design the database wrapper object and let purchased software do the rest.

Figure 10.8 shows the database tables required for mapping the Department Class Schedule to SQL. Note that all the fields in Department Class Schedule are repeated in Section. Thus, there is no longer any need to include a separate Department Class Schedule table, even though it is shown in Figure 10.8.

Figure 10.9 shows the database tables required for mapping the Course-to-Section association. The fields in the three tables of concern (Course, Department, and Section) come from the design class diagram, Figure 10.3. Note that Course has Department Code as a foreign key to Department. Likewise, it may appear that

---

[5]SQL is a standard language that is used by all relational DBMSs.
[6]See, for example, Cay Horstmann, *Core Java*, vol. 2 (Upper Saddle River, N.J.: Prentice Hall, 2000).

FIGURE 10.6 *Load* operation requirements for the Public University Registration System

OBJECT / ASSOCIATION	LOAD PERSISTENCE OPERATIONS
Course	loadCourse (departmentCode, courseNumber)
Department	loadDepartment (departmentCode)
Department Class Schedule	loadDepartmentClassSchedule (term, year)
Professor	loadProfessor (professorIdentifier)
Section	loadSection (departmentCode, courseNumber, sectionNumber, term, year)
Student	loadStudent (studentIdentifier)
Student/Section	loadStudentSection (studentIdentifier, departmentCode, courseNumber, sectionNumber, term, year) – Note that this operation will link the **section** object to the associated **student** object and also link the **student** object to the associated **section** object.
Section/Professor	loadSectionProfessor (departmentCode, courseNumber, sectionNumber, term, year professorIdentifier) – This operation will link the **section** object to the associated **professor** object.
Course/Department	loadCourseDepartment (departmentCode, courseNumber) – This operation will link the **course** object to the associated **department** object.
Department/Department Class Schedule	loadDepartmentDepartmentClassSchedule (departmentCode, term, year) – This operation will link the **department** object to the associated **departmentClassSchedule** object.
Department Class Schedule/Section	loadDepartmentClassScheduleSection (term, year, departmentCode, courseNumber, sectionNumber) – This operation will link the **departmentClassSchedule** object to the associated **section** object.

FIGURE 10.7 *Create* operation requirements for the Public University Registration System

OBJECT	CREATE PERSISTENCE OPERATIONS
Department Class Schedule	createDepartmentClassSchedule (term, year)
Section	createSection (courseNumber, title, units, sectionNumber, meetingTime, meetingPlace, maximumNumberOfStudents)
Student	createEnrollment (studentIdentifier, courseNumber, sectionNumber)

FIGURE 10.8   Mapping Department Class Schedule to a database table

TABLE	DATA
DEPARTMENT	DEPARTMENT_CODE (VARCHAR (03)) – Primary Key NAME (VARCHAR (40))
DEPARTMENT_CLASS_SCHEDULE	TERM (INTEGER) – Primary Key YEAR (INTEGER) – Primary Key DEPARTMENT_CODE (VARCHAR (03)) – Primary Key, Foreign Key
SECTION	SECTION_NUMBER (INTEGER) – Primary Key TERM (INTEGER) – Primary Key, Foreign Key YEAR (INTEGER) – Primary Key, Foreign Key DEPARTMENT_CODE (VARCHAR (03)) – Primary Key, Foreign Key COURSE_NUMBER (INTEGER) – Primary Key, Foreign Key MEETING_TIME (VARCHAR (20)) MEETING_PLACE (VARCHAR (40)) MAXIMUM_NUMBER_OF_STUDENTS (INTEGER) TITLE (VARCHAR (40)) UNITS (INTEGER) PROFESSOR_IDENTIFIER (VARCHAR (20)) – Foreign Key

Section should have foreign keys to Course so that the field **title** is no longer repeated. These table definitions assume that the section number is an external identifier of a particular offering of a course for a particular term. Thus, the section numbers could be numbers such as 1, 2, 3, ...

However, **course** and **section** objects are separate. Because each Section may inherit its title from different Courses over time, it is best to leave all the attributes in Section. It is often the case that a course number is constant for many years but that the course title changes from year to year. Thus, inheritance in this example does not require

FIGURE 10.9   Mapping the inheritance from Course to Section to database tables

TABLE	DATA
COURSE	COURSE_NUMBER (INTEGER) – Primary Key TITLE (VARCHAR (40)) UNITS (INTEGER) DEPARTMENT_CODE (VARCHAR (03)) – Primary Key, Foreign Key
DEPARTMENT	DEPARTMENT_CODE (VARCHAR (03)) – Primary Key NAME (VARCHAR (40))
SECTION	DEPARTMENT_CODE (VARCHAR (03)) – Primary Key, Foreign Key COURSE_NUMBER (INTEGER) – Primary Key, Foreign Key SECTION_NUMBER (INTEGER) – Primary Key TERM (INTEGER) – Primary Key, Foreign Key YEAR (INTEGER) – Primary Key, Foreign Key MEETING_TIME (VARCHAR (20)) MEETING_PLACE (VARCHAR (40)) MAXIMUM_NUMBER_OF_STUDENTS (INTEGER) TITLE (VARCHAR (40)) UNITS (INTEGER) PROFESSOR_IDENTIFIER (VARCHAR (20)) – Foreign Key

any special tables to model the relationship between Course and Section. This is because inheritance always models classes and not objects. Only the classes inherit attributes.

Figure 10.10 shows the final table definitions for the Public University Registration System. Note the addition of foreign keys in the tables Section and Course in order to implement the associations of multiplicity one-to-many. Also note that the table STUDENT_SECTION is created to hold the associations between Student and Section.

A database designer would most likely avoid such a long, concatenated key for Section as illustrated in Figure 10.10. Note that the primary key has five components: DEPARTMENT_CODE, COURSE_NUMBER, SECTION_NUMBER, TERM, and YEAR. A better choice might be to use internal section identifiers that are always unique. The disadvantage is that these numbers would get very large after a few years. For example, after a few years, the section identifiers would look like this: 872634, 872635, 872636 .. . . However, using this approach would simplify the design. Figure 10.11 shows the table requirements using this implementation.

It is now time to define SQL operations for reading from and writing to the data base, as shown in Figure 10.12. These operations are required by the DBMS. It can

FIGURE 10.10 DBMS table definitions for the Public University Registration System

TABLE	DATA
COURSE	COURSE_NUMBER (INTEGER) – Primary Key TITLE (VARCHAR (40)) UNITS (INTEGER) DEPARTMENT_CODE (VARCHAR (03)) – Primary Key, Foreign Key
DEPARTMENT	DEPARTMENT_CODE (VARCHAR (03)) – Primary Key NAME (VARCHAR (40))
PROFESSOR	PROFESSOR_IDENTIFIER (VARCHAR (20)) – Primary Key NAME (VARCHAR (40))
SECTION	DEPARTMENT_CODE (VARCHAR (03)) – Primary Key, Foreign Key COURSE_NUMBER (INTEGER) – Primary Key, Foreign Key SECTION_NUMBER (INTEGER) – Primary Key TERM (INTEGER) – Primary Key, Foreign Key YEAR (INTEGER) – Primary Key, Foreign Key MEETING_TIME (VARCHAR (20)) MEETING_PLACE (VARCHAR (40)) MAXIMUM_NUMBER_OF_STUDENTS (INTEGER) TITLE (VARCHAR (40)) UNITS (INTEGER) PROFESSOR_IDENTIFIER (VARCHAR (20)) – Foreign Key
STUDENT	STUDENT_IDENTIFIER (INTEGER) – Primary Key NAME (VARCHAR) ADDRESS (VARCHAR (40)) GPA (DECIMAL (3,2))
STUDENT_SECTION	STUDENT_IDENTIFIER (INTEGER) – Primary Key DEPARTMENT_CODE (VARCHAR (03)) – Primary Key, Foreign Key COURSE_NUMBER (INTEGER) – Primary Key, Foreign Key SECTION_NUMBER (INTEGER) – Primary Key, Foreign Key TERM (INTEGER) – Primary Key, Foreign Key YEAR (INTEGER) – Primary Key, Foreign Key

be seen that what has happened is a transformation between the data base and the objects using SQL operations hidden behind the interface.

PUBLIC UNIVERSITY – SYSTEM ALTERNATIVES REVISITED

We are now able to extend the discussion of the system design alternatives for the Public University Registration System. The three alternatives introduced at the end of Chapter 7 are shown again as Figures 10.13, 10.14, and 10.15. These alternatives are:

Alternative A, a centralized, single-processor system;

Alternative B, a distributed system with a department database server and a local microcomputer in each department office; and

Alternative C, a two-processor system with one of the processors serving as a database machine.

PARTITIONING THE SYSTEM INTO BATCH AND ON-LINE PORTIONS

The decision about which of the processes will be interactive and which will be batch was presented in Chapter 7. Figures Figure 10.13 through 10.15 have been annotated accordingly.

| FIGURE 10.11 | DBMS table definitions for the Public University Registration System using a unique internal identifier for Section |

TABLE	DATA
COURSE	COURSE_NUMBER (INTEGER) – Primary Key TITLE (VARCHAR (40)) UNITS (INTEGER) DEPARTMENT_CODE (VARCHAR (03)) – Foreign Key
DEPARTMENT	DEPARTMENT_CODE (VARCHAR (03)) – Primary Key NAME (VARCHAR (40))
SECTION	SECTION IDENTIFER (INTEGER) – Primary Key SECTION_NUMBER (INTEGER) TERM (INTEGER) YEAR (INTEGER) DEPARTMENT_CODE (VARCHAR (03)) – Foreign Key COURSE_NUMBER (INTEGER) MEETING_TIME (VARCHAR (20)) MEETING_PLACE (VARCHAR (40)) MAXIMUM_NUMBER_OF_STUDENTS (INTEGER) TITLE (VARCHAR (40)) UNITS (INTEGER) PROFESSOR_IDENTIFIER (VARCHAR (20)) – Foreign Key
STUDENT	STUDENT_IDENTIFIER (INTEGER) – Primary Key NAME (VARCHAR) ADDRESS (VARCHAR (40)) GPA (DECIMAL (3,2))
STUDENT_SECTION	STUDENT_IDENTIFIER (INTEGER) – Primary Key SECTION_ IDENTIFIER (INTEGER) – Primary Key

FIGURE 10.12	DBMS SQL operations for the Public University Registration System

TABLE	SQL STATEMENTS
COURSE	SELECT * FROM COURSE WHERE . . .
DEPARTMENT	SELECT * FROM DEPARTMENT WHERE . . .
PROFESSOR	SELECT * FROM PROFESSOR WHERE . . .
SECTION	SELECT * FROM SECTION WHERE . . .
STUDENT	SELECT * FROM STUDENT WHERE . . .
STUDENT_SECTION	SELECT * FROM STUDENT_SECTION WHERE . . .
SECTION	INSERT INTO SECTION VALUES (SECTION_NUMBER, MEETING_TIME, MEETING_PLACE, MAXIMUM_NUMBER_OF_STUDENTS, TERM, YEAR, COURSE_NUMBER, TITLE, UNITS, DEPARTMENT_CODE, PROFESSOR_IDENTIFIER)
STUDENT_SECTION	INSERT INTO REGISTRATION VALUES (STUDENT_IDENTIFIER, SECTION_NUMBER, TERM, YEAR, COURSE_NUMBER, DEPARTMENT_CODE,)

PARTITIONING THE BATCH PORTION INTO JOBS

The job boundaries are determined by time cycles. Since by definition, the events are independent of each other, the response to the use case associated with each event will be a separate job.

FIGURE 10.13	Alternative A

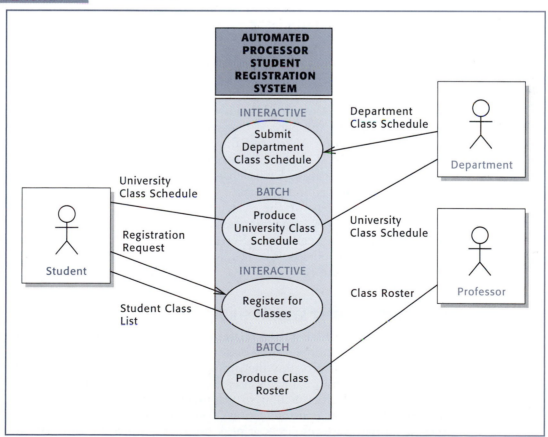

FIGURE 10.14   Alternative B

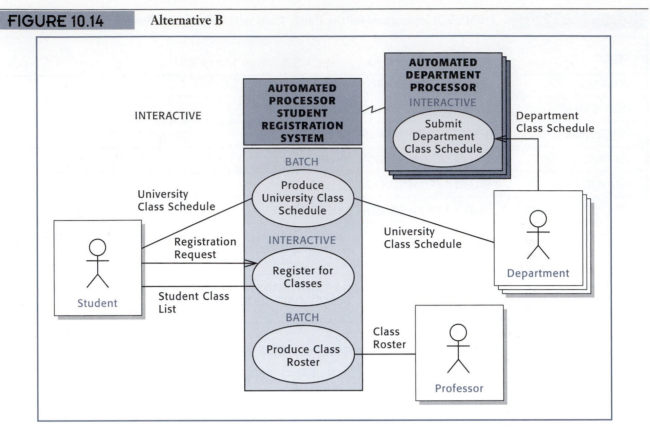

PARTITIONING THE DATA BASE

In the early stages of system design, partitioning can be done at the use case level. As the design is refined, it may be desirable to take the allocation of processes or the data base to the concept or class level.

For example, in both Alternative A and Alternative C, the entire data base is on a single processor. In Alternative B, however, the data base is distributed — part is on the main processor and part on department processors. One way of showing the database allocation for Alternative B is to draw boundaries on the class diagram, as shown in Figure 10.16. In fact, these boundaries also show which classes will reside on each type of processor. Each department processor will have the objects for its own schedule, courses, and sections.

Since the objects of the system are assigned to multiple processors in Alternative C, each department processor will require its own façade object. Some of the operations in the **registrationSystem** object now become responsibilities of the **department** façade objects. The necessary revision of the class diagram is dealt with in Exercises 10–6 and 10–7.

SELECTING THE BEST SYSTEM STRUCTURE

Finally, during the Elaboration phase, the developers select the best system structure. Some of the advantages and disadvantages of each alternative follow.

Alternative A is probably the simplest and most straightforward solution. It is even likely that software for this alternative is commercially available. This could be viable if the university is willing to adapt its operations to the software or if there is opportunity for some customization. There may be some contention for database access and hardware resources at peak use times, especially when departments are

FIGURE 10.15   Alternative C

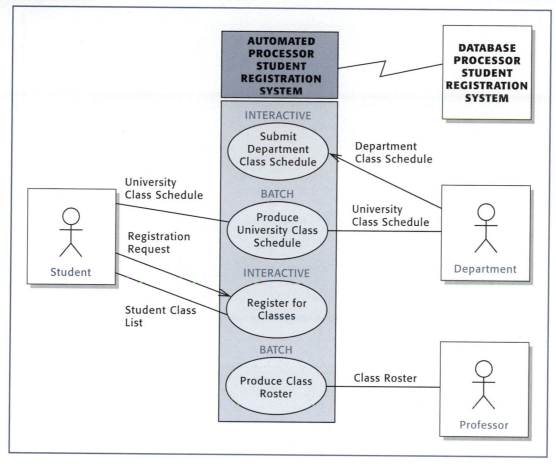

entering schedules or students are registering. A multitasking operating system may be required for the best on-line response.

Alternative B provides some local processing independence. The use of multiple microcomputers may make this alternative more expensive, and the network environment will add some complexity to the software. The partitioning of the data base is relatively clean, with little or no redundant data. This alternative may provide better response time for entry of class schedules and for registration.

Alternative C has the advantage of two processors, each of which could back up the other in the case of emergency. The redundancy is an advantage because of the critical timing of the system's response in the context of the university's academic calendar. A second processor might be required in Alternative A just for backup.

Ultimately, the determination of the best alternative depends on a cost-benefit analysis and on the parallel selection of the hardware.

SUMMARY

The storage layer of the three-tier system architecture implements the requirement for persistent software objects. When the computer is shut down, the persistent memory holds the attributes, associations, and behaviors of objects until the computer is started again.

Computer technology has answered the question of how to store data reliably over time by developing data bases and database management systems (DBMSs).

FIGURE 10.16   Class diagram showing processor and database boundaries

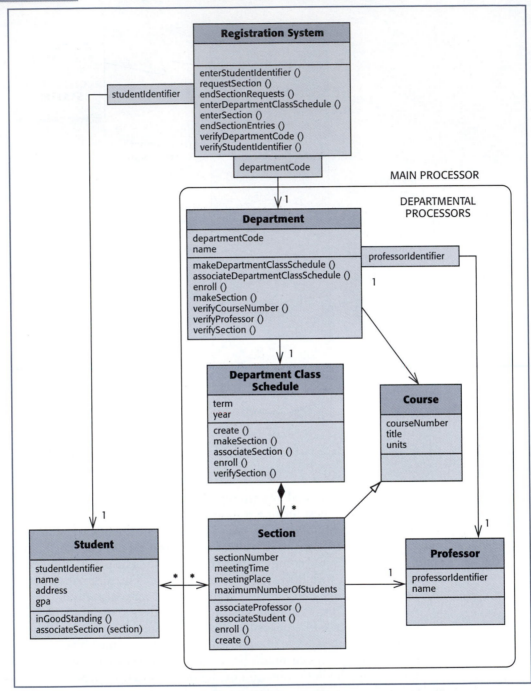

A data base is a systematically partitioned, reusable, integrated collection of data which can be shared by many individual users as well as by multiple software applications. The computer system software and hardware that manage a collection of information and provide for logical and physical data independence are called a database management system. Other major roles of a database management system are to enforce integrity constraints — restrictions that maintain consistency within a data base — and security — restrictions that prevent unauthorized access to the data.

Object database management systems (ODBMSs) are commercially available but still have relatively limited usefulness. In practice, the most common way of organizing a data base is as a collection of tables called a relational data base.

In a database environment, we need a software interface to the data base from the objects in the business layer. This interface between the application and storage layers should selectively access the data required by each user or application program. The interface permits either layer to be changed with relatively little effect on the other.

The generic operations on an object are **create**, **remove**, **store**, and **load**. The generic operations on an association are **create** a link and **delete** a link.

Designing a relational data base to support persistent objects requires us to map the attributes and associations of the objects to a set of tables. However, relational data bases can hold only data and not objects. The class templates cannot be stored. During system start-up, the objects must be reassembled using the class templates. First, new objects must be created in the volatile system memory. When an object is instantiated, the data from the data base is used to populate its attributes. This process is commonly called a **load** operation. Since one does not know when to expect system failures, the **store** operations should be done after each business transaction. In this way, the data base is always up to date.

Database operations require global visibility to the object providing the interface to the data base. This is achieved through the Singleton pattern, which provides a single access point to the DBMS via a single interface object. Operations of the singleton object may be purchased or may be written by the system developers.

KEY TERMS

create operation *291*

data base *289*

database management system *290*

database wrapper *297*

foreign key *293*

load operation *291*

logical independence of data *290*

object database *290*

persistence *289*

physical independence of data *290*

relation (in a data base) *290*

relational data base *290*

remove operation *291*

Singleton pattern *292*

store operation *291*

REVIEW QUESTIONS

10-1. What is persistence and why is it important?

10-2. What are the three principal components of the three-tier architecture?

10-3. What are two kinds of system shutdowns?

10-4. How does a database management system differ from a database?

10-5. What are the major roles of a database management system?

10-6. What do rows and columns represent in a relational database table?

10-7. Explain what each of these generic operations on an object does:
  a. Create
  b. Remove
  c. Store
  d. Load

10-8. Explain what each of these generic operations on an association does:
  a. Create
  b. Delete

10-9. What operations are required during system start-up? During shutdown?

10-10. What operations are necessary because of system failures?

10-11. Why is the Singleton pattern used to represent the DBMS?

EXERCISES AND DISCUSSION QUESTIONS

10-1. What are some of the reasons object data bases are not used by the mainstream systems?

10-2. Why do many companies purchase third-party software to perform the persistence function?

10-3. Suppose you are an information services manager. Explain how you would argue the merits of the three-tier model.

10-4. Add operations to the Public University Registration sSystem to maintain students, departments, and sections. Then create the database table definitions with their corresponding SQL statements.

10-5. Investigate and summarize the maintainability of the three-tier design of the Public University Registration System.

10-6. Consider Alternative B for the Public University Registration System, as shown in Figure 10.14. This alternative allocates the use case Submit Department Class Schedule to separate processors in each department. As a result, the objects and the related data bases are divided among the processors.

a. Discuss the rationale for partitioning the data base in this way.

b. Discuss the implications of this alternative for the registration process. Comment especially on the flow of information between the main registration system processor and the department processors.

10-7. Separate Figure 10.16 into two class diagrams — one for the registration processor and one for a typical department processor. Which operations will shift from Registration System to the façade object for a department processor? Be sure to show this in the diagrams.

10-8. Suppose the Registrar requires a log of incoming registration requests which can capture information about students who cannot register because sections are filled. Which class should have this responsibility? Add the necessary operations or other modifications to the class diagram. If you wish, modify the interaction diagram(s) for Register for Classes as well.

10-9. For backup purposes, it is desirable to log (write to the data base) each enrollment as it occurs. Discuss which class should have this responsibility, what database operation is required, and when the operation will be invoked. (Recall that this is an example of an administrative responsibility, as discussed in Chapter 9.)

10-10. Discuss the advantages and disadvantages of a more fully decentralized alternative in which each student's records would be allocated to a server in the department in which the student majors.

10-11. Extend the scope of the system to include one or more of the capabilities listed below. Prepare revised versions of Figures 10.13 through 10.15 and discuss the impact on each of the system alternatives. You may wish to continue the design by drawing interaction diagrams and revising the design class diagram(s).

a. Withdrawing a student from a section

b. Recording grades at the end of a term

c. Producing grade reports for students and faculty

Assignments

1. Apply the Singleton pattern to the Giant Forest Inn system to provide an interface from the objects in the application layer to the storage layer. Modify the design class diagram accordingly, showing all the operation of the singleton object.

2. Assume that a relational DBMS is used to implement the persistence of the attributes and associations of the objects. Define the structure of the required tables. (See Figure 10.8.)

Assignments

1. Apply the Singleton pattern to the Apache Rent A Car system to provide an interface from the objects in the application layer to the storage layer. Modify the design class diagram accordingly, showing all the operation of the singleton object.

2. Assume that a relational DBMS is used to implement the persistence of the attributes and associations of the objects. Define the structure of the required tables. (See Figure 10.8.)

DESIGNING THE USER INTERFACE — DESIGN PRINCIPLES

11

LEARNING OBJECTIVES

After mastering the material in this chapter, you will be able to

- Describe the principal components of an interactive graphics system and explain the function of each.
- Write down the fundamental control logic for an event-driven interactive system.
- Discuss important characteristics of users which must be accommodated in the design of the user interface.
- State how ergonomics contributes to the design of the user interface.
- Give examples of several hardware devices which can perform each of the following generic functions: locate a position, select an object in the display, enter a quantity, enter text, and select an action.
- Give examples of output devices.
- Recognize common styles of interaction at the user interface.
- State some guidelines for interaction design and give examples of how they may be applied.
- Be able to name common types of windows and controls in an interactive display in the personal computer environment.
- Apply Gestalt principles of visual design to the critique and design of displays and documents.
- Understand and apply the guidelines for the use of color presented in this chapter.

INTRODUCTION

The users' judgment about a computer information system is heavily based on the quality of the user interface. How users feel when they interact with the system affects strongly their acceptance of the system and their ability to use it productively. As far as many users are concerned, the interface *is* the system.

The design of the user interface specifies the dialogue which takes place between a human being and a computer. Designing the user interface is especially challenging because it is a multidimensional and multidisciplinary enterprise. Some of these disciplines — graphic design, psychology, and ergonomics — are oriented toward the human participant in the dialogue. Others address the automated partner. The variety of available devices continues to increase, and the state of the art sets ever more sophisticated and demanding standards.

User interface design establishes the form as well as the permissible content of the interaction at the automation boundary. Before user interface design begins, the automation boundary must be located. That is, the designer must decide which of the essential processes are to be performed by a person and which are to be performed by a computer.

On the machine side of the automation boundary, all the data are in electronic form; on the human side, all the data are in a form which can be understood and processed by people. These two very different types of processors communicate by messages across the boundary. At the boundary are data capture and data display devices which convert messages from each type of processor into a form in which they can be understood and acted on by the other.

Chapters 11 and 12 are concerned with designing the form and structure of the messages crossing the automation boundary as well as with designing the objects in the presentation layer. This chapter addresses the context for user interface design and the components of the interface. It discusses the principal characteristics of the user, the input and output devices, and the software involved in the user interface. It summarizes an overall approach to user interface design, including important principles and guidelines. It also discusses the organization of reports and displays. Chapter 12 presents tools and techniques for modeling the interaction between user and computer during design. It also addresses the design of the presentation layer in an object-oriented system.

These chapters stress a basic approach and fundamental principles which will endure when devices and details change. The intent throughout is to encourage you as a designer to take a broad perspective rather than being immediately constrained by what is familiar. Technology which today seems exotic and expensive may become commonplace sooner than we think.

A BRIEF HISTORY OF USER INTERFACES

The earliest user interfaces for business applications were simple. Input was recorded in a fixed format on forms from which paper tape or cards were punched. Output was mostly tabular reports with a minimum of identifying labels. The limitations of the hardware and software took priority over the convenience of the user. Efficient data entry took precedence over ease of filling out the forms. Forms were processed in batches — with much attention given to editing the input for errors, as processing was time-consuming and long reports often required overnight processing.

Around 1960, application-specific languages were designed for engineering users of computers. Flexible commands in free format replaced fixed-format input sheets. These commands, which incorporated the relevant data, invoked one or more program modules to execute procedures in a sequence determined by the user. These **problem-oriented languages**, as they were called, cast the interaction between user and computer in the form of a dialogue.

The early 1960s saw the first interactive computer graphics systems for scientific and engineering applications on dedicated processors. These computer graphics systems had a more complex interface, combining several modes of interaction and a choice of devices. Consequently, much of what is now known about designing the user-computer interface has been learned from graphics systems. Work at the Xerox Palo Alto Research Center (Xerox PARC) during the 1970s led to the style of interaction now exemplified by the Apple Macintosh — a high-resolution display (originally black-on-white), a mouse, pull-down menus, and extensive use of icons. Interactive business applications and business graphics came more recently. An interactive graphical user interface (GUI) is now the norm. Such a user interface can effectively combine graphics, text, and numeric information.

INTERACTIVE SYSTEMS

The approach to user interface design presented here assumes the broadest context — an interactive system. As noted in Chapter 7, it has been traditional to distinguish between *batch* and *interactive* systems, although this distinction may now be of limited value. (Recall that in a batch system the system inputs are collected and stored at or near the automation boundary. They are then processed as a group, or batch.) As a designer, it is probably more useful to think of the time it takes the automated system to respond to a user's request. Then it is possible to investigate trade-offs among response time, cost, and other design criteria.

In an interactive system:

▮ The hands-on users (as defined in Chapter 2) are typically those whose work is directly supported by the computer application. Examples include bank tellers who accept customer deposits or loan payments, travel agents who make airline reservations, and faculty who access university records in order to advise students.
▮ Information enters the computer one data flow at a time. Time delays or requirements to group data are handled with internal data storage.
▮ As a consequence, error detection and correction also apply to a single data flow, although it may be checked for consistency with the internally stored data.
▮ Response time ranges from milliseconds to a few minutes, depending on the task.

Interactive systems are often further characterized as online and real-time, depending on how rapidly a system must produce its outputs. Originally, *on-line* meant that there was a direct electronic connection between the input-output devices and the central processing unit and that the transmission of input and output took place without delay. In this sense, all interactive systems are on-line systems. The term "on-line" also connotes interaction via a remote workstation or network, often as part of a multiuser system.

A *real-time* system is a system which produces its preplanned responses rapidly enough to affect events in its environment. Real-time systems need not interact with a human user but may receive input from instruments in the environment. Applications of real-time systems include industrial process control, vehicle guidance and navigation, and automated execution of trades in the securities markets.

GENERIC DESCRIPTION OF AN INTERACTIVE SYSTEM

Figure 11.1 shows a block diagram of a basic interactive computer graphics system. There is a single output device — a graphics display capable of presenting text and graphics with colored or shaded areas. However, the system could easily be extended to include audio or speech output and hard-copy devices.

The components in the diagram are functional; they may include both hardware and software. A user enters information through an input device. Signals from the input device are processed by a device handler which converts them to an appropriate internal form. The input stream is then analyzed by a command interpreter to determine what action the user wants and what data is necessary to carry it out. The command directs the application software to accomplish the processing. As part of this processing, the application software receives the input, may request additional information from the database, and produces the essential system output.

Newman and Sproull[1] distinguish between the essential system output, which they call the ***information display***, and other messages crossing the automation boundary which facilitate the dialogue by providing *feedback* to the user. Figure 11.1 shows three types of feedback — device feedback, command feedback, and selection feedback:

- ▎ ***Device feedback*** comes from the input devices. When a key is depressed, a character appears on the display. When a mouse moves, a cursor tracks the motion.
- ▎ ***Command feedback*** confirms that the word or command just entered has been recognized and accepted as valid.
- ▎ ***Selection feedback*** indicates which objects in the display have been selected in preparation for or as the result of the execution of the command.

FIGURE 11.1   Diagram of an interactive computer graphics system

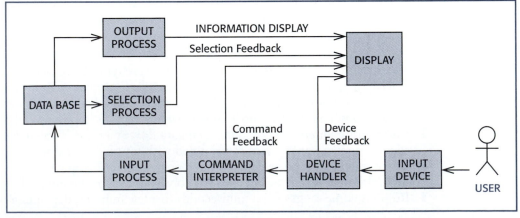

Based on William M. Newman and Robert F. Sproull, *Fundamentals of Interactive Computer Graphics*, 2nd ed. (New York: McGraw-Hill, 1979), 464.

---

[1]William M. Newman and Robert F. Sproull, *Fundamentals of Interactive Computer Graphics*, 2nd ed. (New York: McGraw-Hill, 1979).

In some cases, different devices for essential system output and for feedback may be desirable.

THE FUNDAMENTAL PATTERN OF INTERACTION

Interactive systems have a fundamental pattern of interaction with their users.

> [T]hey tend to be *event-driven*; that is, they wait for the user to do something, react appropriately, and wait again. Essentially, the dialogue consists of a simple loop:
>
> **repeat**
>   provide a choice/pose a question;
>   **wait** for the user to respond with one of n allowed values;
>   **case** — branch on the answer to the appropriate procedure for that
>   answer;
> **until** stop {user responds with STOP}[2]

Wait, act based on a response, and wait some more constitutes the basic abstraction underlying one important model of the user interface — the state transition diagram— discussed in Chapter 12. Recall that at the system level the same abstraction is the basis for event analysis, as discussed in Chapter 3.

UNDERSTANDING USERS

The user interface comprises hardware, software, and, most importantly, users. The next three sections of this chapter discuss each of them in order to provide an overview of the domain of user interface design. We begin by considering the users.

The design of early computer information systems tended to be driven by the characteristics of the hardware and software rather than by the convenience of the user. Memory was restricted; processing was time-consuming; programming languages constrained arrangement of the input and output. Users were willing to accept considerable inconvenience in order to accomplish tasks which were impractical without a computer. It was far easier for a person to adapt to the limitations of the machine than to expect the machine to make interaction easy for its users.

Today larger memories, faster processing power, and low-cost input/output devices enable the designer to focus on the convenience and effectiveness of the user.

CHARACTERISTICS OF USERS

In Chapter 2, we identified four types of users of an information processing system: the system owner, the responsible user, the hands-on user, and the beneficial user. Only the **hands-on user** interacts directly with the system; the **beneficial user** receives and uses system outputs but does not deal with the system directly. Thus, the beneficial user is affected by the design of the outputs, while the design of the interaction must be based on the characteristics of the hands-on user.

People exhibit a wide range of diversity. It is important to take into account this expected variation among the anticipated users of a particular application. The following categories indicate some of the human characteristics which concern the designer of the user interface. These categories are to be understood as continuous, with the possibility of several different profiles for users of a single system.

---

[2]James D. Foley and Andries van Dam, *Principles of Interactive Computer Graphics* (Reading, Mass.: Addison-Wesley, 1982), 27.

Orientation: Computer-Orientation/Application-Orientation

Today's users are primarily application-oriented. They use the computer in both anticipated and unanticipated ways. They not only carry out repetitive, routine tasks but also solve problems and develop the information to support their own decisions and those of others. Although they may appreciate what computers help them do, they wish to accomplish their tasks with as little knowledge of computers as possible.

Personality

People vary intrinsically in their personalities and in their attitudes. Some are secure in their outlook. They are comfortable with both familiar and unfamiliar settings. They are not threatened by change and are willing to learn. Others are insecure. They fear the new and unknown. They may perceive automation as a threat to their jobs or lack the self-confidence necessary to learn new concepts and skills.

Some people are adaptable, while others are rigid and inflexible. The implementation of any new system brings change. New technology and new procedures affect the environment in which people work and with which they interact. People's attitudes toward change vary from seeking out what is new and different (whether or not it is better) to insisting that others first prove the benefits of any change, or even to refusing to make any sort of accommodation to anything different from "the way we've always done it."

Experience: Novice/Expert

People exhibit a range of experience and expertise — from none at all to novice to intermediate to expert. These levels of expertise apply to interacting with computers as well as to familiarity with the application areas supported by the information system.

Continuous/Intermittent

Some users interact with computers regularly. They perform tasks such as data entry, word processing, or financial analysis with a spreadsheet program much of the day. They use a very limited number of application packages — perhaps only a single program. Others use a computer only occasionally — when they need help with a specialized task — possibly once every few months. Intermittent users need extra help in remembering how to communicate with application software.

Supervised Production/Solving One's Own Problems

A person who works in a supervised group is often a continuous user. In addition, others in the group are available to answer questions, provide help when difficulties arise, and explain infrequently used software features. If several software packages are used, the group may contain an "expert" for each package.

A person who works alone or wishes to use special, possibly obscure, features of an application must rely on the quality of the user interface, the documentation, and the help included as part of the software.

Memory Limitations: The Magic Number 7 ± 2

All human beings have limited short-term memory; they are able to pay attention to between about five and nine things at once without losing their train of thought or overlooking significant information. Interaction with the computer must take this limitation into account.

Right/Left Brain

There is evidence that each hemisphere of the brain controls different modes of thinking. The right side is the locus of linear or sequential thinking, including mathematics, language skills, and sequential analysis and reasoning. The left side controls visual thinking, spatial and geometric conceptualization, and artistic expression. Modes of interaction should support rather than inhibit these differing modes of thought.

THE IMPORTANCE OF ERGONOMICS

Ergonomics is the discipline which studies the **human factors** involved in the design of useful objects, especially in the workplace. The best designers have always taken human factors into account, but only recently has knowledge of these factors had a consciously scientific basis. Ergonomics originated in the context of industrial design/industrial engineering, as its Greek root words — *ergos* (work) and *nomos* (law or principle) — indicate. Ergonomics attempts to adapt the work environment to the worker rather than forcing the worker to adapt to the environment.

Ergonomics tries to accommodate the physical characteristics of the human body in order to promote comfort and to minimize fatigue. It reminds the designer of the wide range of human sizes and shapes, and of the fact that many of us are left-handed, are color-blind, or have limited mobility. It also incorporates knowledge of human perception and human psychology to facilitate the use of human senses in recognizing, understanding, and executing the task at hand. It promotes effective information transfer and seeks to minimize boredom.

This concern for users is closely related to the focus on usability discussed in Chapter 12.

Ergonomics has contributed to the design of keyboards, displays, and other devices for human-computer interaction. It is also beginning to have an impact on requirements for software as well as hardware — on the way information is organized for display and on the various styles of interaction between users and computers. Because the field of ergonomics is relatively new, there are many unanswered questions, and much research is necessary. However, specialists in the field are beginning to appear in both industry and universities. These specialists are becoming increasingly important members of the interface design team who make valuable contributions to this complex design task.

HUMAN FACTORS FOR EVALUATING THE USER INTERFACE

Measurable human factors provide important criteria for evaluating the design of the user interface. Shneiderman identifies the following five as central:[3]

1. *Time to learn.* How long does it take for typical members of the user community to learn how to use the commands relevant to a set of tasks?
2. *Speed of performance.* How long does it take to carry out the benchmark tasks?
3. *Rate of errors by users.* How many and what kinds of errors do people make in carrying out the benchmark tasks?
4. *Retention over time.* How well do users maintain their knowledge after an hour, a day, or a week?
5. *Subjective satisfaction.* How much did users like using various aspects of the system?

UNDERSTANDING THE HARDWARE

"To one with only a hammer, the whole world looks like a nail." In the 1960s, the world of input looked like a punched card, and the world of output looked like a report produced on a line printer. By the 1970s, interaction was dominated by a keyboard attached to a monochrome display. Today an almost bewildering variety of input/output devices is available for the user interface. There are high-resolution workstations for commercial art and business presentation graphics with palettes of

---

[3]Ben Shneiderman, *Designing the User Interface: Strategies for Effective Human-Computer Interaction,* 3rd ed. (Reading, Mass.: Addison-Wesley, 1998), 15.

hundreds of thousands of colors. There are laser scanners at the checkout stand in the grocery store and the circulation desk at the library. Devices that recognize or synthesize speech are economically feasible for some office systems. The challenge now is not to stretch a single device to its limits but to select an appropriate combination from an increasingly rich array of devices.

These hardware devices are the physical components of the user interface. They form the outermost portion of the automated system. Their function, as mentioned earlier, is to change information crossing the automation boundary from human readable/processible form to machine readable/processible form and vice versa.

INPUT DEVICES

Because there are so many types, makes, and models of input devices and their technologies and costs change so rapidly, these devices will first be categorized by the generic functions they perform. Then some of the devices currently available to carry out one or more of the generic functions will be listed.

Generic Functions of Input Devices[4]

Input devices perform five generic functions:

1. *Locate.* (Mark a position or orientation.)
2. *Select an object* in the display.
3. *Enter a quantity.*
4. *Enter text.*
5. *Select an action* from a set of choices.

Each of these functions can be accomplished by a variety of physical devices.

Physical Devices

1. Locate a position. The **digitizer tablet** is a natural locator device used to digitize maps or drawings. It has a flat surface with a movable **stylus** or **cursor**. To indicate the desired position, the user presses down on the stylus or pushes a button on the cursor. As the pointing device moves, its position is displayed by a tracking cursor to provide the user with visual feedback. Information from the tablet is obtained at the computer's request, at predefined time intervals, or at movements of the stylus or cursor greater than a prespecified distance.

Other locator devices include the **mouse**, the **trackball**, the **joystick**, and the **touch panel**.

A keyboard may be used to simulate a locator. Up, down, left, and right arrows may be used to position a cursor on the screen; the ENTER or other key may then be used to select the location. Alternatively, the values of coordinates may be entered.

2. Select an object in the display. Most systems use a locator to simulate this function.

3. Enter a quantity. Values may be entered on a keyboard or by moving a dial or slider.

4. Enter text. The **alphanumeric keyboard** is the natural device for entering text. Depression of a key generates a unique code for the corresponding character. Keyboard characteristics include the location and spacing of the keys, the slope of the keyboard, the shape of the key caps, the amount of pressure needed to depress a key, and the feel of the key when it is depressed.

---

[4]See Chapters 2, 3, and 5 of Foley and van Dam, *Principles of Interactive Computer Graphics*. See also Chapter 8 of James D. Foley, Andries van Dam, Steven K. Feiner, and John F. Hughes, *Computer Graphics: Principles and Practice, Second Edition in C* (Reading, Mass.: Addison-Wesley, 1996).

Optical character readers will read typed text, including typefaces specially designed for optical scanning. A voice input unit will recognize words as an alternative to keyed entry. Handwriting recognition is widespread in hand-held devices and continues to improve. Numeric values may be encoded in a magnetic strip (as on the back of a credit card) or read with a bar code scanner or a magnetic character reader (used to scan checks and other financial documents).

5. Select an action. The most common **button** device is the **programmed function key**, often integrated with an alphanumeric keyboard. Buttons are also found on tablet cursors and mice. Since hardware buttons have no predefined meanings, overlays are often used to label the keys for specific applications. If the keyboard is dedicated to an application, such as a cash register in a fast-food store or a teller machine at a bank, the keys may be permanently labeled. **Touch screens** may also be used to select actions. Buttons may be simulated in a display.

Other input possibilities include bar-code scanners, document scanners, mark sense readers, special recording devices (such as those used by meter readers), and instruments which send signals for use in manufacturing and process control applications. Radio-frequency identification (RFID) chips enable retailers and their suppliers to track goods from the factory to the checkout counter, reducing theft, eliminating warehouse staff, and helping to keep items in stock.

Input devices which recognize speech and handwriting continue to improve their accuracy of recognition and the size of their vocabulary and will be increasingly useful in the future.

OUTPUT DEVICES

Output devices may also be grouped into several broad categories — primarily printers, plotters, and displays — with some devices overlapping these categories.

Printers

Printers print characters or images on paper using several techniques, which form a basis for subcategorization.

Inkjet printers form the images by depositing small dots of black or colored ink on the paper. Their capacity is measured in pages per minute. **Laser printers** use a xerographic process involving electrostatic charges to form the images. Their capacity is also measured in pages per minute. Older technologies include **impact printers**, which form characters by striking the paper through a ribbon with a type wheel or type bar. **Dot matrix** printers are impact printers which use small dots to form the characters. Other printers produce characters using thermal action on specially treated paper. The highest-quality devices for printed output are the **photocomposition** machines used in the publishing industry for typesetting operations.

Displays

The most widely used display device has been a **cathode ray tube** (CRT). CRT technology, known as a **raster display**, is similar to that of a television set. The image is produced by an electron beam which activates the phosphor coating of the CRT. Many CRTs permit several levels of intensity. Color displays require at least three phosphor colors (red, green, and blue or magenta, cyan, and yellow).

Flat-panel displays are becoming the current technology. **Liquid-crystal displays (LCDs)** are used extensively in notebook computers. **Plasma** displays provide large flat displays. **Light-emitting diodes (LEDs)** are also used.

The components of these displays are an array of points, called **pixels** (picture elements). There is one pixel for each dot that can be displayed on the screen. This array of pixels is called a **bit map**.

The most important attribute of any display is its **resolution** — the number of points per inch or other unit of measure. The higher the resolution, the finer the detail that can be displayed. (Note that resolution is often cited improperly in terms of the number of points alone. The ability to display 1,000 by 1,000 points in a 1-yard square is quite different from displaying those 1,000,000 points in a 10-inch square.)

Plotters

Plotters produce graphic output — drawings and diagrams — typically on large sheets of paper or film. Lines, curves, and characters are usually drawn as tiny dots or line segments, depending on the technology used and the quality and cost of the hardware.

Many of the technologies used for printers — inkjet, electrostatic, laser, and xerographic — are also used for plotters. High-resolution printers are replacing plotters for many applications where the drawing area is relatively small.

For high-quality images in color, there are **film recorders**, which consist of cameras carefully coupled to CRT displays. These devices are constructed so as to minimize distortion when the CRT image is photographed.

Audio Output

Audio output devices use a synthesizer to produce sound or speech. As the technology improves, computer-originated speech will approach more closely the full quality of natural human speech, allowing messages from the computer which do not interrupt the user's visual focus. For some applications, prerecorded sound is appropriate.

UNDERSTANDING THE SOFTWARE

The software for managing the user interface reflects the expected response time of the system. The batch, on-line, and real-time environments have already been mentioned. They affect the high-level structure of the software. Batch software is typically structured as a sequence of jobs or job steps. Interactive (on-line) software is frequently organized by a menu of high-level options. Real-time software is treated as a coordinated set of concurrent processes, which may be implemented in a number of different ways.

At the lowest level, each input/output device requires its own controlling software, known as a *device driver* or *handler*. Working in conjunction with and under the control of the operating system, a device driver makes possible the transfer of data between a specific input or output device and an application program. Thus, a write statement with appropriate parameters can cause output to be printed, plotted, or displayed on a designated device. Similarly, different read statements can get a line of text from a keyboard, the coordinates of a point from a tablet, or a universal product code from a laser scanner.

The wide variety of available devices, the rapid change in their relative cost with changing technology, and the ability to substitute many physical devices for any given logical class of devices make it especially important to keep the high-level structure of the application software independent of specific devices and their characteristics. This is one motivation for a separate presentation layer in the three-tier system architecture discussed in Chapter 7.

STYLES OF INTERACTION

In *Designing the User Interface*, Shneiderman identifies five primary styles of interaction — direct manipulation, menu selection, form fill-in, command language, and natural language.[5] The advantages and disadvantages of each are shown in Figure 11.2.

---

[5]Shneiderman, *Designing the User Interface*, 71–74. See also Shneiderman, Chapters 6, 7, and 8.

FIGURE 11.2   Advantages and disadvantages of the five primary interaction styles

ADVANTAGES	DISADVANTAGES
Direct Manipulation Visually presents task concepts Allows easy learning Allows easy retention Allows errors to be avoided Encourages exploration Affords high subjective satisfaction	May be hard to program May require graphics display and pointing devices
Menu Selection Shortens learning Reduces keystrokes Structures decision making Permits use of dialogue-management tools Allows easy support of error handling	Presents danger of many menus May slow frequent users Consumes screen space Requires rapid display rate
Form Fill-In Simplifies data entry Requires modest training Gives convenient assistance Permits use of form-management tools	Consumes screen space

Command Language
Is flexible
Appeals to "power" users
Supports user initiative
Allows convenient creation of
    user-defined macros
	Has poor error handling
	Requires substantial training
	    and memorization

Natural Language Relieves burden of learning syntax	Requires clarification dialogue May require more keystrokes May not show context Is unpredictable

From Ben Shneiderman, *Designing the User Interface: Strategies for Effective Human-Computer Interation*, 3rd ed. (Reading, Mass.: Addison-Wesley, 1998), 72, box 2.1.

DIRECT MANIPULATION

High-resolution displays and graphics software provide an opportunity for interaction through direct manipulation.

> When a clever designer can create a visual representation of the world of action, the users' tasks can be greatly simplified because direct manipulation of familiar objects is possible. . . . By pointing at visual representations of objects and actions, users can carry out tasks rapidly and observe the results immediately. Keyboard entry of commands or menu choices is replaced by cursor-motion devices to select from a visible set of objects and actions. Direct manipulation is appealing to novices, easy to remember for intermittent users, and with careful design, it can be rapid for frequent users.[6]

[6]Ibid., p. 71–72.

Direct manipulation is currently the most common interaction style. Examples of applications using direct manipulation include word processing, spreadsheets, video games, and computer-aided design.

Direct manipulation follows a theory of user interface design which Shneiderman calls the Object-Action Interface (OAI) model. Users' tasks are organized as a hierarchy of objects and actions. A user selects an object and then chooses an action which applies to that object.

MENU SELECTION

Menu selection allows the user to choose an action from a list of alternatives displayed on the screen. More detailed choices of options or parameters may subsequently be selected from submenus. The menu may contain icons instead of or in addition to words.

Menu selection is relatively easy for novice and infrequent users. Selection requires few keystrokes and can be facilitated by a mouse or similar device. The designer can limit the list to currently valid choices, thus designing errors out of the interaction. Submenus can restrict the number of options presented at once. Care is required to make the options clear and as nearly self-explanatory as possible. Consistency of user action and system response is important, especially when there are multiple levels of menus. Easy navigation through the hierarchy of menus is an important design consideration.

Advanced dialogue-management tools help build user interfaces based on menu selection. These tools facilitate consistent screen design, validate completeness, and support maintenance.

FORM FILL-IN

Form fill-in is more appropriate than menu selection when the interaction requires extensive data entry.

> Users see a display of related fields, move a cursor among the fields, and enter data where desired. With the form fill-in interaction style, the users must understand the field labels, know the permissible values and the data entry method, and be capable of responding to error messages. Since knowledge of the keyboard, the labels, and permissible fields is required, some training may be necessary. This interaction style is most appropriate for knowledgeable intermittent users or frequent users.[7]

Form fill-in is often implemented on a display which permits the user to enter or reenter data anywhere until all entries are correct. Then the data from the entire screen is transmitted as a block. Software tools are also available to support interaction by form fill-in.

COMMAND LANGUAGE

Command languages are seldom used now that the graphical user interface has become the norm for interaction. However, a command language can be effective for a frequent user with a good grasp of an application area. Initiative and control lie with the user rather than the system. The user specifies the execution of a series of actions without being prompted. Thus, complex tasks can be communicated directly and effectively. But it is necessary to teach users the syntax as well as the interpretation which the system gives to the vocabulary of the application area.

---

[7]Ibid., 73.

Infrequent users often find it difficult to maintain their facility in a command language. It can be difficult to provide good error diagnostics for a command language if the cause of a problem is far back in the command sequence.

NATURAL LANGUAGE

In this interaction style, users communicate with computers in unrestricted natural language. There has been success in applications of limited scope. These systems have infrequent but knowledgeable users who can use the technical vocabulary of the application area precisely. Otherwise, the "clarification dialogue" necessary to eliminate ambiguity or establish a specific context interferes with rapid and effective interaction. Nevertheless, considerable progress has been made over the past decade, and the future of natural language interfaces appears promising indeed.[8]

COMMUNICATING WITH COMPUTERS: THE LANGUAGE ANALOGY

Since the early days of computers, communication between people and computers has been compared to communication among humans via natural language. The built-in instruction set which controlled the sequence of processing operations was called "machine language." This powerful analogy is useful as a basis for designing the user-computer interaction.

Indeed, as Foley and van Dam point out:

> There are really two languages at this interface. With one, the user communicates to the computer; with the other, the computer communicates to the user. The first language is expressed with actions applied to various interaction devices, while the second language is expressed graphically through lines, points, character strings, filled areas, and colors combined to form displayed images and messages.[9]

This double design task is even more challenging than perhaps we realized. Few of us are expert in using our native tongue, yet we are required to specify not just one, but two artificial languages for user-computer interaction. Perhaps this fact helps explain why the task is so difficult and why truly "user-friendly" interfaces are just beginning to emerge after a slow evolution with many mistakes along the way.

It is traditional to describe natural language in terms of both its content, or semantics, and its form, or syntax. It is also necessary to deal with the words of which a language is composed. The field of *linguistics* has technical terms for these aspects and elements of language. A familiarity with these terms is useful not only for discussing user interface design, but also for communicating precisely about programming languages and natural languages.

SEMANTICS: MEANING

Semantics is concerned with the **content** or **meaning** expressed through language. Semantics focuses on **what** is said rather than **how** it is said. To be sure, the conceptual content of language interacts with the forms that express it. However, it is useful to treat meaning as a separate aspect of all language, relatively independent of any specific language and its associated culture.

---

[8]Wade Roush, "Computers That Speak Your Language," *Technology Review* 106, no. 5 (June 2003): 32–39.
[9]Foley and van Dam, *Principles of Interactive Computer Graphics*, 220.

SYNTAX: FORM

Syntax is concerned with the **form** of language. The *grammar* of a language defines the rules for well-formed sentences. Syntax is important to communication because there is a correspondence between syntactic and semantic structures. Clear, correct syntax facilitates understanding. Confused syntax promotes confusion. Ambiguous syntax adds to the burden of interpretation.

PRIMITIVES

A language is composed of *primitives* — elements which cannot be decomposed without losing their significance in the system. In a natural language, the primitive units of form and meaning are the **words** which make up its *vocabulary*.

We can also recognize lower-level constituents of a language which have no meaning until they are combined to form words. In a natural language, these are the distinguishable sounds represented by the letters of an alphabet. In the context of user-computer interaction, we deal with hardware primitives from which the system inputs and outputs are formed. For example, the user of a keyboard constructs words out of characters; each character is associated with one or more keystrokes. Or a character on a display can be referred to by other hardware primitives; it can be pointed at with a cursor controlled by a mouse. Ultimately, the user interface design must be defined to the level of these hardware primitives.

The language of the dialogue at the user interface should be natural to the user, efficient, complete, and extensible.

STEPS IN DESIGNING THE INTERACTION

Foley and van Dam describe a six-step process for designing the user interface.[10] This process is shown in Figure 11.3. The first four steps define the interaction in the dialogue. The remaining two steps complete the design.

While there are advantages of this approach both for presentation and for deferring the low-level, implementation-related details, in practice the process is not so neatly linear. The detailed design decisions affect feasibility and quality and thus interact with high-level decisions.

These activities assume a prior task analysis, in which the data requirements and information processing functions of the application have been identified. They also assume that these functions have been allocated between the human and automated information processors. In addition, the location of the automation boundary is known, as are the essential content and structure of the information flows across it.

The use case narratives prepared during analysis provide the task analysis. The high-level system design locates the automation boundary, and the system sequence diagrams define the essential content and the structure of the messages from the human actors to the system.

FIGURE 11.3	Process for designing the user interface

> 1. Design the user model (conceptual design).
> 2. Design the functionality of the interface (semantic design).
> 3. Design the sequencing of the dialogue (syntactic design).
> 4. Design the hardware bindings.
> 5. Define the conversation protocol.
> 6. Design the user environment.

---

[10]Foley and van Dam, 220–222.

1. DESIGN THE USER MODEL (CONCEPTUAL DESIGN)

This step defines the key concepts which form the user's model of the application domain. These concepts guide the dialogue and help the user to understand it. The user's model usually comprises the interface objects, their properties, the associations between the objects, and the operations on the objects and associations. Much of this analysis is carried out while building the domain model during requirements analysis, as discussed in Chapter 5. The domain model will contain most of the components of the user model and suggest clues to the rest.

For example, in a computer-aided system for producing interaction diagrams, the concepts would include classes, objects, messages, and collaborations. Messages would connect collaborating objects. Operations on an object would include creating it, moving it, deleting it from the diagram, modifying attribute values, and associating two objects.

2. DESIGN THE FUNCTIONALITY OF THE INTERFACE (SEMANTIC DESIGN)

Functional design specifies what operations are performed on each interface object, the information needed from the user or within the automated system for each of these operations, what errors may occur and what to do about them, the results of each operation, and the information to be displayed by the computer for each operation. The emphasis is on the meanings of the operations — not on the form, sequence, or style of interaction.

Even though the style of interaction will be determined later, it is helpful at this stage to think of a set of one or more commands associated with each operation. Then the constituent components of each command can be identified.

The essential information content of each command is defined for each system input and output. In some cases, several commands may be necessary to enter one essential input. Possible errors may be identified by considering how to protect the automated system from the entry of erroneous information. Reporting on errors (or lack of them) at this level constitutes the *command feedback* shown in Figure 11.1.

3. DESIGN THE SEQUENCING OF THE DIALOGUE (SYNTACTIC DESIGN)

The next step is to specify the form in which the units of meaning will cross the automation boundary in both directions. The syntax of the input language defines the sequence in which the primitives of each command will be entered. The most common sequence in today's user interfaces is:

1. Select the object(s).
2. Select the operation or action to apply to the object(s).

The syntax of the output language specifies the layout of the information displayed, plotted, or printed as the result of executing each command. Formal and rigorous specification tools and techniques should be used at this step.

4. DESIGN THE HARDWARE BINDINGS

This design activity binds specific hardware primitives to the hardware-independent components of the input and output languages. In this step, the interaction technique, or alternative techniques, for each user command is defined, working within the framework established by the sequencing design. Similarly, the designer specifies the device-dependent output primitives (such as points, lines, or characters) and their attributes (such as intensity, color, or font) which will be combined to form the messages from the computer to the user. Errors at this level are part of the *device feedback* shown in Figure 11.1. Deferring this binding to the latter stages of interface design keeps the high-level design freer of specific details of the technology for implementing the interaction.

5. DEFINE THE CONVERSATION PROTOCOL

The *conversation protocol* defines the time relationships between the user commands and the system responses. This step incorporates all the various types and levels of feedback, prescribes response times, and thus determines whether the user perceives the system as batch or interactive.

6. DESIGN THE USER ENVIRONMENT

As the dialogue is defined in the earlier steps, the design decisions are recorded and organized as a **reference manual**. This manual is an essential part of the interface specification and will be the basis for acceptance testing of the completed interface.

It is also desirable to prepare a draft **users' manual**, which explains the user model and emphasizes its relationship to the semantic and syntactic levels of the dialogue. This draft will facilitate user review of the design for the interface and can be refined during the construction phase. During construction, a **quick reference guide** will be extracted from the reference manual. Producers of commercial software have largely replaced paper manuals with **computer-based tutorials** and **Help commands** as well as **on-line help**. This is certainly less expensive for the manufacturer as well as the purchaser. However, it may not always be as useful.

The designer may also need to pay attention to the physical environment of the terminal or workstation used in the interaction. Important considerations include an adequate area for the equipment and the user's reference materials; appropriate background and task lighting, ambient noise level, temperature control; and the ability to accommodate both left-handed and right-handed users of a variety of sizes and shapes.

Throughout the process, the work products must be reviewed to detect and correct problems and errors in the design. Informal reviews as well as formal reviews and walkthroughs are used for quality assurance.

GUIDELINES FOR INTERACTION DESIGN

In a complex design domain such as that of the user interface, it is difficult to specify a detailed design method. Instead, the work of the designer is assisted by a set of guidelines, which also serve as criteria for evaluating the quality of the design.

Some of the more important of these guidelines include the following:

▌ Provide *simple and consistent* interaction sequences.
▌ *Show the appropriate options clearly* at every stage of the interaction.
▌ *Give appropriate feedback* to the user.
▌ Allow the user to *recover gracefully* from mistakes.
▌ *Help the user learn the system.*[11]

Each of these will be discussed briefly.

SIMPLE AND CONSISTENT INTERACTION SEQUENCES

There is a consensus that consistency is one of the most important design goals for the user interface. If the same action is always invoked in the same way, the user can learn the system more rapidly and feel more confident of achieving predictable results. The more variations and exceptions there are, the more the user has to remember and the greater the demand for help from the system.

---

[11]Foley, van Dam, Feiner, and Hughes, *Computer Graphics*, 41. See also Foley et. al., Chapters 8 and 9.

According to Foley and his colleagues:

The basic purpose of consistency is to allow the user to generalize knowledge about one aspect of the system to other aspects. Consistency also helps to avoid the frustration induced when a system does not behave in an understandable and logical way. The best way to achieve consistency is through a careful top-down design of the overall system.[12]

One example of consistency is always displaying menu items in the same relative place in the menu. Another simple example is providing generic commands, such as Move, Copy, and Delete, which apply predictably to any object in the system.

SHOW THE APPROPRIATE OPTIONS CLEARLY

Many potential user errors can be designed out of the system. If a menu is displayed, it should include only those options which are allowed at the current stage of the dialogue. Other choices can be grayed out or eliminated from the menu. This makes it impossible for the user to enter an illegal command. Require the user to select from a set of valid entries or actions to prevent input errors.

GIVE APPROPRIATE FEEDBACK TO THE USER

As Figure 11.1 shows, feedback can and should be provided from several locations in an interactive system. These locations correspond to the various levels in the linguistic hierarchy discussed above. At the lowest level (the hardware primitive level), there is **device feedback** from the input devices. When a key is depressed, a character should appear on the display. When a mouse is moved, the cursor should track its movement. At the syntactic level, the computer should provide **command feedback**, confirming that the word or command just entered has been recognized and is valid. This can be done by highlighting an area of the display as well as by showing a confirming message. **Selection feedback** indicates which menu choice or object in the display has been selected. **Semantic feedback** tells or shows the user that the operation requested has been completed. If the requested action will take more than a few seconds to complete, the user should be notified that the system is working to accomplish the request. Ideally, feedback should appear on the screen in the area where the user is looking, rather than in a fixed location, to avoid forcing the user to move the eyes back and forth between the work area and a fixed message area. An alternative is to provide audio feedback.

ALLOW USERS TO RECOVER GRACEFULLY FROM MISTAKES

We all make mistakes. The design of an interactive system should prevent errors where possible. Otherwise, the system should detect errors and make them easy to correct.

Many systems provide backup which makes it possible to undo the most recent command. If a command has serious consequences or would be difficult to cancel, the user may be asked to confirm the user's desire before the action is taken. The classic example is the action of deleting a file, when the user may be asked, "Do you really want to delete this file?" Or the user may be allowed to cancel an action before it has been completed.

---

[12]Ibid., 404.

HELP THE USER LEARN THE SYSTEM

This principle may be incorporated in a system in several ways — through **tutorials**, a **help** facility, and **prompts** or **wizards** to lead the user through the interaction. It is often desirable to let the user control the type and amount of help needed. It is now a common practice to make tutorials and the help facility available to the user on line to assist with the task the user is currently performing.

These five guidelines would appear to be largely common sense and easy to follow in designing the user interface. But Foley and van Dam remind us:

> [T]hese rules may seem obvious. However, when the time comes to design an interactive system, the rules are all too often forgotten or given lip service. The reasons for this are clear enough. Typically, there is pressure to get a system running as soon as possible, which leaves insufficient time for a thoughtful design to be developed. Thus the user interface is consequently designed for ease of implementation rather than for ease of use. . . .
>
> But while the reasons for bad design are understandable, the resulting systems can be deplorable. To design an interactive system, a complete, well-thought-out, and well-documented design is necessary, prepared with clear guidelines . . . in mind.[13]

ORGANIZING REPORTS AND INTERACTIVE DISPLAYS

Designing a report or interactive display is inherently a problem in graphic design as well as in user interface design. Poor graphic design inhibits users' ability to understand and employ information effectively. It can also have a negative impact on user productivity and attitudes. On the other hand, good design can enhance the image of an organization in the eyes of the software's various users as well as increase user effectiveness.

Graphic design is a field with its own traditions, principles, and expertise. Too often designers of the user interface operate without the benefit of a background in graphic design yet do not employ experts in the field. The result can be painfully obvious to graphic designers and users alike.

This section sets out some basic principles of graphic design and applies them to the organization of reports and displays. It also discusses graphic elements of reports and displays as well as technological constraints affecting these graphic media. While an in-depth treatment of report and display design for application software is impossible here, you should at least become aware of the potential complexity of the design decisions to be made and the potential value of involving a professional graphic designer in the process.[14]

---

[13]Foley and van Dam, *Principles of Interactive Computer Graphics*, 238–239.

[14]The definitions below specify our use of the following words. They are all derived from the Greek verb *graphein*, meaning to mark, thus to write or draw.

Graph n. A chart or diagram showing quantitative relationships.

Graphic n. One icon or pictorial symbol. adj. (1) Pertaining to graphics or the graphic arts. (2) Vivid.

Graphical adj. (1) Pertaining to graphs. (2) Pertaining to graphics or the graphical arts (primarily in the case where *graphic* could be interpreted as *vivid*).

Graphic arts n. Arts based on or using drawing, including drawing, painting, lithography, and engraving.

Graphics n. (sing.) The art or science of drawing or producing drawings.

WINDOWS IN THE USER INTERFACE

The graphical user interface is organized as a series of windows which present the application display and support the interaction with the user. This section identifies the most common types of windows and addresses navigation from window to window.[15]

TYPES OF WINDOWS

A *window* is a rectangle containing other graphic elements. More than one window may be displayed at a time. Associated with windows are characteristics of their behavior, such as whether they are movable, are resizable, or can be overlapped by other windows. These characteristics are associated with a specific *window types*.

The window-type definitions here are representative of the Microsoft Windows environment.

Main or Application Window

A *main window*, or *application window*, can overlap other windows and be overlapped by them. It is movable, is resizable, and can be minimized to an icon on the desktop. A main window normally has a menu. Figure 11.4 illustrates a main window.

Pop-Up Window

A *pop-up window* appears on top of another window, which is known as its *parent window*. It may not be overlapped by its parent, but it can be moved, even outside the parent window. It may also be minimized. Figure 11.5 illustrates a pop-up window.

Child Window

A *child window* is similar to a pop-up window. However, a child window may not be moved so that it is visible outside the parent window. If it is minimized, its icon appears in the parent window. Figure 11.6 illustrates a child window.

| FIGURE 11.4 | Main (application) window |

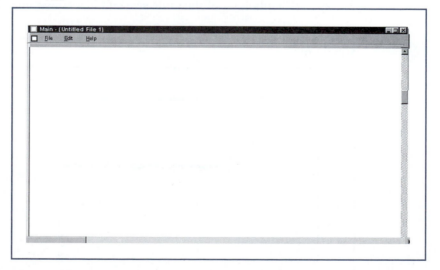

---

[15]This section is based in part on Chapter 11 of David A. Ruble, *Practical Analysis and Design for Client/Server and GUI Systems* (Upper Saddle River, N.J.: Yourdon, 1997).

FIGURE 11.5   Pop-up window

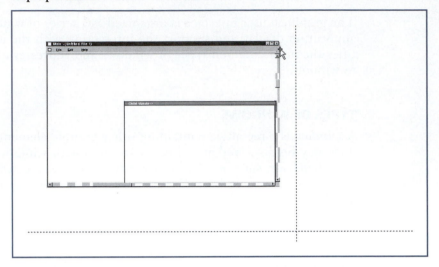

Response Window

A *response window* is not resizable or minimizable. When opened, it inhibits interaction with other windows until it is closed. Figure 11.7 illustrates a response window.

COMPONENTS OF REPORTS AND DISPLAYS

Reports and displays comprise a variety of graphic elements and components. Their content and arrangement will depend on the requirements of each specific application.

Text Components

These components constitute the alphanumerical portion of reports and displays. They are aggregated into words, messages, paragraphs, and tables.

Character. The basic element of text is a single character.

Font. A *font* is a set of characters — letters, numbers, punctuation, and other special symbols — of the same size and in a consistent style so that they can be

FIGURE 11.6   Child window

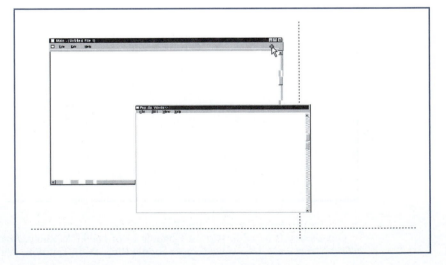

FIGURE 11.7   Response window

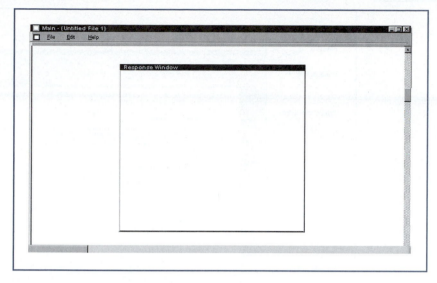

combined. Fonts may be available in a range of sizes. A font may include italic, bold, and oblique characters.

Block of text. Characters are combined to form blocks of text — primarily words, sentences, and paragraphs.

Table. A *table* has a matrix structure. The elements, rows, and columns may have labels and headings. A table may contain numeric data with subtotals and totals for rows or columns.

In addition to text, reports and displays may include:

Icons and special symbols. A report may incorporate a logo or other graphical components as part of its design. Menus for interaction may include *icons*. Interaction through direct manipulation incorporates application-specific graphical elements.

Graphs and charts. Numeric data can be presented concisely and effectively through *graphs* and *charts*. Commonly used formats are bar charts, pie charts, line graphs, and graphs of mathematical functions.

COMPONENTS OF WINDOWS IN AN INTERACTIVE DISPLAY

Earlier in this chapter, output at the user interface was described in terms of information display for the application, device feedback, command feedback, and selection feedback. (See Figure 11.1.) This section looks more closely at the graphic components available to the designer of a graphical user interface. The components and the conventions for their use are illustrated with examples of the **common user interface** of the Windows environment. Conventions for the Macintosh environment are similar.

A typical application in the Windows environment may contain the following graphic elements. Figure 11.8 illustrates some of these elements.

Window

A *window* is a rectangle containing other graphic elements. More than one window at a time may be displayed. Types of windows were discussed in the previous section.

FIGURE 11.8   Display for a typical application in the Windows environment

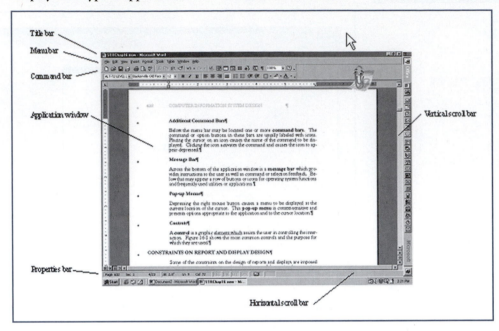

Title Bar

Across the top of a window is a ***title bar*** containing the name of the window. If the window is the main window of an application, the title bar contains the name of the application and usually the name of the current object being displayed (such as a document or spreadsheet).

Menu Bar

Beneath the title bar of an application window is a ***menu bar*** listing the available commands in text. Each item on the menu serves as a button for executing the command. From left to right, the first two commands are "File" and Edit," and the last command is "Help."

Dialogue Boxes

If a command name is followed by an ellipsis (. . .), additional information is needed. A dialogue box may prompt the user for this information. A ***dialogue box*** is a window which provides the user with information or asks the user for a response. It may include a set of buttons labeled with the allowable responses. If so, the button for the default response encloses its label in a dotted rectangle. Among the buttons are usually a CANCEL button and an OK button.

   Avoid a long sequence of dialogue boxes within dialogue boxes. There should be a consistent way of leaving the current menu or dialogue box.

Command Bars

Below the menu bar may be located one or more ***command bars***. The command or option buttons in these bars are usually labeled with icons. Placing the cursor on an icon causes the name of the command to be displayed. Clicking the icon activates the command and causes the icon to appear depressed.

Properties Bar

Across the bottom of the application window is a ***properties bar***, which provides instructions to the user as well as command or selection feedback. Below that may appear a row of buttons or icons for operating system functions and frequently used utilities or applications.

Pop-Up Menus

Depressing the right mouse button causes a menu to be displayed at the current location of the cursor. This *pop-up menu* is context-sensitive and presents options appropriate to the application and to the cursor location.

Controls

A *control* is a graphic element which assists the user in controlling the interaction. Figure 11.9 shows the most common controls and the purpose for which they are used. Figure 11.10 shows a dialogue box with examples of some of these controls.

CONSTRAINTS ON REPORT AND DISPLAY DESIGN

Some of the constraints on the design of reports and displays are imposed by the output media and associated hardware. Others arise from requirements of the application.

FIGURE 11.9   Controls for the graphical user interface

CONTROL NAME	PURPOSE	REMARKS
Text box	Allows a user to enter data from the keyboard.	
Open list box	Displays a list of data (often from a data base) from which the user selects the desired element. Used for data entry.	May contain a scroll bar.
Check box	Displays one of a set of options which are not mutually exclusive.	Clicking a square next to the option toggles a check mark on or off to show whether the option is selected.
Option button (or radio button)	Displays one of a set of mutually exclusive options. Clicking the circle next to the option selects that option and deselects the other options.	
Drop-down list box	Displays a highlighted current selection from a list.	Clicking the down arrow at the right of the list box displays the full list of options and may allow the user to make another selection.
Command button	Displays an action.	Clicking the button executes the action.
Scroll bar (horizontal or vertical)	Allows the contents of an object larger than its window to be moved into the viewable area.	

FIGURE 11.10 Dialogue box with examples of controls

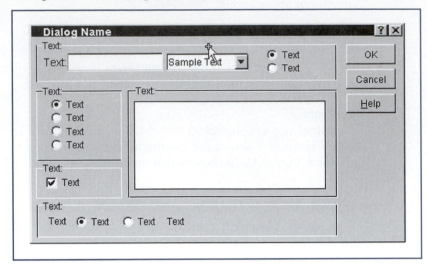

Constraints Due to Output Media and Devices

The major classes of output devices were described earlier in the chapter. This section highlights some of the device and media limitations which may affect the design of displays and reports. Output which must be produced on a variety of devices requires special care to assure that it is compatible with all the target devices.

Printers. The design of printed output is constrained by the number and style of the available fonts, which characters are in the character set, and the size of the characters. It is important to consider whether the printer provides fixed or variable horizontal spacing as well as whether there is any control over the vertical spacing. When output must be reproduced, the resolution of the printer will affect the ability to enlarge or reduce output and have it remain legible. The size of the area that can be printed will limit the size of the report. For some applications, the ability of the printer to generate boxes around text, to overprint, or to print a gray scale may be critical. Graphics printers will be necessary for reports containing charts and graphs.

Paper and Forms. Additional constraints are associated with the paper or forms used or with the interaction between the printer technology and the type of form. Some printers may require a minimum margin between the edge of the paper and the printed area. If multiple copies of a report are required for distribution, an impact printer may require multiple-part forms or necessitate a subsequent copying step. Alternative printer or distribution technologies (such as or Internet distribution) may be worth considering.

Preprinted forms containing repeated information, such as titles, headings, and labels for data, can reduce the amount of information transferred and printed. Forms suppliers can define the detailed constraints on the design of preprinted forms and will often assist in designing these forms. With the advent of laser printers, the use of preprinted forms has decreased. Preprinting is often limited to colored areas which enhance a corporate image.

Displays. Display devices are subject to many of the same constraints as printers — the maximum size of the image, its resolution, the available character sets and fonts, and the range of character sizes. Color displays are now the norm. For some applications, the palette of available colors will be important. The feasibility of some user interface designs will depend on the existence or development of an appropriate library of icons and symbols for the application. Color displays, color film, and color printing span different portions of color space. It is difficult, sometimes impossible, to reproduce colors exactly in different media. Special care is necessary when color from a display must be faithfully reproduced on film or in hard copy.

Application Constraints

Some constraints arise from the requirements of specific applications. Many of these are related to hard-copy output.

Use of the Document. How a document will be used in an information processing application also affects its design.

For example, many billing systems use what are called **turnaround documents**. Part of the bill is designed to be returned by the customer along with the payment. When the seller (or the seller's bank) receives it, this part of the bill will be used for data entry so that the customer's account can be credited with the amount paid.

Sometimes a return envelope is enclosed with the bill. The payment portion should fit conveniently in the envelope. If the envelope has a transparent window, the return address must be located so that it is visible. Also, the location of information on the payment slip should facilitate data entry.

In other applications, output includes bar codes to permit subsequent reading by a scanner.

Forms Control. In some applications, it is necessary to account for output at the level of each individual document. For example, a system which prints checks could provide an opportunity for fraud or theft if blank checks fall into the wrong hands. It is common to have a serial number preprinted on each check. At output time, one of the fields printed on the check is a number which must match the preprinted number.

Corporate Image. Many organizations use graphic design to promote a recognizable corporate image — to the public and within the organization. Consistency of design across the gamut of products and documents associated with the organization is therefore an important objective. Such a corporate design policy will provide further constraints and guidelines. These guidelines can assist user interface design by supplying a predefined framework for graphic design decisions.

WEB PAGES AS A USER INTERFACE

Many applications today are entirely Web-based or use Web pages as a user interface. The principles of good design apply to a Web-based interface as well as to an interface at a workstation. However, a Web interface raises a number of design issues not found in the interface for a workstation.[16] Those issues are outside the scope of this book.

---

[16]Patrick J. Lynch and Sarah Horton, *Web Style Guide: Basic Design Principles for Creating Web Sites*, 2nd ed. (New Haven, Conn.: Yale University Press, 2002), is a concise and valuable guide for user interface design, whether on or off the Internet. However, it does not deal with the use of Web pages for data entry or for obtaining access to data bases. See also Jakob Nielsen, *Designing Web Usability: The Practice of Simplicity* (Indianapolis, Ind.: New Riders, 2000).

Web pages based on HTML (hypertext markup language) provide users with limited flexibility and control over the interaction, making careful design especially important. Newer software, such as XML (extensible markup language) and Java applets, provides both user and designer with greater flexibility and control. Applications based entirely on the Web require no installation on user machines. All that is necessary is a browser.

VISUAL DESIGN PRINCIPLES

The complexity of user interface design goes beyond the complexity of the information to be communicated. Seeing is itself a complex process in which the images can convey complex and subtle cultural and emotional associations.

In Chapter 1, we noted that, when confronted by complexity, people structure and simplify. We attempt to organize information into a small number of things — "7 +/− 2" — to think about simultaneously. To make many things comprehensible, we often create hierarchical structures. These observations apply to visual phenomena as well as to other modes of thought.

GESTALT PRINCIPLES OF VISUAL ORGANIZATION

In the early part of the 20th century, some European researchers developed theories about the structures of human visual perception. When they studied the way people see things in two dimensions, they noticed that what we see is organized into objects on a background. Moreover, our visual processes seem to group the objects in the visual field so as to simplify their apparent structure.

These Gestalt[17] psychologists stated a set of principles of visual organization for objects seen in two dimensions. These principles describe the bases on which objects are grouped, providing insight which can be applied to two-dimensional design problems such as report and screen layout.

Objects seen in two dimensions are grouped according to the following principles: proximity, similarity, direction, common motion, continuation, and closure. Many of these principles were understood as examples of a more inclusive law: "Of several geometrically possible organizations, that one will occur which possesses the best, simplest, and most stable shape."[18]

Proximity
Visual elements are grouped when they are close to each other. For example, in the United States, telephone numbers are ten digits long. They are grouped as a three-digit area code followed by a three-digit prefix followed by a four-digit number. Long numbers are easier to read when subdivided by commas into three-digit groups. In Figure 11.11, the arrays of dots are seen as vertical lines because the vertical distance between dots is less than the horizontal distance.

---

[17]Gestalt (pronounced with a hard *g* and accented on the final syllable: Ghe-*shtahlt*) is a German word meaning form, shape, configuration, or pattern. The wholeness and unity of the pattern is emphasized. These investigators of visual phenomena stressed that "the whole is greater than the sum of its parts." The group included Wolfgang Koehler, Kurt Koffka, and Max Wertheimer. The Gestalt psychologists had a significant impact on 20th-century architecture and art through their influence on education at the Bauhaus. "Principles of Perception," a translation of Wertheimer's 1923 paper, may be found in David C. Beardslee and Michael Wertheimer, eds., *Readings in Perception* (Princeton, N.J.: Van Nostrand, 1958).
[18]Kurt Koffka, *Principles of Gestalt Psychology* (New York: Harcourt Brace, 1935), 138.

FIGURE 11.11   Proximity

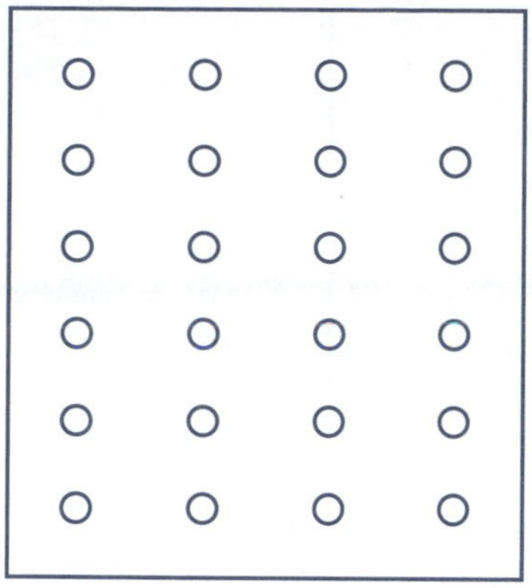

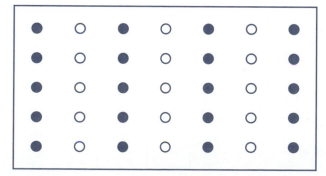

Similarity

Visual elements are grouped when they are similar to each other. The basis for grouping the elements may be any shared attribute, such as shape, size, or color.

In the above numeric examples, the principle of proximity is reinforced by the principle of similarity. In long numbers, one similar group consists of the digits; the other consists of the commas. In a telephone number, the digits and the punctuation marks form separate groups. In Figure 11.12, the array appears as alternating vertical stripes of dark and light dots.

Closure

Visual elements are grouped to form simple, closed figures. Thus, even if a group lacks a few elements of a simple structure, the group will be organized as if the missing elements were present. The matrix of Figure 11.11 is structured as a square; that of Figure 11.12 is structured as a rectangle. Figure 11.13 is understood as a circle even though there is a gap.

Common Motion

Visual elements are grouped when they move together. Items on a screen which blink together or are highlighted at the same time are seen together, in contrast to the part of the screen which does not blink or is not highlighted.

FIGURE 11.12   Similarity

FIGURE 11.13   Closure

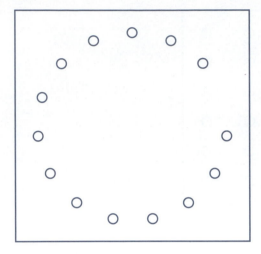

Continuation

Visual elements are grouped to preserve smooth continuity instead of abrupt change. A group of elements may establish a direction which we expect to be continued when another element is added to the group. Figure 11.14 is seen as two intersecting curves instead of two V-shapes with a common vertex.

Figure/Ground Segregation

Other principles describe the distinction between figure and background:

▌ The smaller of two adjacent areas is seen as the figure, the larger as the ground.
▌ An area surrounded by another is seen as the figure against the surrounding area, which is seen as the ground.
▌ Symmetrical areas are seen as figures against asymmetrical backgrounds.
▌ Horizontally or vertically oriented areas are seen as figures.

CORRESPONDENCE OF VISUAL STRUCTURES AND DATA STRUCTURES

The Gestalt principles of organization describe the structuring of visual phenomena apart from any nonvisual information or semantic content. They can be used to make objects in the visual field difficult to see, as in camouflage, or to aid visual communication.

In arranging information in two dimensions so that it can be easily scanned and understood, it is important to make the purely visual organization correspond to the

FIGURE 11.14   Continuation

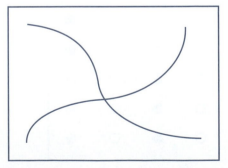

logical or semantic organization of the information. In this way, the two sets of structures will reinforce each other and assist the viewer to comprehend what is being presented. Thus,

> **Visual structures should reinforce data structures.**

In laying out reports and screens, the arrangement of the information on the page or screen should be guided by the composition of the data structures to be printed or displayed. Data structure is thus the starting point for report and screen design.

Visual indications of hierarchy, such as indentation or explicit tree structures, can aid in presenting hierarchical data structures. Variations in typography can also show levels in a hierarchy (as in the sections of this book).

LAYOUT AND TASK PERFORMANCE

Report and screen layout is also related to the kinds of tasks the user must perform.

Mixed upper- and lower-case characters are easier to read than upper-case characters alone. A well-designed *typeface* assures that similarly shaped characters, such as **g** and **q** or **b** and **h**, are easy to distinguish.

The grouping of numeric data into groups of three or four digits facilitates data entry.

A common interactive task is searching for a specific item on a display. This task may be aided by emphasizing the item in a variety of ways: making it blink, displaying it in reverse video, increasing its intensity, making it move, giving it a unique shape or size, or making it a distinctive color. A distinctive color is generally better than a difference in shape, size, or brightness and better than identification by alphanumeric characters or letters.[19]

In some applications, it is necessary to code the items displayed so the user can differentiate between categories of items. Means of coding include color, size, intensity, width of line, style of line, shape, and blink rate. Shape and color coding allow more items to be displayed simultaneously than other coding strategies.

Color coding is a more accurate means of coding than shape, size, or intensity, but color coding is up to 50 percent less accurate than alphanumeric coding.[20]

Redundant coding increases discrimination among categories. It may be especially desirable with color coding because, as noted below, some users may be color-blind.

METRICS OF COMPLEXITY

Researchers have tried to develop metrics for layouts so that screens and reports can be evaluated quantitatively as well as qualitatively.

For example, Tullis proposed four metrics for monochrome screen layouts consisting of alphanumeric characters — overall density, local density, grouping, and layout complexity. He then experimented to determine how well the metrics were correlated with the time it took to perform searches. He also asked the participants in the experiment for a subjective rating of their satisfaction with the various layouts.[21]

---

[19]R. Christ, "Review and Analysis of Color Coding Research for Visual Display," *Human Factors* 17, no. 6 (1975): 542–570.
[20]Ibid.
[21]T. S. Tullis, "Predicting the Usability of Alphanumeric Displays" (Ph.D. diss., Rice University, 1984).

KEY TERMS

batch system *309*

chroma *337*

conversation protocol *322*

ergonomics *313*

font *327*

hue *337*

icon *327*

intensity *337*

linguistic *319*

online system *309*

primitive *320*

real-time system *310*

saturation *337*

semantics *319*

syntax *320*

turnaround document *331*

typeface *335*

value *337*

vocabulary *320*

REVIEW QUESTIONS

11-1. What is the purpose of the user interface to a computer information system?

11-2. What are the three principal components of the user interface?

11-3. What must be specified in the design of the user interface? What system requirements (or design decisions) are prerequisite to the design of the user interface?

11-4. State some of the human factors to be considered in designing the interaction between a person and an automated information processing system.

11-5. Why is the understanding of an interactive system the principal basis for user interface design?

11-6. State some of the most important characteristics of batch, interactive, and real-time systems.

11-7. What are the five generic functions performed by input devices? Name some devices which can perform each of these functions.

11-8. What are the three major categories of output devices? Give examples of some of the technologies used within each of these categories.

11-9. Identify the six steps in user interface design. Describe each briefly.

11-10. How is quality assurance achieved during user interface design?

11-11. State four guidelines for user interface design. Explain why each of them is important.

11-12. State five primary styles of interaction. What are the advantages and disadvantages of each?

11-13. What constraints on report and screen design are imposed by each of the following output devices or media?
   a. Printers
   b. Paper and forms
   c. Displays

11-14. Name and explain five principles of visual organization formulated by the Gestalt psychologists.

11-15. What quantifiable physical attribute of light is related to each of the following: hue, value, and chroma?

11-16. State at least five advantages and five disadvantages of using color in interactive displays.

11-17. What are the consequences of using large, contrasting areas of red/green, blue/yellow, green/blue, or red/blue?

11-18. What kinds of backgrounds are appropriate for light viewing conditions? For dark viewing conditions?

11-19. What visual elements of a screen or report should contrast most highly with the background?

EXERCISES AND DISCUSSION QUESTIONS

11-1. Name the type(s) of software associated with each of the following components of Figure 11.1: data capture (input) devices, information display, and application database.

11-2. Observe a user interacting with a computer to perform each of the five generic input functions (see Review Question 11–7). What device or devices were used for each of these functions? In the application you saw, was a single device being used to perform several of these generic functions? If so, what was the device and for what functions was it used? Comment on the apparent ease with which each device was used.

11-3. Explain how a mouse (a locator) can be used to simulate each of the other four generic input device types.

11-4. Collect a variety of printed and graphic output. See if by careful examination you can identify the technology involved. What clues led to a successful identification?

11-5. What is meant by the term "event-driven"? How is it related to the technique of event analysis? Write down the overall logic for a typical interactive program.

11-6. Investigate and summarize the application of ergonomics to the design of one or more of the following: a specific input device currently on the market, furniture to accommodate a personal computer, and optical character fonts.

11-7. Some application software permits the use of a keyboard only or a keyboard augmented with a mouse. Examine one such package and comment on the relative ease of use with and without the mouse. If possible, find test data for both cases comparing the interaction with respect to such characteristics as productivity, fatigue, and user satisfaction.

11-8. The technology and cost of input/output devices change rapidly. Identify several reliable sources of current information about the cost, capacity, and major features of available devices. (You may need to go to different sources for different types of devices and for different system sizes.)

11-9. Using some of the sources identified in Exercise 11–8, prepare a table summarizing information about the following classes of devices. Show the following information about each class of devices as a range of values: device type, physical dimensions, information transfer rate across the boundary, size of data capture/display area, class of host system, resolution (where applicable), and cost.

a. Keyboard
b. Mouse
c. Bar-code scanner
d. Touch screen
e. Impact printer
f. Dot matrix printer
g. Character printer

      h. Laser printer
      i. Inkjet printer
      j. Color raster display
      k. Liquid crystal display
      l. Light emitting diode display
     m. Plasma display

11-10. To what type(s) of users is each of the five interaction styles best suited? Relate your answers to the user characteristics discussed in this chapter.

11-11. For each of the five interaction styles, identify one example of a program which uses that interaction style. Who are its intended users?

11-12. Use one or more programs to which you have access and do the following:

    a. Identify the hardware used in the interaction.
    b. Identify at least one example of a design decision made during each of the six steps of interface design.
    c. Identify the style(s) of interaction.
    d. Describe what you liked and disliked most about the interaction.
    e. Give a brief critique of the interface in terms of the four design principles presented in this chapter.

11-13. The graphical user interface based on the desktop metaphor has become the preferred style for user workstations. What advantages and disadvantages does it provide over other interaction styles? Based on your answer, discuss why knowledge of the principles of interactive computer graphics and of graphic design is or is not important for designers of software for business applications.

11-14. Select an interactive software package with a graphical user interface and with which you are familiar. Locate examples of the following:

    a. Title bar
    b. Menu bar
    c. Pull-down menu
    d. Open list box
    e. Drop-down list box
    f. Pop-up menu
    g. Dialogue box
    h. Command button
    i. Check box
    j. Option button
    k. Scroll bar
    l. Message area
   m. Device feedback
    n. Command feedback
    o. Selection feedback

11-15. Identify some examples of commercially available software tools which support the design and construction of the user interface. Which style or styles of interaction does each product support?

11-16. Investigate and describe the difference in usage of the term "font" in traditional typography and in computer jargon. Can you explain the reason for this difference?

11-17. Which of the arrangements of the alphabetically ordered list in Figure 11.19 is better for searching it? Why?

11-18. According to Shneiderman, effective screen designs contain a middle number of groups (6 to 15) that are neatly laid out, surrounded by blanks, and similarly structured. Discuss and explain this statement in terms of

FIGURE 11.19   **Alternatives for an alphabetical search**

ADAM	ESAU	ONAN
ABEL	JEHU	RUTH
AMOS	JOEL	SABA
BOAZ	MOAB	SAUL
CAIN	NOAH	SHEM
ADAM	ABEL	AMOS
BOAZ	CAIN	ESAU
JEHU	JOEL	MOAB
NOAH	ONAN	RUTH
SABA	SAUL	SHEM

the Gestalt principles of visual organization. Name the principles which apply and explain to what part of the statement each applies.

11-19. Investigate Gestalt principles for segregating the figure from the background. State and illustrate four of these principles.

11-20. Find two utility bills of different design and compare them. Which is better? Why? State what could be done to improve the design of each and why the proposed design is an improvement.

11-21. Find two property tax bills of different design and compare them. Which is better? Why? State what could be done to improve the design of each and why the proposed design is an improvement.

11-22. Consider the article in Figure 11.20 on the development of the customer relationship management system (CRM) at Blue Cross and Blue Shield of Minnesota:

   a. The article does not define a customer relationship management system. Investigate what is meant by a CRM system. What are its purpose and functions?

FIGURE 11.20   **Connecting with Customers**

Connecting with Customers

For Blue Cross and Blue Shield of Minnesota, building self-service Web capabilities meant the difference between winning and losing several major clients, including retailer Target, Northwest Airlines, and General Mills.

"Without it, they would not do business with us, "explains John Ounjian, CIO and senior vice president of information systems and corporate adjudication services at the $5 billion insurance provider.

So when Ounjian explained to executives that the customer relationship management (CRM) project would cost $15 million for the first two phases, they didn't blink.

St. Paul-based Blue Cross and Blue Shield of Minnesota learned the importance of communicating with business units during the design phase of the Web self-service screens. Ounjian and his technical team designed drop-down boxes that they thought were logical, but a focus group of end users found the feature cumbersome and the wording hard to understand. "We had to adjust our logic," he says.

Overall, CIOs agree that disruption to the organization is inevitable with CRM projects and that the entire company should be prepared. "Management must understand that pots and pans are going to fall off the shelf," Ounjian says. "These transformations are disruptive and need an initiative right at the heel to add quality improvements, which will bring stability."

Adapted from "Connecting with Customers,"Computerworld, January 6, 2003, 19

b. To what extent could this system be considered to be a strategic information system for Blue Cross and Blue Shield of Minnesota?

c. Why would CRM projects be disruptive to an organization?

d. What technique was used to help end-users evaluate the design of the user interface?

e. What did the developers learn as a result of the user evaluation, and how did they respond to what they learned?

f. Discuss the problem with the design of the drop-down boxes in relation to some of the user interface design principles discussed in this chapter.

CASE STUDIES FOR PROJECT ASSIGNMENTS

Assignment

1. Design a portion of a class diagram which will produce the hotel bill shown in Figure 3.8.

2. Design a screen or screens for a graphical user interface to be used for the registration of a guest on arrival. Be sure to permit the registration of guests with or without a reservation.

Assignment

1. Design an itemized bill to be given to the customer when the car is returned to Apache, showing the charges for the rental.

2. Design a portion of a class diagram which will produce this bill.

3. Design a screen or screens for a graphical user interface to be used for entering the information required when a customer picks up a car. Be sure to permit the rental of cars with or without a reservation.

12 DESIGNING THE USER INTERFACE — DESIGNING THE PRESENTATION LAYER

INTRODUCTION

When defining the essential model of a computer information system, the emphasis is on the essential messages which cross the system boundary going to or from the environment. Similarly, after the automation boundary has been located, the focus is on the essential messages between the user and the automated portion of the system. The overall structure and specific information content of these messages are captured in the use case narratives and shown in the system sequence diagrams produced during analysis.

When the system is implemented, as we have noted, the data capture operations for interactive input to the automated system involve a dialogue between the user and the computer. Often there is a dialogue related to system output as well, to allow the user to select the desired output or perhaps to control the content and format of the desired output.

As we have seen, the design of the user interface is concerned with the neighborhood of the automation boundary. From the outside, it involves the dialogue between the user and the computer. Just inside the automation boundary is the presentation layer, which manages the dialogue at the user interface. (See Figure 12.1.) Objects within the presentation layer translate messages from human-processible form to machine-processible form and vice versa. Inputs are then passed to the application layer for validation and processing via a façade controller (or other interface object), as discussed in Chapter 8. Outputs are returned from the façade controller to the presentation layer for display, printing, or other output medium. (Compare Figure 12.1 with Figure 7.5.)

In designing the user interface, it is important to be able to define with some precision the significant characteristics of the interactions in the user interface zone. This chapter presents tools and techniques for modeling those features of the user interaction of most interest to the designer. These include state transition diagrams for modeling the user-computer dialogue as well as window navigation diagrams for modeling the paths through menus and windows. These models are applicable to a variety of user interfaces — such as windows or screens, web pages, cell phones, and other wireless devices.

The chapter also includes an outline for a specification of the external design of the user interface and some brief comments on testing the interface.

The chapter concludes with a high-level discussion of the software design for the presentation layer and its connection to the business layer.

LEARNING OBJECTIVES

After mastering the material in this chapter, you will be able to

- Describe which features of the user-computer dialogue should be included in a design model for the user interface.
- Explain the components of a state transition diagram (statechart) and what each of them represents.
- Use a coordinated pair of state transition diagrams to model the user-computer interface.
- Explain the conventions for window navigation diagrams.
- Use a window navigation diagram to model the navigation through a series of windows or web pages.
- Discuss the importance of testing the interface for usability.
- Describe the Model-View Separation pattern and discuss the advantages it provides.

FIGURE 12.1   Automation boundary and the three-tier model of the application software

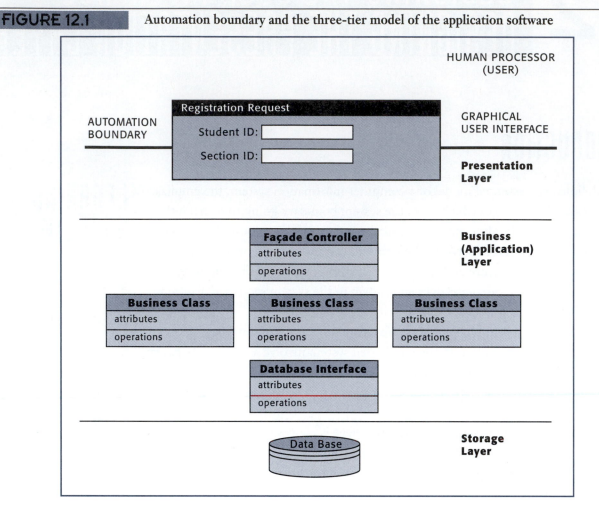

REQUIREMENTS FOR A MODEL OF THE USER-COMPUTER DIALOGUE

What are some of the requirements for a model of the user-computer dialogue? What features of the dialogue should be represented in the model of the interaction?

GENERAL REQUIREMENTS

A model of the user interface, like other design models, may serve several purposes. It may permit the designer to assess the performance of the interface and determine whether that performance is acceptable. It may also help determine whether the proposed interface can be constructed within the constraints on the development project.

Models of the user interface, like all representations, must be internally consistent and consistent with the other models describing the same system or system components. They should be as simple as possible, easy to modify and maintain, and easy to understand.

In addition, because the user interface is the part of the system visible to users, some portions of the user interface model must allow users to preview and critique the dialogue. The more successful these parts of the interface model are in conveying what the constructed interface will be like, the more value the users' crucial decisions about the interface design will have.

FEATURES TO BE MODELED

In the most general sense, the user-computer dialogue consists of messages transmitted back and forth across the automation boundary between two processors — one a human, the other a computer. Each processor carries out actions in response to each message received from the other. There must be some means of coordinating the actions of the two parties to the dialogue as well as some means of appropriately sequencing the actions within each processor.

Thus, a model of a user-computer dialogue should incorporate a representation of the following features of the dialogue.

Messages Containing Data

These are the messages containing application-related data elements — user inputs or information display.

Messages Controlling the Dialogue

These messages may include several types of control information:

- An instruction to the user (from the computer),
- An instruction to the computer (from the user): a command or selection,
- An identification of an error detected by either partner in the dialogue,
- A report to the other processor on a processor's current status, and
- A report to the other processor on the result of a processor's action.

Material Inputs and Outputs

In some systems, the dialogue may involve a flow of material as well as of messages. For example, the user may insert a card, a key, or other object and may receive a ticket, cash, or merchandise.

Operations or Procedures

Transformations in both processors receive or produce the data, control, or material flows.

Coordinating and Sequencing the Actions of the Processors

The actions of user and computer require synchronization. This is accomplished by flows which trigger transformations at the appropriate time or in the appropriate sequence. The actions within a processor must be sequenced by the familiar control structures of sequence, selection, and iteration.

STATE TRANSITION DIAGRAMS

A state transition diagram provides a convenient and rigorous model of the user interface. A state transition diagram (also known as a *state diagram* or *statechart*) is part of the Unified Modeling Language (UML) and has other uses besides modeling interaction at the user interface.

A *state transition diagram* views a process (or the processor which carries it out) as consisting of a finite set of states. The states are mutually exclusive; the process may be in only one state at a time. While in a state, the process either waits or carries out some operation. The transition to another state is dependent on the occurrence of an event or the satisfaction of a condition. Accompanying the transition are one or more outputs — control flows (also known as event flows). A state transition diagram shows the possible states of a process, the permissible transitions between states, the events or conditions which trigger the transitions, and the output flows accompanying each transition.[1]

The finite-state processor has **no state memory**. This means that in its current state it has no knowledge of its history — of how it entered that state. Thus, a transition out of a state depends only on the current state and on the event or condition which triggers the transition.

AN EXAMPLE OF A STATE TRANSITION DIAGRAM

The following example (for a physical system) introduces the basic features of a state transition diagram.

Figure 12.2 shows a state transition diagram for controlling a three-way incandescent lamp. The lamp has two filaments, one of 50 watts and the other of 100 watts. A rotating switch controls the lamp to turn each of the filaments on and off in the following sequence: both off, 50-watt on and 100-watt off, 100-watt on and 50-watt off, both on. Each of these four levels of illumination is a *state* of the lamp (shown by the capsules). The *event* or condition which causes the lamp to change from one state to another is a turn of the switch. Such a change of state is called a *transition* and is shown by an arrow. **The name of the event causing the transition is written next to the arrow; the names of the actions executed during the transition are written after the event name with a slash to separate them.** The result of turning the switch depends on the current state of the lamp. The initial state of the lamp is Off; this is shown by the arrow which points toward it without coming from another state.

FIGURE 12.2   State transition diagram for a three-way lamp

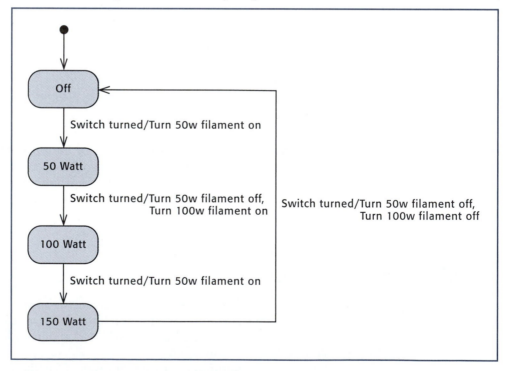

---

[1]There are a number of alternatives for presenting the information in a state transition diagram. In *Diagramming Techniques for Analysts and Programmers* (Englewood Cliffs, N.J.: Prentice-Hall, 1985), James Martin and Carma McClure discuss the state transition matrix and the fence diagram (see pages 219–230). In *Structured Development for Real-Time Systems*, 3 vols. (New York: Yourdon, 1985), Paul T. Ward and Stephen J. Mellor discuss the transition table and the action table (see pages 1:64–78; 2:50–55; and 3:96–109).

COMPONENTS OF A STATE TRANSITION DIAGRAM

A state transition diagram represents the behavior of a processor which controls and coordinates the work of a set of transformations. A state transition diagram depicts two types of components — **states** and **transitions** from one state to another. Associated with each transition is an **event** which triggers the transition and one or more independent *actions* associated with the output at the time of the transition.

Each state represents a unique, observable status of the control processor in which it waits until a control flow triggers the next transition. While the processor waits, the system may be executing transformations. Information about each state is retained in the memory of the processor while that state is active.

One state may be identified as the *initial state*; one or more states may be identified as *final states*.

A transition is a change from one state to another. In general, a transition is allowed to occur between any pair of states, including a return to the same state. Specific constraints on permissible transitions are system-dependent — these constraints are precisely what a state transition diagram depicts.

CONVENTIONS FOR STATE TRANSITION DIAGRAMS

There are a variety of conventions for drawing state transition diagrams. There is a choice of whether to depict the states as nodes and the transitions as arcs or vice versa. *Mealy diagrams* (the representation used in the UML) represent the states as nodes; *Moore diagrams* show them as arcs.

The representation for state transition diagrams presented here is that of the UML. By this convention, a state is depicted as a capsule; a transition is shown as an arrow with right-angled changes of direction. Next to each transition arrow is a label. The label consists of two parts. The first is the name of the event which *triggers* the transition; the second is the independent action or actions which occur at the time of the transition. The event name and actions are separated by a forward slash. (See Figure 12.2.) If more than one event is shown, the occurrence of any one of them will trigger the transition. If more than one action is shown, all the actions are performed. These actions are assumed to occur simultaneously and instantaneously. If the sequence in which the actions occur is significant, then additional states must be introduced.

An event causing a transition may be constrained by a guard. A *guard* is a condition which must be true in order for the transition to occur. A guard may be a conditional expression or the name of a control flow, such as Pin Is Valid or Pin Is Invalid. Guards are enclosed in square brackets, as shown below in Figure 12.9.

The initial state, if there is one, is identified by an arrow with a black circle at its tail which points toward it without coming from another state. A final state is one with no transition out of it. A final state is identified by a symbol like a "bull's eye" composed of two concentric circles; the inner circle is black. (See Figure 12.7.) If there is no final state, a state transition diagram will contain a loop traversing one or more states.

Components of state transition diagrams are named as follows:

▌ State names often include the event which will cause a transition out of the state, e.g., Wait for Entry of Pin Number. Sometimes the name describes what the processor is doing while waiting for the event, such as Validate Pin Number or Validating Pin Number. Idle is frequently used as the name for a state in which nothing is happening in the processor. Whatever the name, it is important to remember that the action named is usually being performed by an operation inside the system; the system is waiting while the operation executes.

■ Events associated with transitions are named with short sentences. A verb in the active voice permits an actor to be included as the subject of the sentence, or the sentence may be in the passive voice. For example, Customer Enters Pin or Pin Entered.

■ Actions associated with transitions are named with imperative sentences. These names often include the name of an operation which is being activated, such as Trigger Validate Pin Number. Sometimes the word "Trigger" may be omitted without ambiguity.

DECOMPOSING STATE TRANSITION DIAGRAMS

A state transition diagram may be decomposed into subdiagrams to reduce its complexity.[2] This is equivalent to decomposing the corresponding control transformation, whether or not the control transformations are shown explicitly.

The simplest way to decompose a state transition diagram is by pulling out a sequence of states to form a separate diagram. The process is analogous to making a separate operation out of a sequence of actions in an algorithm for a more inclusive operation.

Figure 12.3 shows schematically the decomposition of a state transition diagram. The partitioning introduces two additional control flows so that each diagram can trigger the other. This permits the sequence of states in the partitioned diagram to be equivalent to that of the states in the unpartitioned diagram. An additional state, in which one process waits while the other process is active, is added to each transition

FIGURE 12.3   Decomposition of a state transition diagram

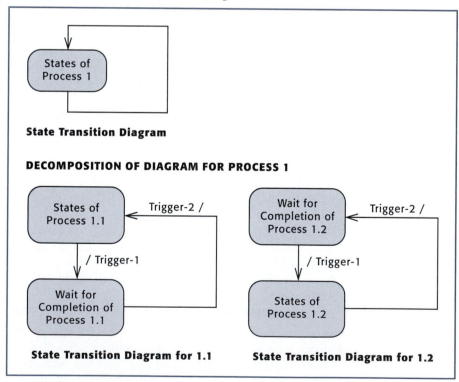

[2]See David Harel, "Statecharts: A Visual Formalism for Complex Systems," *Science of Computer Programming* 8 (1987): 231–274. This is the source of the UML term "statechart." See also Meilir Page-Jones, *Fundamentals of Object-Oriented Design in UML* (Reading, Mass.: Addison-Wesley, 2000), 167–171.

diagram. The transition into this wait state triggers the execution of its transition diagram. The transition out of the wait state requires a trigger produced by the other process to signal that it has completed its execution. Note where each trigger appears on both transition diagrams.

Figure 12.3 suppresses all details except those related to transitions between the two diagrams.

For an example, see the relationship of Figure 12.7 to Figure 12.8 in the automated teller machine example later in the chapter.

MODELING THE USER-COMPUTER DIALOGUE WITH STATE TRANSITION DIAGRAMS

There is one state transition diagrams (or set of state transition diagrams) for each processor — one for the user and one for the computer. To reduce the complexity of the diagrams, there will probably be a pair of diagrams for each system-level event.

When modeling the user-computer dialogue with state transition diagrams, we need to specify the following:

- The events to which each processor must respond,
- The actions to be taken by each processor as a result of each condition, and
- When one processor will be waiting for another processor to complete the next step of the dialogue.

In the case of the user, we note that:

- The events are what the user perceives which will cause him to act. These are usually computer displays or messages.
- The actions are what the user does next. These are usually the manual transformations performed by the user or control information telling the computer what to do.
- The states describe the time the user is waiting or deciding what to do next.

In representing the computer, we note that:

- The events are what the computer detects — usually data or control information coming from an input device.
- The actions are what the computer does in response — often ending in feedback or information display. (See Figure 11.1.)
- The states show when the computer is waiting for the user or deciding which action to take.

QUESTIONS AND ANSWERS

Following are some of the questions which arise about the use of state transition diagrams:

- *How many state transition diagrams are necessary to model the interaction?* A minimum of one per processor.
- *How complex should an interaction model based on state transition diagrams be?* In general, as simple as possible to adequately describe the interaction. First, use one state transition diagram for the user and one for the automated processor; when necessary, decompose the state transition diagrams.

A DIALOGUE WITH AN AUTOMATED TELLER MACHINE

The following example illustrates a dialogue with an automated teller machine (ATM). The dialogue has been simplified considerably. After validation of the user's card and personal identifier, the only permissible transaction is a withdrawal in a multiple of $20. It is assumed that the user has only one account with the bank.

Relationship of the State Transition Diagram to Analysis and Design Models

Before examining the state transition diagrams for a withdrawal from the ATM, we should look at the analysis and design models on which they are based. The most relevant analysis models are the essential use case narrative for Withdraw Funds (Figure 12.4) and the corresponding system sequence diagram (Figure 12.5). They show the necessary input data as well as the principal alternative flows of events. Note, however, that the analysis models are intentionally free of decisions about the implementing technology. If desired, we could prepare a *real* (or *implementation*) *use case narrative* (Figure 12.6), filling in our decisions about technology. Note the difference between the two use case narratives (see Exercise 12–2).

Sometimes it may be useful to work from the contracts or the interaction diagrams as well. While those models should be consistent with the use case narrative and system sequence diagram, they may provide additional details about the validation of inputs and the sequencing of the system's response.

FIGURE 12.4	Expanded essential use case narrative for Withdraw Funds

---

Use case:	**Withdraw Funds**
Actors:	Customer
Purpose:	Withdraw cash from the customer's account.
Overview:	A Customer requests a withdrawal of funds from the Customer's account. The system records the transaction. On completion, the system provides the Customer with the cash and a receipt for the transaction.
Type:	Essential
Preconditions:	Customer has an account.
Postconditions:	The withdrawal transaction was recorded.
Special Requirements:	None

Flow of Events

ACTOR ACTION	**SYSTEM RESPONSE**
1. This use case begins when a Customer desires to withdraw funds from an account.	
2. The Customer provides the Customer's account number and the amount of the desired withdrawal.	3. Records the withdrawal transaction.
	4. Provides cash to the Customer and produces withdrawal receipt.
5. The Customer receives the cash and the withdrawal receipt.	

Alternative Flow of Events

Line 3: Invalid account number entered. Inform the Customer. Terminate the transaction.

Withdrawal amount exceeds the permissible amount (based on minimum remaining balance or maximum withdrawal amount). Inform the Customer. Terminate the transaction.

FIGURE 12.5

System sequence diagram for the Withdraw Funds use case

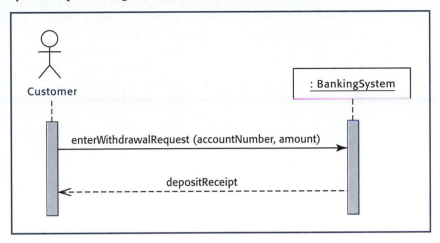

FIGURE 12.6

Expanded real use case narrative for Withdraw Funds at ATM

Use case:	**Withdraw Funds at ATM**
Actors:	Customer
Purpose:	Withdraw cash from the customer's account.
Overview:	A Customer requests a withdrawal of funds from the Customer's account. The system records the transaction. On completion, the system provides the Customer with the cash and a receipt for the transaction.
Type:	Real
Preconditions:	Customer has an account and a valid ATM card.
Postconditions:	The withdrawal transaction was recorded.
Special Requirements:	The withdrawal amount must be a multiple of $20.

Flow of Events

ACTOR ACTION	SYSTEM RESPONSE
1. This use case begins when a Customer desires to withdraw funds from an account.	
2. The Customer provides the Customer's account number by putting the ATM card in the slot and then enters the Customer's PIN (personal identification number).	3. Records the withdrawal transaction.
4. The Customer enters the amount of the desired withdrawal.	5. Dispenses cash and a withdrawal receipt and returns the ATM card.
6. The Customer receives the cash, the withdrawal receipt, and the ATM card.	

Alternative Flow of Events

Line 3: Invalid account number or PIN entered. Inform the Customer. Terminate the transaction and return the ATM card.

Line 5: Withdrawal amount not a multiple of $20. Inform the Customer. Return to Step 4. Withdrawal amount exceeds the permissible amount (based on minimum remaining balance or maximum withdrawal amount). Inform the Customer. Terminate the transaction and return the ATM card.

State Transition Diagrams

We are now ready to present and discuss the state transition diagrams for the ATM example. Figure 12.7 shows a state transition diagram for the user, and Figure 12.8 shows a state transition diagram for the machine.

In Figure 12.8, the details of the withdrawal transaction are suppressed. They are shown in Figure 12.9. Even this relatively simple situation seems to require the decomposition of the state transition diagram for the ATM to keep it from becoming too complex. Note that Figures 12.8 and 12.9 are coordinated by control flows. Trigger-Withdrawal, shown as an action in Figure 12.8, appears in Figure 12.9 as the condition which causes withdrawal instructions to be displayed. End-of-Withdrawal (Figure 12.9) is the condition which reacti-

---

FIGURE 12.7   **State transition diagram for user of ATM**

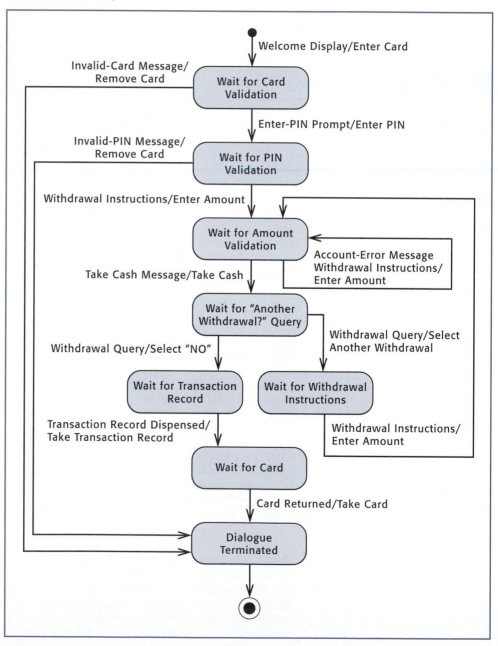

FIGURE 12.8   State transition diagram for ATM

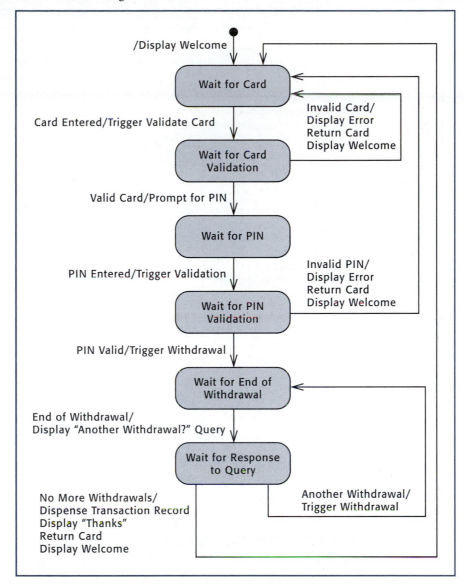

vates Figure 12.8. That is, Trigger-Withdrawal corresponds to Trigger-1 in Figure 12.3, and End-of-Withdrawal corresponds to Trigger-2. Note also in Figure 12.9 the use of square brackets to enclose a condition, also known as a guard, such as [Amount exceeds limits], on a transition. This permits us to use a guard instead of or in addition to an event to further restrict when a transition may occur.

Let us extend the example to allow the user to select from several types of trans-actions. The display of the menu of options and the user's selection must be added to the dialogue. In this case, it seems natural to decompose the diagrams by separating them sequentially into a log-in dialogue, an option dialogue (with only the with-drawal transaction detailed), and a concluding log-out dialogue. This leads to Figures 12.10, 12.11, and 12.12. Note that Figure 12.9, detailing the withdrawal, is still compatible with Figure 12.11.

FIGURE 12.9   State transition diagram for withdrawal (ATM)

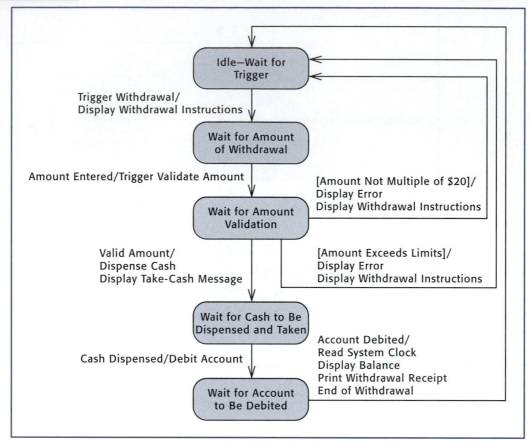

Decomposing the state transition diagram for the user into separate diagrams for log-in, option selection, a withdrawal transaction, and the ending dialogue is left as an exercise (Exercise 12–6).

WINDOW NAVIGATION DIAGRAMS

Navigation is the process of moving through the windows of the graphical user interface with the aid of the menus, dialogue boxes, and command buttons or icons. A well-designed interface facilitates navigation. It is important to design the navigation carefully and to provide the user with a clear sense of his or her current location on the path of navigation. From there, the user must be able to return to a previous window or reach the window for the next task.

For applications of any complexity, an explicit model of the navigation through the user interface is an important part of the design. The navigation model supplements the state transition diagrams, which define the detailed interaction at the user interface.

A *window navigation diagram* represents each window or screen as a rectangle. One set of conventions for a window navigation diagram appears in Figure 12.13. Each window is labeled with its title and may be labeled with its window type. An arrow shows the path from one window to another. An arrow with a head at each end means that the user must return to the calling window. Navigation diagrams also show when users are expected to save their work to a data base. The word **"Save"** may apply to a single window or to a group of windows.[3]

---

[3]See Page-Jones, *Fundamentals of Object-Oriented Design in UML*, 198–200, for a slightly different set of conventions for window navigation diagrams.

FIGURE 12.10   State transition diagram for log-in (ATM)

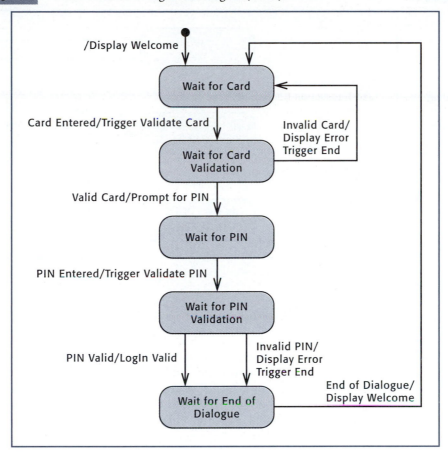

FIGURE 12.11   State transition diagram for option selection (ATM)

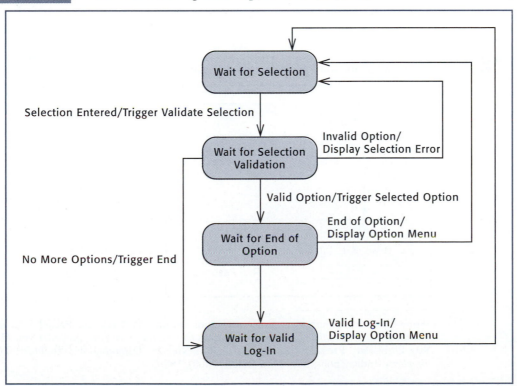

FIGURE 12.12   State transition diagram for end dialogue (ATM)

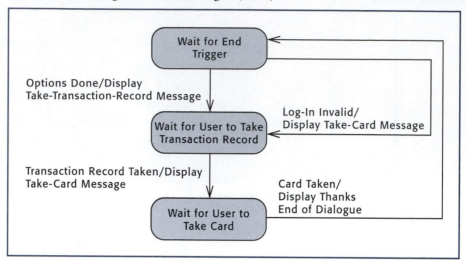

A window navigation diagram often shows the navigation paths through the user interface for a single use case.[4]

Figure 12.14 is an example of a window navigation diagram for the Register for Classes use case. The main screen for the use case (labeled M) is reached by selecting a menu option (not shown). If the student is unknown or ineligible to register, the screen informing the student of the fact is the final screen of the use case. If the student can register, selection of the department code from a pull-down list opens a pop-up window (labeled P) which displays the available sections offered by that department. The student is required to respond in order to confirm the selection. Upon confirmation, the student is enrolled in the selected section. When the student ends the selection of classes, the end of registration screen displays the schedule and gives the student the option of printing it. These two screens are terminal screens for the use case.

FIGURE 12.13   Conventions for window navigation diagrams

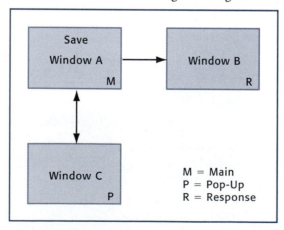

---

[4]For a discussion of how to organize navigation within a Web site, see Patrick J. Lynch and Sarah Horton, *Web Style Guide: Basic Design Principles for Creating Web Sites*, 2nd ed. (New Haven, Conn.: Yale University Press, 2002). See also Jakob Nielsen, *Designing Web Usability: The Practice of Simplicity* (Indianapolis, Ind.: New Riders, 2000), 188*ff.*

FIGURE 12.14   Window navigation diagram for the Register for Classes use case

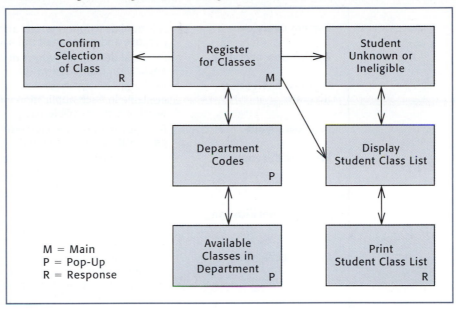

SIMULATIONS

The most effective means of communicating the design of the interface to users is a simulation of the interaction. A simulation of the user-computer interface can range from very simple to very sophisticated. A talk-through of the interaction scenario with paper or transparent mock-ups of reports or screen layouts has been used since the earliest days of software design.

A facsimile of a screen or report can also serve as the design specification of one or more information flows, presenting the format of the flows as well as their content.

Note that in simulating user-computer interaction the aim is to present the interaction to the reviewer as realistically as possible within the constraints on a specific design project. A separate description of the interface design may be desirable thereafter for use by those who will construct the interface. A familiar example of this is a screen or printer layout chart — a rectangular grid filled with x's and 9's to depict alphanumeric and numeric fields, respectively. Such a chart may be an effective definition of the design of the report for a programmer but is a poor way to show a prospective user what a sample of system output will look like.

Software for generating displays can allow users to see a proposed design or design alternatives and to participate more actively in the interaction scenario. In some cases, the interface will be simulated primarily to present the design so that users can see and critique it. Simulations can also help designers estimate response times for the various portions of the dialogue.

If prototyping is used extensively in the system development process, then the prototypes may include the evolving user interface as well.

SPECIFYING THE DESIGN OF THE GRAPHICAL USER INTERFACE

Ruble emphasizes the importance of a written specification for the external design of the graphical user interface. Figure 12.15 presents his outline for that document.

FIGURE 12.15   Outline for the external design specification of the graphical user interface.

System overview	A textual description which orients the reader to the purpose and function of the system.
Application overview	A textual description which defines the features of each application contained within the system.
Window navigation diagram	A diagram which shows which windows are available in each application within the system and which are the possible navigation paths between them.
Window layout	A depiction of how each window on the navigation diagram will appear to the user.
Window description	The text which accompanies each window layout and describes the window's function and features so that a potential user can understand the behavior of the design.
Window specification	A technical specification which defines the behavior for opening and closing the window as well as for enabling and executing each button, control, and menu item.
Field specification	A definition of the fields and associated edits for any data element which appears on the window. The field specification should include how the data is to be acquired, a list of table names and column names, an indication of how to join tables, and a description of how to apply any selection criteria.

Adapted from David A. Ruble, *Practical Analysis and Design for Client/Server and GUI Systems* (Upper Saddle River, N.J.: Yourdon, 1997), 306.

TESTING THE USER INTERFACE DESIGN

The critical nature of the user interface makes careful testing of the design of utmost importance. Unfortunately, testing the user interface appears to be the first casualty of a development project which is behind schedule.

Many professional software developers find it impossible to put themselves in the place of a user. They also tend to lack the expertise in ergonomics or human factors which would facilitate user-centered design of the interaction. Therefore, it is essential to involve users in review, evaluating, and testing of the interaction. Walk-throughs of the design models, prototyping, and acceptance testing apply to the user interface as well as to other aspects of the system. Users must participate in testing the prototypes and in the acceptance tests. They should be representative of the spectrum of users of the system.

EVALUATION CRITERIA

Testing the quality of the user interface design should be based on the following five measurable criteria rather than on vague notions of "user friendliness":[5]

- Time to learn specific functions,
- Speed of task performance,
- Rate of errors by users,
- User retention of knowledge over time, and
- Subjective user satisfaction.

---

[5] See Ben Shneiderman, *Designing the User Interface: Strategies in Effective Human-Computer Interaction*, 3rd ed. (Reading, Mass.: Addison-Wesley, 1998), 15.

Acceptance tests for the user interface should include at least one test for each of these criteria. The tests must be stated in quantified, observable terms.

USABILITY TESTING

Usability testing attempts to evaluate users' satisfaction with a tool or product. The *usability* of a system is a collective term for all aspects of an activity's performance which can be affected by the use of technology. Cox and Walker believe that a **usable** tool is one which the user controls, which becomes transparent to the user, and which is flexible and easy to learn. They state three defining principles of *usability testing*:[6]

- Usability testing requires a user.
- Usability testing is done by observing people doing tasks with the product being tested.
- Interpreting observations always requires judgment, and such interpretations will vary depending on the circumstances. Usability measures are imprecise, and there is no prescription that tells us how usable an artifact is.

Cox and Walker also cite three methods of observation — cooperative user observation, observations in a controlled environment, and observations in a natural environment.

- In **cooperative observation**, the designer watches a user use the system and takes notes. The designer may ask the user to explain unexpected actions. The user may ask the designer questions about how to do things. The user may make suggestions. User and designer work together to improve the product.
- In **observation in a controlled environment**, the user is assigned specific tasks and thinks out loud. The user states what he is doing and why he is doing it. The interaction is recorded in writing, with a tape recorder, or with a video camera. The designer watches with or without interacting with the user.
- In **observation in a natural environment**, the user performs tasks in the workplace or other setting in which the software product will be used.

Observation yields information about the quality of the design which may be impossible to gather any other way. When they have difficulty, users often assume that they are stupid or have done something wrong. They mistakenly blame themselves instead of the design of the software and the interface.

DESIGNING THE INTERFACE TO THE PRESENTATION LAYER

The discussion thus far has dealt with the design of the user interface from an external perspective. We have described what the user sees and what the user does to interact with the computer. We have presented state transition diagrams to model the user-computer dialogue and window navigation diagrams to define the paths through the various screens and menus.

---

[6]Kevin Cox and David Walker, *User Interface Design*, 2nd ed. (Singapore: Prentice-Hall, 1993), 81–83. See also Shneiderman, *Designing the User Interface*, 127–132.

We now turn to the design of the objects which connect the presentation layer to the business layer. The treatment is relatively high-level. It reinforces the importance of the three-tier architecture shown in Figure 12.1 and introduces principles for maintaining its integrity.

THE MODEL-VIEW SEPARATION PATTERN

How should we connect the application layer to the presentation layer? What kind of visibility should the classes of the graphical user interface have to the application layer? How should the objects in the business layer communicate with the user interface?

These questions are answered by the Model-View Separation pattern (Figure 12.16). It states that objects in the application domain should not have direct knowledge of or be directly coupled to objects in the presentation layer. (Here, *model* refers to the objects in the application layer, as in a class diagram). *View* refers to presentation objects, such as windows, applets, and reports. Business objects should not know about the objects in the user interface. Therefore, they should not be able to send messages to presentation objects. Indirect communication from the application layer to the presentation layer is permissible.[7]

Window objects are responsible for accepting input and displaying output but must not maintain data or contain application logic. However, they may have visibility to objects in the business layer — ideally as few objects as possible.

ADVANTAGES OF MODEL-VIEW SEPARATION

Chapter 7 introduced the three-tier system architecture. Chapter 10 discussed how to connect the application and storage layers. The application and presentation layers should be separated to:

- Minimize the impact of interface changes on the application layer;
- Minimize the impact of changes to the application logic on the user interface;
- Permit multiple views of the same application object, such as a spreadsheet and a chart;
- Permit the application layer to be used with another kind of user interface;

FIGURE 12.16	The Model-View Separation pattern

Pattern Name:	**Model-View Separation**
Problem:	How can we minimize the impact of changes to the windows in the user interface on the objects in the business layer?
	How can we minimize the impact of changes to the objects in the business layer on the windows in the user interface?
Solution:	Define the classes in the business domain (the model) so that they do not have direct visibility to the window (view) classes. Maintain all the application logic and data in the classes in the business layer.

[7]As might be expected, the details of the communication between the application and presentation layers depend on the software environment for which the graphical user interface is developed. See the discussion of the Observer pattern in Erich Gamma, Richard Helm, Ralph Johnson, and John Vlissides, *Design Patterns: Elements of Reusable Object-Oriented Software* (Reading, Mass.: Addison Wesley, 1995), 293–303, for a more detailed treatment of indirect communication from the application layer to the presentation layer.

▌ Allow parallel development of the user interface and application layer, as mentioned in Chapter 7; and

▌ Allow execution of the application logic apart from the normal user interface.

MODEL-VIEW SEPARATION IN THE PUBLIC UNIVERSITY REGISTRATION SYSTEM — AN EXAMPLE

Figure 12.17 shows an example of Model-View Separation for the Public University Registration System. It illustrates the pattern without providing a detailed design for the presentation layer. It shows a portion of the system's response to the use case Register for Classes. A student has just entered a department code, course number, and section number and has clicked the Add button.

Clicking the Add button is a low-level user interface event which sends the message **onAddSection ()** to a window object, **registrationWindow**. The window object in turn sends the system operation message **requestSection (departmentCode, courseNumber, sectionNumber)** to **registrationSystem**, the façade object in the business layer. Then **registrationSystem** asks the appropriate **department** object to enroll the student. For the remaining collaborations in the business layer for **requestSection**, see Figure 8.38.

| **FIGURE 12.17** | Connecting the presentation layer to the application layer |

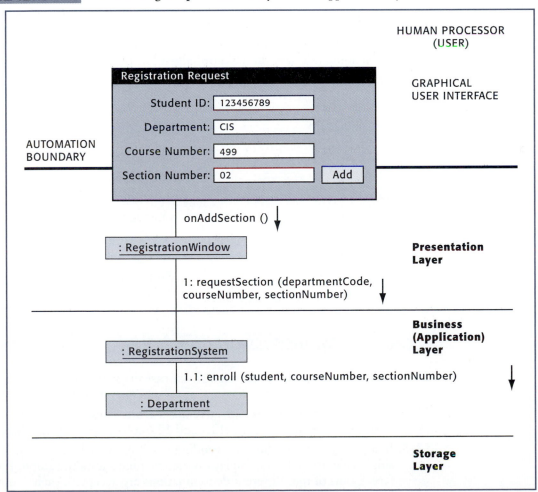

SUMMARY

A model of the user-computer dialogue must show the interaction between the human and the automated processors. Some models have as their major purpose presenting the interface design to a prospective user. Others are used to specify the interaction in sufficient detail for it to be constructed. In general, the interaction model shows the information flows which cross the automation boundary as well as the response of each processor to the messages received from the other.

The external design of the user interface should be recorded in a written specification.

Testing the design of the user interface throughout the development process is critical to success. Acceptance testing must be based on quantified, observable measures of criteria for quality. There is no acceptable substitute for observing users as they interact with prototypes as well as with the completed user interface.

Three types of interaction models are useful in the design of the user-computer interface: state transition diagrams, window navigation diagrams, and simulations of the interaction. A state transition diagram (one or more for each processor) depicts the states of a processor, the permissible transitions from one state to another, and the events triggering each transition. For complex interactions, it may be necessary to supplement state transition diagrams with other diagrams depicting control transformations for each processor in the interaction. Navigation through the displays of the user interface should be modeled with a navigation diagram. Window navigation diagrams show the navigation paths through menus and windows as well as the transitions between these components of the graphical user interface. Simulation techniques range from paper mock-ups of displays to sophisticated prototypes.

The Model-View Separation pattern guides the connection of the presentation layer and the business layer. It states the design principle that objects in the application domain should not have direct knowledge of or be directly coupled to objects in the presentation layer.

KEY TERMS

action *351*

event *350*

event flow *350*

final state *351*

guard *351*

initial state *351*

Mealy diagram *351*

Model-View Separation pattern *364*

real use case narrative *354*

state *350*

state transition diagram *349*

transition *350*

trigger *351*

usability testing *363*

window navigation diagram *358*

EXERCISES AND DISCUSSION QUESTIONS

12-1. Describe the relationships among a use case diagram, an essential use case narrative, a system sequence diagram, and a model of user-computer interaction.

12-2. How does a real use case narrative differ from an essential use case narrative? Compare Figures 12.4 and 12.6 to illustrate these differences.

12-3. In a subway station, there are vending machines which sell tickets for a single ride. Initially, the display on the machine shows the amount of the full fare. Coins of four different denominations are accepted; each denomination has a separate slot. The machine requires exact change. As each coin is introduced, the display changes to show the remaining amount to be deposited. When the amount reaches zero, a ticket is dispensed, and the display returns to the full fare amount.

Draw two state transition diagrams, one for the vending machine and one for the user. Assume that the machine operates perfectly and that only legitimate coins are introduced.

What are some of the errors which can be expected to occur during this interaction? Modify the diagrams to consider and respond to these errors.

12-4. Exercise 12–3 assumes that the subway rider will deposit exact change. Extend the diagrams to permit the machine to make change. Remember to consider any error conditions associated with this new requirement.

12-5. A municipal parking lot contains an automated cashier. On entering the garage, the patron presses a button which raises the entrance gate and dispenses a ticket with a magnetic stripe encoding the date and time of entry. To pay the parking charges before leaving the garage, the ticket is inserted in the machine. The machine computes the charges based on the length of time the car was parked and displays the amount due. Coins are inserted (see Exercise 12–3) until the amount due is reduced to zero; the machine will make change if required. The ticket is then encoded to show that the charges have been paid and returned to the patron, who then uses it to operate the exit gate.

Draw state transition diagrams for the interaction between the patron and the automated cashier. (*Note*: When does this dialogue begin and end?)

12-6. Draw state transition diagrams for an ATM user for log-in, option selection, a withdrawal, and the ending dialogue. Be sure that they are consistent with the state transition diagram for the user (Figure 12.7) as well as with the state transition diagrams for the ATM (Figures 12.8 through 12.12).

12-7. Modify the state transition diagram for a withdrawal from the ATM (Figure 12.9) to check for additional errors. What happens if there is no money in the machine? If there is insufficient money to dispense the amount requested? If there are no more slips for printing the transaction record?

12-8. Modify the model of the dialogue with the ATM so that the user selects whether to withdraw from a checking account or a savings account. Be sure to consider the additional errors which are now possible.

Many ATMs use a standard options menu. How might some of the errors you just identified be prevented?

12-9. Discuss the advantages and disadvantages of each of the interaction models described in this chapter for communicating the design of the interface to users and to system constructors.

12-10. State transition diagrams are constructed of the structured programming constructs of sequence, selection, and iteration. Draw a primitive state transition diagram for each of these constructs, showing the minimum number of states. Describe a rule for generating a diagram from these primitive constructs. (*Hint*: Think of how sequence, selection, and iteration may be combined to form a structured program.)

12-11. Compare and contrast a state transition diagram and a window navigation diagram.

12-12. Develop a window navigation diagram for the ATM example in this chapter. Be sure that it is consistent with the state transition diagrams. If you feel the design can be improved, revise both the state transition diagrams and the window navigation diagram.

12-13. Find a Web site with no more than ten pages. Develop a navigation diagram for the Web site showing the links between pages within the Web site. Does the navigation diagram help you evaluate how usable the Web site is?

12-14. Why is it important for users to be involved in testing the user interface?

12-15. What is the value of usability testing?

12-16. Discuss some of the advantages and disadvantages of each of the three methods of observation for usability testing.

12-17. Using specific examples from the Public University Registration System, explain the advantages of the Model-View Separation pattern.

12-18. What is the purpose of each component of an external specification of a graphical user interface?

12-19. Consider the article in Figure 12.18 about the inadequate usability of enterprise resource planning software:

    a. What were some of the tasks involved in Forrester Research's usability testing?

    b. Do you think it was valid to test the software without any user training? Why?

    c. What are some of the consequences of software which is difficult or frustrating to use?

    d. How do you react to the suggestion that revenue from training reduces a vendor's incentive to improve the usability of its software?

FIGURE 12.18   Business Applications Get Bad Marks in Usability

Business Applications Get Bad Marks in Usability

Business applications from major software makers are often difficult for the average office worker to use, costing companies millions of dollars and compromising many corporate software projects, according to a new study conducted by Forrester Research.

The software usability study is part of a bigger report the firm is publishing that evaluates software companies that sell enterprise resource planning (ERP) applications.

ERP applications are a type of business management software designed to help companies automate day-to-day tasks, such as taking orders, keeping books, and managing human resources.

In their usability evaluation, Forrester analysts tried to perform a number of standard tasks with applications from 11 different ERP companies, including SAP, PeopleSoft, Oracle, J.D. Edwards, Microsoft and Lawson. The tasks included changing security profiles, which are used to control access to the applications and to sensitive data.

The analysts also attempted to modify the software to reflect changes in a company's organization, such as a plant closing, and they tried to download software patches for bugs and updates via the vendor's customer support Web site.

In its report, Forrester said several applications required "inordinate patience and expertise" to complete the tasks, and many fell short on overall usability.

"It's a frustration factor for customers," said Forrester's Laurie Orlov, one of the analysts involved in the study. "But once the software's implemented, there's not much you can do."

Forrester analysts received no user training before testing the software. Companies typically invest in extensive training for their workers, spending between 10 percent and 15 percent of their project budgets on average, according to Forrester. However, the analysts tested what they thought of as "straightforward" tasks that shouldn't require training, Orlov said.

Forrester receives many complaints from businesses about the poor design of ERP software. While such complaints aren't necessarily on the rise, in a depressed market for corporate applications, now is the time to improve the situation. "In a buyer's market, customers should be demanding better usability," Orlov said.

The costs to businesses that use poorly designed software are huge, according to Orlov. Companies often end up investing tens of thousands of dollars in additional training they hadn't budgeted for. A ponderous interface can also disrupt worker productivity. In the worst case, it can cause workers to abandon the software all together in favor of manual processes, negating the benefits of projects in which businesses typically invest millions.

Most software companies have little incentive to make their applications more intuitive because their training programs are an important source of revenue, Orlov said. SAP, the biggest seller of ERP software, refuted the notion that it's not doing enough to improve usability. "We're constantly in the process of talking to customers and incorporating their feedback in our products," SAP spokeswoman Bonnie Rothenstein said.

Adapted from Alorie Gilbert, "Business Applications Get Bad Marks in Usability," CNET News.com, January 14, 2003

Giant Forest
INN

Assignment

Develop a coordinated pair of state transition diagrams to model the details of the interaction between a hotel clerk and the automated system for guest registration. Base these diagrams on the screen design you prepared for the assignment in Chapter 11.

APACHE
Rent-a-Car

Assignment

Develop a coordinated pair of state transition diagrams to model the details of the interaction between an Apache employee and the automated system for picking up a car. Base these diagrams on the screen design you prepared for the assignment in Chapter 11.

PART FOUR

SUPPORTING THE OBJECT-ORIENTED ANALYSIS AND DESIGN PROCESS

Parts II and III explained UML models and related techniques as part of a six-step process for object-oriented systems analysis and design. The two chapters in Part IV discuss some other important activities which support the system development process. Chapter 13 deals with how to collect the information necessary to construct the object-oriented analysis and design models. Chapter 14 addresses critical issues for the management of object-oriented software development projects.

GATHERING, MANAGING, AND REPORTING INFORMATION

INTRODUCTION

Chapter 2 discussed how to determine the feasibility of a system development project. Chapters 3 through 5 explained how to model the new system requirements. These activities require large quantities of information to be collected, evaluated, managed, and communicated. Although the quantity of information and its details vary from project to project, it should now be clear what information is needed during the feasibility study and system requirements definition.

This chapter focuses on how to gather, manage, and present the information needed by users, analysts, and other participants in the process. It describes sources of information, techniques for collecting it, and criteria for evaluating it. Aids to manual and automated management of changing information throughout the iterative process of system analysis are also described. The important considerations in communicating information and presenting the results of the feasibility and analysis activities are discussed. Throughout the chapter the emphasis is on the principles for collecting, maintaining, and reporting information. The skills and techniques summarized here are applicable in many other contexts besides systems analysis.

GATHERING INFORMATION

The task of system development depends on information gathered by the development team. Ultimately most of this information has to come from the system's users. They are the experts on what their business is about and what they expect an information system to do. They own this information, and the success or failure of the entire development effort depends on their ability to communicate it to the system developers clearly, accurately, and completely.

WHAT INFORMATION TO GATHER

Analysts and designers must focus their search on the information which is essential to their task of system development. Users' requirements are the major determinant of what information to gather. The critical information for object-oriented systems analysis is the information needed to carry out event analysis, identify the use cases, write the expanded use case narratives, and construct the domain model.

INFORMATION SOURCES

Some of the sources of information for analyzing and specifying system requirements have been mentioned in previous chapters. These include documents and information displays that are part of the current system — input forms, graphic displays, reports, and other system outputs. They include written statements of procedures, organizational goals, and policies, as well as applicable laws and regulations. If the existing system is automated, there may be some existing system documentation. That documentation may use diagrams and models developed before the days of object-oriented systems — such as system flowcharts, module hierarchy charts, program flowcharts, file and record descriptions, system reference manuals, or users' manuals. There may also be portions of a data dictionary and perhaps, for systems developed using structured methods, even data flow diagrams and entity-relationship diagrams.

Other sources may also be helpful. Among these are annual reports and brochures, which often contain summaries of an organization's goals, objectives, principal activities, and functions, as well as graphs of trends and projections for the future. Business- and industry-oriented publications deal with the general business climate and with trends in the environment of the new system. These sources as well as books and periodicals about information systems describe a variety of applications, the state of the art in hardware and software, and commercially available application software packages and turnkey systems.

People are the other major information sources. They provide information not available in photographs, drawings, and writing, and can suggest other information sources. People not only describe the current system, but also identify its problems and deficiencies. They state future opportunities; they imagine how a future system could operate; they express hopes and fears, state policies, and articulate goals and objectives. People also explain, interpret, and give perspective to the information they provide. They can withhold information and, as they choose, express or conceal their interests in system change. Users of the system, as described in Chapter 2, are the most important people to talk to during system development. However, it is often beneficial to consult users and analysts outside the organization who have had experience with using or developing similar information processing systems.

INFORMATION-GATHERING METHODS AND TECHNIQUES

In addition to collecting information from the written sources listed above, the most common methods by which analysts gather information are interviews, observation, and questionnaires. In some situations with very ill-defined system requirements, it may be helpful to present users with simulated or actual systems to obtain their reactions. One such approach, prototyping, is discussed in Chapter 14.

Interviews

An *interview* is a conversation in which questions are asked in order to gather information. An interview may involve only two people or a small group. It is preferable for interviews to be conducted face to face, to permit both interviewer and interviewee to communicate nonverbally. However, it may sometimes be necessary to interview by telephone. A successful interview builds rapport between analyst and user as well as collecting information. Perhaps the most important requirement for an interview is that the participants **listen** to each other. In preparing for and conducting an interview, an analyst should make every effort to assure that listening takes place. Evaluation of the information must wait.

Preparing for an Interview. Preparation for an interview includes selecting the people to be interviewed, scheduling time for one or more sessions, and planning the questions to be asked. Identifying whom to interview and obtaining an appointment are often some of the most difficult aspects of interviewing. You need to find out who are the system owner and responsible users, as you are likely to interview them first. However, they are likely to be the busiest users.

During the feasibility study, the system owner will be interviewed to obtain an understanding of the relationship of the proposed system changes to the goals and policies of the organization, the principal reasons for system change, and constraints on the system or its development. System owners can provide a long-range view of the future of the organization. They may be able to suggest some alternatives for the new system and why each alternative is desirable or undesirable. System owners may also identify specific people in the organization whom they wish the analyst to interview.

Responsible users have a more detailed view of the system's operation, but their perspective is still that of a manager. If the responsible users have sufficient expertise, there may not be a need to talk to hands-on users in the early stages. However, discussions with hands-on users may be necessary to pinpoint deficiencies in the current system. Later, when the new system is being modeled, interviews primarily involve the responsible and hands-on users (and perhaps an occasionally beneficial user). System owners may need to be interviewed again only if the objectives, constraints, and approaches defined during the feasibility study are called into question by the detailed information gathered later.

A memorandum from user management announcing the interviews and explaining their purpose often precedes scheduling them. Otherwise, when an analyst makes an appointment, a brief statement of the purpose of the interview is a good idea.

Individual sessions should be kept short — under 30 minutes to an hour — with the shorter time limit for managers and the longer sessions where details of system operation are being investigated. If possible, leave enough time between interviews to summarize the information collected in the first and review the plan for the second.

It is important to make a list of the questions to be asked during the interview. This frees you to listen instead of thinking about what you are going to say next. It also helps you carry out your responsibility for directing the conversation. Try to arrange the questions in a logical sequence and estimate the time it will take to answer them so that you can keep to the allotted time. Allow some time for unanticipated questions. Some questions will restrict the responses to "Yes," "No," or a limited number of specified alternatives. Others will provide an opportunity for freer response and reactions.

Conducting an Interview. Courtesy, tact, and a businesslike attitude during an interview will demonstrate that the analyst is a professional. A period of light conversation at the beginning may encourage relaxation and rapport, but it should be appropriate to the position and personality of the person being interviewed and should be kept brief to avoid wasting time. Follow the questions prepared in advance and make notes of the essentials of the answers. Record attitudes and opinions as well as facts. Ask if documents are available to keep your notes from duplicating the information they contain.

Attentive and focused listening is critical if you are to understand and absorb what the person being interviewed has to tell you. You cannot really listen if you are preoccupied with what you will ask or do next. Listen carefully to sense what may be left unsaid. Be alert to unanticipated responses and new ideas and follow them up with additional questions. Look for nonverbal cues such as tone of voice, facial expression, and body language to interpret what is being said. If you believe a question was not understood, paraphrase it. If you do not understand an answer, say so, or restate it for confirmation. Provide feedback to demonstrate that you have understood. Often a neutral restatement of the answer to one question can introduce the next.

Sometimes your presence itself may be felt as a threat. In that case, you may have to spend part of the time, especially during an initial interview, to explain the purpose of the interview and reassure the interviewee that the information is being collected to help the organization. Unless a primary purpose of the interview is to obtain reactions to system changes or develop a new system description, do not propose solutions to system deficiencies. Do not attack the credibility or evaluate the opinions of the interviewee.

Conclude the interview with a brief summary of what was covered and express thanks for the other person's assistance or cooperation. State whether another session is necessary, and arrange to schedule it. After the interview is formally concluded, the person interviewed may volunteer further insights. For this reason, many analysts plan to end an interview a few minutes early, particularly if it is with a person whose time is tightly scheduled.

As soon as possible, review your interview notes, transcribe them if necessary for legibility, and add impressions and observations that you were unable to record at the time or that have resulted from reflecting on the interview. Occasionally, it may be appropriate to send a written summary of the interview to the interviewee for written confirmation, if the discussion was significant, and you need to make it a matter of record.

Questionnaires

A *questionnaire* is a list of questions to which written answers are requested from several respondents. If the questions are asked orally, the technique is called a *survey*. A questionnaire is used in situations in which it is impractical or undesirable to hold individual interviews. This is the case when there are many people to be surveyed, when they are located far away, or are geographically dispersed. Perhaps there is a lack of suitable interviewers or not enough time to schedule interviews before the answers are needed.

An interview usually focuses on information that a person is uniquely qualified to provide because of position, expertise, or experience. The intent of a questionnaire, on the other hand, is to ask everyone surveyed the same questions. Those chosen to receive the questionnaire may be selected from a larger population so that their answers will be representative of the entire group. For example, a business might mail or distribute questionnaires to its customers who will be beneficial users of a new system.

In comparison to an interview, a questionnaire is shorter and more highly structured. A long list of questions discourages people from giving thoughtful answers and sometimes from responding at all. Most often, answers to a questionnaire are true/false or multiple choice. It is often desirable to include open-ended questions in order to cover what is missed by the other questions. However, the open-ended questions should solicit a brief, focused comment, not an essay.

The design of a questionnaire requires great care if the results are to be valid. The questions must be stated clearly so that they are self-interpreting. The questions and the choice of responses must not bias the answers. Respondents must be encouraged to ignore questions that they feel incompetent to answer, perhaps by offering choices such as "Don't Know," "No Opinion," or "Insufficient Information to Answer."

If the recipients of a questionnaire are chosen to represent a larger class of people, a statistician should prescribe the selection procedure to assure a valid sample. A statistician may also be helpful in interpreting the significance of the replies after they have been tabulated.

Whether or not the respondents are anonymous, there is no way to assure that their answers are honest. A questionnaire provides none of the nonverbal cues inherent in an interview. However, it is possible to include in a questionnaire of moderate length some questions to detect inconsistent responses.

Since few questionnaires achieve a 100 percent response, there is always uncertainty as to whether the answers of those who failed to reply would have differed significantly from the replies that were received.

When using a questionnaire, be sure to allow enough time for prepare the questions, identify the respondents, distribute the questionnaires, receive the replies, and tabulate and interpret the results. Seek expert advice and assistance if reliable answers are crucial to the system development project.

Observation

Observation is a natural and direct way of gathering information about an existing system. It is a good way to learn about manual information-processing procedures by following the flow and transformation of information. Observation of the interface between the manual and automated portions of a system is also beneficial.

Watching what happens is a good way of confirming or correcting information collected by other techniques. A current system description should show what occurs, even if that differs from what official policies or procedures say should occur. In most cases, the discrepancies involve physical aspects of the system. A difference that affects the essential system description is more important to look for.

An observer without some knowledge of a system may miss important features or may misinterpret what is seen. Another problem with observation is that, when people know they are being watched, their behavior may change. This possibility must be considered when interpreting what is observed.

Preparation is important to observation as well as to interviews and questionnaires. Knowing what you want to look for or confirm will help you focus on the appropriate situations.

Record observations with notes or sketches. It may also be appropriate to take photographs or use film or videotape. In that case, advance arrangements should be made.

An analyst should also be alert to informal opportunities for observing what happens in an information processing system and the organization it supports.

JOINT APPLICATION DEVELOPMENT (JAD)

User involvement in the system development process is critical to an accurate specification of users' requirements and to user satisfaction with the completed system.

One approach to ensure that users actively participate in system development is Joint Application Development (JAD).[1] JAD is a technique originated by IBM in

---

[1]Also known as Joint Application Design. See Jane Wood and Denise Silver, *Joint Application Development*, 2nd ed. (New York: John Wiley, 1995). Also see Steve McConnell, *Rapid Development: Taming Wild Software Schedules*, (Redmond, Wash.: Microsoft Press, 1996), ch. 24.

1977 to create a consensus among the participants in system development. In this approach, users and developers participate in an intensive three- to five-day workshop, called a *session*. JAD has most often been used to define system requirements and the preliminary design of the new system, but it may assist in other system development tasks as well. JAD provides a structure to support and encourage user involvement.

JAD manages user participation so as to avoid conflicts or situations in which the user's involvement becomes an obstacle instead of a benefit. The process is highly scripted and disciplined, and the sessions are carefully documented. There is an *executive sponsor*, who has decision-making authority for all aspects of the project and who can assure the availability of all the attendees. An impartial *facilitator* is responsible for keeping the JAD sessions on track and avoiding irrelevant and unproductive discussions. There is also a *scribe*, selected from the project team or from a staff group set up to support JAD for many projects. The scribe takes notes as directed by the facilitator and collects work products generated during the session to create a permanent record for subsequent review and use. The remaining *full-time participants* are decision-makers for the project. They are committed to attendance during the entire session. Others may be *on-call participants*, who attend only when their expertise on a specific topic is needed. There may also be *observers*, who attend but do not participate except when requested to answer a question.

Figure 13.1 shows a typical setup for a room in which a JAD session is held. The tables are arranged in an open rectangle. Only the facilitator and the scribe sit at the front table near the magnetic board. One of the side walls has a projection screen; the other provides space for flip charts. There is also an easel for a flip chart pad. In the center is projection equipment for overheads and computer-generated images of documents, charts, "slides," and UML or other system models. The center space is accessible via an opening in the table next to the facilitator.

JAD helps foster a sense of ownership in the system by its users and closely links them to the decisions about the appearance and performance of the system. Users are also more likely to understand the technical issues which arise in the process.

However, the benefits of JAD depend on intensive and time-consuming user participation. The JAD session itself is preceded by careful planning and followed by preparation, review, and approval of a final document, which contains all the decisions and agreements made during the session. This can be burdensome for both users and the organization unless mitigated by careful planning and realistic expectations on the part of both user managers and information technology managers.

Although JAD pre-dates object-oriented software development, it has been used with some success for defining requirements for object-oriented systems.

EVALUATING INFORMATION

Regardless of its source or the methods used to collect it, information must always be evaluated. The analyst's expertise, the time available, and the project budget constrain the selection of the evaluation procedures. In evaluating information, the following questions must be answered, whether the procedures are formal, sophisticated, and quantitative, or less formal and more qualitative.

What Does the Information Say?

The information content must be known before it can be analyzed, evaluated, and used. The ability to write a summary or paraphrase is a good test of an analyst's or user's comprehension of information, especially when technical terms have been used. The summary should try to maintain the precision of technical language while eliminating jargon.

FIGURE 13.1   Arrangement of a meeting room for a JAD session

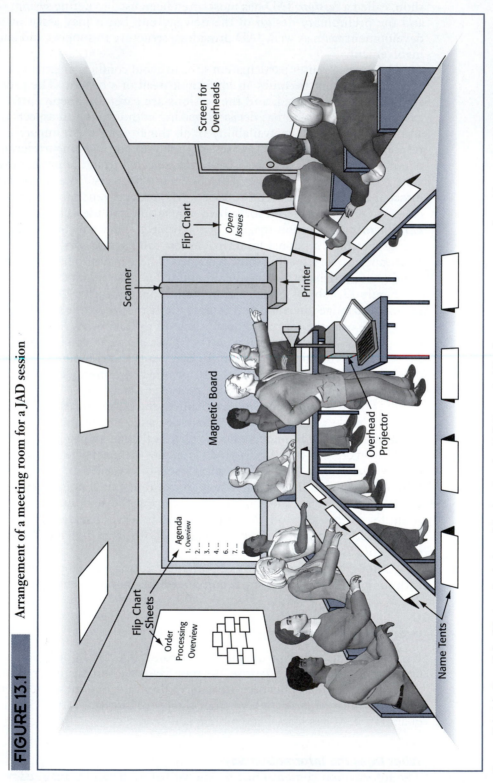

Source: Valacich, *Essentials of System Analysis and Design*, Prentice Hall, Upper Saddle River, NJ © 2004, p-137; adapted from F7.6 of Wood & Silver, Joint Application Development, Wiley, 1989, p-111.

What Does the Information Mean?

Here the emphasis shifts from content to understanding. What are the implications of this information for the organization and system being studied? How is it related to other information? To what extent is it reinforced or contradicted by other information? Is it primarily a statement of fact, opinion, perceptions, or feelings?

Is the Information Relevant?

This question is concerned with how the information can help in identifying user needs and specifying system requirements. Some information may contribute to formulating the system's objectives; to defining performance requirements; to identifying, generating, or comparing system alternatives; or to modeling the current or new system. Other information may reveal people's attitudes toward changing the system, thereby suggesting problems and opportunities associated with integrating the system into the operations of the organization. Sometimes information can be immediately discarded as extraneous; at other times the relevance of information becomes apparent only later.

Is the Information Reliable?

Information is not always reliable. Systems and procedures may have been changed without revising documentation and policy statements. Information gathered directly from people may also be unreliable. It may be intentionally misleading or unconsciously biased by its source or the methods used to gather it. It may be colored by emotion or self-serving motives. It may be only partially true, or it may omit significant information.

    Generally, the information which people use to make decisions and then act is incomplete, contradictory, partly false, and partly unreliable. The best we can do is to be aware of this situation and try to compensate for deficiencies in the information we use. Clues to the reliability of information can be found in the competence and credibility of the information sources as well as in the number of independent sources supporting it. That is why it is desirable to use more than one method of gathering information, to corroborate by observation when possible, and to cross-check written and oral sources of information with each other.

MANAGING INFORMATION

For even a modest system development project, a large amount of information is gathered, evaluated, and used. Because some of the information collected is irrelevant, and because information from several sources is desirable to assess its reliability, analysts must manage more information than is contained in the feasibility report and requirements statement. Moreover, it is usually impossible to control the information-gathering process so closely that each stage is limited to obtaining precisely the information needed next. Some means of organizing and managing this information during system development is essential.

    Information management is necessary for reasons other than the quantity of information. The complexity of the information to be managed is related to the complexity of an information processing system and its development. In addition, since development is an iterative process, the amount of information grows, and the details often change at each iteration. The documents and models produced in early stages of system development must keep their identity and be retained for use in later stages of the process. The additional understanding of a system and additional detail developed in modeling the new system cause the tentative decisions made during the feasibility study as well as the estimates of costs, benefits, and project schedules to be reviewed and revised. The result is increased reliability. The new system models produced in analysis should be kept as a statement of user requirements so that they can be compared to the system as designed and delivered for user acceptance.

Clearly the means of maintaining information must facilitate changes. There must be orderly procedures for changing the system requirements during design and construction.[2]

MANUAL METHODS OF INFORMATION MANAGEMENT

Information management during systems analysis is concerned with organizing the information collected, as well as maintaining and modifying the various system descriptions produced in the process. Organizing the notes, documents, and other material is mostly a matter of setting up and keeping the discipline established by a good filing system. There should be a central place for maintaining the manual files for the project, even though most of the project participants will keep their own copies of the documents as well. Take notes in a legible hand, transcribing them if necessary so that you and others can read them later. Learn to make clear, professional-quality sketches. In this time of ubiquitous xerography, everything committed to paper, such as notes, diagrams, drawings, and reports, should be recorded with sufficient contrast to yield clear, clean copies.

In a manual system, the elimination of redundancy is especially important. Every duplication of information, every cross-reference, is one additional item which must be maintained and one additional opportunity for an inconsistent system description.

AUTOMATED AIDS TO INFORMATION MANAGEMENT

Information systems analysts, like the proverbial shoemaker's children, were slow to benefit from their own technology. However, the widespread availability of information technology makes possible and indispensable automated aids to information management. Word processing software can facilitate changes to the documents produced during system development. Computer graphics makes it easy to create and modify diagrams. Database management systems can organize and maintain the information needed for a system development project. Combined with selective query and report-generating capabilities, a database management system can help in monitoring project progress and in presenting the results of system studies.

Today, integrated development environments (IDEs) extend computer-aided software development considerably beyond information management. They support the entire development process from project inception and requirements analysis through design, code generation, testing, performance monitoring, and deployment into the organization. These environments integrate analysis and design models with program code. For example, changes to a class diagram or interaction diagram generate consistent changes to the code, and vice versa. Code can be reverse-engineered to produce the design models. IDEs typically incorporate a variety of products from multiple vendors. They can generate code in multiple object-oriented languages for deployment and implementation in a variety of operating systems on a variety of hardware platforms. The benefits of these environments include improved software quality through keeping the models consistent during software development, enhanced communication among members of the software development team, and increased productivity through partial automation of development tasks. Current examples of IDEs are Rose, from the Rational Software Corporation, and Borland's Together ControlCenter.

---

[2]See Edward Yourdon, *Managing the System Life Cycle*, (New York: Yourdon Press, 1982), and Philippe Kruchten, *The Rational Unified Process: An Introduction*, 2nd ed. (Reading, Mass.: Addison-Wesley, 2000), 215ff.

REPORTING INFORMATION

The importance of communicating to and interacting with users, analysts, and others throughout system development makes it imperative for systems analysts to become skilled at reporting and presenting information as well as at acquiring and maintaining it. Written, oral, and graphic communication skills are all necessary. Though they are distinguished below, in practice they are combined to produce the best results.

For the most part, the primary purpose of reports and presentations made by systems analysts is to help others to understand — so that they can critique, confirm, or make decisions about what is presented. Usually analysts should present findings and recommendations objectively, relying on the intrinsic merit of what is reported. Occasionally it is important for analysts to become advocates of a recommendation — to persuade as well as to present.[3]

MODES OF COMMUNICATION

The principal modes of communicating information are written, oral, and graphic.

Written Reports

The most common written documents prepared by analysts during system development are the feasibility report, use case descriptions, and documents recording walkthrough findings. If there are models of the current system, they should be available as a separate document. There may also be a document containing details of the alternatives for the new system. This provides a record of all the system descriptions but eliminates nonessential detail from the presentation of the chosen alternative. In addition, there will be a variety of memoranda, both technical and related to project management. Reports also include project proposals and plans.

Oral Reports

Although oral communication is involved in information gathering as well as throughout system development, oral presentations consist primarily of walk-throughs and management briefings or reports.

Graphic Communication

The effectiveness and desirability of graphic communication have already been emphasized. Advertisers exploit the visual impact of television and use photographs and strong graphics in newspapers and magazines. Even radio, a nonvisual medium, frequently tries to create visual images for its listeners. This power of images is one reason that the UML provides use case diagrams, domain models, interaction diagrams, class diagrams, and statecharts for use during analysis and design. The UML also offers activity diagrams (not covered in this book) as a way to represent the logic of business rules and procedures. Similarly, charts and graphs should be used in preference to narrative for summarizing information, reporting trends, comparing costs and benefits of system alternatives, and presenting project budgets and schedules.

PRINCIPLES OF COMMUNICATION

Understanding and putting into practice the following principles should result in clear, effective communication. Some of them are valid for all kinds of communication; others are directed toward specific media or situations.

---

[3]See Chapters 13 through 15 of Thomas H. Athey, *Systematic Systems Approach* (Englewood Cliffs, N.J.: Prentice-Hall, 1982), for a discussion of the issues involved.

Know Your Audience

To whom are you speaking or writing? What is their general background and level of education? How much expertise do they have in the subjects being dealt with? It is insulting to be talked down to, yet too high a level of discussion impedes or prevents communication. Sometimes only a little extra background or introduction will allow the reader or listener to follow the presentation. Try to put yourself in the place of your audience. Determine what you would want to know if you were in their position.

Answer the Basic Questions

These questions are summarized in verse by Kipling:

> I keep six honest serving men
> (They taught me all I knew);
> Their names are What and Why and When
> And How and Where and Who.[4]

Though Kipling recommends them for information gathering, these questions are also basic for reporting information. Perhaps in a business context, we should also add "At what cost?" In any case, providing the answers to these questions is fundamental.

Seek Simplicity

Clarity, directness, and simplicity reinforce each other. Writing and speaking clearly, directly, and simply require effort; making simplicity habitual requires years of discipline.

Use paraphrase or everyday language instead of technical language for a non-technical audience. For example, a use case diagram is a "picture of the interaction between users and the system"; a domain model shows "the essential business concepts in the application and what information the system needs to know about them." Otherwise, define technical or other unfamiliar terms and the concepts behind them in simple language. On the other hand, users often have their own vocabulary and jargon; be sure to learn it well enough to use it correctly.

Control the rate of information transfer. This is especially important in oral presentations, where listeners must rely on their memories of what was said earlier. The accompanying visual material should also be kept simple. To put so much information on a slide that it becomes too small to read is self-defeating. When time is limited, limit the number of topics to be covered or points to be made accordingly.

Organize and Plan the Report or Presentation

Organizing a presentation or report gives it a structure, defining its components and arranging them in an appropriate sequence.

Begin with an overview which states the principal points or topics and then develops these in detail. Reports or presentations to management often begin with a concise summary, which includes recommended decisions or actions when appropriate. Details supporting the recommendation or summary follow, perhaps at several levels. This permits the reader of a report to choose the areas and levels of detail to be investigated further. A table of contents with the outline made explicit throughout the document facilitates skimming and selective reading. Similar principles apply to oral presentations.

It is also important to arrange the components of the report in a logical sequence, to be sure that new concepts and terms are defined as they are introduced, and that each lays the groundwork for the next.

---

[4]Rudyard Kipling, "The Elephant's Child," in *Rudyard Kipling: The Complete Verse* (London: Kyle Cathie, 2002), 493.

The plan should also consider the selection of examples, the coordination of written and graphic material, and appeal to the senses and to the imagination. It may require you to make a schedule to allow time for typing documents, preparing charts and slides, and reproducing reports or presentation aids before the deadline.

Prepare and Rehearse the Presentation

An effective oral presentation requires careful preparation and rehearsal. The more powerful the audience and the more critical the outcome, the more important it is to spend time getting ready. This means that visual aids must be ready early. If possible, practice in the place where the presentation will be given. Have others listen and comment on both the strengths and the weaknesses, but remember that the purpose of a run-through is to identify and improve the weaknesses. If a video camera or tape recorder is available, use it to monitor the rehearsal. Practice until you feel comfortable. Be sure that you can stay within the allotted time; plan what to leave out if time runs short. Try to anticipate questions and prepare an answer for them.

Make a Final Check

Take the time for a final check, but provide enough leeway to correct deficiencies. Are there enough seats located where their occupants can see? Is all the equipment in place? Will the cords reach the power source? Are there spare lamps for the projectors? Are the slides, transparencies, charts, and handouts at hand, along with pens if you plan to write? A few minutes spent in this way can prevent last-minute panic and allow you to concentrate on what you are saying rather than worrying about what has gone wrong.

Watch for Feedback

In oral presentations it is important to notice the clues your listeners give as to how well they are receiving what you are saying to them. Watch their expressions and their body language. These clues can help you decide whether you are moving too rapidly or too slowly for your audience so that you can adjust your pace accordingly. Provide an opportunity for them to ask questions. If you repeat or paraphrase a question, you have additional time to understand it and to prepare your answer. This also assures that everyone has heard these questions, particularly if the group is large. In some cases, you may be able to ask questions of the audience.

SUMMARY

Skills in gathering, managing, and communicating information effectively complement skills in system modeling — all are required for successful information system development.

Users' requirements are the major determinant of what information to gather. The critical information for object-oriented systems analysis is the information needed to carry out event analysis, identify the use cases, write the expanded use case narratives, and construct the domain model.

The skilled analyst gathers information from a variety of sources, including people and documents. Principal methods of information gathering consist of interviews, questionnaires, and observation.

Joint Application Development (JAD) defines system requirements and a preliminary system design. It is a highly structured process requiring intensive sessions involving developers and key users.

Regardless of its source or the methods used to collect it, information must always be evaluated for content, meaning, relevance, and reliability.

The amount of information to be managed during systems analysis is so large, and its rate of change so frequent, that automated aids are highly desirable, probably even essential. Integrated development environments can support software development from project inception through deployment while improving software quality and increasing the productivity of the developers.

In reporting information, written, oral, and graphic communication skills are all necessary. Important principles to remember in communicating information include: know your audience; answer their basic questions; seek simplicity; organize, plan, prepare, and rehearse presentations; make a final check before issuing a document or giving a presentation; and watch for feedback.

KEY TERMS

interview *374*

Joint Application Development *376*

observation *376*

questionnaire *375*

REVIEW AND DISCUSSION QUESTIONS

13-1. Identify some sources of information for systems analysis and requirements specification.

13-2. Name and give a definition for three information gathering techniques used in systems analysis.

13-3. Why is it desirable to use a variety of sources and techniques to collect information?

13-4. What kind of information would you expect to from each of the following types of users (as defined in Chapter 2)?:
a. System owner
b. Responsible user
c. Hands-on user
d. Beneficial user

13-5. State what you would do to prepare for an interview.

13-6. Some authors suggest the use of a tape recorder during interviews. What are the advantages and disadvantages? Under what circumstances might a tape recorder be appropriate?

13-7. In what circumstances is a questionnaire an appropriate technique for gathering information?

13-8. What role does a statistician play when questionnaires are used?

13-9. Discuss reliability and relevance in relation to information collected through:
a. Interviews,
b. Questionnaires, and
c. Observation.

13-10. What are some of the benefits and disadvantages of Joint Application Development?

13-11. What advantages can automated aids provide to maintaining a system description?

13-12. List three basic forms of communicating information. Give important features of each.

13-13. Briefly explain each of the following principles of communication:

   a. Know the audience.
   b. Answer the basic questions.
   c. Seek simplicity.
   d. Organize and plan the report or presentation.
   e. Prepare and rehearse the presentation.
   f. Make a final check.
   g. Watch for feedback.

13-14. Consider the article about information overload (see Figure 13.2):

   a. What does McGovern believe is the cause of information overload?
   b. What are some of the effects of information overload on organizations?
   c. How does McGovern view the relationship between the quantity of decisions and their quality?
   d. Is the system development process subject to information overload? If so, what strategies can be used to mitigate the problem of information overload?

FIGURE 13.2   Spinning Around

Spinning Around

Another day in the office, which, according to one recent study, consists of handling 46 phone calls, 25 e-mails, 16 voice-mails, 23 items of post, eight inter-office memos, 16 faxes and nine mobile phone calls. It's even more alarming to think that those figures — taken from a 2000 survey of companies employing between 100 and 499 staff conducted by Pitney Bowes in partnership with the US-based forecaster, the Institute for the Future — are likely to have risen since.

Enough to send you barmy? You may be right. Experts say information overload is a serious problem in many companies, adding to stress levels and resulting in a downturn in productivity.

Irish website content management author Gerry McGovern believes that information overload stems from the fact that since the founding of civilisation man has been operating on the premise that more is better. "[It's] the-more-the-merrier kind of concept. . . if we create more, we create more value," McGovern says. "Information overload is a reflection of that almost genetic historic desire to do more."

"But I think the rules that operate within a digital economy are different from those which operate within the physical economy. Part of that is there is essentially no scarcity or there is very little scarcity in a digital economy. The constant movement is towards cheaper, faster processes, infinitely cheaper storage devices that can store vastly [greater] quantities of content or data."

McGovern, who spoke on the subject at this year's Australian Computer Society conference at Lorne, on Victoria's southwest coast, says that something like 70 per cent of most websites goes unread. Despite that, when putting content on the web, "rarely do we ask the question: is anybody interested in reading that?"

McGovern is in no doubt that the glut of information has led to less productivity. "I think, to some degree, long-term or medium-term strategic thinking is being smothered by the necessity to react to the onslaught of short-term data," he says. "A lot of managers are spending so much of their time coping with data that's coming through today that they don't have as much time as they should have to properly analyse that and put that in perspective."

McGovern cites the dotcom boom and bust as an example of what can happen when people refuse to adopt long-term thinking. "Planning went out the window in the whole dotcom boom and we saw the result of what happened," he says. "Trillions were lost during that period and what is there to show?"

McGovern also believes a "macho" element, which sprang from the culture of Silicon Valley, is helping to fuel the increasing demand for information. People were seen as smarter if they handled a greater number of calls or e-mails or more productive if they worked 18-hour days and never took holidays. But McGovern believes people aren't making better decisions simply because they are making more decisions.

"You might be making better decisions if you were making five decisions," he says.

Take e-mails. A study last year by Rogen International and Goldhaber Research Associates found that in 1995, employees sent an average of three e-mails a day and received five. By 2002, employees were sending 20 a day and receiving 30. (The same study also found that about half of an e-mail user's time was wasted dealing with spam.)

McGovern believes most people could halve the number of e-mails sent in a day without any ill effect to their business. "Most companies succeed or fail because of a lot of decisions over a reasonably long period of time."

Adapted from an article by David Adams, *Sydney Morning Herald*, May 20, 2003, 7.

MANAGING OBJECT-ORIENTED SYSTEM DEVELOPMENT

14

LEARNING OBJECTIVES

After mastering the material in this chapter, you will be able to

- Discuss some of the reasons why information system development projects fail.
- Describe the goals of project management.
- Name some of the risk factors associated with users, the development team, and the project itself.
- Explain why it is important to manage users' expectations for a project.
- Discuss how risk, coverage, and criticality can contribute toward developing a project strategy.
- Read a Gantt chart and a critical path model.
- Discuss how object-oriented software benefits software development.
- Explain why the Unified Process creates a detailed project plan for the next iteration only.
- Identify the disciplines in the Unified Process which are related to project management.
- Discuss issues related to preparing estimates of project costs and resources.
- Explain the use of prototyping in object-oriented software development.
- Discuss some alternatives to custom software development.

INTRODUCTION

The preceding chapters in this book have described the development process for object-oriented information systems and explained the models and techniques of object-oriented analysis and design. This chapter discusses some of the most important issues in managing any software development project. It also addresses concerns which are specific to object-oriented systems.

Clearly, project management is far too complex to be dealt with fully in a single chapter. All we can do is to provide an overview of the topic and refer you elsewhere for additional detail.

We begin with a discussion of why projects fail. This motivates the primary goal of project management as a way to complete a project successfully. One important concern is therefore to identify and respond to a project's major risks. Ranking the tasks to be done in terms of their importance to the success of the project becomes the basis for preparing a project plan and schedule. Current best practices in software development recommend a process which is incremental and iterative, as discussed in Chapter 2. The Rational Unified Process (Unified Process) provides a flexible and adaptive framework for achieving the advantages of incremental, iterative development. We discuss some of the ways in which object-oriented technology further facilitates such an approach to system building. There is a summary of important principles for estimating, monitoring, and controlling project costs. Next we outline some of the issues related to the re-use of objects.

Thus far, this book has described a simplified but relatively complete process of development for custom object-oriented application software. This chapter discusses briefly the selection of packaged software as an alternative to complete custom design. It also examines how prototyping can support object-oriented system development.

WHY SOFTWARE DEVELOPMENT PROJECTS FAIL

The history of software development is full of examples of failed projects. Some projects have been abandoned after months — or even years — of effort and expense without delivering a system. Other projects have delivered software which did not work, lacked all the required functionality, was unstable, filled with errors, or failed to meet the specified performance standards. Even projects which satisfied the users' requirements were often delivered late or far exceeded their budgets. The most devastating failures seem to occur with large and complex projects.

The situation is even bleaker if we define failure broadly as "performance that does not meet expectations."[1]

If we are to learn from past failures, as suggested in Chapter 6, we should have some understanding of the reasons for these failures. Lack of technical competence on the part of information technology professionals is seldom the primary cause of a failed software development project. Instead, more important reasons for unsuccessful software projects include:

- The failure of users to communicate requirements completely and accurately,
- Insufficient commitment of users to the project,
- Lack of support for the project by a top management champion,
- Unrealistic project budgets and schedules, and
- Inadequate attention to identifying and mitigating risks to the project.

However, in Tom DeMarco's opinion, the chief cause of failure lies elsewhere:

In my years of auditing software projects, I have seen many total failures. . . . I have known project managers who excelled in those characteristics that I associate with good management. . . . Yet their projects failed. Why? . . . In most cases they simply failed to fulfill original expectations. I am convinced that most project failures are of this very nature, and, in most cases, it is not the fault of the project team at all. It is rather the fault of inflated and unreasonable expectations.[2]

GOALS OF PROJECT MANAGEMENT

Given all these reasons for projects to fail, we would expect the primary goal of software project management to be a successful outcome for a project. Ideally, this means to deliver a system which not only meets users' reasonable expectations, but also is produced on time and within the budget.

This primary goal involves several secondary goals:

- To identify risks to the project and avoid or mitigate them,
- To prepare project plans,
- To monitor project progress against the plans,
- To earn the trust of the system's users and maintain it through continuing communication, and
- To manage users' expectations.

---

[1]Kenneth L. Carper, *Why Buildings Fail* (Washington, D.C.: National Council of Architectural Registration Boards, 2001) 4.
[2]Tom DeMarco, *Controlling Software Projects: Management, Measurement, and Estimation* (Englewood Cliffs, N.J.: Yourdon, 1982) 4.

RISK ANALYSIS

A *risk* is any uncertainty which has a significant probability of preventing the successful completion of a project milestone. There are risks associated with each phase of a project and with each discipline in the Unified Process as well as with each project iteration. More specifically, risks associated with requirements include technical complexity, uncertainty of effort, poor specification, political problems, and usability. Risks associated with construction include new technology or components, adequate performance, and integration of hardware or software components of the system.[3]

RISKS ASSOCIATED WITH USERS

Some of the risks associated with a project's users include the types of users, the users' knowledge of the application, the users' prior experience with system development, and the users' tolerance for risk. It is often desirable to develop a profile of the users in order to identify the associated risks.

In Chapter 2, users were classified as system owners, responsible users, hands-on users, and beneficial users. The initial step in producing a user profile is to determine an individual user's type.

When evaluating the users' knowledge of the application, consider not only years of experience, but also the variety of experience. Remember that ten years of the same experience are not the same as a sequence of 10 years of different experience.

Users' prior experience with system development will have a bearing on how much time is needed to educate users about the system development process and their roles in it. Be sure to consider whether or not these users and system developers have worked together previously. Users who trust the system developers are much more likely to be satisfied with the results. Also try to determine if the users know what their roles will be during the course of analysis and design.

Knowledge of the extent to which a user is willing to take risks can also have an impact on the choice of a strategy for systems analysis and design. One concern here is whether the users can decide to adopt the proposed system based on a relatively abstract system description or whether a more concrete presentation of the proposed system is required. Graphical representations of various aspects of the system, including work flows, often make it easier for users to understand the system and how it works.

RISKS ASSOCIATED WITH THE DEVELOPMENT TEAM

A profile of the analysts, designers, and programmers will help identify and assess the risks associated with the development team. Important factors include the developers' knowledge of the application domain and their experience in system development, especially of object-oriented software.

The analysts' knowledge of the application domain will have a significant bearing on the analysis process. If this is the analysts' first exposure to a particular application domain, they will not only have to spend more effort learning about the application, but will also be more dependent on the users. If, on the contrary, the analysts have considerable experience, less effort will have to be spent in learning for this specific project. Analysts with little or no prior experience in object-oriented systems analysis will require more time and be less confident in the outcome.

---

[3]For a fuller treatment of risks in the context of the Unified Process see Philippe Kruchten, *The Rational Unified Process: An Introduction*, 2nd ed. (Reading, Mass.: Addison-Wesley, 2000).

How much experience the designers and programmers have with the application domain or similar domains will lead to similar risks, as will their degree of familiarity with designing and constructing object-oriented software.

RISKS ASSOCIATED WITH THE PROJECT ITSELF

The additional risks associated with the project itself are due to factors which are largely uncontrollable by either the users or the developers. These factors include the stability of the project environment, the pressure to produce immediate tangible results, and the complexity of the system.

Environmental stability includes such external factors as the competitive situation, legislative requirements, and considerations of social responsibility. Influences generated within the organization include pressures to produce results and the need for accurate schedules or budgets.

Much research is continuing in order to find reliable measures of system complexity. These measures are likely to be based on the structure of the analysis and design models and therefore are not available (except as estimates) until the project is well under way.

By no means have we given an exhaustive list of factors. Rather, you should be aware that we can systematically describe and analyze the risk factors which affect the system development process.

MANAGING USERS' EXPECTATIONS

A major threat to the success of a project is users' unrealistic expectations. Perhaps users' first questions about a new project are "How much will it cost?" and "When will it be completed?" — even though the requirements are still unspecified. The Unified Process defers firm commitments about cost and delivery date until the Initiation and Elaboration phases are complete. By then, the system requirements and system architecture are sufficiently stable.

Building and maintaining the users' trust is one of the most critical factors in successful system development. Trust is built by demonstrating professionalism and by explaining the development process so that users understand their roles and those of the developers. Trust is maintained by continuing communication and candor so that there are no unpleasant surprises. Difficulties along the way can be overcome if users and developers can trust each other to tell the truth about the state of the project. Trust and credibility are key to managing users' expectations.

PROJECT STRATEGY

Listing the known risks to a project, assessing their severity, and developing responses to each are key ingredients in preparing a strategy for the project. Once risks have been identified, they can be ranked in order of their potential threat to the project. Other factors to consider are coverage and criticality.

These three factors — degree of risk, coverage, and criticality — can be used to organize both requirements and iterations. Early iterations might address those parts of the project which have the greatest risk.

Coverage refers to how much of the system is included. Early iterations might include all the major parts of the system — though perhaps not in much depth.

Criticality deals with functions with high business value. The greater the business value of a function, the greater the consideration that should be given to implementing it early.[4]

PROJECT PLANNING AND SCHEDULING

A project plan and schedule are the basis for managing a software development project. The project plan allocates tasks and responsibilities to a team of people. This makes it possible to monitor progress relative to the plan and to detect potential problems with the project.

A *project plan* includes a breakdown of the work to be done, the time dependencies among the project tasks, and the assignment of personnel and other resources to each of the tasks.

A *project schedule* is a set of project artifacts or deliverables listed in the sequence in which they are to be produced. The units of work in a project schedule are known as *tasks* or *activities*. A project activity is defined by its deliverables. *Milestones* in the schedule mark major project accomplishments, such as delivering a first version of the system or passing a design review. The schedule specifies how the deliverables are to be obtained as well as the resources needed to carry out each task.[5] Each task occurs only once in a schedule. Its status is either "complete" or "not complete."

The Unified Process, described in Chapter 2, and the more detailed object-oriented analysis and design method presented in Chapters 3 through 9 are necessarily generic. Many organizations which develop software have their own standards for planning, executing, and managing the process. But each project is unique. A "one size fits all" approach will not work. It is critical to tailor project plans and schedules to the scope, complexity, and risks of every individual project.

NETWORK PLANNING MODELS

The project plan provides a list of tasks, known as *activities*, and the order in which they are to be carried out. Some tasks must be completed before others can begin. These time dependencies among tasks permit the project plan to be modeled as a network. After the planned *duration* of each activity has been determined, it is possible to generate a project schedule from the network. Fixing the starting date of the first task will allow the starting and ending dates for all the other tasks to be calculated. This project network is often called a *critical path model* or *critical path network* because it identifies which activities must be completed without delay in order to prevent the delay of the entire project.

Figure 14.1 illustrates the fundamentals of critical path analysis with a small network for an iteration within the Construction phase. It shows one of a variety of diagramming conventions.

Associated with each node are four times or dates, depending on the units in which the duration of each activity is measured. The *earliest start time* is the earliest time at which the activity can begin, which is the same as the minimum time in which all the preceding activities can be completed. This turns out to be the maximum duration of the path from the initial activity to the node. The *earliest finish time* is the soonest the activity can be completed, calculated by adding its duration to the earliest start time. Its earliest finish time becomes the earliest start time for each

[4]Craig Larman, *Applying UML and Patterns: An Introduction to Object-Oriented Analysis and Design and the Unified Process*, 2nd ed. (Upper Saddle River, N.J.: Prentice-Hall, 2002), 110, 576.
[5]Adele Goldberg and Kenneth S. Rubin, *Succeeding with Objects: Decision Frameworks for Project Management* (Reading, Mass.: Addison-Wesley, 1995), 144*ff.*

FIGURE 14.1 Critical path network for an iteration in the Construction phase.

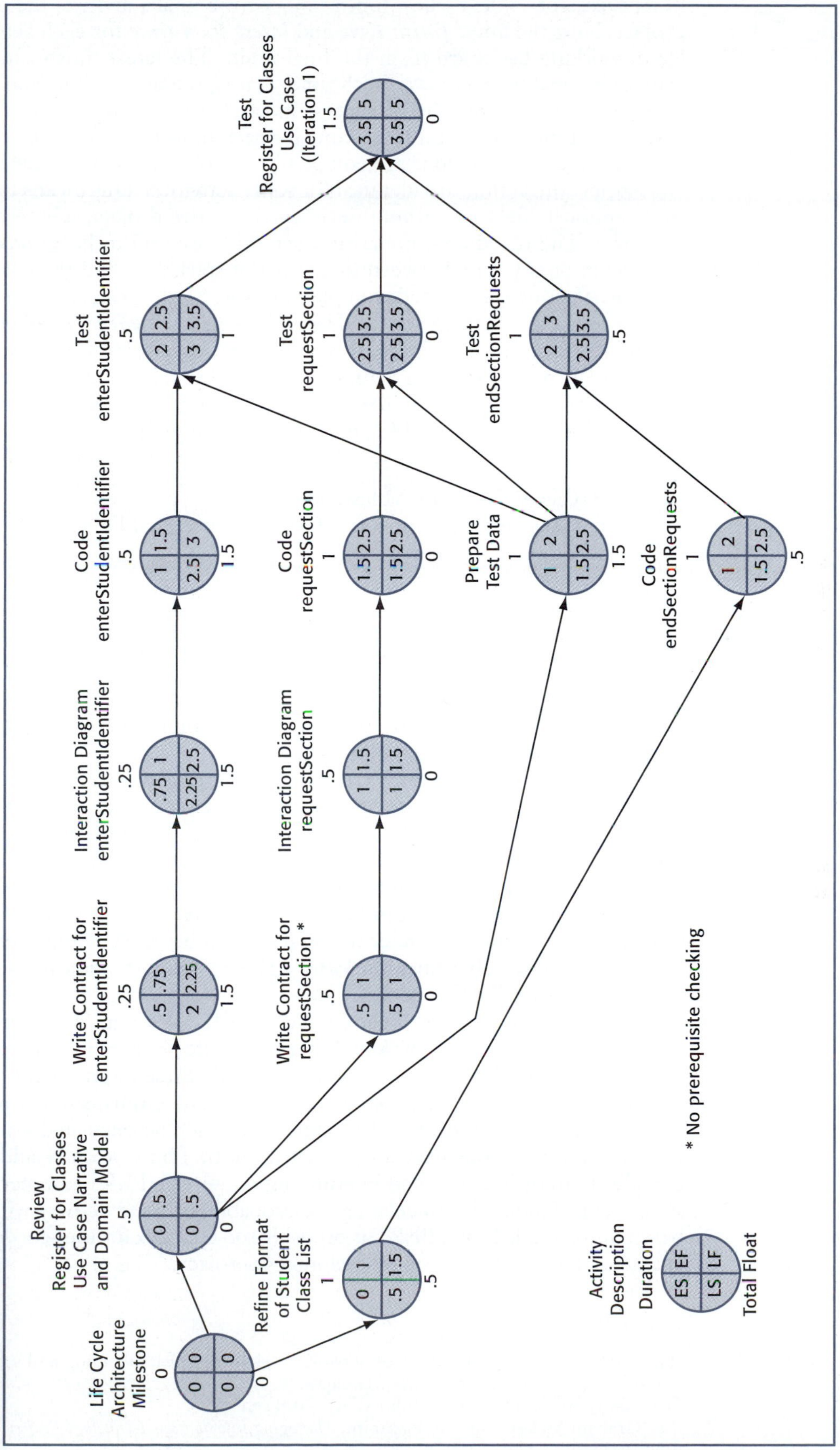

of its successors. The earliest finish time for the final activity is the duration of the project. Next the *latest finish time* and *latest start time* for each activity are calculated, working backward from the final node. The latest finish time for the final activity is equal to its earliest finish time, that is, the project duration. Its latest start time, without delaying the project, is its latest finish time minus its duration. Its latest start time is the latest finish time for each of its predecessors.

After these calculations are completed, we observe that the earliest start times and earliest finish time are identical for some activities. This means that those activities cannot be delayed without delaying the entire project. These are the *critical activities*. The remaining, noncritical activities are said to have *slack*; that is, they may begin at any time between their earliest start time and their latest start time without affecting the project's completion time. Slack is calculated as the difference between an activity's latest start and its earliest start. The *free float* between an activity and its successor is the earliest start of the successor minus the activity's earliest finish. If one of the critical activities is delayed, the start and finish times of their successors can be recalculated to determine a revised completion time for the project.

For example, in Figure 14.1, the critical activities are:

- Life Cycle Architecture Milestone
- Review Register for Classes Use Case Narrative and Domain Model
- Write Contract for requestSection
- Interaction Diagram requestSection
- Code requestSection
- Test requestSection
- Test Register for Classes Use Case (Iteration 1)

If any of these activities is not started or finished on time, this iteration and perhaps the entire project will be completed late.

Costs and personnel or other resource requirements may also be associated with each activity. This permits cost and labor or other resource profiles to be calculated for the project as well. Slack in the scheduling of the noncritical activities may be exploited to level the resource requirements over time.

The activity durations and completion times must be monitored and recorded regularly so that the model can be kept up to date. Any departures from the initial schedule require the remainder of the model to be recalculated. Fortunately, software has been available since the early 1960s to facilitate the extensive calculations required by critical path models.[6]

A variation on the critical path model is PERT (Program Evaluation and Review Technique). It is used for projects where estimates of activity durations are highly uncertain. In PERT, the project planners provide three estimates for the duration of each activity — a most likely estimate, an optimistic estimate, and a pessimistic estimate. An expected estimate of the duration can then be calculated using the assumption that the durations have a beta distribution. This obviously adds considerable complexity to maintaining and interpreting the model. PERT also permits the use of statistical techniques for calculating the probability that an activity will be completed before its scheduled date. PERT is probably too complex for the scheduling and management of information system development projects.[7]

---

[6]For further discussion of the use of network models in project planning and scheduling, see, for example, Harold Kerzner, *Project Management: A Systems Approach to Planning, Scheduling and Controlling*, 7th ed. (New York: John Wiley, 2001) ch. 12.

[7]See Graham McLeod and Derek Smith, *Managing Information Technology Projects* (Danvers, Mass.: Boyd & Fraser, 1996) 163*ff*.

FIGURE 14.2   Phase plan showing milestones with a Gantt chart for an iteration plan

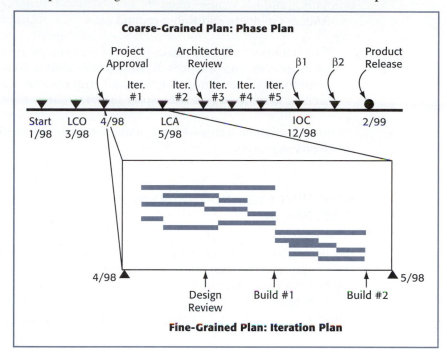

GANTT CHARTS

An older, simpler way of presenting a project schedule is a ***Gantt chart***. It shows the components of a project as horizontal bars on a vertical time grid. It does not show the interdependencies among components as explicitly as a network model. However, the lack of the extra detail may make it more suitable for communicating an overview of the major features of a project schedule.

An example of a Gantt chart based on the Unified Process appears as Figure 14.2.[8] In this figure, LCO marks the milestone for the life cycle objective at the end of the Inception phase. LCA is the milestone for the life cycle architecture, the end of the Elaboration phase. IOC shows the initial operational capability at the end of the Construction phase, when the system is beta-tested.

PROJECT MANAGEMENT FOR OBJECT-ORIENTED SYSTEM DEVELOPMENT

Software project management predates object-oriented technology. In 1975, Brooks published the classic account of what he learned managing the development of OS/360. Among other things, he demonstrated that adding people to a project at the wrong time can further delay the project's completion.[9] Another pioneer of iterative development and other best practices in software project management is Gilb.[10]

---

[8]Kruchten, *The Rational Unified Process*, 117.

[9]Frederick P. Brooks, Jr., *The Mythical Man-Month* (Reading, Mass.: Addison-Wesley, 1975; republished in 1995 in an anniversary edition).

[10]See the classic Tom Gilb, *Principles of Software Engineering Management* (Harlow, England: Addison-Wesley, 1988).

Also, over the years, Boehm has focused on improving the development process, cost estimating, and risk management.[11]

And, as Goldberg and Rubin remind us:

> The important ideas of object-oriented technology are mature ideas, based on experience and practices developed over almost 20 years. But the basics seem to have been ignored in many nineties commercial organizations seeking to build large and complex software systems.[12]

Object-oriented technology, when used properly, can facilitate an effective software development process.

HOW OBJECT TECHNOLOGY SUPPORTS BEST PRACTICES IN SOFTWARE DEVELOPMENT

Over the years, system developers have in fact learned from spectacular failures of the past. Some of the current best practices were introduced in the overview of the system development process in Chapter 2. They address the need for rapid application development even though requirements are not well defined. They adapt to uncertainty and complexity by means of incremental and iterative development. They timebox the iterations to force the developers to achieve visible, measurable progress in a relatively short time. This assures that a project cannot remain off the track for very long without detection. Another best practice uses prototypes, discussed later in the chapter, to investigate areas of uncertainty as the final system evolves.

Object-oriented software brings the following benefits to software development:[13]

▎ Objects are a means of attacking complexity. We cannot always eliminate complexity. Instead, we must try to organize it. We can build software out of relatively simple objects which interact to carry out the system's relatively complex behavior.

▎ Objects build systems resilient to change. Objects encapsulate attributes and behaviors inside well-defined interfaces. We can modify an object's operations without affecting the interface. Good object-oriented design practice will minimize the ripple effect when an object is modified. When the system is changed, even if the change is the wrong one, the system keeps running.

> Goldberg and Rubin provide the following example:

> As early as 1973, Smalltalk played a central role in the research at Xerox PARC. In 1977–78, . . . the Smalltalk–76 system was selected as the basis for creating a hands-on software learning laboratory with which the president of Xerox and his top directors could each compose different simulations of Xerox copier-duplicator centers, factory production lines, document work flow, and so on. . . . Close to show time, we discovered that the memory manager, a critical systems-level object,

---

[11]Barry W. Boehm, "A Spiral Model of Software Development and Enhancement," *IEEE Software*, May 1988; "Software Risk Management: Principles and Practices," *IEEE Software*, January 1991, 32–41. Also see Barry W. Boehm and P. Papaccio, "Understanding and Controlling Software Costs," *IEEE Transactions on Software Engineering*, October 1988.

[12]Adele Goldberg and Kenneth S. Rubin, *Succeeding with Objects: Decision Frameworks for Project Management* (Reading, Mass.: Addison-Wesley, 1995) 15.

[13]Ibid., 52*ff.*

could not handle the high degree of subclassing used by the simulation framework. A change in the implementation of the memory manager was proposed, without a change in its interface. The proposal was reviewed, implemented, and tested within a few days. The revised software learning laboratory was used without a glitch.[14]

- Objects allow partial systems to work. A system can function without all the required capabilities in the current version. We can build a system implementing only some of the use cases or having only a subset of the full behavior of a given use case. We can extend the scope of the system incrementally in later iterations of development as we add new objects or new responsibilities to existing objects.
- Objects represent natural units for re-use. One of the promises of object-oriented systems is that objects can be re-used to reduce the effort required to develop new systems or to modify old ones. Because they model concepts in the problem domain and implement their behaviors in software, objects lend themselves to re-use. Achieving objects' potential for re-use is often difficult. Some of the issues related to re-use are discussed later in this chapter.

PROJECT PLANNING IN THE UNIFIED PROCESS

The Unified Process incorporates the critical insights of current best practices in order to provide flexibility and adaptability. Unlike more traditional approaches to project planning, the Unified Process rejects the idea of planning the entire project in detail in advance. Instead, there is a high-level **Phase Plan**, which specifies the major milestones and estimates their completion dates. An **Iteration Plan** provides a detailed plan for one iteration at a time.

As Larman describes it:

> One of the big ideas of iterative development is to adapt based on feedback, rather than to attempt to predict and plan *in detail* the entire project. Consequently, in the [Unified Process], one creates an Iteration Plan for only the **next** iteration. Beyond the next iteration the detailed plan is left open, to adaptively adjust as the future unfolds. In addition to encouraging flexible, opportunistic behavior, one simple reason for not planning the entire project in detail is that in iterative development not all the requirements, design details, and thus steps are known near the start of the project. Another is the preference to trust the planning judgment of the team as they proceed.
>
> However, there *are* still goals and milestones; adaptive development doesn't mean the team doesn't know where they are going, or the milestone dates and objectives. In iterative development, the team does still commit to dates and objectives, but the detailed path to these is flexible.[15]

MANAGEMENT-RELATED DISCIPLINES IN THE UNIFIED PROCESS

The importance of project management to the Unified Process is emphasized by the fact that it was revised in 2001 to add three core disciplines related to project management — Configuration and Change Management, Project Management, and Environment.

---

[14]Ibid., 53.
[15]Larman, *Applying UML and Patterns*, 579.

Configuration and Change Management
(Manage the Artifacts of the Evolving System)

This discipline manages the artifacts produced during system development. It is concerned with the product and the process as well as project management. The discipline has three key aspects. *Configuration management* deals with the various versions of the artifacts produced during system development. Because the artifacts are interdependent, a change to one artifact usually results in changes to others. *Change request management* is responsible for managing requests for change, assessing their impact on the system and the project, and tracking approved changes. Change requests are closed out when the change has been completed, tested, and incorporated in a release. *Project status and measurement* extract information about the development process, especially the changes, for use in project management.

Following are some of the artifacts associated with configuration and change management:

▌ The Configuration Management Plan. The configuration management plan is part of the software development plan. It sets forth the configuration management policies and practices for the project. It also defines the responsibilities of the Change Control Board, which decides which change requests to approve.

▌ The Project Repository. The project repository holds a data base of the various versions of the project artifacts as well as the change requests.

▌ The Change Request. A change request is a request to change one or more artifacts of the system. Change requests are initiated and then evaluated for their impact. If approved, a change request is assigned for implementation. After implementation and testing, it is included in a release of the system.

Project Management (Manage the Development Process)

This discipline plans all the phases of a software development project from Inception to Transition. It also plans each iteration in detail. It is concerned with identifying and managing the risks associated with development. It tracks and measures the progress of a project in order to detect problems as well as to provide a basis for estimating resource requirements for future projects.

Following are some of the artifacts associated with project management:

▌ The Business Case. The business case is created during the Inception phase and refined during the Elaboration phase. It includes the business context for the system, the business criteria for project success, and a forecast of the financial impact of the system.

▌ The Software Development Plan. The software development plan contains a product acceptance plan, a risk list and risk management plan, a problem resolution plan, and a measurement plan. The software development plan is developed by the project manager early in the Inception phase and revised as necessary following each iteration. It is formally reviewed by the project reviewer to assess its feasibility and acceptability to stakeholders.

▌ The Iteration Assessment. An iteration assessment occurs at the end of an iteration. It evaluates whether the objectives of the iteration were met.

▌ The Status Assessment. A status assessment is a regular report on the current status of the project.

Environment (Support the Development Process with Processes and Tools)

This discipline provides and supports an organization's software development environment. It selects, acquires, installs, and configures software development tools. It provides standards for the organization and guidelines for individual projects. It is responsible for improving the organization's development process. It also supports that process with technical and administrative services. The process engineer is the person responsible for the development process.

The most important artifact associated with the environment discipline is:

▮ The Development Case. The Development Case is the artifact which tailors the system development process for the individual project. For each discipline, the development case specifies which artifacts to use and how to use them.

PROJECT ESTIMATING, MEASURING, AND CONTROLLING

Monitoring the progress of a project is a challenging endeavor. Tom DeMarco's classic, *Controlling Software Projects: Management, Measurement, and Estimation*, was written before object-oriented systems became mainstream. Nevertheless, his approach to project estimating and control is still valuable apart from the structured analysis and design perspective from which he wrote. This section summarizes DeMarco's most important principles and ideas.

DeMarco's fundamental principle is "You can't control what you can't measure."[16] This implies that project management requires quantitative measurements of project progress.

ROLE AND RESPONSIBILITIES OF ESTIMATORS

An *estimate* is a prediction of effort or cost which is equally likely to be above or below the actual result. Success for the estimator must be defined as a function of convergence of the estimate to the actual, **and of nothing else**.

The estimator should be responsible for measurement. Moreover, the estimating function should be separate from the rest of development. Members of the project team should not record data about their own work. There are too many pressures to fudge the numbers.

Ultimately, estimates of the resources required for project tasks must be derived from a data base of accurate costs. Cost data from one organization is seldom directly applicable to another organization's development process. Thus, an organization's cost data base should capture its own history of project development.

It is appropriate for estimators to belong to an organization's standards group, which should have the responsibility for project tactics, as contrasted with project strategy.

ROLE AND RESPONSIBILITIES OF THE PROJECT TEAM

The project team should be responsible for all project **strategy**. After evaluating the project's risks, the team should prepare the project plan.

An appropriate goal for the project team is to maximize the quantity and quality of useful function delivered. Stated more precisely, this means to maximize the amount of total function delivered (weighted by the years of useful system life) per dollar of total system lifetime cost.

How would we measure the components of this goal? A metric of useful function should be based on an implementation-independent model of system size.[17] This in

---

[16]Tom DeMarco, *Controlling Software Projects: Management, Measurement, and Estimation* (Englewood Cliffs, N.J.: Yourdon, 1982) 3.

[17]One approach is the use of **function point analysis**, developed by Allan Albrecht at IBM in the late 1970s. A function point is associated with one end-user business function. See Goldberg and Rubin, *Succeeding with Objects*, 447*ff*., for a discussion of the applicability of function point analysis to object-oriented software development.

turn can be derived from the primitive components of the analysis models. Similarly, metrics which predict the effort (and thus the initial cost) of an implementation should be based on the design models.

OBJECT RE-USE

The re-use of objects promises to yield considerable improvement in programmer productivity. Re-use not only saves the time and cost of building an object again and again, but also should improve quality by incorporating components which have already been thoroughly tested.

In some cases, objects may be re-used as is. In others, an existing object becomes the starting point for customization to meet the needs of a new application.

Yet effective re-use is a challenging task in practice.[18] Reusable objects do not just happen; they must be carefully designed with re-use in mind. Reusable objects should be based on sound, robust abstractions. The principles of coupling and cohesion are particularly important when designing reusable objects. Moreover, merely keeping track of objects available for re-use can be a major challenge to an organization. There must be a library or repository of reusable objects with adequate documentation of the operations and limitations of each object.

DOMAINS OF OBJECT CLASSES

Page-Jones categorizes object classes into four major domains. They are listed here in order from the domain with the least likely candidates for re-use to the domain with the most likely candidates for re-use:

- The application domain — classes valuable for a single application,
- The business domain — classes valuable for an industry or company,
- The architecture domain — classes valuable for a single implementation, and
- The foundation domain — classes valuable across all businesses and architectures.[19]

Thus, because they are industry-specific, the objects in the business layer are less likely to be reusable than those which can be shared across industries and architectures.

ACQUIRING REUSABLE OBJECTS

There are several options for acquiring reusable objects:

- Purchase existing objects from a commercial vendor,
- Contract with a vendor who will develop reusable objects,
- Share the development of reusable objects with another internal project, or
- Build your own reusable objects as part of a single internal project.[20]

In this regard, Goldberg and Rubin state:

> **It's your business**. No one knows your business better than you. You have to provide the strategic insight on your business abstractions. You have to turn to your own internal resources for domain expertise. You have to be

---

[18]See *ibid.*, chs. 9–11, for an extensive discussion of issues related to object re-use.
[19]Page-Jones, *Fundamentals of Object-Oriented Design in UML*, 234*ff*.
[20]Goldberg and Rubin, *Succeeding with Objects*, 230.

prepared to build the assets yourself. Or you have to convince your competitors to cooperate in building those assets that are shareable in the industry, but that do not represent unique competitive advantage.[21]

Today, however, business-domain objects can be purchased for some industries. In the future, they should be more widely available. Nevertheless, some objects will continue to be unique to an industry or to provide a strategic advantage and therefore will continue to be developed in house.

PROTOTYPING

Prototyping is inherent in best practices of software development. It is a key technique for reducing some of the risks in the development process.

WHAT IS PROTOTYPING?

Prototyping is an approach to system development in which software simulates one or more aspects of a proposed information processing system. A *prototype* is a partial or limited version of a system.

The prototyping process is characterized by the rapid development of many prototypes. It implies an iterative approach in which the system requirements are approximated more completely and more precisely at each step. Prototypes may be used in the design and construction of the system as well as in systems analysis.

TYPES OF PROTOTYPES

There are a variety of types of prototypes. Goldberg and Rubin list the following four:

- *Analysis prototypes.* This kind of prototype allows potential users to interact with a partial mock-up of the system. It can help clarify the users' requirements and may simulate the proposed user interface. The prototype itself may become part of the documentation for the system requirements.
- *Design prototypes.* A design prototype explores the architecture for the system implementation, especially during the Elaboration phase of development. It may help identify inconsistencies in the design. It may also focus on system performance in order to identify bottlenecks.
- *Vertical prototypes.* A vertical prototype examines a slice through a problem and its solution. It is applicable when a complete implementation of this portion of the system is needed to understand or explain it.
- *Feasibility prototypes.* A feasibility prototype helps determine whether some aspect or portion of the system can in fact be implemented successfully.[22]

WHY PROTOTYPE DURING ANALYSIS?

Prototypes are especially beneficial in defining users' requirements for an information processing system. Among the most important reasons for using prototypes during analysis are the following.

---

[21]Ibid.
[22]Ibid., 98–99.

Facilitate Communication Between Users and Analysts

Some users find it difficult to envision what a proposed system will look like when it is described as abstractly as in a use case description or a Unified Modeling Language (UML) model. This may be especially true for users with little experience as participants in system development. As a consequence, these users may be unable to determine whether their needs will be met by the proposed system.

Prototyping attempts to bridge the gap between the users' view and the analysts' view of the requirements. Through prototyping, the essential and significant features of a system description can be quickly realized in a concrete form which simulates the proposed system. In this way, users can "play" with a mock-up of the new system and suggest changes. Users can see the proposed input and output formats as well as evaluate the proposed scenarios for interaction with the automated system.

Users often find it difficult to state their requirements completely and accurately without seeing what the inputs and outputs will look like and how they will interact with the completed system. Most users cannot easily visualize the operation of a complex system from looking at documents used by analysts and designers. Even if they learn to read the UML diagrams, they may be unable to envision the finished software. Prototypes offer an alternative means of communicating the appearance and behavior of the system to users. Prototypes permit users to execute commands and see portions of the system in operation, complete with displays and simulations of reports generated by the system. They capture the "look and feel" of the software as well as demonstrate the functionality of the system.

Shorten the Analysis Process

The prototype is an effective means for analysts to learn about the system requirements. Numerous alternatives may be considered in a very short time. Each time the prototype is altered, its presentation of the requirements may be seen and evaluated.

Decrease the Cost of Defining Requirements

With appropriate development tools, each new version of the prototype is not only developed quickly, but also requires only a small additional amount of resources. Active user participation in the process facilitates rapid convergence on a correct set of requirements.

Reduce the Risk of a Failed System Development Project

As we have seen, many system development projects fail because their requirements were specified incorrectly or incompletely. Others have failed because the development process took so long that the requirements changed and the completed systems were no longer useful or cost-effective. Improved communication and capture of user requirements, better definition of requirements, and shorter analysis times all serve to decrease the risk of project failure and thus prevent costly mistakes.

HOW PROTOTYPED REQUIREMENTS AFFECT DESIGN

Prototyping is used to capture users' requirements for an information processing system when the application is new to the users or when users have difficulty in communicating their requirements to analysts. In some cases, the prototype itself is the only definitive statement of the requirements. In other cases, analysts choose to prepare a separate statement of requirements based on the completed prototype approved by the users.

If the latter course is followed, analysts must faithfully translate the explicit and implicit requirements incorporated in the prototype into the requirements specification. Requirements in addition to those defined by the prototype must also be captured. Then design may proceed just as in the absence of a prototype. The availability of the prototype may affect the system acceptance tests.

Because a prototype for defining requirements will have its own user interface, it must be clear whether the style of interaction (see Chapter 11) embodied in the prototype is to be regarded as required or whether it is merely a consequence of the prototyping technique and subject to replacement by a more appropriate style of interaction in the completed system.

WHY PROTOTYPE DURING DESIGN?

At least three kinds of prototypes may be appropriate to address important design issues. They are concerned with the design goals of satisfactory performance and realizability as well as the design of the user interface.

If designers feel that the performance of a portion of a system is critical, it may be desirable to build a prototype to evaluate performance. Perhaps there are no good models for the critical feature. Perhaps available models ignore factors considered to be important. Perhaps there is sufficient complexity that a model would be difficult to build or interpret. A prototype of the selected portion can provide a more realistic evaluation of expected performance.

If a design or alternative designs propose innovative structures, there may be some question about whether the software can be constructed. Or it may be necessary to determine whether the proposed structure can be built using the prescribed programming language or in the prescribed operating environment. In such cases, a prototype to confirm realizability is appropriate.

A third type of prototype allows users to preview the design of the user interface to determine whether the proposed style of interaction and detailed-level design will be acceptable to them. This may be especially desirable where designers have considerable latitude in designing the user-computer interaction or where an earlier prototype has influenced user attitudes toward the style of interaction.

Prototyping may also be used during design to evaluate system performance, resolve questions of realizability or feasibility, and preview the user interface.

PROTOTYPING STRATEGIES

There are two basic strategies in prototyping — building a mock-up of the new system which is discarded when the construction of the actual system is complete and letting the prototype system evolve into the new system. The first strategy is often called *throwaway prototyping*; the second is known as *evolutionary prototyping*.[23]

Throwaway prototypes allow us to gain a better understanding of system requirements or to investigate design and construction issues. They are not intended to function in a production environment. Thus, they do not necessarily need to be very robust or reliable or to handle the same volume of transactions or the same quantity of data as the new system.

Evolutionary prototypes, on the other hand, are designed to gradually become the production version of the system. The strategy for the transition usually entails adding capabilities to the prototype and refinements to the user interface as the system evolves. Thus, in evolutionary prototyping, the developers must first acquire the users' requirements and then design the system with adequate robustness for the production environment. This implies that iterations during analysis will refine the correctness and completeness of the system requirements. More resources are invested during analysis; thus, evolutionary prototyping is more resource-intensive than throwaway prototyping.

---

[23]See Steve McConnell, *Rapid Development: Taming Wild Software Schedules* (Redmond, Wash.: Microsoft Press, 1996) chs. 38 and 7.

Both methods can be used on a single project. Those areas of the system which are well understood can employ evolutionary prototyping, while poorly understood areas can be initially explored through throwaway prototyping.

Design with Evolving Prototypes

If the prototype evolves into the operational application software, there are a number of design issues to be addressed:

▌ The prototype or the techniques used to develop it implicitly bias the system design. Are users and designers aware of these biases and willing to live with their consequences?

▌ Is the prototype capable of expansion to accommodate the size of the data base or the volume of transactions required by the operational system?

▌ Will the prototype or prototyping techniques result in software which is robust enough to detect and withstand the kinds of errors expected of users under real-world operating conditions? How difficult will recovery from such errors be?

▌ Is the structure of the prototype sufficiently clear to permit the software to be modified during development and after operation begins? Is it desirable to model the design of the system structure to facilitate understanding as well as structural change?

▌ Is development using an evolving prototype subject to the same rigorous management and quality controls with defined schedules and deliverables as in more conventional design and development?

PROTOTYPING TOOLS

Both prototyping strategies depend on the availability of software development tools that permit the rapid construction of software applications and the rapid integration of system components. Speed is important to the process because the applications will be built and rebuilt many times, seeking improvement at each iteration.

There is clearly a relationship between the choice of a prototyping strategy and the selection of prototyping tools and development environments.

Tools for Throwaway Prototyping

In throwaway prototyping, the tools are chosen for the speed and ease with which prototypes can be created and modified. For example, special-purpose tools can simulate interaction at the user interface. After the prototype has served its purpose, it is then converted into an implementation language more suited for the production environment.

Tools for Evolutionary Prototyping

In evolutionary prototyping, it is usually desirable to develop the prototypes with the language and tools to be used for the production version. This eliminates the need for conversion during the system development process. However, the prototypes may be developed on microcomputers, with the production version operating on a mainframe or a network. Many languages permit applications to be moved from one hardware platform to another without recoding. Some languages incorporate one version which supports rapid modification and another which provides more efficient execution.

Object-oriented languages, including Java and C++, are an appropriate choice for evolutionary prototyping. Object-oriented systems support rapid development, reusable and easily modified software components, and interactive icon-based user interfaces.[24]

Goldberg and Rubin comment:

> Object-oriented technology changes the role of prototyping. . . . But the typical object-oriented development environment invites prototyping of full functionality — actual working functionality that can be used and commented upon by the target customers. It is appropriate to prototype at this deep level to make sure that the feedback from the target customer informs the analyzers and designers about work flow, function details, and performance. But the implementation of a prototype is not necessarily product quality, designed for long-term maintainability. Rather, it is often quickly glued together, to be tried and then rewritten.[25]

PITFALLS IN PROTOTYPING

Thus far, we have described the rationale for and advantages of prototyping. But prototyping also has its potential pitfalls.

Many of the factors which contribute to success of the prototyping process can also have a negative impact on it. One such factor is the close involvement of users. In most situations, users are expected to be intensively involved in prototyping while carrying out their primary jobs at their usual level of effort. The stress and strain of this overburdened situation may adversely affect users' morale and health. It may reduce the quality of the users' participation in specifying requirements as well as the quality of work done in their primary jobs.

Another potential pitfall is that the process of iteration may be difficult to halt. Resources will be wasted if the process is not terminated when there is no significant change in the system requirements from one iteration to the next. Cosmetic changes to the user interface can be so easy to make that both the users and the analysts are tempted to tinker with the system's appearance while ignoring the fundamental purpose of these prototypes — understanding and specifying the essential system requirements. It is the project manager's responsibility to limit the amount of effort spent on changing the details of the user interface.

Quality assurance is especially critical during prototyping. Each iteration permits the introduction of additional defects in the requirements. Nevertheless, the process itself supports quality assurance because each iteration allows users to confirm their agreement with the results of analysis thus far. The process also permits users to see the requirements as defined by the prototype many times, thus increasing the probability that, if an error exists, it will be discovered.

Poorly planned and managed prototyping can fragment the time of users and developers into too many short sessions. Sessions can also degenerate into unproductive running of the prototype with no improvement in understanding users' needs or the system requirements. Many small changes to the structure of the data base, rather than a few, logically grouped changes, can needlessly tie up the database administrator assigned to the team.

The prototyping process naturally causes the team to revisit concepts and issues discussed in previous iterations. If the number of items about which there is disagreement and the degree of disagreement on each point is not reduced in successive iterations, there are problems with the process. If disagreements are increasing, two possibilities are likely. Either the analysts are unable to understand

---

[24]John L. Connell and Linda B. Shafer, *Object-Oriented Rapid Prototyping* (Englewood Cliffs, N.J.: Yourdon, 1995).
[25]Goldberg and Rubin, *Succeeding with Objects*, 99.

and interpret the users' requirements, or there are personality conflicts between users and developers. Note that personality issues become much more important in prototyping because of the frequent, intense interaction among members of the prototyping team.

The greatest problems in prototyping arise from the failure to conduct adequate analysis prior to constructing the prototype and from the failure to adequately control the overall process. This is particularly true in large or complex systems. Both these failures are derived from the following overly hopeful and overly simplistic view of prototyping:

> When a system is prototyped, it is unnecessary to obtain accurate information from the user or environment initially, because it will eventually be obtained through the many iterations that are characteristic of prototyping. Furthermore, . . . the need for substantial documentation of the system is greatly diminished. Updating the system description would be difficult anyway because of the many versions of the prototype that must be built before the final version is accepted.

This false view of prototyping causes major problems in the prototyping process and in prototyped systems. In many cases, although users may get something faster, the ultimate delivery of the final product may be unpredictable. In some cases, the new system will arrive much later than if prototyping had not been used.

Pure prototyping or evolutionary development without prior design merely gets poorly designed systems implemented faster. Maintenance on a particular bug can be done much faster, but, again, there are more iterations. Thus, careful needs assessment and solid systems analysis are essential to the construction of an adequate system, regardless of whether or not it is developed using prototyping. Adequate, well-documented analysis becomes even more critical in a prototyping environment and must be done if the system is to be viable.

CONCLUDING ADVICE

We close this discussion of prototyping with some advice from Fred Brooks, the director of IBM's OS/360 project. In his classic book, *The Mythical Man-Month*, Brooks advises system developers to "plan to throw one away; you will anyhow."[26]

He warns that if this advice is not followed, the first version of a system will turn out to be a prototype instead of a production system. Sooner or later it will be replaced by a system that corrects the shortcomings of the first system. (One of our colleagues comments that his organization usually creates a system three times — the first system works, the second system is tuned for performance, and the third system is easy to maintain.)

ALTERNATIVES TO CUSTOM SOFTWARE DEVELOPMENT

Thus far, this book has described a simplified but relatively complete process of development for custom object-oriented application software. However, custom software development is not always the best approach to acquiring needed software. This section presents some alternatives for software acquisition.

---

[26]Brooks, *The Mythical Man-Month*, 116.

One major alternative to custom software development is the use of packaged software for the new system. Software which can be customized or configured for a specific organization occupies the middle ground between packaged and custom software.

PACKAGED SOFTWARE

For some common applications, such as accounts payable/receivable, general ledger, and payroll, software packages are commercially available for a variety of processors and operating systems. If one of these packages satisfies the users' requirements or if users are willing to adjust their requirements, then custom software is unnecessary. The best of these packages are likely to be well documented with good users' manuals, carefully tested, and supported by the vendors.

If a software package satisfies most of the requirements but lacks critical features, it may be possible to modify the package or supplement it with custom software to support these additional features. Some vendors are willing to make modifications; others will supply source code; sometimes the software contains interfaces for enhancements by the users' organization. In still other situations, the enhancements may be added as separate programs.

After the users and analysts have arrived at an appropriate scope of automation for the new system, they can prepare a request for proposal (RFP). The RFP asks vendors of application software packages to propose solutions to the automation requirements for the system.

System Requirements for Packaged Software

This approach still requires a statement of system requirements as a basis for evaluating and comparing the vendors' proposals. However, the requirements statement can often be simpler than one intended for custom development. An RFP may include suggested or required algorithms for certain critical business processes, specific interface or performance requirements, and budget constraints. In response to the RFP, the vendor is required to state the extent to which his package satisfies the new system requirements, whether it can be modified to meet the requirements, and what the cost of the necessary changes will be. An unfortunate ramification of this approach is that, in general, the vendor is free to use **any** system description technique when answering an RFP. Some organizations require that responses to RFPs adhere to stringent guidelines in order to facilitate comparison of the various vendors' system descriptions.

The Impact of Software Packages on Design

By using a software package, the design effort can be substantially eliminated or greatly reduced. It is still wise to review the package carefully against the requirements specification and to make sure that the users understand the trade-offs they are making and the limitations of the package. Thorough training is still necessary. An acceptance test is desirable if the terms of license or purchase permit it. Any modifications or enhancements require design, construction, and testing, as they remain custom software.

Design by RFP

Another option, which bypasses in-house design, is to issue an RFP based on the requirements specification, perhaps leaving respondents free to supply a software package, a modified software package, or custom software. The RFP needs to control the form and content of the response so that the proposals can be compared on a consistent and fair basis.

CUSTOMIZABLE OR CONFIGURABLE SOFTWARE

Customizable software is an alternative between as-is use of a package and "start-from-scratch" custom development. Many software vendors incorporate ways to extend their packages or to tailor them to the users' unique requirements. For complex applications, such as enterprise resource planning systems and customer relationship management systems, the ability to customize may be essential. Successful customization requires careful analysis. Users, with the help of analysts, must define to what extent their business practices can change to fit the software and to what extent the cost of custom modifications is justified.

SUMMARY

Effective project management can make the difference between successful system development and a failed project. The history of software development is full of examples of failure, especially if we define failure broadly as performance which does not meet expectations. The most devastating failures seem to occur with large and complex projects.

Lack of technical competence on the part of information technology professionals is seldom the primary cause of a failed software development project. Instead, more important reasons for unsuccessful software projects include unreasonable user expectations, the failure of users to communicate requirements completely and accurately, insufficient commitment of users to the project, unrealistic project budgets and schedules, and inadequate attention to risks.

In order to deliver a system which not only meets users' reasonable expectations but also is produced on time and within the budget, project management seeks to identify risks to the project and avoid or mitigate them, to prepare project plans, to monitor project progress against the plans, to maintain continuing communication with the system's users, and to manage users' expectations.

A risk is any uncertainty which has a significant probability of preventing the successful completion of a project milestone. There are risks associated with each phase of a project and with each discipline in the Unified Process as well as with each project iteration. Some of the risks are associated with users, others with the development team, and still others with the project itself. In preparing a project strategy, it is important to consider not only the degree of risk but also coverage and criticality.

A project plan and schedule are the basis for managing a software development project. The project plan allocates tasks and responsibilities to a team of people. This makes it possible to monitor progress relative to the plan and to detect potential problems with the project. A project schedule is a set of project artifacts or deliverables listed in the sequence in which they are to be produced. The units of work in a project schedule are known as tasks or activities. A project activity is defined by its deliverable. Each task occurs only once in a schedule. Its status is either "complete" or "not complete." Milestones in the schedule mark major project accomplishments. It is critical to tailor project plans and schedules to the scope, complexity, and risks of every individual project.

Object-oriented technology, when used properly, can facilitate an effective software development process. Objects are a means of attacking complexity, objects build systems resilient to change, objects allow partial systems to work, and objects represent natural units for re-use.

The Unified Software Development Process contains three core disciplines related to project management — Configuration and Change Management, Project Management, and Environment. Configuration and Change Management manages the artifacts produced during system development. Project Management plans all the phases of a software development project from Inception to Transition. It also plans each iteration in detail. Environment provides and supports an organization's software development environment.

The Unified Process incorporates the critical insights of current best practices in order to provide flexibility and adaptability. Therefore, the Unified Process does not plan the entire project in detail in advance. Instead, there is a high-level Phase Plan, which specifies the major milestones and estimates their completion dates. An Iteration Plan provides a detailed plan for one iteration at a time.

Project management requires quantitative measurements of project progress. These measurements should be based on the project artifacts and made by estimators who are not part of the project team. Success for the estimators must be defined as a function of convergence of the estimate to the actual. Success for the project team should be defined as maximizing the amount of function delivered (weighted by the years of useful system life) per dollar of total system lifetime cost.

The re-use of objects can yield considerable improvement in programmer productivity as well as system quality. However, reusable objects do not just happen; they must be carefully designed with re-use in mind. Objects may be acquired by purchasing existing objects, having a vendor develop objects, or building the objects in house. In the future, business-domain objects for a variety of industries should become widely available.

Prototyping is inherent in best practices of software development. A prototype is a partial or limited version of a system. Prototypes may address questions of analysis, design, or feasibility or may provide a vertical slice through the system. There are two basic strategies in prototyping — throwaway prototyping and evolutionary prototyping. Object-oriented languages are an appropriate choice for prototyping. Object-oriented systems support rapid development, reusable and easily modified software components, and interactive icon-based user interfaces.

Not every system development project requires custom analysis, design, and construction. One major alternative to custom software development is the use of packaged software for the new system. Software which can be customized or configured for a specific organization occupies the middle ground between packaged and custom software. These alternatives can have a significant impact on both the system development process and the completed application software.

KEY TERMS

coverage *389*	project estimate *397*
critical path model *390*	prototype *399*
criticality *390*	prototyping *399*
evolutionary prototype *401*	risk *388*
Gantt chart *393*	throwaway prototype *401*

REVIEW QUESTIONS

14-1. In order to facilitate comparison of vendor proposals, what steps should be taken to ensure that responses to an RFP adhere to specified guidelines for system description?

14-2. Considering Brooks's advice to "throw one away," discuss the prototyping approach with respect to each of the following:
   a. Sophisticated versus naive users,
   b. Evolutionary versus throwaway prototypes, and
   c. Availability of prototype development tools

14-3. Explain the difference between throwaway and evolutionary prototyping.

14-4. State two alternatives to custom software design.

EXERCISES AND DISCUSSION QUESTIONS

14-1. Discuss the potential impact of each of the following factors on the analysis process:

a. Concerns of the various types of users;
b. Extensive versus limited user knowledge of application;
c. Extensive versus minimal user experience with system development;
d. Risk-averse versus risk-taking users;
e. Extensive versus limited developers' knowledge of application;
f. Extensive versus minimal developers' experience with system development;
g. Stable versus unstable organizational environment; and
h. Complex versus less complex system.

14-2. DeMarco states that the goal of the project team should be to maximize the total amount of useful function delivered over the life cycle cost of the system. His original metrics were derived for non-object-oriented systems. Discuss what you might use as similar metrics for object-oriented systems:

a. A metric of useful function based on an implementation-independent model of system size and derived from the primitive components of the analysis models;
b. Metrics which predict the initial cost of the system, based on the design models; or
c. Metrics for the cost of the system over the remainder of its useful life.

14-3. How does prototyping modify the phases of system development?

14-4. How may prototypes be used in specifying system requirements? What impact does this have on design?

14-5. What are some of the purposes of design prototypes?

14-6. Consider the article in Figure 14.3 about the IT turnaround at the Chicago Board of Trade (CBOT):

a. What situation did Bill Farrow find when he became CIO of the CBOT in July 2001?
b. How did he begin to deal with these problems? Comment specifically on the areas of relationships with the business managers, software quality assurance, and management of IT projects and personnel assignments.
c. What would be likely to happen now if one of the CBOT's primary systems were in trouble while the exchange was in operation?
d. How was Farrow able to maintain a flat budget during the turnaround?
e. Discuss the role of return on investment (ROI) considerations in the turnaround.

FIGURE 14.3   Market Rally

Market Rally

An IT turnaround has brought the Chicago Board of Trade, the world's oldest commodities exchange, back to profitability.

Picture 3,000 traders in "the pit" waving their hands and screaming orders for stocks, bonds, and commodities. Millions of dollars in investments are changing hands every minute. Suddenly, screens freeze; orders won't execute. Mayhem reigns as millions of dollars are lost with every tick of the clock.

"That's the worst thing that can happen," says Carol Burke, executive vice president and chief of staff at the Chicago Board of Trade (CBOT). But two years ago, trading-floor systems were crashing almost weekly because of a deteriorating infrastructure. Trading-floor systems capture the Buy and Sell orders, match them with Sell and Buy orders, route them to completion, and send back acknowledgments. The crashes were costing the exchange and its members millions of dollars.

In July 2001, after two years of operating in the red, the board of directors brought in a new management team, including Executive Vice President and CIO Bill Farrow. A total IT revamp got the exchange back to in-house profitability. By 2002, its profit had risen to $25 million, trading-system crashes were virtually unheard of, and CBOT was bullish on technology.

Farrow walked into a situation that was grim. The infrastructure was ancient, unreliable, and undocumented. For example, the phone system was 20 years old. "We literally had to put someone in a van and send him to Colorado to get parts for it," Farrow recalls. Desktops ran a version of Windows no longer supported by Microsoft Corp. Nearly every key process was routed through a group of old, midrange Tandem computers in an environment so complex that developing a new process took 90 steps.

IT was full of silos and fiefdoms, so there were no economies of scale. Morale was low. Other than Y2K, IT hadn't completed a single project in four years. As a result, people had no experience in project management disciplines, and return on investment was a foreign concept.

Farrow began by taking inventory of what he had. He documented systems and technical architecture, nailed down vendor relationships and service-level agreements, and evaluated security systems.

Simultaneously, he faced the bigger challenge of building new relationships with the skeptical business people. He assigned IT managers to counterparts on the business side to brainstorm regularly about how technology could support business goals. Replacing the ancient Tandems with Sun Unix servers and Oracle data bases, a process that was expected to take two years, got done in half the time because IT's business partners helped with the analysis, legwork, and scope.

Farrow boosted quality assurance with additional software testing and backed it up by putting IT troubleshooters on the trading floor every day when the market opens.

Farrow established a project office to centralize the project portfolio and the IT skills pool. He chose enterprise change management software to automate processes and provide real-time status reports on projects. The office gives a broad view of how IT skills are needed and used across the exchange, enabling him to deploy human resources efficiently. It also helps the business people understand IT resources. "If they want additional staff hours, they can see that [it's] at the expense of something else," Farrow explains.

Farrow also brought ROI to project agendas. "We [know] a lot more in terms of what projects will provide as returns on investments," says Brian Durkin, senior vice president of operations at CBOT.

Durkin is particularly happy with a new master-antenna system for the trading floor. "It gives us an immense amount of growth for wireless technology on the floor," he says. "There's been a phenomenal growth of activity."

In 2002, IT completed 66 projects. The projects have made the business managers believers in IT. In February, CBOT handled 33 million contracts — 33% more than in the previous February. "We have a much more stable and robust environment with fail-over abilities," says Durkin. "If there were a problem in a primary system, it would fail over to a backup and be seamless to the marketplace."

Throughout the turnaround, IT has maintained a flat budget. "If you are wasting 35% of your money and you can make that 35% productive, that's a lot of money to put back into the technology to make it robust," Farrow says.

Adapted from Kathleen Melymuka, "Market Rally," *Computerworld*, April 7, 2003, 40

APPENDIX: UML NOTATION AND OBJECT-ORIENTED ANALYSIS ARTIFACTS

This appendix contains a summary of the UML notation presented in this book. It also contains examples of work products of object-oriented analysis which are not part of the UML or for which the UML does not specify a standard format.

USE CASE DIAGRAM

FIGURE A.1   UML notation for use case diagrams

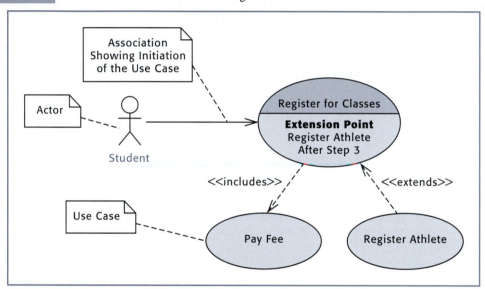

UML COLLABORATION DIAGRAM

FIGURE A.2   An example of a UML collaboration diagram

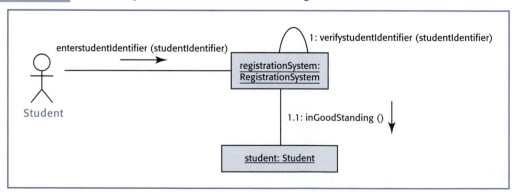

UML SEQUENCE DIAGRAM

FIGURE A.3	The UML sequence diagram equivalent to Figure A.2

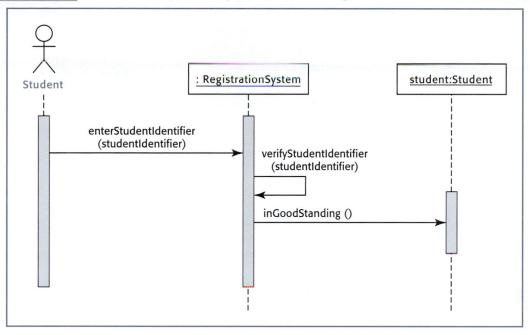

UML CLASS DIAGRAM

The UML makes no formal distinction between class diagrams used to model the problem domain (domain models) and design class diagrams. Domain models contain no operations. In them the associations represent connections between concepts. In class diagrams used for design, the associations represent links or message paths.

CLASS DIAGRAM NOTATION

FIGURE A.4   UML notation for class diagrams (domain models or design class diagrams)

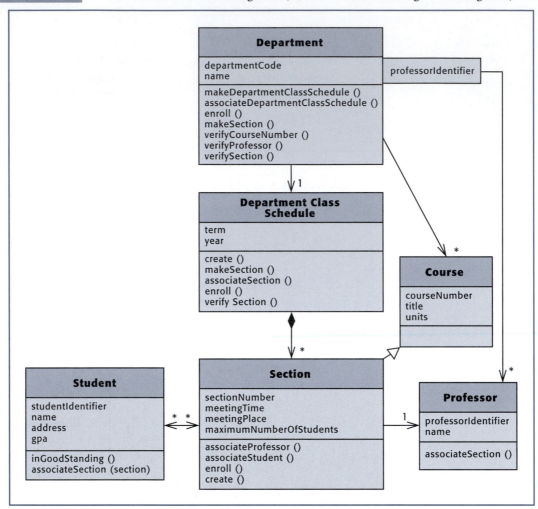

CLASS NOTATION

FIGURE A.5   UML notation for a class in varying degrees of detail

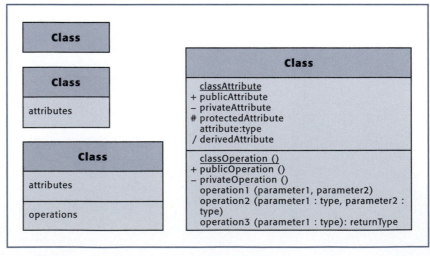

ASSOCIATIONS IN CLASS DIAGRAMS

FIGURE A.6   UML notation for an association

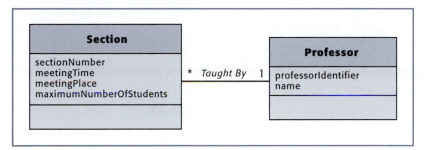

FIGURE A.7   UML notation for a reflexive association

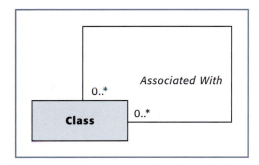

FIGURE A.8   UML notation for whole-to-part associations

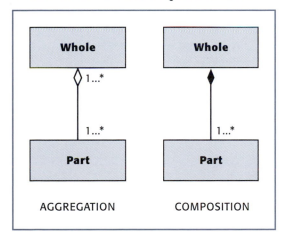

MULTIPLICITY

FIGURE A.9   UML notation for multiplicity

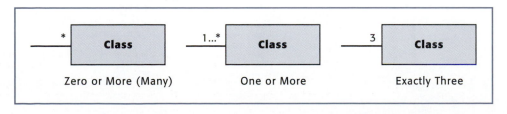

ASSOCIATION CLASSES

FIGURE A.10　UML notation for association classes

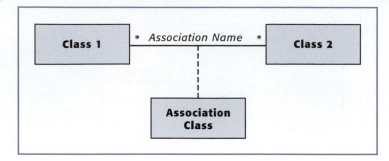

GENERALIZATION-SPECIALIZATION HIERARCHIES

FIGURE A.11　UML notation for generalization-specialization hierarchies

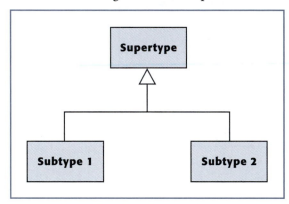

USE CASE NARRATIVE

FIGURE A.12   Sample expanded essential use case narrative

Use case:	**Register for Classes**
Actors:	Student
Purpose:	Register a student for classes and record the student's schedule.
Overview:	A Student requests the sections of class desired for a term. The system adds the Student to each section if there is space available. On completion, the system provides the Student with a list of the classes in which he or she is enrolled.
Type:	Essential
Pre conditions:	Class schedule must exist.
Post conditions:	Student is known by the system.
	Student was enrolled in the Section.
Special Requirements:	Student must get a system response within 10 seconds.

Flow of Events

ACTOR ACTION	SYSTEM RESPONSE
1. This use case begins when a Student desires to register for classes.	
2. The Student provides the Student's identifier and a list of the department code, course number, and section number for each section desired.	3. Adds the student to the section if there are seats available.
4. On completion of entry of the section requests, the Student indicates that the request is complete.	5. The system produces a student class list for the student.
6. The Student receives the student class list.	

Alternative Flow of Events

Line 3: Invalid department code and course number entered. Indicate error. Return to Step 2. Invalid section number entered. Indicate error. Return to Step 2. No seats remaining. Inform the student. Return to Step 2.

SYSTEM OPERATION CONTRACT

FIGURE A.13   Sample system operation contract (for *requestSection* system operation)

Contract Name:	**requestSection** (departmentCode, courseNumber, sectionNumber)
Responsibilities:	Enroll the Student in the Section
Type:	System
Exceptions:	If the combination of department code, course number and section number is not valid, indicate that it was an error.
	If no seats are available, inform the Student.
Output:	
Pre conditions:	Department and Section are known to the system.
Post conditions:	A new instance of the Enrolled-in association was created linking the Student and Section.

abstraction.
(1) The extraction of essential information relevant to a particular purpose.
(2) The essential information thus selected.

acceptance test. *See* system acceptance test.

access.
(1) A flow of information to or from a data store.
(2) To store information in or retrieve it from a data store.

actor. A person, organization, or system in the environment which sends a message (input) to the system or receives a message (output) from the system.

aggregate. In an aggregation, the class representing the whole.

aggregation.
(1) A process of assembling a system using a set of elementary components.
(2) An association between classes representing a part-to-whole relationship in which the parts and the whole may exist independently and in which a single part may be associated with more than one whole at the same time.

algorithm. The step-by-step specification of the operations or actions which accomplish a transformation.

alias. An alternate name for an item; a synonym.

alternative (course of action). In an expanded use case description, a conditional action of the system which differs from the typical flow of events.

analysis. The process of determining the structure of an object or system; decomposition. (*See* systems analysis.)

application layer. The layer of information system architecture which carries out the operations in the business or application domain.

application program. Software which causes general-purpose hardware to carry out transformations required by users.

arc. A component of a network which connects two nodes.

architectural baseline. A component of a network which connects two nodes.

artifact.
(1) An object or system devised by human beings.
(2) A work product or deliverable in the system development process.

association.
(1) A significant connection between problem-domain concepts or between classes.
(2) A connection between use cases.

association concept. A concept whose existence depends on an association between other problem-domain concepts.

attribute. A named characteristic of an object which may take on a value.

automation boundary. A boundary which partitions an information processing system into automated and manual portions.

beneficial user. A person who has no direct contact with an automated information processing system but who provides system input or receives system output.

break-even point. The time at which the present value of the net benefits of a project equals the present value of the cost of the project.

brightness. *See* value.

business event. A system-level event in a business problem domain.

button. An input device which initiates an action.

channel. A generic hardware component whose function is to transport data.

chroma. Saturation; the position of a color on a scale from its weakest to its most vivid variant. It is related to the proportion of white light mixed with light of the dominant wavelength.

class. A group of objects which have an identical set of attributes and an identical set of behaviors.

client (client/server system). A component of a client/server system which requests services from another component.

client (object). An object which sends a message to a server object.

client/server system. An information processing system consisting of clients and servers connected by a communication network. The clients request services from one or more servers.

closure. The Gestalt principle that visual elements are grouped to form simple, closed figures.

cohesion. A measure of how strongly related and focused the responsibilities of a class are.

collaboration. The fulfillment of a responsibility by two or more objects through client/server relationships.

collaboration diagram. An interaction diagram showing the messages between interacting objects and classes as a network model.

command feedback. A message from a command interpreter indicating that a command just entered has been recognized and accepted or that there is an error in its syntax.

command interpreter. A component of an interactive system which assembles (parses) input primitives into commands.

command language. A style of interaction at the user interface in which the user specifies the execution of a series of tasks without being prompted.

common motion. The Gestalt principle that visual elements are grouped when they move together.

component. In a composition, the class representing one of the parts.

composite. In a composition, a class representing the whole.

composition.
(1) (Of a system input or output) Its content (data elements) and structure (how they are organized).
(2) An association between classes representing a whole-to-part relationship in which the parts may belong to only one whole at a time and the whole does not exist without its parts.

computer aided software engineering (CASE). Software for maintaining interrelated models of an information processing system during the development process.

concept. A person, idea, or thing in the problem domain which is significant for an information system.

conceptual class. A UML term for a constituent of a class diagram. (*See* concept.)

constituent. In an aggregation, a class representing one of the parts.

constraint. A condition or requirement which must be satisfied (by a proposed problem solution or system design) for the system to be acceptable.

container. A generic hardware component whose function is to store data.

context diagram. A diagram of a system, its environment, and their interactions. More specifically, it is a diagram showing the system as a single object, all its inputs and outputs, the actors who provide the inputs, and the actors who receive the outputs.

continuation. The Gestalt principle that visual elements are grouped to preserve smooth continuity rather than abrupt change.

contract. A description of a behavior which a system component commits itself to carry out; a commitment by the receiver of a message to satisfy the postconditions of an operation if the sender of the message makes sure that the preconditions of the operation are satisfied.

control flow. Information which activates or terminates the execution of an operation or which controls the sequence of execution of the procedure for the operation.

coupling. A measure of how strongly one class is connected to, has knowledge of, or relies on other classes.

Creator pattern. A pattern which assigns the responsibility of requesting a class to create a new object — i.e., which assigns the responsibility of sending a **create** message.

criterion (*pl.* criteria). A measurable or observable factor used to compare alternatives.

critical path model. A network model for project planning and scheduling. It shows sequential dependencies between activities and which activities cannot be delayed without delaying the entire project.

data base. A systematically partitioned, reusable, integrated collection of data which can be shared by many users.

database management system. The computer system software which manages a data base, providing for logical and physical data independence, controlling redundancy, and enforcing integrity constraints, privacy, and security.

data capture device. Hardware which transforms automated system inputs from human-readable form to machine-readable form.

data element. A data structure primitive; an item of information which does not require any decomposition in the system of which it is a part.

data flow. A movement of application-specific information within a system or across the system boundary.

data type. The UML term for the description of an attribute of a class. Data types are always either primitive data types or value objects.

design.

(1) A process which creates descriptions of a newly devised artifact.
(2) The product of the design process — a description which is sufficiently complete and detailed to assure that the artifact can be built.

design class diagram. A class diagram which shows attributes, operations, and navigability.

design sequence diagram. A sequence diagram which shows interactions of classes within the system.

device driver (handler). Software which controls an input or output device.

device feedback. A message from a device driver which displays or tracks input primitives.

direct manipulation. A style of interaction at the user interface in which the user manipulates directly objects of interest in the display.

discipline. In the Rational Unified Process, a sequence of activities which produce an observable result of value to an actor (formerly known as workflow).

display. An output device, either in general or one which produces an image.

domain model. An analysis model which represents real-world concepts in a problem domain. A domain model is a static model which shows concepts in the problem domain, their attributes, and associations among them.

economic feasibility. The feasibility of a project based on financial criteria.

encapsulation. Using an interface to protect an object's internal attributes and behaviors from external access.

environment (of a system). Whatever lies outside the system; often something outside a system which affects or interacts with the system.

ergonomics. The discipline which studies the human factors involved in the design of useful objects, especially in the workplace.

essential.

(1) A model or model component which avoids specifying the technology with which a system is or will be implemented.
(2) A necessary system requirement or component.

event. An occurrence which takes place at a specific time and initiates or triggers a predetermined response from a system.

event analysis. A technique for systems analysis which considers the purpose of an entire information processing system to be responding to a selected set of occurrences in the system's environment.

event flow. A signal which notifies a system that a particular event has occurred.

expanded use case narrative. A detailed use case narrative, including a typical flow of events, exceptions, and pre- and postconditions.

Expert pattern. A pattern which assigns a responsibility to the object which has the attributes needed to carry out the responsibility.

«extends». A conditional association between use cases such that the extension augments the use case which it extends.

external event. An event which occurs outside the system boundary.

façade (controller). An object which coordinates the work of the objects in the application layer and serves as an interface to the presentation layer.

Façade pattern. A pattern which assigns to a single object representing the system as a whole the responsibility for receiving messages from an initiating actor.

feasibility report. The product of a feasibility study (the activity of making the business case, containing both technical and management guidelines for a system development project, including a summary of system alternatives).

feasible. Satisfying all the constraints on a system.

figure/ground segregation. The perception of some visual elements (the figure or foreground) as being in front of or separate from others (the background).

flow of events. The part of a use case narrative which presents the sequence of actions of the actors and the corresponding responses of the system.

font (printing). A complete assortment of type in one face and size.

font (software). A complete assortment of characters of one design in many faces and sizes.

form fill-in. A style of interaction at the user interface in which the user sees a display of related fields, moves a cursor among the fields, and enters data where desired.

future value. The value of a benefit or cost incurred at a future time.

Gantt chart. A horizontal bar chart showing the scheduling of project activities or tasks.

generalization-specialization. A hierarchical construct in which every instance of a subtype is also an instance of its supertype. Subtypes share (or inherit) the attributes and operations of the supertype.

«generalizes». An association between use cases which implies that the child use case contains all the attributes, sequences of behavior, and extensions of the parent use case.

Gestalt principles. Principles of visual perception which stress the unity of visual shapes and patterns.

Gestalt theorists. A group of early–20th-century psychologists who studied perception, including Koehler, Koffka, and Wertheimer.

global visibility. A type of visibility in which an object is obtained from a class by the object requiring visibility to it.

guard. A condition or constraint.

hands-on user. A person who interacts directly with the data capture and data display devices for an automated information processing system.

hierarchy. A system structure in which every system component except the one at the top is subordinate to exactly one immediate superordinate.

hue. A color as perceived. It is related to the dominant wavelength of the light.

human factors. *See* ergonomics.

icon. A pictorial symbol.

«includes». An unconditional association between use cases such that the included use case always occurs whenever the use case which includes it occurs.

infeasible. Not feasible; failing to satisfy one of the constraints on a problem or system.

inheritance. The ability of a subclass to have all the attributes and operations of its superclass.

initiating actor. An actor who initiates a use case.

instance. A specific member of a class or an individual occurrence of an association.

interaction diagram. A dynamic model shown in a diagram which depicts the messages between objects or classes in a program.

interactive system. A system in which the user interface is event-driven; the user and the computer communicate through a dialogue.

interface.
(1) A shared boundary.
(2) To connect or be connected.
(3) A connection or interaction between two components or systems.

internal event. An event which occurs inside the system boundary.

iteration.
(1) A control structure for an operation: the process of repeatedly executing a given sequence of programming language statements until a given condition is met or while a given condition is true.
(2) A single execution of a loop.

Joint Application Development (JAD). A process for obtaining agreement on critical decisions about system requirements and design during an intensive workshop for all the relevant users and developers.

Law of Demeter. A design principle which states that a client should give its server the responsibility for collaborating with other objects.

linearity (of a display). A measurement of whether straight lines appear straight.

link. An instance of an association.

local visibility. A type of visibility in which an object is obtained locally by capturing an object returned from a message.

man-machine boundary. The automation boundary.

menu. A list from which a user selects the desired action.

menu selection. A style of interaction at the user interface which allows the user to choose an action from a list of alternatives displayed on the screen.

message. A request from one object to a second object to carry out a behavior or execute an operation belonging to the second object.

method.
(1) An organized process for accomplishing a task.
(2) (In the UML) A specific implementation of or an algorithm for an operation.

milestone. The completion of a phase of system development. It is marked by the delivery of a defined set of artifacts (models or other work products).

model. An abstraction or representation of an object or system.

Model-View Separation pattern. A pattern which states that objects in the application layer should not send messages directly to objects in the presentation layer.

multiplicity. The number of instances of a concept or class which can be associated with one instance of another concept or class.

natural language (interaction style). A style of interaction at the user interface in which the user controls the interaction in a natural language, such as English.

navigability. The ability of a client object to know the identity of a server object with which it collaborates. (Also known as visibility.)

net present value. The present value of a benefit minus the present value of a cost incurred at the same time.

network. A structure comprising a set of nodes connected by arcs.

node. A point within a network.

object. The basic structural component of object-oriented software.

on-line system. A system in which each data flow entering the automated portion is processed as soon as it is received.

operation. A service which can be requested from an object; an implementation of or an algorithm for a procedure.

organizational feasibility. The feasibility of a project based on the politics and culture of the using organization.

package. A set of use cases, objects, or classes comprising a system or subsystem.

parameters (of a message). The data elements transmitted as part of the message.

parameter visibility. A type of visibility in which an object is provided by a message as a parameter.

participating actor. An actor who is involved in a use case but does not initiate it.

pattern. A named statement of a design problem together with its solution.

persistence. The need for an object to continue in existence for a long time.

pixel. A point in a raster display.

phase. In the Rational Unified Process, one of four sequential subdivisions of the system development process. Each ends with the delivery of a set of artifacts and a decision about whether to continue to the next phase or to terminate the project.

plotter. An output device which produces drawings.

polymorphism. The ability of objects in different classes to respond differently to messages of the same name.

postcondition. A condition which states the required effect of an operation on a system.

precondition. A condition which must be true before an operation or use case can be performed successfully.

presentation layer. The layer of information system architecture which manages the user interface, transporting data to and from the application layer.

present value. The value of a future cost or benefit after discounting it for the time value of money.

primitive. An elementary component of a system or language — one which is not decomposed further.

primitive data type. A data type which can be directly represented in computer hardware.

private (attribute or operation). An attribute or operation which is available only from within an object and cannot be accessed by other objects.

prototype. A partial or limited working version of a system.

proximity. The Gestalt principle that visual elements are grouped when they are close to each other.

public (attribute or operation). An attribute or operation which can be accessed by other objects.

qualified association. An association which uses a qualifier at one end to select one or a subset of instances on the other end.

qualifier. An attribute of a class which has a unique value for each object in the class.

quality assurance. Procedures and techniques for minimizing defects and maximizing the quality of a product or system.

random-scan display. A vector display.

raster display. A display organized as a grid of points (pixels).

Rational Unified Process. A system development process for object-oriented software created by Jacobson, Booch, and Rumbaugh and their colleagues at Rational Software Corporation. (Also known as the Unified Process.)

real-time system. A computer system which processes data according to time requirements imposed by an outside process.

real use case narrative. A use case narrative which includes details of the implementing technology.

reference object. An object whose unique identity is meaningful.

reference visibility. A type of visibility in which the client object has a pointer or reference to the server object.

relational data base. A data base structured as a set of tables.

requirement.

(1) A condition or capability needed by a user to solve a problem or achieve an objective.

(2) A condition or capability which must be met by a system or system component to satisfy a contract, standard, specification, or other formal document.

requirements specification. A document produced during systems analysis containing the requirements for a new system.

resolution (of a display). The number of points per inch or other unit of measure which can be displayed.

resource feasibility. The feasibility of a project based on the availability of the required people, materials, equipment, and other resources.

response. What a system does when an event occurs.

responsibility. An obligation of an object to provide services to other objects.

responsible user. A low- to middle-level manager with direct day-to-day responsibility for the business functions supported by an information processing system.

return on investment. The ratio of the overall net present value of a project to the net present value of all the costs.

risk. An uncertainty which has a significant probability of preventing the successful completion of a project milestone.

saturation. *See* chroma.

scenario. A description of a single occurrence or instance of a use case.

schedule feasibility. The feasibility of a project based on whether the project can be completed in time to meet the business requirements of its users.

selection feedback. A message indicating which objects from the data base have been selected in preparation for or as the result of the execution of the command.

semantic feedback. A message indicating to the user that the operation requested has been completed.

sequence diagram. An interaction diagram which shows the messages between interacting objects and classes in a fence format.

server (client/server system). A component of a client/server system which provides services to another component.

server (object). An object which receives a message from a client object.

signature. A complete definition of the message associated with an operation. It consists of an access specification, the name of the operation the names and data types of the parameters, and the name and type of the object or value returned.

similarity. The Gestalt principle that visual elements are grouped when they are similar to each other.

simulation. The use of a model, often a working model, to represent a system or its behavior.

Singleton pattern. A design pattern which provides a class with a single object; used to provide global visibility or a controlled interface.

software engineering. The discipline concerned with the development of computer software.

special requirement. A system requirement which addresses aspects other than actions of the system, such as response time and reliability.

state. The condition of a system or process between events.

state transition diagram. A network model of a finite-state machine, showing its legal states and the transitions between them.

stimulus. A message or signal which reports the occurrence of an event and triggers a system to respond.

storage layer. The layer of information system architecture which manages the data base, providing access to the data from the application layer.

subclass. A class in a generalization-specialization hierarchy. Its objects have all the attributes and all the operations of its superclass.

subsystem boundary. The limit dividing a subsystem from the rest of a system.

superclass. A class in a generalization-specialization hierarchy. It is the parent of its subclasses.

synthesis. The creation of a whole from components.

system. An interrelated set of components which are viewed as a whole.

system acceptance test. A test of a completed system to determine whether it meets the stated system requirements.

system architecture. The structure of the system; the set of significant decisions about what the software components are and how they are to be organized.

system boundary. The limit dividing the interior of the system from what is outside the system.

system design.

(1) The process of defining the structure and components of a system which satisfies the specified users' requirements.
(2) The result of the system design process; a description of a system which satisfies the specified requirements and that is adequate for constructing the system.

system development process. A conceptual framework for understanding and managing the activities involved in information system development and use.

system input. A message or information flow which crosses the system boundary to enter a system.

system model. An abstraction of a real-world system which shows the significant components and their relationships. This abstraction is often used to study and predict the behavior or performance of the system.

system operation. An operation which a system carries out in response to a system input.

system operation contract. A description of the changes in the overall state of a system when a system operation is carried out.

system output. A message or information flow which crosses the system boundary to leave a system.

system owner. A high-level manager and decision maker for the business area supported by an information processing system.

systems analysis. The process of studying user needs to arrive at a definition of system or software requirements.

system sequence diagram. A type of sequence diagram which shows only the interactions between a system and its actors.

technical feasibility. The feasibility of a project in terms of its ability to be constructed.

temporal event. An event which occurs at a prespecified time.

three-tier system architecture. A system architecture consisting of a presentation layer, an application (or business) layer, and a storage layer.

timebox. A limited period of time for accomplishing a specified task or tasks.

transaction. A stimulus which triggers a response from a system. Any element of data, control, signal, event, or change of state which causes, triggers, or initiates some action or sequence of actions.

transition. A change from one state to another.

UML. *See* Unified Modeling Language.

Unified Modeling Language (UML). A standard notation for describing and modeling object-oriented systems.

Unified Process. *See* Rational Unified Process.

use case. The sequence of actions which occur when an actor uses a system to complete a process.

use case diagram. A graphical model which shows the use cases of a system in relation to the actors in its environment.

use case narrative. A narrative presenting the sequence of internal actions by which the system responds to actions of an actor.

use case scenario. An instance of a use case.

user interface. The hardware and software at the automation boundary.

value (color). Brightness; intensity; the position of a color on a gray scale — that is, its lightness or darkness independent of the particular hue. Value is related to the amount of luminous energy in the light.

value object. An object whose unique identity is not meaningful.

visibility. The ability of a client object to know the identity of a server object with which it collaborates. (Also known as navigability.)

walkthrough. A group review of a work product for the purpose of judging its completeness, correctness, consistency, and adherence to standards.

window navigation diagram. A model of the navigation paths between windows or screens in a workstation display or between web pages.

workflow. *See* discipline.